Americans and
Chinese Communists, 1927–1945

A PERSUADING ENCOUNTER

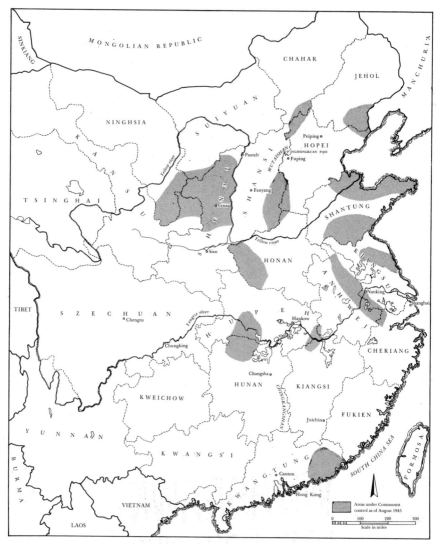

MONGOLIAN REPUBLIC

SINKIANG

CHAHAR

JEHOL

MANCHURIA

NINGHSIA

SUIYUAN

K A N S U

TSINGHAI

S H E N S I

S H A N S I

W U T A I S H A N

Paoteh

Peiping

HOPEI

CHINGHSINGKUAN PASS

Fuping

Fenyang

Yenan

SHANTUNG

K I A N G S U

Sian

HONAN

A N H W E I

Yellow river

Yellow river

TIBET

S Z E C H U A N

Yangtze river

Chengtu

H U P E H

Hankow

Nanking

Shanghai

Chungking

CHEKIANG

Changsha

HUNAN

KIANGSI

C H I N G K A N G S H A N

FUKIEN

KWEICHOW

Juichin

Y U N N A N

K W A N G S I

B U R M A

K W A N G T U N G

Canton

SOUTH CHINA SEA

F O R M O S A

Hong Kong

VIETNAM

LAOS

Areas under Communist
control as of August 1945

Scale in miles

0   100   200   300

CHINA

Americans and
Chinese Communists, 1927–1945

★ A PERSUADING ENCOUNTER

Kenneth E. Shewmaker

Cornell University Press

ITHACA AND LONDON

International Standard Book Number 0-8014-0617-X
Library of Congress Catalog Card Number 70-144031

PRINTED IN THE UNITED STATES OF AMERICA
BY VAIL-BALLOU PRESS, INC.

To Liese and to
Richard W. Leopold

Acknowledgments

It is a pleasure to acknowledge the many people and institutions that have contributed to this book. I wish to express my gratitude to the Committee on Research of Dartmouth College for typing expenses, to the East Asia Language and Area Studies Center of Dartmouth College for research and travel expenses, and most especially to the Joint Committee on Contemporary China of the Social Science Research Council and the American Council of Learned Societies for a generous grant which allowed me a year of uninterrupted writing and research. Dr. Bryce Wood of the Social Science Research Council merits a special word of appreciation for his helpfulness.

I wish to thank the staffs of the Historical Office of the Department of State, the Hoover Institution on War, Revolution and Peace, the Division of Manuscripts of the Library of Congress, the Office of the Chief of Military History, the Western History Collection of the University of Oklahoma Library, and the Franklin D. Roosevelt Library for their help in locating records and for permission to use certain manuscript materials. Mr. Jack Haley of the University of Oklahoma Library was particularly generous with his time in assisting me in examining the Patrick J. Hurley papers. I also am indebted to the editors of *The China Quarterly, Journalism Quarterly,* and *Pacific Historical Re-*

view for permission to use materials previously published in their journals.

I am particularly grateful to those who have read the entire manuscript and given me the benefit of their discerning criticisms: Professor Dorothy Borg of Columbia University, Professor Leo Ou-Fan Lee of Chung Chi College, Professor Jonathan Mirsky of Dartmouth College, Professor James E. Sheridan of Northwestern University, and Professor James C. Thomson, Jr., of Harvard University. I also am indebted to Professor Louis Morton of Dartmouth College and Professor Russell Weigley of Temple University for reading certain chapters of the book and providing valuable suggestions, and to the staff of Cornell University Press for their kindly cooperation and skillful editing.

My greatest debts of gratitude are to the two people to whom this volume is dedicated. In addition to creating the atmosphere in which this book could be written, my wife Liese read the manuscript several times and provided many helpful suggestions. Our children, Richard and Nancy, also deserve a very special word of thanks for their cheerfulness and patience.

I had the good fortune to begin this study under Richard W. Leopold and to benefit from his impeccable scholarship and constant support. For his sustaining interest and sound advice, I am deeply grateful. No author could have had a better mentor.

K. E. S.

Hanover, N.H.
February 1971

Contents

PART IV. PERSUADING ENCOUNTER

Illustrations

Introduction

This study of the first contacts between Americans and Chinese Communists is part of an increasingly common type of historical inquiry that as yet has no adequate name. It can be called diplomatic history, but it bears little resemblance to the traditional concern of the diplomatic historian with the foreign policies of various countries. It can be called intellectual history, but it is focused less on ideas than on assumptions, images, and perceptions. Yet it is diplomatic history in that it seeks to describe the direct encounter between Americans and Chinese Communists, and intellectual history in that it tries to grasp the different value systems that underlay such interaction. The Sino-American relationship comprises all the direct and indirect contacts between individual Americans and individual Chinese. And international relations, as Akira Iriye wrote, "are nothing if not relations among men." [1]

Perhaps Iriye has best described the nature and goal of this new kind of bicultural historical inquiry. "All diplomatic history," he observes, "is hyphenated history." But to make meaningful contributions to an understanding of American–East Asian relations, scholarship ought to be "hy-

[1] Akira Iriye, "The Twenties (1922–1931)," unpub. paper, American–East Asian Relations Research Conference, Cuernavaca, Mexico, January 2–4, 1970, p. 2.

phenated in more than one way." It should be "diplomatic-
intellectual-psychological history." [2] Only when United
States relations with China are seen as a complex intellectual
problem of communication will it be possible for us to liberate ourselves from the burden of the past and look forward
to a more peaceful world.[3]

Iriye's suggestion that foreign relations should be seen primarily as an intellectual problem seems particularly appropriate to a study of the experiences and writings of Americans who came into direct personal contact with the Chinese
Communists from 1937 to 1945. Against a background of
twenty-five years of intense Chinese Communist–American
hostility and mutual recrimination, it may be difficult for
some to imagine that the relationship could ever have been
different. But it was different in the years 1937–1945. This
was the period of the united front against Japan in China,
the era when the Sino-Japanese conflict became a part of the
Second World War. Outside aggression had temporarily prevented the Kuomintang (KMT) and the Chinese Communist Party (CCP) from settling their accounts on the field of
battle. Japanese expansionism also had temporarily allowed

[2] *Ibid.,* p. 15.

[3] Iriye, *Across the Pacific: An Inner History of American–East Asian
Relations* (New York, 1967), p. 329. Other works representative of the
kind of historical inquiry under consideration include John K. Fairbank, *China: The People's Middle Kingdom and the U.S.A.* (Cambridge, Mass., 1967), and "Assignment for the '70's," *American Historical Review,* LXXIV (February 1969), 861–879; Waldo H. Heinrichs,
Jr., *American Ambassador: Joseph C. Grew and the Development of
the United States Diplomatic Tradition* (Boston and Toronto, 1966);
James C. Thomson, Jr., *While China Faced West: American Reformers in Nationalist China, 1928–1937* (Cambridge, Mass., 1969); Tang
Tsou, *America's Failure in China, 1941–50* (Chicago, 1963), and "The
American Political Tradition and the American Image of Chinese
Communism," *Political Science Quarterly,* LXXVII (December 1962),
570–600; Marilyn B. Young, *The Rhetoric of Empire: American China
Policy, 1895–1901* (Cambridge, Mass., 1968).

Americans to think of Chinese, whether Nationalist or Communist, as allies in the world-wide defense of freedom and self-determination.

From 1937 to 1944, the United States government had no official contact with the CCP. Before Chiang Kai-shek authorized the establishment of an American military mission in Yenan, Foreign Service officers had to base their assessments of Chinese communism largely on secondhand information.[4] The first contingent of the Yenan Observer Group did not arrive in the Communist areas of China until July 22, 1944.[5] Shortly thereafter American policy as implemented by Ambassador Patrick J. Hurley succeeded in alienating the CCP from the United States. By July 1945, the CCP had publicly denounced Hurley and other "imperialist elements" in the United States for giving unilateral support to the KMT.[6] Chinese Communist–American relations assumed the pattern of enmity and exclusion that has persisted to the present. Since 1949, Jonathan Mirsky has noted, "no American, except for Edgar Snow, has traveled widely in the People's Republic and written about it."[7] Those Americans

[4] Herbert Feis, *The China Tangle: The American Effort in China from Pearl Harbor to the Marshall Mission* (Princeton, 1953), pp. 157–165. See also Dorothy Borg, *The United States and the Far Eastern Crisis of 1933–1938: From the Manchurian Incident through the Initial Stage of the Undeclared Sino-Japanese War* (Cambridge, Mass., 1964), pp. 196–234.

[5] Colonel David Barrett, Yenan, August 14, 1944, to the Commanding General, United States Army, China-Burma-India Theater, APO 879, "Dixie Mission" papers.

[6] Cited in Stuart R. Schram, *The Political Thought of Mao Tsetung* (rev. and enlarged ed., New York, Washington, and London, 1969), pp. 400–404. See also the excerpts from a New China News Agency broadcast from Yenan on June 26, 1945, in *Foreign Relations of the United States: Diplomatic Papers, 1945. The Far East and China* (Washington, D.C., 1969), pp. 418–421.

[7] Jonathan Mirsky, "Report from the China Sea," *New York Review of Books,* XIII (August 21, 1969), 35.

who traveled to Yenan before 1945 knew a different Communist China, one that was reasonably well disposed toward the United States.

The first American visitors to Red China were not diplomats and other governmental officials. Most were journalists, but others were businessmen, doctors, educators, military observers, missionaries, even a housewife. Whatever their background, they almost invariably returned from Yenan aglow with praise for China's Communists. Though it may seem strange today, there is reason to believe that the Chinese Communists were as impressed by Americans as Americans were by them.[8]

Although this book concentrates on Americans and Chinese Communists, I have attempted to present a representative cross section of Western opinion. Accordingly, I have devoted considerable attention to the Europeans who had face-to-face encounters with the Chinese Communists. Their observations are useful and important in that they provide a means of comparison and contrast. Nonetheless, since most of the foreigners who traveled in the Communist regions of China during these years of war and human misery were Americans, the story is truly theirs.

Anyone who attempts to treat the relationship between Americans and Chinese Communists is confronted with certain difficulties, perhaps the most important of which is the controversial nature of the subject. As Ross Y. Koen observed in 1960, "United States policy toward China is more deeply involved in domestic politics than any other aspect of American foreign affairs." [9] After 1949, Chinese communism

[8] See Feis, *The China Tangle*, p. 206; Schram, *Mao Tse-tung* (New York, 1966), pp. 209–210; Warren I. Cohen, "The Development of Chinese Communist Policy Toward the United States, 1922–1933," *Orbis*, XI (Spring 1967), 219–237, and "The Development of Chinese Communist Policy Toward the United States, 1934–1945," *ibid.* (Summer 1967), 551–569.

[9] Ross Y. Koen, *The China Lobby in American Politics* (New York, 1960), p. vii.

became a hotly debated issue in the United States. Senator Arthur H. Vandenberg, the Republican spokesman on foreign policy, excluded China from the scope of bipartisanship. He wrote about "the China 'crime' " of selling Chiang Kai-shek "down the river" and emphatically disassociated himself from the Far Eastern programs of Presidents Franklin D. Roosevelt and Harry S Truman. While Senator Vandenberg recognized that it was quite easy to look backward and to condemn, he personally was "not disposed to do much of it." [10] Some of Vandenberg's colleagues, however, most notably Senator Joseph R. McCarthy, were less restrained when it came to discussing the China story. As a consequence, many of the men and women who appear in this study became prime targets in the anti-Communist crusade of the 1950's.

While the intense emotionalism of the 1950's has abated, the subject of American contact with the Chinese Communists is still one that can conjure up images of dark conspiracy and rampant un-Americanism. Historians of the right, such as Anthony Kubek, have labored to keep the mistakes of the past before the American public.[11] Contemporary reporters occasionally find parallels between our current involvement in Vietnam and the earlier experience of the United States in wartime China. Thus, for example, Lee Hall labeled the designation of American military personnel in Vietnam as "advisers" as "possibly the most inaccurate description since the Chinese Communists were termed 'agrarian reformers.' " [12] The subject of this study, then, remains

[10] Arthur H. Vandenberg, Jr., ed., *The Private Papers of Senator Vandenberg* (Boston, 1952), pp. 535, 543.

[11] Anthony Kubek, *How the Far East Was Lost: American Policy and the Creation of Communist China, 1941–1949* (Chicago, 1963). See especially Chapter XVI, "Subversion Along the Linotype Front: Reviewers at Work."

[12] Lee Hall, "Capt. Gillespie Goes Out After the Viet-cong," *Life*, LVII (November 27, 1964), 33. Hall is the Paris bureau chief for *Life* magazine.

controversial and sensitive. When I was engaged in research in the files of the Department of State, an affable official made a casual inquiry about the nature of my project. I replied that I was interested in the problem of American reporting on the Chinese Communist movement. The official's response, "Oh, my God," is a revealing commentary on the continuing status of the American experience in Red China as a topic for inquiry.

A second difficulty is related to the first. One might assume from the plethora of charges and countercharges that were common in the 1950's that Americans have always been deeply concerned about Chinese communism. Actually, throughout most of the period under examination, only a handful of Americans were reasonably well informed about the CCP. Chinese communism, moreover, was scarcely front-page news during these years. The present colors the past, and one of the historian's tasks is to understand events in their proper context. It should be recognized at the outset that hindsight has tended to distort our perspective on the American experience in Red China. Not until very late did the Chinese Communists attain a degree of prominence before the bar of American public opinion. While the CCP emerged from obscurity to a kind of recognition by 1945, relatively little was known about them when the war against Japan ended. When most people thought of China, they thought of Generalissimo Chiang Kai-shek, his attractive wife, and the Flying Tigers. As the chaplain for General Claire Chennault's Flying Tigers recalled, the Chinese Communists "were always a side issue." [13] This is the setting in which the Chinese Communist movement must be understood.

A third problem is semantics. I have used a number of terms that are commonplace in the literature of American reporting on the Chinese Communist movement but that

[13] Paul Frillmann and Graham Peck, *China: The Remembered Life* (Boston, 1968), p. 221.

might be confusing to the reader of this book. For example, the word "Red," as in the Chinese Red Army or the Chinese Reds, is not meant to be a pejorative. Although some first-hand observers used the term in a negative way, others such as Edgar Snow did not, and a popular song in the People's Republic proclaims that "red is beautiful." No particular connotation is intended when the author employs that colorful word. The designations Red China, Communist China, CCP China, and the Border Regions or Border Areas have been used interchangeably. Since Communist rule did not extend over all of China proper until after 1945, these appellations refer only to those parts of the country that were under CCP domination at specific times. The abbreviations KMT and CCP are often used in their broadest sense to refer to Chinese Nationalists and Chinese Communists respectively. After 1937 the Red Army was known as the Eighth Route Army, the Eighteenth Group Army, or the Paluchun. I have restricted myself to the two most common usages, Red Army and Eighth Route Army. The phrases "news blockade" and "news blackout" are not meant to be taken literally. They pertain to a specific state of affairs that was characterized by stringent news censorship and prohibitions against foreign travel in certain restricted locales. It should be recognized, however, that a bona fide military barrier replete with blockhouses and picket lines did in fact surround the Communist strongholds during most of the period 1937–1945. Finally, I have used the terms "reporters" and "reporting" in two ways. "Reporter" means either simply someone who retells or a person who is authorized by a news agency to gather information and regularly to submit written accounts. "Reporting" is associated with a professional correspondent's finished product, or, more broadly, with an account, published or unpublished and by a particular individual, that provides information about the Chinese Communists. I hope that these various usages will become adequately clear in context.

The organization of any book causes problems, and

ordering this book proved to be no exception. Part One provides a background sketch of foreign reporting on the Chinese Communists prior to 1937. It tries to place the subject in historical perspective and does not pretend to be exhaustive. The few individuals of this early period whose writings were important at a later date, such as Agnes Smedley, have been treated at some length. Part Two is a narrative history of firsthand encounters with the Chinese Communists from 1936 to 1945. Although I have been mainly occupied in this section with the questions *who* and *when,* I have also attempted to describe briefly the significant literary productions of the period and to suggest contemporary reactions to these writings. Part Three discusses this literature in a more thematic and more detailed fashion, particularly with respect to the "agrarian reformer" myth. The last section is concerned with the totality of the American experience in Red China. It focuses on the question *why* Westerners responded to China's Communists as they did and tries to suggest certain patterns of intercultural contact.

American involvement with the Chinese Communists is a subject of never-ending fascination. Why? One writer has speculated that the distinctiveness of Sino-American relations is a case of the "attraction of opposites." [14] An examination of the firsthand encounters of Americans and Chinese Communists, at least in the period 1937–1945, suggests the opposite conclusion. By analyzing the writings of travelers who had direct contacts with China's Communists during these years, I have sought to understand why Americans perceived Chinese Communists as they did and to see how closely their perceptions corresponded to reality. My major purpose is to provide an equitable and orderly account of a controversial topic in Sino-American history, and a reasoned explanation of why things happened and why people behaved as they did.

[14] Fairbank, *China,* p. 67.

★ PART I

FOREIGN REPORTING ON
THE CHINESE COMMUNIST
MOVEMENT, 1927-1936

[1]

Before the Blockade: 1927

In the early hours of April 12, 1927, the Kuomintang abruptly ended its revolutionary entente with the Chinese Communist Party by seizing and executing scores of Communists in Shanghai. From 1923 to 1927 the two parties had participated in an uneasy alliance that was in reality little more than a marriage of convenience. Communists individually acquired membership in the KMT, but the CCP retained its independent organization and apparatus. The White Terror unleashed by Chiang Kai-shek in 1927 exposed the façade and inaugurated a civil war which bled China until 1937. The heritage of distrust resulting from the Shanghai coup was never overcome. Only in 1949, when the Communists had driven the Nationalists from the mainland, did peace return to China.

To the foreign eye, there was not much to distinguish Communist from Nationalist before 1927. Few observers were aware of the impending split, and Americans generally assumed that the KMT was subject to powerful Communist influence.[1] It was true, moreover, that the Soviet Union had been the mainstay of the KMT, providing it with military advisers and economic assistance. The KMT had even been

[1] Dorothy Borg, *American Policy and the Chinese Revolution, 1925–1928* (New York, 1947), p. 256; James E. Sheridan, *Chinese Warlord: The Career of Feng Yü-hsiang* (Stanford, 1966), p. 170.

admitted to the Communist International and granted a consultative status. Until Chiang Kai-shek's rupture with the CCP, suspicion of the Chinese Nationalist movement was commonplace in the West,[2] and many Americans and Europeans were relieved when Chiang turned against his erstwhile collaborators.[3]

After disbanding the Communist organizations in Shanghai, Chiang Kai-shek set up a government in Nanking on April 18 to rival the established left-wing KMT regime at Hankow. This so-called Wuhan government was a coalition of Chinese Communists and liberal KMT elements under the leadership of Wang Ching-wei. The CCP hoped to withstand Chiang's opposition by cementing their alliance with the left-KMT, but this hope crumbled when the powerful warlord Feng Yü-hsiang defected to Nanking. In mid-July the Wuhan Nationalists outlawed the CCP. Michael Borodin and his fellow Soviet advisers quickly made their exit from China.[4] The Chinese comrades were left to fend for themselves and were soon fighting for survival against a purged KMT. In less than six months, membership in the

[2] See, for example: Putnam Weale [Bertram Lenox Simpson], *Why China Sees Red* (New York, 1925), p. 89 *et. seq.;* H. G. W. Woodhead, Julean Arnold, and Henry Kittredge Norton, *Occidental Interpretations of the Far Eastern Problem* (Chicago, 1926), pp. 47, 60–69, 217–228; Edward Thomas Williams, *China Yesterday and Today* (rev. ed., New York, 1928), pp. 539–540.

[3] A. T. Steele, *The American People and China* (New York, Toronto, and London, 1966), p. 24. For contemporary examples see: Williams, *A Short History of China* (New York and London, 1928), pp. 607, 610–612; Grover Clark, *In Perspective: A Review of the Politico-Military Situation in China in the Summer of 1927* (Peking, 1927), pp. 3–9; O. D. Rasmussen, *What's Right With China: An Answer to Foreign Criticisms* (Shanghai, 1927), p. 222; Stanley K. Hornbeck, *China To-day: Political* (Boston, 1927), pp. 438–440; Thomas F. Millard, *China: Where It Is Today and Why* (New York, 1928), pp. 44–48.

[4] Sheridan, *Chinese Warlord*, pp. 219–233; Jonathan Spence, *To Change China: Western Advisers in China, 1620–1960* (Boston and Toronto, 1969), p. 203.

CCP fell from more than 50,000 to less than 25,000.[5] A phase in the history of the CCP had come to an end. The Chinese Communists were no longer even nominally a part of the KMT. From 1927 until the second united-front agreement of 1937, the Communists marched under their own tattered banners.

Prior to the climactic events of the spring and summer of 1927, most reporting on the Chinese Communists had been hostile and based on secondhand sources. Thereafter, it became almost impossible for Western reporters to contact Chinese Communists. Between the Shanghai coup in April and the expulsion of the Communists from Wang Ching-wei's short-lived regime in July, however, three Americans were able to observe China's Communists firsthand. Earl Browder's *Civil War in Nationalist China,* Anna Louise Strong's *China's Millions,* and Vincent Sheean's *Personal History* are atypical in being based on extensive personal contact with leading Communist figures and in being written from a point of view not unfriendly to the CCP. Browder's, Strong's, and Sheean's observations acquire an added significance because nearly a decade was to elapse before other Westerners had face-to-face encounters with the Chinese Communists.

Earl Browder scarcely requires an introduction. In 1927 the future secretary-general of the American Communist Party was part of the International Workers' Delegation (IWD) to China. He was also a Comintern agent. Accompanied by his comrades, the Briton Tom Mann and the Frenchman Jacques Doriot, Browder arrived at Canton on February 17, 1927. In the five months from February to June, the IWD traveled through the provinces of Kwangtung, Kiangsi, Hupeh, and Honan.[6] Although their on-the-

[5] Jerome Ch'en, *Mao and the Chinese Revolution* (New York, 1967), p. 125.

[6] Earl Browder, *Civil War in Nationalist China* (Chicago, 1927), pp. 9–10.

spot communiqués parroted the Comintern line in supporting Chiang Kai-shek and the united front, these Western Communists did not, as Harold R. Isaacs has written, miss the importance of what they observed.[7]

Browder's pamphlet, *Civil War in Nationalist China,* is an interesting account in the form of a diary of the IWD's experiences in China. The author is long on description and short on analysis, a quality that makes *Civil War in Nationalist China* rather unusual for a Communist publication. Browder is, moreover, sparing in his use of Leninist slogans and keeps Marxist theorizing to a minimum. The sources he used include personal observations, interviews with KMT and CCP leaders, and reports made available by the chief Soviet adviser, Michael Borodin. Browder's emphasis is on civil strife within the KMT.

Most of the sixty-one pages of Browder's essay constitute a vivid portrayal of the breakdown of Chinese unity and the ascendancy of Nanking. At nearly every stop on the road, he recorded such portents as KMT police suppressing trade and peasant unions. The only bright spot on the itinerary had been Kianfu, Kiangsi, "a revolutionary oasis in a desert of counter-revolution." Although Browder recognized that the Chinese Communists had suffered a reverse at the hands of Chiang Kai-shek, he ended *Civil War in Nationalist China* on a note of dialectical optimism. The setback was not permanent. Rather, Browder proclaimed, it was only a matter of time before the workers would lead their peasant and petty bourgeois allies in a successful drive to revamp Chinese society.[8] The interpretation may not have been original with Earl Browder, but he did embellish it with a wealth of fascinating eyewitness political observations of China from Canton to Hankow during a decisive period in KMT-CCP relations.

[7] Harold R. Isaacs, *The Tragedy of the Chinese Revolution* (2nd rev. ed., Stanford, 1961), p. 158.

[8] Browder, *Civil War in Nationalist China,* pp. 19, 59–61.

By the time Anna Louise Strong arrived in Shanghai in May 1927, she was predisposed to accept Communists as oracles whose crystal balls dialectically reflected the substance of human reality. Miss Strong could trace her lineage deep into America's colonial past, but she was a modern, emancipated woman. Her father, Dr. Sydney Strong, was a Congregationalist minister who advocated the teachings of Charles Darwin; her mother was a graduate of Oberlin. Anna Louise, who was born in Friend, Nebraska, in 1885, followed in the footsteps of her parents. At the age of twenty-three she had won a doctorate, *magna cum laude,* from the University of Chicago and then found employment with the Russell Sage Foundation as a specialist in child-welfare exhibits.[9] Experience led her to conclude that capitalism was an inefficient way of organizing society. At first seeking an intellectual substitute in the kind of utopian socialism offered in Edward Bellamy's *Looking Backward,* she eventually drifted into a career of journalism and became an advocate for militant labor groups in the Pacific Northwest. American participation in the First World War and the failure of the Seattle general strike of 1919 left her disillusioned and ripe for the Communist alternative.

A conversation with Lincoln Steffens in 1920 convinced her that she must see the brave new world being created in the Soviet Union. From the autumn of 1921 until her mysterious expulsion from the U.S.S.R. in 1949, she made a second home in Moscow. She became the Russian correspondent for Hearst's International News Service, attended the Fourth Comintern Congress of 1922, and began a career as free-lance writer. As roving journalist she divided her time between lecturing American audiences on the virtues of the Soviet experiment and visiting the world's trouble spots, always returning to her spiritual mecca, Moscow. By 1927,

[9] Miss Strong's doctoral thesis was published by the University of Chicago. See Anna Louise Strong, *A Consideration of Prayer from the Standpoint of Social Psychology* (Chicago, 1908).

then, Anna Louise Strong had accepted the Russian Communists as the engineers of the future, constantly turned to them for advice and guidance, and was driven by an intense desire to be a useful instrument in the cause of international socialism.[10]

She had first visited China in 1925. While en route from Moscow to the United States, she met Fanny Borodin in Peking. The wife of the Comintern adviser to the KMT persuaded her that a brief detour to revolutionary Canton would be worth the inconvenience. After spending a few days in the strike-bound city, she continued on to her original destination. She did not return to China until after the Shanghai coup had seriously damaged the CCP.[11]

China's Millions is semi-autobiographical and recalls the events Miss Strong witnessed in the spring and summer of 1927. Shortly after her arrival in Shanghai, she made her way to "Red Hankow." Here the Communists who had escaped extermination at the hands of Chiang Kai-shek were trying desperately to preserve their shaky entente with the Wuhan Nationalists. While at Hankow, she stayed with Madame Sun Yat-sen and spent much of her time interviewing leading Communist figures like Borodin, Chen Tu-hsiu, and Li Li-san. Borodin had introduced her to Chen Tu-hsiu, the secretary-general of the CCP, with a prophetic remark: "Miss Strong is unlucky in her revolutions. She came too late for the Russian revolution and now she has come too soon for China." [12]

China's Millions is full of romantic tales of heroic personal sacrifice, confident predictions that the future of China lay in the hands of the awakened worker and peasant masses,

[10] Strong, *I Change Worlds: The Remaking of an American* (New York, 1935), pp. 1–227; Philip Jaffe, "The Strange Case of Anna Louise Strong," *Survey*, LIII (October 1964), 129–130.

[11] Strong, *I Change Worlds*, pp. 227–237; Jaffe, "The Strange Case of Anna Louise Strong," 130.

[12] Strong, *I Change Worlds*, p. 261.

and criticisms of the feudal militarists and bourgeois politicians who had betrayed the Chinese revolution. Although based on firsthand observations. it does little more than recapitulate in travelogue fashion the author's experiences as she witnessed the last gasp of revolutionary *élan* in a China that was moving toward domination by the Nanking regime. Anna Louise Strong accepted Borodin's dictum that the Chinese upheaval failed because the workers and peasants had placed too much trust in the petty bourgeoisie. Like him, she grieved over lost comrades but took hope in the inevitable socialist future. The time, however, was not ripe. When Borodin hastily departed Hankow for Moscow on July 27, she accompanied his small party. The weary traveler breathed a sigh of relief when she was once again in Russia and the "great, dark chaos" of China was far behind her.[13] Not until 1938 did she return to China.

Although Vincent Sheean shared Anna Louise Strong's contempt for the Chinese bourgeoisie and her admiration for Borodin and those who labored at his side, their personalities and approaches were dissimilar. While Miss Strong tried to emulate proletarian virtues, Sheean was something of a dandy who smoked Egyptian cigarettes and dressed ostentatiously. Anna Louise Strong tried to analyze the forces that gave the Chinese revolution its impetus and accounted for its failure, but Sheean was not really interested in the upheaval itself. His forte was the dissection of the human personality. It was flesh and bone that attracted him, not abstractions. Sheean's *Personal History,* which became a popular book in the United States, was just what its title suggested—a semi-autobiographical exercise in political journalism dominated by colorful character sketches.

Early in his career Sheean worked for several prominent newspapers, among them the *Chicago Daily News.* In 1927 the North American Newspaper Alliance sent him to China.

---

[13] Strong, *China's Millions* (New York, 1928), p. 412.

He arrived in mid-April, shortly after Chiang Kai-shek had launched his anti-Communist crusade. The twenty-seven-year-old reporter was appalled by the misery and exploitation he saw in Shanghai, sickened by the ruthlessness of the KMT's counterrevolutionary terror, and critical of missionaries who tried to impose an alien God on the Chinese and of the assumptions of superiority that characterized the thinking of Western businessmen.

Arriving at the seat of the Wuhan government about the same time as Anna Louise Strong, Sheean was also moved by the dedication of such individuals as Borodin, Madame Sun Yat-sen, and Rayna Prohme. Rayna and her husband, William, were radical American journalists who ran Hankow's *People's Tribune* as a propaganda organ for the Communists and the left-wing KMT. Sheean considered Mrs. Prohme the most significant personal influence he had ever encountered. Although he was unable to accompany Borodin's party when it left China, by September he had rejoined his Hankow friends in Moscow.[14]

Sheean summarized his depressing experience of five months in China by saying that everything he believed "worth a damn had gone to pot." The right-wing KMT had triumphed over the forces that had captured his sympathy— the Russian Bolsheviks and their Chinese comrades. But Sheean faced an even greater disappointment in Moscow. Rayna Prohme died of encephalitis shortly before she was to become a member of the Communist Party.[15] It was not until late 1941 that Sheean returned to China and resumed his condemnations of the KMT.

While the books of Browder, Sheean, and Anna Louise Strong were based on intimate contact with Communist functionaries, they did not constitute substantial sources of information on Chinese communism. All three accounts

[14] Vincent Sheean, *Personal History* (New York, 1935), pp. 203–204, 208, 230.

[15] *Ibid.*, p. 259.

were entertaining, but they were generally unenlightening when it came to questions involving the nature of the CCP. Neither Miss Strong nor Sheean paid much heed to the Chinese. It was the Soviet advisory personnel, particularly Borodin, who commanded their attention. The schematic nature of *China's Millions* and the preoccupation of its author with descriptive trivia limited its value as a source of information. Sheean's overriding concern with personality made his work unsatisfactory for readers who sought an understanding of the larger historical forces that contributed to the growth of the Chinese Communist movement. Browder's book was the most detailed and perceptive of the three. Although he was committed to a stereotyped interpretation of history, he meticulously recorded the events that he witnessed.[16] Whatever their shortcomings, *Civil War in Nationalist China, China's Millions,* and *Personal History* were uniquely valuable works, if only because not until 1936 were other Westerners able to write about the CCP from the standpoint of firsthand observation.

[16] For an interesting statement of Earl Browder's philosophy of history see Browder, "The American Communist Party in the Thirties," in *As We Saw the Thirties: Essays on Social and Political Movements of a Decade,* ed. Rita James Simon (Urbana, Chicago, and London, 1967), pp. 245, 252–253.

[2]

From Revolutionaries to
Bandits: 1928-1936

The 1927 coup and the ensuing counterrevolution nearly obliterated the Chinese Communist Party. It was only with considerable effort that the remnants of the CCP were able to survive. The Communist movement split into two currents: the urban-oriented, Moscow-directed underground group of conspirators who made their secret headquarters in Shanghai, and the less orthodox, peasant-oriented band of enthusiasts who established guerrilla bases in the mountainous regions of Southeastern China. Following the disastrous Comintern line of urban insurrection, the first group suffered one crushing defeat after another at the hands of Chiang Kai-shek's superior forces. This branch of the Communist movement had all but disappeared by 1932. Its survivors were incorporated into the more successful group directed by the comrades who operated from partisan bases deep within the relatively inaccessible hinterlands of China.

In the winter of 1927–1928, Mao Tse-tung and Chu Teh combined their 10,000 remaining followers into one unified force. This action inaugurated one of the most remarkable movements in modern history. In the mountainous Chingkangshan region on the Hunan-Kiangsi border, the Mao-Chu combine established a territorial base, created a Red Army, and developed a "Maoist" strategy which fused civil-

ian peasant support behind mobile guerrilla bands. At Juichin in Kiangsi, a Chinese Soviet Republic was proclaimed
on November 7, 1931. Its radical constitution provided for
extensive land redistribution and appealed to the class interests of the poor. Mao Tse-tung and Chu Teh rose to domi-
nate the Chinese Communist movement by virtue of their
own tenaciousness and drive. They were not simply Moscow's obedient creatures.

Chiang Kai-shek cordoned off the Communist base with a
ring of blockhouses and attempted to wipe out the Red disease before it infected other parts of the body politic. After a
series of extermination campaigns and the expenditure of
much blood and treasure, the Generalissimo was finally able
to dislodge his opponents from their mountain strongholds.
In October 1934, 100,000 Communist veterans surged forth
from the Kiangsi redoubt, broke through the KMT blockade, and began the 6,000-mile Long March which has become an epic in the history of human endurance. In the
midst of this ordeal, at the Tsunyi Conference of the Politburo in January 1935, Mao Tse-tung gained supreme leadership of the CCP. By late October of the same year, he had
arrived in the northwestern province of Shensi, where he
commenced an expansion of the Communist enclave which
had been established by Liu Chih-tan.[1] Foreigners knew little of these momentous events.

For all practical purposes, direct foreign contact with the
Chinese Communists had come to an end when Anna Louise
Strong retreated from Wuhan with Borodin. The years from

[1] John King Fairbank, *The United States and China* (rev. ed., New
York, 1958), pp. 230–234; O. Edmund Clubb, *20th Century China*
(New York and London, 1964), pp. 190–202; Robert C. North, *Moscow
and Chinese Communists* (2nd ed., Stanford, 1963), pp. 92–167; Jerome
Ch'en, *Mao and the Chinese Revolution* (New York, 1967), pp.
116–200; Mark Selden, "The Guerrilla Movement in Northwest China:
The Origins of the Shensi-Kansu-Ninghsia Border Region," *China
Quarterly*, Nos. 28–29 (October-December 1966, January-March 1967),
63–81, 61–81.

1928 to 1936 were a time of general uncertainty about the Chinese Communist movement. Otto Braun, a German military adviser smuggled into Kiangsi by the Comintern in 1933, was the sole Westerner in intimate contact with the Chinese Soviet base areas, and he was not providing information for the outside world.[2] While KMT troops were blockading the Soviet region, it was impossible for Western observers to acquire substantial evidence about developments in Red Kiangsi. Consequently, reports on Chinese communism published in the period 1928–1936 are characterized by vagueness and unsubstantiated generalizing.

An examination of *Pacific Affairs,* a journal published by the Institute of Pacific Relations (IPR), constitutes a case study in the uncertain quality of reporting on the Chinese Communist movement to 1936. *Pacific Affairs* was designed to be primarily the news bulletin of the Institute. It also offered its readers a forum for exchanging opinions on the problems of the Pacific region and provided a monthly article of a scholarly nature. From its first issue in May 1928, until its editorial reorganization in 1934, *Pacific Affairs* included extensive bibliographical abstracts of contemporary books and articles on Asian developments. Furthermore, one of the journal's regular features was a news compendium titled "Pacific Items." Usually written by the magazine's editor, Elizabeth Green, this section is a testimonial to the inadequacy of available information about Chinese communism.

The CCP was first mentioned in "Pacific Items" in July 1930. Editor Green wrote that although the Communists

---

[2] Until very recently, Otto Braun was a man shrouded in mystery. Since he always used the Chinese party name "Li Teh," even his real name was unknown. Braun revealed his identity, but little else, in an article criticizing current developments in China in an East Berlin newspaper. See Otto Braun, "In wessen Namen spricht Mao Tse-tung?" *Neues Deutschland,* May 27, 1964. This article is cited in Stuart Schram, *Mao Tse-tung* (New York, 1966), p. 166.

seemed to be only a minor problem in Chiang Kai-shek's continuing struggle against war-lordism, " 'red' uprisings and banditry" had been reported in the vicinity of Hankow.[3] The August installment spoke of brigandage in south and west China, and in September there appeared a news item to the effect that "so-called Communist bands" had inflicted widespread damage and looting on Changsha.[4] Vague references to KMT extermination campaigns and so-called Communist insurrections appeared in "Pacific Items" more or less continuously through 1930 and 1931. By the summer of 1931, Miss Green spoke of "the perennial bandit and communistic disturbances" which troubled Chinese internal affairs.[5]

The Communist problem was first accorded prominence as the leading news item in Miss Green's column of August 1931. She observed that although press cables on the "so-called bandit-communist menace" had been singularly uninformative, Chinese internal developments had centered around the Generalissimo's efforts to eradicate the Reds.[6] During 1932 and 1933, however, her current events commentary, which had been retitled "Pacific Trends," included only a few nebulous references to Chinese civil strife.[7] Until Miss Green's replacement as editor of *Pacific Affairs* in early 1934, the reader of her column could conclude only that the Chinese Communists were sporadically a cause of at least some concern to the Nanking regime. It is pertinent to recognize, furthermore, that she based her news reports largely on official Chinese press releases. The KMT chose to call the Communists "bandits" and to minimize their signifi-

[3] "Pacific Items," *Pacific Affairs*, III (July 1930), 676–677.
[4] *Ibid.*, (August 1930), 770–771; (September 1930), 868–869.
[5] *Ibid.*, IV (June 1931), 523.
[6] *Ibid.*, (August 1931), 713–714.
[7] For example, see "Pacific Trends," *ibid.*, V (June 1932), 514–515; *ibid.*, VI (February-March 1933), 98–101.

cance on the Chinese scene. Elizabeth Green's descriptions of China's Communists were an accurate reflection of the inadequacy of her sources.

The feature articles which appeared in *Pacific Affairs* from 1927 to 1934 did not provide the reader with much more information about the Chinese Communist movement than did "Pacific Items." In the journal's first number, Shao-chang Lee, professor of Chinese history at the University of Hawaii, referred to lawless Communist bands which were creating trouble in various parts of China.[8] David Z. T. Yui, chairman of the China Council of the IPR and a prominent Y.M.C.A. figure, praised Chiang Kai-shek for liberating his nation from the " 'Communist nightmare.' " He viewed Bolshevism as an alien theory imported from Russia and employed to cloak sinister intrigues.[9] L. K. Tao, director of Peiping's Institute of Social Research, believed that communism was one of three influential ideas in modern China. Aside from asserting that the doctrine was attractive to Chinese-youth, Tao had little to say that was not of an abstract nature.[10] In his surveys of relations between the United States and China, T. A. Bisson briefly alluded to the Chinese Communist movement. This research expert for the Foreign Policy Association concluded that the KMT's large-scale offensives demonstrated the vitality and strength of the CCP.[11]

[8] Shao-chang Lee, "In the Orient View: A Survey of the Periodical Press of China and Japan," *ibid.,* I (May 1928), 24–25.

[9] David Z. T. Yui, "China and the Pacific World," *ibid.,* III (January 1930), 35–36, 42.

[10] L. K. Tao, "Social Changes in China," *ibid.,* IV (August 1931), 669–670.

[11] T. A. Bisson, "The United States and the Far East: A Survey of the Relations of the United States with China and Japan—September 1, 1930, to September 1, 1931," *ibid.,* V (January 1932), 67; "The United States in the Pacific: A Survey of the Relations of the United States with Pacific Countries from September 1, 1931, to September 1, 1932," *ibid.* (December 1932), 1049.

There was only one noteworthy exception to the usually brief and unspecific analyses of Chinese communism. In accordance with the journal's policy of presenting the viewpoints of various countries without regard to political considerations, *Pacific Affairs* published a symposium on the CCP from Russian sources in its issue of October 1931. As was to be expected, the Soviet writers discerned a burgeoning Chinese revolutionary upheaval spearheaded by the CCP. Red Kiangsi was depicted as a progressive utopia governed by a 60,000-strong, reform-minded CCP, behind which, the Russians argued, China inevitably would gain its freedom.[12]

In March 1934, *Pacific Affairs* appeared under new management and in a different format. "Pacific Trends" had no place in a journal which now emphasized interpretation over factual reporting. The bibliographical abstracts which had been a cache of information gave way to lengthy book reviews. Owen Lattimore superseded Elizabeth Green as editor. Almost the only carry-over from earlier days was the magazine's disclaimer of a commitment to any specific political, social, or economic point of view. In terms of quantity, commentary on the Chinese Communists did not increase noticeably through 1936. The essays on the CCP in the revamped journal were, however, of a different genre. They were somewhat longer, more analytical, and more skeptical about the official bandit thesis disseminated from Nanking.

Harold R. Isaacs' Trotskyist critique of the Chinese Communist movement was the first article devoted specifically to the subject.[13] Although Isaacs based his study largely on Comintern sources, he borrowed most of his ideas from a decidedly antagonistic observer. Isaacs, an American journalist and former editor of Shanghai's radical *China Forum,* did little more than add factual supports to the interpretive

[12] "The Soviet in Asia," *ibid.,* IV (October 1931), 910–913.
[13] Harold R. Isaacs, "Perspectives of the Chinese Revolution: A Marxist View," *ibid.,* VIII (September 1935), 269–283.

framework provided by Leon Trotsky in *Problems of the Chinese Revolution*.[14] Like Trotsky, Isaacs assumed that proletarian hegemony over the nonsocialist peasantry was the indispensable ingredient in the Marxist formula for revolution. Isaacs charged that before 1927 the Comintern-directed CCP had substituted class collaboration for class struggle. After 1927, he asserted, the CCP had followed a criminal "adventurist" line of urban insurrections which had no possibility of success. Isaacs concluded that whatever else the peasant-oriented Chinese Communist Party might be, it certainly was not "a genuine working-class party, pursuing sound, Marxist proletarian policies." [15]

Only one article other than Isaacs' addressed itself specifically to the subject of Chinese communism in the period 1934–1936. In September 1936, *Pacific Affairs* published a detailed bibliographical study of the literature of the Chinese Soviet movement. A large number of books, pamphlets, and articles from both Communist and non-Communist sources were listed, categorized, and described briefly.[16]

If nothing else, *Pacific Affairs* under the editorship of Owen Lattimore did provide for an exchange of opinions. The journal opened its pages to critiques by those who disagreed with the writers of its feature articles. Thus, for exam-

[14] Leon Trotsky, *Problems of the Chinese Revolution* (trans. Max Shachtman; New York, 1932).

[15] Isaacs, "Perspectives of the Chinese Revolution," 283. Isaacs' dramatic *The Tragedy of the Chinese Revolution* (London, 1938) is a classic expression of the Trotskyite point of view. Isaacs had more respect for facts than his Stalinist opponents, but the analyses of both camps are marred by doctrinaire assumptions. In the subsequent editions of his book, Isaacs abandoned his wholehearted allegiance to Trotsky's brand of Bolshevism. Nevertheless, his interpretive critique remains fundamentally unaltered. See particularly *The Tragedy of the Chinese Revolution* (2nd rev. ed., 1961), pp. vii–xix.

[16] "Pacific Affairs Bibliographies: No. III—Literature on the Chinese Soviet Movement," *Pacific Affairs*, IX (September 1936), 421–435.

ple, Chi Ch'ao-ting, an underground member of the CCP
and a regular contributor to the left-wing New York periodical *China Today,* furnished a Stalinist refutation of Isaacs'
Trotskyist analysis.[17] Also, the enlarged book reviews af-
forded a convenient forum for the interplay of different
viewpoints. In one critique, a former editor of the *North
China Daily News* discounted the proposition that China
would succumb to communism by asserting that there was
no reason to doubt that the Chinese Communists would be
suppressed.[18] Finally, the editor of *Pacific Affairs* would occasionally write an analysis of current issues. In one of these
analyses, Lattimore stated that the real power of the Communists did not lie "in weight of numbers, but in the quality of their leaders and their ability to win support in the
territories they occupy." [19]

Pacific Affairs mirrors the scarcity of authoritative accounts of the Chinese Communist movement. In terms of
the quality of reporting on communism in China and the
meager proportion of available space devoted to the subject,
the journal can hardly be rated as an outstanding source of
information. Nonetheless, in comparative terms, the official
organ of the IPR paid about as much—or more accurately as
little—attention to the Communist problem as did the
books on China published from 1928 to 1936. They too were
circumscribed by the dearth of firsthand appraisals.

One of the manifestations of the shortage of eyewitness information on the CCP was an acceptance by some Far Eastern experts of the official Nationalist position that the Com-

[17] Hansu Chan [Chi Ch'ao-ting], "Another Perspective," *ibid.,* VIII
(December 1935), 477–481. For an excellent biographical sketch of Chi
see Howard L. Boorman, ed., *Biographical Dictionary of Republican
China,* I (New York and London, 1967), 293–297.

[18] O. M. Green, review of *The Case for Manchoukuo* by George
Bronson Rea in *Pacific Affairs,* VIII (September 1935), 376.

[19] Owen Lattimore, "Comment and Opinion: The Inland Gates of
China," *ibid.* (December 1935), 468–473.

munist remnants in the hinterlands had disintegrated into gangs of roving bandits. Nathaniel Peffer, a specialist on China at Columbia University, echoed KMT propaganda to the effect that the "so-called Red armies" were little more than pillaging gangster organizations.[20] While accepting Nanking's contention that the Communists were simply bandits, other writers disagreed with the Chinese government in assessing their strength and potential. Hallett Abend, a correspondent for the *New York Times*, thought that the Red guerrillas were merely powerful outlaw bands which had appropriated some Marxist slogans. He was alarmed, nevertheless, that China might be ripe for their blandishments. Decades of intolerable misrule and oppression, Abend explained, had made the peasant masses receptive to the agitations of the "so-called Communists."[21]

The lack of reliable firsthand information about the CCP also affected the writings of those who believed that the so-called bandits were in fact genuine Marxists dedicated to the communization of China. In 1935, Anna Louise Strong's *China's Millions* was published in an expanded and revised edition. After altering some of her seven-year-old statements with the apparent purpose of bringing them into line with current Comintern interpretations and refurbishing Borodin's speeches with invectives against Chiang Kai-shek, she added a new section on events since 1927. While this enlargement of *China's Millions* may have increased the book's propaganda value, it made almost no contribution to the world's fund of knowledge about the Chinese Communist movement. For the most part, she offered the reader little

[20] Nathaniel Peffer, *China: The Collapse of a Civilization* (New York, 1930), p. 179. See also Arthur N. Holcombe, *The Spirit of the Chinese Revolution* (New York, 1930), pp. 61, 118–119 and Reginald E. Sweetland, "The Strength of Communism in China: II—Banditry in a New Guise," *Current History*, XXXIII (January 1931), 526–529.

[21] Hallett Abend, *Tortured China* (New York, 1930), pp. 23, 44, 78. For a similar appraisal see Ralph Townsend, *Ways That Are Dark: The Truth About China* (New York, 1933), pp. xiv, 200, 214–218, 254.

more than stereotyped generalizations about the march of progress in the guerrilla areas.[22] Even Pavel Mif, the director of Sun Yat-sen University in Moscow and formerly the Communist International's top agent to the Central Committee of the CCP, seemed to know very little about what was happening in the Kiangsi Soviet. His history of Chinese communism before 1931 bogged down in Stalinist rationalizations of the failure of the Comintern line, but contained factual data which reflected an intimate knowledge of what had taken place prior to the suppression of the Shanghai group. Mif's account of Red Kiangsi, however, was brief, general, and based on sparse documentation. Although the Russian expert on the CCP doctrinairely proclaimed that Chinese Communists were fellow Marxists in whose hands the socialist future of China inevitably lay, he had to qualify descriptions of developments after 1931 with such telltale phrases as "judging from the information received." [23]

The widespread assumption that communism was irrelevant to China is the most significant manifestation of the lack of authentic information. There were a few scholars like the University of Chicago's Harley Farnsworth MacNair and

[22] Anna Louise Strong, *China's Millions: The Revolutionary Struggles from 1927 to 1935* (New York, 1935), pp. 37, 252–253, 417–457. For similar impoverished stereotypes by an editorial writer for the New York *Daily Worker* see Harry Gannes, *When China Unites: An Interpretive History of the Chinese Revolution* (New York, 1937), pp. 276–281.

[23] P. Mif, *Heroic China: Fifteen Years of the Communist Party of China* (New York, 1937), pp. 89–92. The ill-informed nature of Communist writings is further illustrated in two Communist tracts for the time: Ray Stewart, *War in China* (New York, 1932) and M. James and R. Doonping [Chi Ch'ao-ting], *Soviet China* (New York, 1932). Stewart's contribution to the "International Pamphlets" series amounts to little more than a few glowing generalizations. James and Chi are well informed on events prior to 1928. For developments after 1928, however, they had to rely on the *New York Times* for most of their material.

Columbia's Paul Monroe who believed that a peasant brand of Marxism was a genuine possibility.[24] But most writers were able to discover a variety of reasons why communism was peculiarly unsuited to China. One analysis anchored itself on the notion that the Chinese cultural milieu was inherently anti-Communist. Grover Clark, the American editor of the Peking *Leader,* knew that CCP spokesmen claimed to be Leninists. He believed, however, that China offered "only very stony ground" for Bolshevism. The Marxian concept of subordinating the individual to the community, he reasoned, was basically antipathetical to deeply rooted Chinese traits of property consciousness, individualism, and family solidarity.[25] A British journalist similarly concluded that communism was "alien to Chinese culture." [26]

Other writers thought that it was simply absurd to contemplate Leninism in a nation of peasants. Leon Trotsky, who had long held a low opinion of the revolutionary potential of the *muzhik,* caustically remarked that to accept the possibility of a real Soviet development in China was to "believe in miracles." [27] While Nathaniel Peffer had little else in common with the creator of the Russian Red Army, he did share Trotsky's conviction that it was unreasonable to anticipate the growth of Bolshevism in an agrarian society. Peffer defined Chinese communism as an "exotic growth, brought in from outside, from a different soil and climate,

[24] Harley Farnsworth MacNair, *China's International Relations and Other Essays* (Shanghai, 1926), pp. 158–169, and *China in Revolution: An Analysis of Politics and Militarism Under the Republic* (Chicago, 1931), pp. 188–219; Paul Monroe, *China: A Nation in Evolution* (New York, 1928), pp. 226–227.

[25] Grover Clark, *The Great Wall Crumbles* (New York, 1935), pp. 333–335.

[26] Gerald Yorke, *China Changes* (New York, 1936), pp. 217–218.

[27] Trotsky, *Problems of the Chinese Revolution,* pp. 304–306. See also Isaac Deutscher, *The Prophet Unarmed: Trotsky, 1921–1929* (London, New York, and Toronto, 1959), pp. 328, 422–424.

and thrust in barely under the surface." The number of so-called Communists who had even the most remote conception of Marxism was infinitesimal, Peffer said, and he had no doubt whatever that China was impenetrable to the foreign doctrine of communism.[28]

Many observers, then, felt that it was highly improbable that communism would take root in what one of them described as the "unsympathetic soil of China." [29] By framing estimates, either explicitly or implicitly, on an identification of the Soviet Union as the authoritative model for Marxism, it was easy to conclude that Chinese communism could not evolve along orthodox Leninist lines. If nothing else, the seeds which later would come to fruition in the agrarian reformer myth had been planted. Furthermore, the proposition that Marxism was not an alternative for peasant China reinforced the bandit-remnant interpretation.

The unsubstantial character of the Western literature on Chinese communism can be summarized by examining the most detailed and heavily documented study on the subject to appear in the years from 1927 to 1936. General Victor A. Yakhontoff, formerly an officer in the Imperial Russian Army and military attaché at the Russian Embassy in Tokyo, published *The Chinese Soviets* in 1934.[30] The book contains a detailed account of Chiang Kai-shek's annihilation campaigns through early 1934, an analysis of political and economic developments in Kiangsi, and a cataloguing of the military and social policies of the Chinese Communists. Yakhontoff traveled to China, Soviet Russia, Japan, and Man-

[28] Peffer, "The Chinese Idea of Communism," *Current History,* XXXVI (July 1932), 400–404.

[29] Henry Kittredge Norton, *China and the Powers* (New York, 1927), p. 92.

[30] General Yakhontoff, born in 1881, was a member of the Russian general staff during the First World War. He served as assistant secretary of war in Alexander Kerensky's short-lived government of 1917. Yakhontoff left Russia for the United States in 1918 and became a naturalized American citizen.

choukuo in his search for materials. Although the KMT censorship on information about the CCP prevented this conscientious Russo-American from obtaining all that he desired, he could justly claim that his bibliography overlooked little. The text, however, is discursive, rambling, and lacks focus. Yakhontoff's penchant for quoting long excerpts from his sources, his arid style, and his bias in favor of Comintern appraisals of Chinese communism do not improve the presentation. Most important, as Yakhontoff himself admitted, the paucity of available evidence made it impossible to arrive at entirely sound judgments about developments in the guerrilla regions. The General may have been convinced that Chinese Communists were progressive revolutionary reformers, but the inconclusive nature of his sources reduced this partisan interpretation to an educated guess.[31]

In the absence of firsthand observations of the Chinese Soviet regions, Far Eastern specialists were generally compelled to formulate their assessments from sources that were neither informative nor balanced. According to KMT propagandists, Chinese Communists were nefarious bandits. Comintern functionaries propagated equally stereotyped and misleading images. Uncommitted authorities like Nathaniel Peffer found themselves in a quandary. Despite all that had been said about the Communist movement, he complained in 1935, "we actually know nothing about it." He felt that because of the absence of an adequate means of gaining substantiated data about the Soviet areas, one had to rely more on rumor than on evidence. Everything that had been written on the subject could be categorized as "propaganda, special pleading, guesswork or hearsay." Therefore, Peffer despaired, "what you believe about communist China still depends on whom you prefer to believe—whose sympathies you share or whom you respect enough to accept his intelli-

[31] Victor A. Yakhontoff, *The Chinese Soviets* (New York, 1934), pp. viii, 1–13.

gent estimate as carrying weight."[32] Reporting on the CCP must be understood, then, in the overall context of a factual uncertainty that bordered on sheer ignorance.

Before 1927, Western observers had been slow to recognize that the Chinese Communists were a distinct element in the KMT. From 1928 to 1936 they could not see much beyond the Nationalist-inspired bandit-remnant thesis. These were truly years of uncertainty about the Chinese Communists. With a few unspectacular exceptions, foreign accounts of the Chinese Communist movement were characterized by speculative theorizing, unsubstantiated generalizing, and partisan reporting. It seems clear, moreover, that Chinese communism was not a topic of international concern. Most journalists, for example, were unperturbed about the lack of available information. Even American diplomats serving in China did not go out of their way to analyze what appeared to be an unimportant movement. From 1932 to 1936 only one Foreign Service officer, the vice-consul at Hankow, tried to provide Washington with a continuous analysis of the Chinese Communist movement.[33] This myopic state of affairs is attributable to an absence of persuasive data on the CCP. Bottled up in Kiangsi by the KMT, China's Communists were nearly forgotten by the world outside.[34] In Western eyes, they were rebels without a cause or an informed audience.

[32] Peffer, review of *The Chinese Soviets, China's Red Army Marches,* and *The Fundamental Laws of the Chinese Soviet Republic* in *Pacific Affairs,* VIII (June 1935), 223–226.

[33] Dorothy Borg, *The United States and the Far Eastern Crisis of 1933–1938: From the Manchurian Incident Through the Initial Stage of the Undeclared Sino-Japanese War* (Cambridge, Mass., 1964), pp. 196–234. See also O. Edmund Clubb, *Communism in China: As Reported from Hankow in 1932* (New York and London, 1968).

[34] A. T. Steele, *The American People and China* (New York, Toronto, and London, 1966), p. 24.

[3]

The Bandit-Remnant Thesis
Questioned: 1931-1936

Despite a general indifference about Chinese communism
and a lack of authoritative information on the subject, by
1936 there was a growing skepticism of the bandit-remnant
interpretation. As early as 1931, Yang Chien and William
Prohme had disputed the bandit thesis. Yang, the Assistant
Director of the National Research Institute, based his analysis on documents captured from the Communists in Kiangsi
during the annihilation campaigns. Critical of his own government for publishing misleading communiqués about
"decimated remnants," he assessed the Chinese Communists
as dedicated Marxists tenaciously scheming to install the "Soviet Republic of China." [1] Less sure of his ground than
Yang, William Prohme implied that Chinese Communists
were not brigands. The former editor of Hankow's *People's
Tribune* described the Chinese Soviet development as something "still unclarified, still haphazard." He believed, however, that the Chinese Communists possessed the "semblance

[1] Yang Chien, *The Communist Situation in China* (Nanking, 1931),
pp. 1, 11. See also Dorothy Borg, *The United States and the Far Eastern Crisis of 1933–1938: From the Manchurian Incident Through the
Initial Stage of the Undeclared Sino-Japanese War* (Cambridge, Mass.,
1964), pp. 196–234.

of an ideology" and that their leaders were agrarian revolutionaries, not gangsters.[2]

Throughout the early 1930's a handful of observers like Yang Chien and William Prohme questioned the bandit-remnant thesis. Perhaps the most important of these was a young American woman of very radical convictions. Agnes Smedley is one of two foreigners whose ashes are buried in Red China's equivalent to Arlington Cemetery, the National Revolutionary Martyrs Memorial Park. The simple inscription placed to honor her reads: "Agnes Smedley, revolutionary writer and friend of the Chinese people." [3] The terseness of the epitaph scarcely does her justice, for the Chinese Communists had no better foreign friend than the American woman who gave of herself unstintingly in her efforts to further their cause.

By any standard, Agnes Smedley was extraordinary. The most radical American journalist in China, she pursued a career as fascinating as any in recent history. Anna Louise Strong was a well-bred, middle-class intellectual who had to observe the downtrodden from afar before she consciously adopted revolutionary convictions. Miss Smedley was a social malcontent long before she had heard of Karl Marx or Vladimir I. Lenin. Her burning class hatreds were rooted in the childhood experiences of a sensitive daughter of indigent parents who worked in the mining camps of Colorado. As Chalmers A. Johnson has observed, Agnes Smedley was "educated in the original school of hard knocks." [4] Her fictionalized autobiography, *Daughter of Earth*, constitutes an indictment of an environment which taught its author that the life of a hillbilly family promised little more than poverty and

[2] William Prohme, "Soviet China," *New Republic*, LXVII (August 12, 1931), 334–335.

[3] Edgar Snow, *The Other Side of the River: Red China Today* (New York, 1962), p. 77.

[4] Chalmers A. Johnson, *An Instance of Treason: Ozaki Hotsumi and the Sorge Spy Ring* (Stanford, 1964), p. 63.

uncertainty. "We belonged to the class," Agnes Smedley
wrote, "who have nothing and from whom everything is always taken away." [5] She never forgot the humiliations that
were part of the everyday life of a second-class citizen in a
land of plenty, and she bitterly resented being deprived of
an adequate education. A brutalized childhood instilled in
her a spirit of rebellion against all forms of constituted authority.[6]

When Agnes Smedley arrived in China as special correspondent for the liberal *Frankfurter Zeitung* in late 1928,
her life had amounted to little more than a series of disap-
pointments. Lacking a high-school education, she had made
haphazard attempts to improve herself by attending evening
lectures at New York University and a summer session at the
University of California.[7] After wandering from a job to job
and after a short and unhappy marriage, she became involved with a group of Indian revolutionaries in New York
City. Her connection with the Indian nationalists led to a
brief imprisonment in 1918 for violations of American neutrality law, a stormy eight-year liaison in Germany with one
of their leaders, a nervous breakdown and attempted suicide,
and, finally, a contract as the *Zeitung*'s China reporter.[8]
Eric Hoffer's profile of the potential true believer motivated
by a desire to discard an unwanted self and find a new
sense of purpose by identification with a utopian cause seems
particularly applicable to Agnes Smedley.[9] Not many years

[5] Agnes Smedley, *Daughter of Earth* (rev. ed., New York, 1935), p.
58. According to one of Miss Smedley's acquaintances, she wrote the
first draft of *Daughter of Earth* as part of a case history for her psy-
choanalyst in Europe; Mrs. Helen Foster Snow to the author, May 1,
1965.

[6] Anna Wang, *Ich kämpfte für Mao: Eine deutsche Frau erlebt die
chinesische Revolution* (Hamburg, Germany, 1964), pp. 86–89.

[7] F. W. Deakin and G. R. Storry, *The Case of Richard Sorge* (New
York, 1966), pp. 70–71.

[8] Smedley, *Battle Hymn of China* (New York, 1943), pp. 1–27.

[9] Eric Hoffer, *The True Believer: Thoughts on the Nature of Mass
Movements* (New York, 1951), pp. 12–16, 53–55.

were to lapse before this intense militant found her cause. Miss Smedley's initial impressions of Nationalist China convinced her that she was in a feudal cesspool where a decadent KMT exploited the subjugated masses in the interests of a small privileged class. By one means or another, she made the acquaintance of Chinese Communists in Shanghai. Thus, for example, at a dinner held for the renowned novelist Lu Hsün, she listened to the editor of a Communist underground newspaper present a report on the activities of the CCP. Driven by a Quaker heritage that prompted her to place conscience above Chinese civil law, she came to consider it an honor to assist those who were "fighting and dying for the liberation of the poor," China's Communists.[10]

As previously noted, Anna Louise Strong's retreat from China with Borodin symbolized the end of direct outside contact with the CCP. Agnes Smedley, however, provides a qualified exception to the absence of personal encounters after 1928. Her connections developed to the point where a wounded Red Army commander, Chou Chien-ping, spent his period of convalescence at her home telling her stirring tales of Communist heroism.[11] Although it was not until 1937 that she actually entered the Soviet regions and viewed the Chinese Communist movement firsthand, she was covertly supplied with testimonials by Communist agents in Shanghai. Agnes Smedley's contemporaries knew that she was the only Western journalist receiving information directly from CCP sources before 1936. This gave her writings a notoriety that they did not otherwise merit.[12]

Chinese Destinies and *China's Red Army Marches* are the most important literary expressions of Agnes Smedley's clandestine encounters with the CCP. The former is a collection

10 Smedley, *Battle Hymn of China*, p. 81; Mrs. Snow to the author, May 1, 1965.

11 Smedley, *Battle Hymn of China*, pp. 123–124.

12 James Bertram, *Return to China* (London, Melbourne, and Toronto, 1957), p. 5; Anna Louise Strong, *China's Millions: The Revolutionary Struggles from 1927 to 1935* (New York, 1935), p. 440; Snow, *The Other Side of the River*, p. 263.

of unconnected anecdotes that are riddled with stereotypes. Capitalists and landlords are always fat and greasy, Communists lean and unselfish. Miss Smedley's approach is that of a proselytizing novelist. Her characters tell their own stories in a fashion not overly complimentary to the KMT. Thus, one of her soldier-heroes is made to say that Chiang Kai-shek's mother "slept with a dog, and he is the result!" [13] While Agnes Smedley's prose is vivid enough, her fictionalized characterizations and extreme bias render *Chinese Destinies* an ineffectual instrument for relaying either information or propaganda.

Although one authority has called *China's Red Army Marches* "pure propaganda," this second morality play does represent an improvement over her first effort.[14] She was more specific as to names and places and even included interesting details on CCP procedures and developments. Nonetheless, *China's Red Army Marches* remains a storybook primer in which iron battalions of dynamic Communist guerrillas invariably triumph over KMT legions of depraved mercenaries led by Fascist officers. Agnes Smedley might rightly claim to have based her tales on "actual events" and to have drawn her materials from "actual participants," but they were exactly what she called them— "stories" provided by informants who understandably chose to remain anonymous.[15]

For all her banality and lack of balance, Agnes Smedley did provide an alternative to KMT propaganda. Her heroes are the progressive, idealistic, hard-fighting men of the Red Army; the bandits are the depraved, rape-minded troops of Chiang Kai-shek. Such ideas earned Miss Smedley sharp at-

---

[13] Smedley, *Chinese Destinies: Sketches of Present-Day China* (New York, 1933), p. 267.

[14] Samuel B. Griffith, II, *The Chinese People's Liberation Army* (New York, Toronto, London, and Sydney, 1967), p. 325, note 22.

[15] Smedley, *China's Red Army Marches* (New York, 1934), pp. viii, xiii.

tacks from the official Chinese press, the disquieting attention of the KMT police, and a trip to the Soviet Union in 1933 to recover her shattered nerves. In 1934 she returned to the United States. By 1936, however, she was back in China serving the cause which had given her life meaning and purpose.[16]

Unlike Agnes Smedley, the Reverend Rudolf Alfred Bosshardt had no affinity for Chinese communism. Like the American journalist, however, this Swiss missionary had an unusual encounter with the Chinese Communists before 1936. In early October 1934, Bosshardt and five other members of the China Inland Mission were kidnapped and held for ransom by a detachment of Ho Lung's Second Front Army. Although the other captives were soon released, Bosshardt and the Reverend Arnolis Hayman were compelled to accompany their captors on marches through Kweichow, Szechuan, Hupeh, Hunan, and Yunnan provinces. Although, according to Bosshardt, Chinese prisoners were beaten, degraded, and executed, he and Hayman were provided with the best available food, clothing, and accommodations. The Communists released Hayman on November 18, 1935, but Bosshardt was not given his freedom until April 12, 1936. Within a few months of the release, Bosshardt related the story of his ordeal in a volume entitled *The Restraining Hand: Captivity for Christ in China*.[17]

One might assume that his year and a half in the midst of the Chinese Communists would have enabled Bosshardt to gather a great deal of valuable information. This was not the case, however. Regularly confined to quarters, he had few opportunities to talk with any Chinese Communists other than his guards. The Swiss missionary's dogmatic opposition to communism also posed a barrier to any meaningful dialogue with his captors.

[16] Smedley, *Battle Hymn of China*, pp. 79, 92–98.

[17] R. A. Bosshardt, *The Restraining Hand: Captivity for Christ in China* (London, 1936), pp. 11, 18, 23, 56–57.

The China Inland Mission was known for its fervent anti-communism.[18] If Bosshardt was one of its typical representatives, its reputation was deserved. He viewed communism as a doctrine "utterly void of love" and found Communists rude and discourteous, being particularly offended by their "continual swearing and filthy talk." Chiang Kai-shek's soldiers, whose company he much preferred, did not hurl about such epithets as "Devil," "Dog," and "Imperialist." He did, however, give the Communists a superior rating as propagandists.[19]

Despite the many reports which referred to them as robbers and bandits, Bosshardt regarded the Red Army cadres as "disciples of Marx and Lenin." Their religion was communism, their true motherland the Soviet Union. The aroused missionary called for a spiritual rearmament to resist the devilish Red menace to home, to church, and to civilization.[20] Since *The Restraining Hand* went unnoticed by both Far Eastern authorities and the American press, it is doubtful that Bosshardt's appeal had much effect. Such indifference is understandable. Except for his pointed comments about the bandit-remnant thesis, Bosshardt said almost nothing about the programs and policies of the CCP.

While lacking the experiences and prejudices of Agnes Smedley and Bosshardt, other writers shared their conviction that the bandit-remnant thesis was inadequate. The skillful maneuvers of the Red Army on the Long March deeply impressed Norman Hanwell. Dismissing KMT statements as useless for even "rearranging pins on a campaign map," he asserted that it was imperative that Nanking's propaganda be replaced with a "more plausible" explanation of the Chinese Communist movement.[21]

[18] Fox Butterfield, "A Missionary View of the Chinese Communists, 1936–1939," in *Papers on China*, XV (Cambridge, Mass., 1961), 178–179.

[19] Bosshardt, *The Restraining Hand*, pp. 23, 34, 78, 264–265.

[20] *Ibid.*, p. 12.

[21] Norman Hanwell, "The Chinese Red Army," *Asia*, XXXVI (May 1936), 317.

Norman Hanwell had been in China since 1934 doing research on rural development and local government. In 1936 he put aside his research and made a determined effort to find that more believable interpretation. Hanwell interviewed newspaper correspondents, Chinese who had lived in the Soviet regions, and missionaries who had fled before the advancing Communists. But most of his information was obtained from a report on conditions in Szechuan made by a Chinese investigator after the withdrawal of the Red Army. Hanwell tried to verify his secondhand data by making excursions to the areas that had been passed through during the Long March. He spent three months in Szechuan and traveled extensively in the provinces north of the Yellow River.

Hanwell's findings were published in a series of articles that the editors of *Asia* magazine advertised as the most thorough and reliable account of the Chinese Red Army so far to appear in print.[22] Yet Hanwell himself stated that secondhand reports on the CCP were terribly unreliable, differing according to the prejudices of their originators.[23] Not only did Hanwell forego an assessment of the strength of Chinese Communists for lack of credible data, he also declined to offer an alternative to the Red-bandit interpretation.[24] He did discover that the Communists were reputed to be highly mobile and disciplined, to be advocates of land reform and progressive taxation, and, above all, to be expert organizers.[25] But while he had no doubt that the term bandit was a "misnomer," Hanwell was unwilling to go beyond his evidence.[26] He did not try to replace the Chinese government's

[22] Hanwell, "The Chinese Red Army," 317–322; "When Chinese Reds Move In," *ibid.* (October 1936), 631–634; "Within Chinese Red Areas," *ibid.*, XXXVII (January 1937), 58–61.

[23] Hanwell, "When Chinese Reds Move In," 631; "The Chinese Red Army," 321.

[24] Hanwell, "The Chinese Red Army," 320.

[25] Hanwell, "The Chinese Red Army," 320–321; "When Chinese Reds Move In," 632–634; "Within Chinese Red Areas," 61.

[26] Hanwell, "The Chinese Red Army," 322.

description of Chinese Communists with a more plausible one.

Reizo Otsuka, a member of the staff of the South Manchuria Railway Company, shared Hanwell's conviction that the available sources of information about the Chinese Communists were unreliable. He deplored the absence of any first-hand missionary or newspaper correspondent's accounts and confessed that he had been forced to turn to the self-interested literature of the KMT and CCP. "Unfortunately," he explained, "there are practically no other sources or documents upon which one might rely." [27] Nevertheless, in a data paper prepared for the Sixth Conference of the Institute of Pacific Relations which met at Yosemite National Park in the summer of 1936, Reizo rejected the KMT interpretation. Warning that the "menace of sovietization in China" had not been diminished by the Long March, he emphasized the organic relationship of the CCP to the Comintern. He even called on China to join hands with Japan in a cooperative effort to suppress the Chinese Communists.[28]

Reizo's paper occasioned a suggestive debate at the Yosemite meeting. The Chinese delegates contested the assertions that the CCP was still obedient to the Comintern and represented a serious threat to the internal stability of their country. They argued that the importance of communism had been purposely exaggerated by the Japanese "as a pretext for unwarranted interference in China." [29] Because of the controversial nature of the subject, the editors of the proceedings of the Yosemite Conference prefaced Reizo's essay with

[27] Reizo Otsuka, "Recent Developments in the Chinese Communist Movement," in *Problems of the Pacific, 1936: Aims and Results of Social and Economic Policies in Pacific Countries, Proceedings of the Sixth Conference of the Institute of Pacific Relations, Yosemite National Park, California, 15–29 August 1936*, ed. W. L. Holland and Kate L. Mitchell (Chicago, 1937), p. 348.

[28] *Ibid.*, pp. 355, 375.

[29] "Summary of Conference Discussions," in *Problems of the Pacific*, pp. 171–172.

a precautionary footnote disclaiming any responsibility for his interpretations on the part of either the Secretariat of the Institute of Pacific Relations or the Japanese Council. The paper was being printed, the editors stated, in the hope that it would provide "useful information on a relatively little-known question." [30]

Hallett Abend was less certain than Reizo Otsuka as to what should replace the bandit-remnant interpretation. But the passage of six years had convinced him that Nanking's propaganda was obsolete. Abend found it difficult to believe that the CCP's impressive record of resistance to Chiang Kai-shek was inspired merely by love of plunder. The *New York Times'* China correspondent concluded that the charge that the Red Army was made up of "bandits" was contradicted by a morale and vitality strong enough to withstand the onslaughts of incomparably better equipped forces.[31]

Edgar Snow's sentiments were identical to those of Abend. In a letter to Ambassador Nelson T. Johnson, Snow wrote that he had ceased believing in the brigand cliché prior to his entry into the Soviet regions. The general propaganda about the Communists, Snow reflected, "simply didn't make sense: one could not believe that mere bandits, interested only in loot and slaughter, could defy all Nanking's forces for nearly 10 years." There must, Snow concluded, "be a powerful something holding them up." [32] The course of events, then, had convinced a few observers that the gangster thesis was bankrupt some time before *Red Star over China* gave the myth its *coup de grâce*.

[30] Reizo, "Recent Developments in the Chinese Communist Movement," p. 343n.

[31] Hallett Abend and Anthony J. Billingham, *Can China Survive?* (New York, 1936), pp. 240–242.

[32] Snow to Johnson, February 6, 1937, Nelson T. Johnson papers.

★ PART II

FIRSTHAND ENCOUNTERS
WITH THE CHINESE
COMMUNISTS, 1936-1945

[4]

The Bandit-Remnant Thesis
Destroyed: 1936-1937

By 1936 the nature of Chinese communism had become,
as Norman Hanwell wrote, a controversial topic of great interest to those in the Far East.[1] The debate, however, was
rather inane. Apart from KMT communiqués, the only accounts that even pretended to be authoritative were those
from Communist sympathizers like Agnes Smedley. The inadequacy of Nanking's propaganda had been highlighted by
such dramatic events as the Long March, and the bandit-
remnant thesis had been questioned. But Western ignorance
about the CCP precluded the emergence of a clear alternative. It was against this background that China's Communists found their Boswell in the person of Edgar Parks Snow.

Edgar Snow was born in Kansas City, Missouri, where his
family owned and operated a printing company. One of his
ancestors, Captain Samuel Snow, had been commissioned by
President James Madison to serve as the first resident American consul at Canton. Aside from that fact, Edgar Snow had
little reason to go to the Far East. But he possessed a trait
characteristic of most foreign correspondents, wanderlust.
After graduating from the University of Missouri's school of
journalism, Snow decided to take a trip around the world.

[1] Norman Hanwell, "The Chinese Red Army," *Asia*, XXXVI (May
1936), 317.

He had planned to stay in China for only six weeks, but he was not to see the United States again for thirteen years.[2] When Snow arrived in Shanghai in the summer of 1928, he was twenty-two years old and his only practical experience in journalism was as a campus correspondent for the *Kansas City Star*. Nevertheless, he was hired as an assistant to John B. Powell, the editor of the *China Weekly Review*. Snow spent most of the years before 1936 traveling in the Far East and contributing articles to various newspapers and magazines. During the 1930's he wrote a regular column for the New York *Sun,* became the London *Daily Herald's* special correspondent, and served as part-time lecturer in journalism at Yenching University. When he married the attractive Helen Foster in 1932, there were two talented writers in the family. From 1933 to 1937 the Snows made their residence in Peiping.[3]

A comfortable upbringing in the American Midwest left Snow unprepared for the harsh realities of Asia. One of his early assignments was to cover a famine in northwest China. It was a formative experience for him. He saw children starving and human flesh being sold openly in the marketplace, and he saw usurers and landlords profiting from this misery. Snow responded to the famine of 1929 with intense solicitude for fellow beings in distress. Many foreigners became inured to the commonplace suffering of the Chinese people. Significantly, this was not true of Edgar Snow. One of the hallmarks of his thinking and writing is a concern with man's inhumanity to man. He believed that all men are brothers and should behave as brothers.[4]

[2] Edgar Snow, *Journey to the Beginning* (New York, 1958), pp. 1–2, 11–15.

[3] *Ibid.,* pp. 3–5, 102–106, 129. See also Stanley J. Kunitz and Howard Haycraft, eds., *Twentieth Century Authors: A Biographical Dictionary of Modern Literature* (New York, 1942), pp. 1309–1310.

[4] Snow, *Journey to the Beginning,* pp. 3–11. For an unusually vivid recollection of the 1929 famine see *Red Star over China* (New York, 1961), pp. 226–227.

Snow grew increasingly disillusioned with the Nanking regime. At first, he accepted the pro-Nationalist views of John B. Powell. Like the editor of the *China Weekly Review,* Snow believed that Chiang Kai-shek had saved China from mob rule and that right was on the side of the KMT. His travels and his contacts with people like Madame Sun Yat-sen (Soong Ch'ing-ling), however, gradually convinced him that the Nationalist government was a corrupt, inefficient, and dictatorial regime in a troubled land that desperately needed revolutionary leadership.[5]

While Snow's humanitarianism and distaste for the KMT are obvious, his philosophical convictions are harder to define. As a college student, he distrusted dogmatism in any form, was indifferent to sectarian religious beliefs, and called himself a "rationalist." In the mid-1930's he adopted the tenets of Fabian socialism. Although he had done some reading in Marxist works, Snow maintained that "it was not Marx or Lenin or Stalin or Mao Tse-tung who reached me with the logic of Socialism." Rather, it was the Fabian vision of George Bernard Shaw.[6] Whatever the sources, Snow's thought came to be characterized by a curious kind of indeterminate determinism. While he claimed to perceive direction in the historical process, he always demurred at the point of saying that its outlines were fixed and unalterable. This uncertain certainty is best illustrated by Snow's interpretation of the Chinese revolution. He concluded a dialectical analysis of it by saying that his speculations were colored by human subjectivity and were, therefore, open to error and miscalculation.[7]

In 1933, Snow published his first book, *Far Eastern Front.* This account of the Sino-Japanese clash in Manchuria summarizes his political views prior to his entry into the Chinese

[5] Snow, *Journey to the Beginning,* pp. 24–27, 37–42, 47–54, 83–95, 134–138.
[6] *Ibid.,* pp. 11–15, 31, 73, 134–138.
[7] Snow, *Red Star over China,* p. 495.

Soviet regions. He dismissed as sadly mistaken the hope that
the KMT's ascendancy meant a bright vista of reform for
China. After 1927, Snow philosophized, the party of Sun
Yat-sen had degenerated to a "warlord prototype." The Nationalists had not only massacred thousands of progressive
Chinese, he wrote, but also crusaded against the very tenets
of liberal thought. He registered his agreement with the conviction of one Chinese historian that the KMT had become
"a lifeless body, soulless and spiritless, the private chancery
of a military dictator." Snow asserted, however, that the
"logic of history" portended a transition from the decadent
feudalism of China's present to a better, more modern future.[8]

Snow's discussion of Chinese communism in *Far Eastern
Front* is of particular interest. His comments on the CCP
were based on secondary works by scholars like Nathaniel
Peffer and T. A. Bisson. Like them, Snow had only a frag-
mentary knowledge of the Chinese Communist movement.
He echoed Peffer's opinion that the Chinese Communists
were a group of desperate men who lacked even an elementary understanding of Marxism. Snow interpreted the
Chinese Soviet development as a peasant revolt rooted in
mass distress. He referred to "agrarian communism" and
stated that its success would only mean the "triumph of och-
locracy." But such a grim prospect seemed remote. Snow
doubted that the Communists could gain control over
China, even if the Nanking regime should collapse.[9]

Far Eastern Front is a testimonial to the honesty of Snow's
later statements that he knew little of China's Communists
before 1936 other than the names of their leaders.[10] In that

---

[8] Snow, *Far Eastern Front* (New York, 1933), pp. 155, 162, 327.

[9] *Ibid.*, pp. 165–169, 328–329. See also Snow, "The Strength of Communism in China: I—The Bolshevik Influence," *Current History*,
XXXIII (January 1931), 521–526.

[10] Snow, *Random Notes on Red China, 1936–1945* (Cambridge,
Mass., 1957), n.p., author's preface; *Journey to the Beginning*, p. 152.

year even the simplest points about the CCP were in dispute. Credible evidence was just not available. Snow was to alter this situation dramatically.

It was an unusual condition which permitted the American journalist to enter Red China in the summer of 1936. In 1934, Snow's publisher, Harrison Smith, had offered him a contract to write a book on the Chinese Communists. Although he collected material pertinent to the subject, Snow finally decided against the project on the grounds that he was unable to obtain any firsthand information. In 1935, the London *Daily Herald* was eager to finance a trip to the Communist strongholds. Once again, Snow demurred because of the impossibility of gaining access to the Soviet regions. Near the end of May 1936, however, Snow received reliable news, probably from Madame Sun Yat-sen, about a covert truce between the Communists and Marshal Chang Hsüeh-liang's Tungpei Army. This was the extraordinary situation which enabled the adventurous American to enter the Communist districts in north Shensi.[11]

When the Communists relocated their base of operations in Shensi following the Long March, Chang Hsüeh-liang's Northeastern Army was assigned the task of barricading and annihilating them. Chang Hsüeh-liang, the "Young Marshal," and his troops had been driven from Manchuria by the Japanese in 1931. These intensely anti-Japanese Manchurians were less interested in exterminating Chinese Communists than they were in regaining their homeland. As early as 1932 the Communists had declared war against Japan. Although this declaration was largely a symbolic act, the Communist slogan of "Chinese should not fight Chinese" made good sense to the Manchurian exiles. The Young Marshal and his soldiers were subverted from their anti-Red campaign, which was not going too well anyway, by the CCP's call for a united anti-Japanese front. The result was

[11] Snow to Johnson, February 6, 1937, Nelson T. Johnson papers.

that by the summer of 1936 an unofficial truce had been agreed to by Chang's Bandit Suppression Headquarters and those he was under orders to suppress.[12] Thus, as Snow wrote, he was confronted with a "powerful temptation—a world scoop on a nine-year-old-story." He did not "know of anything quite like it as an opportunity in modern journalism." [13] The chance was too good to pass up.

As John King Fairbank has suggested, *Red Star over China* "is a classic because of the way in which it was produced." [14] Snow's personal adventure in breaking the KMT blockade helps to give the book its dramatic impact. All was sheer melodrama. Madame Sun Yat-sen made most of the arrangements. Hsu Ping, a professor at Tungpei University and an underground Communist agent, provided the determined journalist with a letter of introduction to Mao Tse-tung—written in invisible ink by a Red Army commander whom Snow had never met.[15] In Sian he unexpectedly encountered an American doctor who also hoped to enter the Soviet stronghold. Dr. George Hatem had been a specialist in venereal diseases in Shanghai since 1933. Understandably dissatisfied with his Shanghai calling, Hatem learned of the Communists' desperate need for medical assistance. Agnes Smedley helpfully made the proper connections

[12] Lyman P. Van Slyke, *Enemies and Friends: The United Front in Chinese Communist History* (Stanford, 1967), pp. 43, 71–72.

[13] Snow to Johnson, February 6, 1937.

[14] Professor Fairbank made this remark in the unpaginated introduction to the paperback edition of *Red Star over China.*

[15] Snow, *Journey to the Beginning,* p. 152; *Random Notes on Red China,* n.p., author's preface; *Red Star over China,* pp. 8–9, 18; *The Other Side of the River: Red China Today* (New York, 1962), p. 337. The "invisible ink letter" was written by K'e Cheng-shih and authorized by Liu Shao-ch'i, then chief of the underground North China Bureau of the CCP. Snow did not meet him until 1960, at which time he learned that Liu was the source of his introduction to Mao Tse-tung. See *Red Star over China* (rev. and enlarged ed., New York, 1968), pp. 419, 471.

for him.[16] At the Sian Guest House a mysterious person call-ing himself "Pastor Wang" met the Americans.[17] Then, one July morning, a Tungpei officer escorted the wary foreigners to the edge of what Snow called "the great unknown." Snow entered the Communist territory with "little but ten years of horror stories" to cheer him on his way and wondering whether his investigations "might be rudely interrupted" by his demise. His apprehensions, however, "happily turned out to be quite absurd."[18]

It was, then, an apprehensive journalist in search of a big story who entered the Soviet regions of North Shensi in early July 1936. Snow was neither for nor against China's Commu-nists. He had a plethora of questions but few answers. Yet, in a sense, Snow was predisposed to find favorable answers to his questions. Prior to the encounter with Chinese Commu-nists, he had acquired seven years of experience in China, a general knowledge of, and responsiveness to, Marxist theory, a humanitarian sympathy for the reformist aspirations of the CCP, an aversion to Japanese expansionism, and a bitter dis-illusionment with the Nanking government. Predictably, when he returned from terra incognita in October, he had a reportorial scoop of gigantic proportions. He was also com-mitted. Four months of travel in the Communist-controlled enclaves in Shensi, Kansu, and Ninghsia convinced the American that he had caught a glimpse of China's future.

Snow had arrived in Red China at a propitious moment. During his stay in the Northwest, there was a lull in border

[16] Snow, *The Other Side of the River*, pp. 261–271. Hatem entered Red China with Snow, and he is still there today. For a biographical sketch of Hatem see *Red Star over China* (Rev. and enlarged ed.), p. 486.

[17] Snow, *Red Star over China* (New York, 1961), pp. 18–19; *Journey to the Beginning*, pp. 153–155. The mysterious "Pastor Wang" was Wang Hua-jen, an official of the Chinese Red Cross, a member of the KMT, and a genuine pastor. See *Red Star over China* (rev. and en-larged ed.), p. 419n.

[18] Snow to Johnson, February 6, 1937.

fighting and political activity. The Communist leaders had time enough to converse with their attentive visitor. Most important, the CCP was anxious to breach the KMT censorship. The American reporter provided the medium through which the Chinese Communists could finally speak to the outside world and spread their gospel of a united front to save China from the Japanese.[19] As subsequent events demonstrated, Snow was a very able medium.

Snow wasted little time in providing the public with its first authentic look at the Chinese Communist movement. Within a month of his return from the Soviet areas, his stories and interviews were being published both in China and overseas. The London *Daily Herald* featured a series of Snow's articles on their front page and made him their chief Far Eastern correspondent.[20] *Time-Life* paid the Missourian a near-record price for seventy-five of his best photographs.[21] Anyone who looked at the giggling wives of leading Communist officials, the contented children of Soviet society, and the trimly uniformed cadres of the Red Army—all of whom were a part of *Life*'s pictorial drama—would have difficulty in believing that these were merely bandits.[22] American journals which published articles by Snow included *Amerasia, Asia,* the *New Republic, Pacific Affairs,* and the *Saturday Evening Post.*[23] The *China Weekly Review* featured the

[19] See the remarks reputedly made by Mao Tse-tung about *Red Star over China* in Snow, *Random Notes on Red China*, p. 21.

[20] Snow, *Journey to the Beginning*, p. 191.

[21] Snow to Johnson, February 6, 1937.

[22] "First Pictures of China's Roving Communists," *Life*, II (January 25, 1937), 9–15; "An Army of Fighting Chinese Communists Takes Possession of China's Northwest," *ibid.* (February 1, 1937), 42–45.

[23] Snow, "Chinese Communists and World Affairs: An Interview with Mao Tse-tung," *Amerasia*, I (August 1937), 263–269; Snow, "Direct from the Chinese Red Area," *Asia*, XXXVII (February 1937), 74–75. *Asia* also published Mao Tse-tung's autobiography as told to Edgar Snow in four parts and Snow's account of the Long March in two installments. See *Asia*, XXXVII (July-November 1937), 480–484,

American's interviews with Mao Tse-tung, and the *Shanghai Evening Post and Mercury* printed in full a speech which Snow had delivered before the Men's Forum of Peking Union Church.[24] The harassed journalist was besieged by urgent requests for material from a number of magazines. Snow felt that such widespread interest confirmed his belief that the trip had been worth the risks involved.[25]

If the immediate response to Snow's dispatches was impressive, the public reception of *Red Star over China* simply "astounded" him.[26] It was widely recognized as a masterpiece of eyewitness reporting. A well-known American literary critic credited Snow with the "greatest single feat performed by any journalist of our century." [27] Owen Lattimore called *Red Star over China* the biggest journalistic coup in years.[28] Edward C. Carter, the secretary-general of the Institute of Pacific Relations, declared that the book marked an epoch in Western understanding of China.[29] Pearl Buck, the celebrated author of *The Good Earth*, felt

---

570–576, 619–623, 682–688, 689–692, 741–747. Snow, "Soviet China," *New Republic*, XCI–XCII (August 4, 11, 18, September 8, 1937), 351–354, 9–11, 42–44, 124–125; Snow, "Soviet Society in Northwest China," *Pacific Affairs*, X (September 1937), 266–275; Snow, "I Went to Red China: The Inside Story of China's United Front Against Japan," *Saturday Evening Post*, CCX (November 6, 1937), 10–11, 98, 100–103.

[24] Snow, "Interviews with Mao Tse-tung, Communist Leader," *China Weekly Review*, LXXVIII (November 14, 21, 1936), 377–379, 420–421. Snow, "Reds and Northwest: A Visitor to Communist Areas Tells His First-Hand Observations," *Shanghai Evening Post and Mercury*, February 3, 4, 5, 1937, 10–11.

[25] Snow to Johnson, February 6, 1937.

[26] Snow, *Journey to the Beginning*, p. 191.

[27] Malcolm Cowley, "Red China," *New Republic*, XCIII (January 12, 1938), 287.

[28] Owen Lattimore, "The Chinese Communists," *Yale Review*, XXVII (Summer 1938), 814.

[29] Edward C. Carter, review of *Red Star over China* in *Pacific Affairs*, XI (March 1938), 110.

that every page of Snow's extraordinary account was significant.[30] A reviewer for the *New York Times* confided that his reading of Snow's book had been a "shattering experience."[31] One student of Far Eastern affairs heralded *Red Star over China* as the most reliable account of the Chinese Soviet movement in the English language.[32] Another scholarly critic noted that Snow's work constituted a "prime source for historians of contemporary China."[33] Others described *Red Star over China* as "absorbing," "amazing," "brilliant," and "superb."[34] Perhaps the greatest compliment was paid by the anti-Communist Far Eastern authority for the *New York Herald Tribune,* Rodney Gilbert. He accepted most of Snow's conclusions and christened him "the" Occidental authority on Chinese communism.[35]

Red Star over China was the right book, on the right subject, published at the right time. Far Eastern specialists had been made receptive to Snow's detailed account of the Chinese Communist movement by the inadequacy of Nanking's increasingly stale propaganda. As for the timing, it could not have been better. The American edition was published in the wake of the heroic Chinese stand against the

[30] Pearl S. Buck, "Asia Book-Shelf," *Asia,* XXXVIII (March 1938), 202–203.

[31] R. L. Duffus, "A Remarkable Survey of the Red in the Map of China," *New York Times Book Review,* January 9, 1938, 3.

[32] E. Herbert Norman, "Some Recent Books on China," *Amerasia,* I (February 1938), 573.

[33] C. H. Peake, review of *Red Star over China* in *American Historical Review,* XLIII (June 1938), 948.

[34] Eliot Janeway, "Red in the East," *Nation,* CXLVI (January 8, 1938), 48; N. B. Cousins, "The World Today in Books," *Current History,* XLVIII (February 1938), 2; Freda Utley, "Communists in China," *New Statesman and Nation,* XIV (November 6, 1937), 766; Walter H. Mallory, "Red Star over China," *Atlantic Monthly,* CLXI (May 1938), n.p.

[35] Rodney Gilbert, "A Chinese State Hitherto Unknown to Us: The First Authentic Report of What Goes on among China's Reds," *New York Herald Tribune Books,* January 2, 1938, 1–2.

Japanese at Shanghai, the sinking of the American gunboat *Panay,* and the terrifying rape of Nanking by Japan's triumphant legions. As Snow himself recognized, *Red Star over China* conveniently appeared just when Western concern and sympathy had been aroused by the onset of the Sino-Japanese War.[36] The manuscript, he recalled, was completed in July 1937, "to the sound of gunfire by Japanese troops outside the walls of Peking, where I lived." [37]

Within a few weeks of publication, *Red Star over China* had sold over a hundred thousand copies in Great Britain. Although the figure for the first American edition was only approximately fifteen thousand, this was the largest sale of any nonfiction work about the Far East hitherto published in the United States. Some 65,000 copies have been sold in America since 1938.[38] The book was translated into half a dozen languages and had a considerable political influence on the youth of China. Because of the KMT censorship, many Chinese first learned of the CCP's programs in the writings of Edgar Snow.[39] Almost the only unfavorable reception of Snow's international best-seller came from the American Communist Party. Apparently, the party did not appreciate the book's remarks about the bungling character

[36] Snow, *Red Star over China* (New York, 1961), n.p., author's preface. The initial edition was published by V. Gollancz in London in 1937. Random House issued the first American edition on January 3, 1938. A revised edition was published by Random House in late 1938. In 1944 another edition, which incorporated slight revisions of the 1938 revised edition, was issued by Random House. The paperback edition published by Grove Press in 1961 was a reprinting of the 1944 edition. The revised and enlarged edition of 1968 also was published by Grove Press.

[37] Snow, *Red Star over China* (rev. and enlarged ed., 1968), p. 15.

[38] A. T. Steele, *The American People and China* (New York, Toronto, and London, 1966), pp. 171–172; Snow, *Journey to the Beginning,* p. 24.

[39] Stuart Schram, *Mao Tse-tung* (New York, 1966), p. 193; Snow, *Red Star over China* (New York, 1961), n.p., author's preface.

of the Comintern's China policy. They banned it from their book shops.[40]

But the significance of *Red Star over China* cannot be adequately measured by the number of copies sold. Harold R. Isaacs' study indicates that it was second only to Pearl Buck's *The Good Earth* as a major source of American impressions of the Chinese.[41] Even as *The Good Earth* provided Americans with their first real understanding of ordinary Chinese people, *Red Star over China* gave Westerners their first authentic look into the lives of Chinese Communists.[42] In a sense, Snow created the Chinese Communists for a generation of Americans. His was an image-making and an image-breaking book. Snow utterly demolished the notion that Chinese Communists were bandits and promoted them to the status of dynamic Marxist revolutionary reformers. He also contested the idea that the CCP was simply a subservient puppet of Moscow. Rather, he asserted, the CCP had developed a unique and indigenous brand of communism.[43]

As they emerged from the pages of *Red Star over China*, China's Communists were an engaging composite of positive adjectives. They were young, democratic, popular, patriotic, progressive, and orderly. This "incredible brotherhood" was dissimilar to anything the American had seen during his seven years in the Far East. In comparison to standard con-

[40] Snow, *Random Notes on Red China*, p. 20; Freda Utley, *China at War* (New York, 1939), p. 74. For a hostile Marxist review of *Red Star over China* see " 'Asiaticus' Criticizes 'Red Star over China,' " *Pacific Affairs*, XI (June 1938), 237–244.

[41] Harold R. Isaacs, *Images of Asia: American Views of China and India* (New York, 1962), pp. 155n., 162–163. Isaacs bases his conclusions on a series of interviews which he began in 1954. Instead of examining a random sampling of the body politic, Isaacs interviewed a carefully selected group of Americans, many of whom were prominent professionally and publicly. For a thorough description of Isaacs' methodology see *ibid.*, pp. 11–35.

[42] Steele, *The American People and China*, p. 19.

[43] Snow, *Red Star over China* (1961), p. 119.

ceptions of the Chinese, Snow felt that they were "more direct, frank, simple, undevious, and scientific-minded." [44] As depicted by Edgar Snow, the spirited cadres of the Red Army were not unlike Robin Hood's legendary folk heroes. General P'eng Teh-huai best projected this image when he told Snow that "we are nothing but the fist of the people beating their oppressors!" [45] Such imagery is significant because *Red Star over China* established patterns of thinking and reporting on the Chinese Communist movement which endured for over a decade. It had a seminal impact on intellectuals. As Isaacs concluded, *Red Star over China* imprinted upon many minds a contrasting picture of austere, patriotic Chinese Communists and corrupt, unreliable Chinese Nationalists. [46]

There are a number of additional reasons for the influential character of Snow's work. One was his approach to the subject. Snow describes his effort as "mostly the work of a scribe." [47] To some extent, this is an apt characterization of *Red Star over China*. It is atypical for a journalist's account in that the author does not dwell on himself. For page upon page Snow simply wrote down what he was told by those he interviewed. [48] He was content to let the Communists tell their own story, an assignment at which they were most adept. Basically, *Red Star over China* is a history of the Chinese Communist movement as seen through the eyes of the Chinese Communists. Yet, there is more. While Snow did play down the autobiographical aspect of his enterprise, *Red Star over China* is also the personal adventure of an uncertain reporter in the remote hinterlands of China. For a decade the amazing story of China's Communists had gone untold. It is difficult to imagine a more effective approach in

[44] *Ibid.*, p. 409.
[45] *Ibid.*, p. 305.
[46] Isaacs, *Images of Asia*, p. 163.
[47] Snow, *Red Star over China* (1961), n.p., author's preface.
[48] Snow, *Red Star over China* (rev. and enlarged ed., 1968), p. 16.

revealing this timely journalistic scoop than the combination of autobiography and biography which Snow employed. Perhaps the most important factor contributing to the persuasive character of Snow's volume is the nature of its sources. *Red Star over China* is based on interviews, documents, personal observations, and secondary works. Snow was the first Westerner to interrogate leading Communist political and military figures like Mao Tse-tung, Chou Enlai, P'eng Teh-huai, and Ho Lung. *Red Star over China* is still a basic source for the autobiography of Mao.[49] About the only outstanding official that Snow was unable to interview was the commander-in-chief of the Red Army, Chu Teh. But the American was more than a scribe, he was also a scholarly journalist. He examined primary sources such as legislative and executive decrees, newspapers, magazines, pamphlets, and reports. Snow's writing also reflects an acquaintance with secondary works by American, Chinese, and Russian authorities. In all of his investigations, furthermore, Snow took pains to assure that his reporting would be as detailed and accurate as possible. The texts of the interviews with Mao Tse-tung, for example, were twice translated into Chinese and submitted to Mao for revision before being rendered into the final version in English.[50] The quality of Snow's research and methodology gave *Red Star over China* a ring of authenticity which could hardly go unnoticed even by those with only a casual knowledge of Chinese affairs.

The book has its shortcomings. Parts of it are overly dramatic. Nearly every reviewer singled out Snow's description of the Long March as one of the great adventure stories of modern times. Edward C. Carter said that it made "Xeno-

---

[49] When Snow was in Peking in 1960, Mao told him that he had no intention of writing an autobiography and that the story of his life as recounted in *Red Star over China* was the "only one of its kind." See *Red Star over China* (rev. and enlarged ed., 1968), p. 488.

[50] Snow, *Red Star over China* (rev. and enlarged ed., 1968), p. 487.

phon's heroes shrivel into chocolate soldiers." [51] Snow himself concluded that Hannibal's trek over the Alps looked like a "holiday excursion" beside the Anabasis performed by the Reds.[52] He emphasized the combat, as opposed to the survival, aspect of the 6,000-mile trek. Based on interviews with the participants, Snow's account quite naturally reflected their heroic view of the Long March.[53] Furthermore, Snow was uncritical of his sources. With very few exceptions, he accepted as true all the statements and interpretations given him by the Chinese Communists. Finally, Snow's sympathies are decidedly on the side of China's Communists. When the American first entered the Soviet redoubt, he was uneasy and even feared that a group of curious villagers might practice "communism" by redistributing his belongings. When he left North Shensi, however, he felt that he "was not going home, but leaving it." [54] *Red Star over China* is colored by the author's undisguised admiration for the Chinese Communists.

In spite of its defects, *Red Star over China* remains one of the most important and influential books of our time. It made Snow himself a kind of institution, firmly establishing his reputation as a leading interpreter of the Chinese Communist movement.[55] It continues to have a substantial im-

[51] Carter, review of *Red Star over China* in *Pacific Affairs*, XI (March 1938), 111.

[52] Snow, *Red Star over China* (1961), p. 216.

[53] Snow, *Red Star over China* (rev. and enlarged ed., 1968), p. 431. For antidotes to Snow's romantic version of the Long March see Anthony Garavente, "The Long March," *China Quarterly*, No. 22 (April-June 1965), 89–124; John M. Nolan, "The Long March: Fact and Fancy," *Military Affairs*, XXX (Summer 1966), 77–90; Barrington Moore, Jr., *Social Origins of Dictatorship and Democracy: Lord and Peasant in the Making of the Modern World* (Boston, 1967), 222–223.

[54] Snow, *Red Star over China* (1961), pp. 36, 427.

[55] Fairbank, *China: The People's Middle Kingdom and the U.S.A.* (Cambridge, Mass., 1967), pp. 84–85.

pact on historical scholarship. Jerome Ch'en, for example, relied heavily on it in preparing his major study of Mao Tse-tung and the Chinese revolution.[56] Snow's work was much more significant in its own time. Not only non-Chinese but the Chinese people themselves, including many members of the CCP, got their first authoritative view of the Chinese Communist movement by reading translations of Snow's work.[57] Critics have even suggested that had it not been for *Red Star over China* the Chinese Communist revolution would never have occurred.[58] If nothing else, the book took much of the guesswork out of evaluations of Chinese communism and provided the West with a favorable introduction to Chinese Communists.

[56] Ch'en goes so far as to say that Snow's work constitutes an embodiment of objectivity. See Jerome Ch'en, *Mao and the Chinese Revolution* (New York, 1967), p. 13.

[57] Snow, *Red Star over China* (rev. and enlarged ed., 1968), pp. 16, 487.

[58] Fairbank, *China: The People's Middle Kingdom and the U.S.A.*, pp. 84–85.

1. Yenan, 1937. (Courtesy of Helen Foster Snow.)

2. Agnes Smedley in a Red Army uniform, Yenan, 1937. (Courtesy of James Bertram.)

3. Helen Foster Snow with General Hsiao K'eh (*seated at center of picture*) and General Chu Teh (*right*), Yenan, 1937. (Courtesy of Helen Foster Snow.)

4. Americans with Mao Tse-tung, Yenan, 1937 (*left to right:* Owen Lattimore, Philip Jaffe, Mao Tse-tung, Agnes (Mrs. Philip) Jaffe, T. A. Bisson, Helen Foster Snow). (Courtesy of Helen Foster Snow.)

5. James Bertram with General Hsiao K'eh, North Shansi, 1937. (Courtesy of James Bertram.)

6. Evans F. Carlson with General Chu Teh, 1937 or 1938. (Courtesy of Helen Foster Snow and Dean Evans C. Carlson.)

7. A press conference with General Joseph W. Stilwell, Chungking, 1943 (*left to right:* General Stilwell, A. T. Steele, Reilly O'Sullivan, Brooks Atkinson, an unidentified ABC correspondent, Robert Martin, Theodore H. White, "Newsreel" Wong, Norman Soong, James L. Stewart). (Courtesy of Brooks Atkinson.)

[5]

The "Blockade Runners": 1937

An accident of history profoundly influenced Western reporting on the Chinese Communist movement. Renewed foreign contact with the Chinese Communists came at just the time when the CCP was in the process of making a major policy shift away from the hard, revolutionary line of the Kiangsi period. As early as May 5, 1936, the CCP had appealed directly to the Nanking government for a cessation of civil war.[1] In accord with the general Comintern strategy, the Chinese Communists adopted a united-front policy which emphasized patriotic resistance to the Japanese and moderate agrarian reforms. Mao Tse-tung explained the logic of the CCP's new position: *"For a people being deprived of its national freedom, the revolutionary task is not immediate Socialism, but the struggle for independence. We cannot even discuss Communism if we are robbed of a country in which to practise it."* [2]

In late 1936 the Communists were given an opportunity to demonstrate the genuineness of their patriotic professions. In the same month that Snow left the Soviet regions, Chiang Kai-shek journeyed to Sian. The Generalissimo discussed

[1] Lyman P. Van Slyke, *Enemies and Friends: The United Front in Chinese Communist History* (Stanford, 1967), p. 60.

[2] Edgar Snow, *Red Star over China* (New York, 1961), p. 455. The italics are Snow's.

plans for a renewed anti-Communist campaign with Chang Hsüeh-liang. Chang, however, argued for an end to Chinese internal strife and a united front against the national enemy. A dissatisfied Chiang left Sian determined to have his way and put first things first by exterminating the Reds. The Generalissimo returned to Sian on December 7, 1936, intent on launching the sixth bandit-suppression crusade. The issue was joined. On December 12, Chiang Kai-shek was kidnapped by the rebellious Manchurian exiles. For a time, his life was in danger. Presumably on orders from Moscow, the Chinese Communists used their influence with the Tungpei mutineers to secure the Generalissimo's release.[3] The way was paved, thereby, for a KMT-CCP reconciliation.

On Christmas Day Chiang Kai-shek returned to Nanking. The projected bandit-suppression expedition was canceled. While KMT-CCP relations continued to be uncertain for several months, nine years of internecine strife had been supplanted by a tacit truce. The Lukouchiao Incident of July 7, 1937, the event which ignited the Sino-Japanese War, made the continuance of this uneasy armistice a necessity. On September 22, Nanking and Yenan announced the formation of a united front. Japanese aggression had compelled the Chinese antagonists to postpone their day of final reckoning. For a time, Nationalists and Communists would fight side by side against a major threat to China's survival as a nation.

During the period of tacit truce between the Sian Incident and the formal inauguration of a united front in September of 1937, a number of foreign correspondents tried to emulate

[3] Snow, *Random Notes on Red China, 1936–1945* (Cambridge, Mass., 1957), pp. 1–14; John King Fairbank, *The United States and China* (rev. ed., New York, 1958), pp. 234–235; O. Edmund Clubb, *20th Century China* (New York and London, 1964), pp. 202–210; Robert C. North, *Moscow and Chinese Communists* (2nd ed., Stanford, 1963), pp. 177–178. For interpretations which argue that Moscow was not primarily responsible for the stance adopted by the CCP at Sian, see Van Slyke, *Enemies and Friends*, pp. 75–85, and Charles B. McLane, *Soviet Policy and the Chinese Communists, 1931–1946* (New York, 1958), pp. 87–88.

the success of Edgar Snow. The unusual circumstances which had allowed Snow to penetrate the KMT blockade lasted until a few weeks after Chiang Kai-shek's release from captivity. By early 1937, however, troops loyal to Nanking were in control of Sian and the highways leading into the Red stronghold. Military orders once again closed the Communist areas to journalists. But times had changed. Their curiosity whetted by reports filtering through the KMT censorship, some newsmen were willing to risk the displeasure of the Chinese government. The handful of adventurers who took a chance and made their way to Yenan in the uncertain months between the Sian kidnapping and the fall of 1937 have been designated collectively as the "blockade runners." Like Snow, they saw an opportunity which could not be passed up.

On January 8, 1937, a photograph of Agnes Smedley ornamented the front page of the *New York Herald Tribune.* The newspaper referred sensationally to suspicious activities and dark intrigues. Miss Smedley was reported to be abetting rebellion by conducting radio programs for the Communists and appealing for recruits in a forthcoming conspiracy against Nanking.[4] Edward Wingerter, an American aviation specialist working for the Chinese government, similarly told of inflammatory antireligious and pro-Communist radio broadcasts by Agnes Smedley.[5] The *New York Herald Tribune* and Mr. Wingerter were correct in at least one respect. Agnes Smedley was in Sian. Indeed, she was probably the only Western journalist in Sian at the time of Chiang Kai-shek's arrest.[6]

Although some missionaries thought that Miss Smedley had organized the Sian mutiny, the events of December came

[4] "American Woman Recruits Reds for Revolt in Northwest China," *New York Herald Tribune,* January 8, 1937, 1, 4.

[5] *Foreign Relations of the United States: Diplomatic Papers, 1937,* III (Washington, D.C., 1954), p. 11.

[6] Van Slyke, *Enemies and Friends,* p. 80.

as a complete surprise to her.[7] Aside from having her room
at the Sian Guest House looted by rampaging Chinese
troops, she witnessed few of the significant events of those
momentous days. Nonetheless, she was able to establish direct contact with the Chinese Communists. She gave medical
assistance to released Communist political prisoners and
held conversations with the CCP spokesmen who had been
sent to negotiate in behalf of the Generalissimo's release,
Chou En-lai and Yeh Chien-ying.

In all of her years in the Far East, Agnes Smedley had
never been in the Communist regions, and she had been in-
furiated when Edgar Snow became the first Western correspondent to gain access to them.[8] On January 12, 1937, with
the Red Army only thirty-five miles north of Sian, she seized
an opportunity to hitch a ride on an army truck bound for
Yenan. While in Yenan, the energetic Miss Smedley spent
much of her time directing a rat-extermination campaign
and writing letters to other journalists, inviting them to visit
Red Shensi. Failing health compelled her to return to Sian
in late September.[9]

As had been reported, Agnes Smedley did broadcast news
over Station XGOB. This was done, however, under the auspices of the Tungpei Army, not the Communist Army. Furthermore, hers was not the only foreign voice indistinctly
heard over Sian's jammed air waves. A New Zealander,
James M. Bertram, assisted the notorious American radical
in her attempts to tell the outside world what was going on
in China's remote interior.

---

[7] Anna Wang, *Ich kämpfte für Mao: Eine deutsche Frau erlebt die chinesische Revolution* (Hamburg, Germany, 1964), p. 88.

[8] James M. Bertram to the author, April 1965.

[9] Agnes Smedley, *Battle Hymn of China* (New York, 1943), pp.
133–151; Bertram, *First Act in China: The Story of the Sian Mutiny*
(New York, 1938), pp. 157, 178, 214–215; Wang, *Ich kämpfte für Mao*, pp.
109–110. The Communists laughed at Miss Smedley's crusade against rats
—until she won the backing of Mao Tse-tung.

Bertram was quite unlike Agnes Smedley in many ways, and yet they were kindred spirits. Where the American had hardly any formal schooling, the New Zealander had been educated at Oxford. If Agnes Smedley adopted radical convictions because of unhappy personal experiences, Bertram seems to have accepted casually the socialist abstractions which were prevalent among Oxford students in the 1930's.[10] Despite their dissimilar unbringings, the two shared a sympathy for the downtrodden Chinese peasant and an aversion to the Nationalist regime. As Bertram wrote: "We had met by chance, and had little enough in common by background and training. Agnes had an instinctive distrust of intellectuals; the detached study of a subject was meaningless to her. But we shared—and this was perhaps the one thing that made her tolerate me—an unbounded admiration for the common Chinese people." [11]

James Bertram first came to China in early 1936 as a Rhodes scholar. While studying the Chinese language at Yenching University, he became a friend of Edgar Snow's. Shortly after Chiang Kai-shek's kidnapping, Snow appointed Bertram special correspondent for the London *Daily Herald*. Due to many frustrating delays, it was not until December 27, 1936, that Bertram reached Sian. The show was already over and most of the principal actors had left the scene. Bertram compensated for this unfortunate state of affairs by padding his circumstantial account of the Sian mutiny with pleasant descriptions of the topography. Through the good offices of Agnes Smedley, however, he was able to make the acquaintance of several Chinese Communists.[12]

The fledgling correspondent accompanied Miss Smedley on her errands of mercy to the freed Communist political

---

[10] Bertram, *Beneath the Shadow: A New Zealander in the Far East, 1939–46* (New York, 1947), pp. 1–9.

[11] Betram, *First Act in China*, pp. 216–217.

[12] *Ibid., passim;* Snow, *Journey to the Beginning* (New York, 1958), p. 189.

prisoners. This moving experience led him "to understand Agnes Smedley's enthusiasm for the Red Army." Also, Chinese Communists would occasionally drop by the radio station for a friendly chat. Bertram was anxious, however, to observe the Red Army in the field. Since some Communist forces were garrisoned in the countryside around Sian, he determined to have a look for himself. Accompanied by a Chinese student interpreter, Bertram set out on a bicycle. The travelers eventually chanced upon a propaganda unit of the Fourth Front Army and were greeted warmly by the cordial Communists. Bertram's contact with these warriors was brief but persuasive. He was impressed by their dynamism, intelligence, and political sophistication. Although he did not accompany Agnes Smedley on her pilgrimage to Yenan, he did manage, then, to have a minor firsthand encounter with China's Communists.[13] Shortly after Nanking's troops arrived in Sian in February 1937, Bertram left the Northwest.[14] In the not too distant future, however, he was to become the first non-American journalist to tour the Communist regions.

It was considerably more difficult to establish contact with Chinese Communists once Nationalist troops occupied Sian and its environs. After Chiang Kai-shek's return from the Northwest, a group of Shanghai correspondents tried to obtain permission to travel to Yenan. The Nanking government quickly informed them that Red China was off limits to Western newsmen. Nevertheless, between February and September 1937, several American journalists were able to evade the Sian police and make their way to Yenan.[15]

Encouraged by a letter from Agnes Smedley to come to

---

[13] Bertram, *First Act in China*, pp. 173, 176, 237–251.

[14] Bertram to the author, April 1965.

[15] Nym Wales [Helen Foster Snow], *Inside Red China* (Garden City, N.Y., 1939), p. 9; Wales, *My Yenan Notebooks* (Madison, Conn., 1961), pp. 10–11; *Foreign Relations of the United States, 1937*, III, pp. 107–108; Smedley, *Battle Hymn of China*, pp. 177–179.

Yenan and meet the Chinese Communists at first hand, Victor Keen of the *New York Herald Tribune* disregarded the Nanking government's restrictions on travel. Although it almost cost him his American passport, Keen slipped past the border sentries at Sian and spent ten days in Yenan in the spring of 1937.[16] He marveled at the educational programs of the Communist regime and was startled to find that there were no beggars in the Red capital.[17] Above all, Keen was impressed by the devotion of CCP leaders to the ideal of communism.[18]

One day in Yenan rid Earl Leaf's mind of the idea that the Chinese Communists might be bandits. This correspondent for the United Press discovered that the Communists were pleasantly informal and that they observed complete equality of sex and rank. Yenan reminded him of a "Boy Scout summer camp where a spirit of fun" pervaded every aspect of daily life. "Here there is much work and study to be done and no drones are allowed, but there is also ample opportunity for play." [19]

[16] For an amusing account of the unsuccessful attempt of the Sian police to confiscate Keen's passport, see Wang, *Ich kämpfte für Mao*, pp. 106–110.

[17] Victor Keen, "Chinese Soviet Goes to School: 60% Politics and 40% Education Is Recipe in the Mental Diet," *New York Herald Tribune*, June 13, 1937, II, 4.

[18] Keen, "Chinese Soviet's Youthful Army a Merger of Private Battalions," *New York Herald Tribune*, June 6, 1937, II, 5. See also Keen, "China's Reds Offer Olive Branch in Belief that Anti-Japan Front Is More Vital Than Class Fight," *ibid.*, May 23, 1937, II, 7, 14.

[19] Earl H. Leaf, "Chinese Reds in Shensi Work and Play Hard; Soviet Capital Scene of Much Laughter, Fun and Sports," *North China Star*, April 26, 1937, 1. See also Leaf, "Persons and Personages: Six Women of China," *Living Age*, CCCLIV (March 1938), 40–42. Shortly after his trip to Yenan, Leaf left the United Press and became an adviser and publicity agent for the Nationalist government. In 1939 he registered with the United States government as a person employed in the service of a foreign country. See Memorandum of a Conversation with Mr. Earl Leaf, July 12, 1939, 793.94/15229, Department of State files.

Like Keen and Leaf, Harrison Forman also managed to circumvent the Nationalist blockade. This young American photographer was at Ho Lung's headquarters on the fateful evening of July 7, 1937. Forman remained long enough to secure some first-rate snapshots of China's Communists.[20] Although he may not have realized it, another foreigner, Mrs. Edgar Snow, was also in Soviet China when the Sino-Japanese War erupted.

Helen Foster Snow was born in Utah in 1907. Both of her parents were civic-minded, small-town leaders. Her father, John Moody Foster, was a graduate of Stanford University and the University of Chicago law school. As a science teacher and lawyer, Mr. Foster actively participated in public affairs. The Foster family had a distinguished genealogy; their English ancestors were part of the Puritan migration to Massachusetts Bay. Helen Foster identified strongly with the traditions of the seventeenth century, especially those associated with Oliver Cromwell and American Puritanism. Like her Presbyterian progenitors, who had subdued a continent "with nothing but an axe and a Bible," Helen Foster believed in morality, God, enterprise, and hard work.[21]

As far back as she could remember, Helen Foster had always wanted to become a "Great Author." She was interested in history, determined to publish books, and eager to journey to distant lands. In 1931, after attending the University of Utah and passing the civil service examinations, Miss Foster went to China. She secured a position as clerk in the American consulate at Shanghai and became private secretary to the consul general, Edwin S. Cunningham. In late 1932 she married a man who shared her desire to write and travel. The Snows settled in Peiping in 1933. From 1934 to

[20] Harrison Forman, *Report from Red China* (New York, 1945), pp. 9, 127, 129; "The Camera's Story of History-in-the-Making: China's Communists," *Current History*, XLVIII (February 1938), 66–69.

[21] Helen Foster Snow to the author, April 19, 1965. See also Nym Wales, "Old China Hands," *New Republic*, CLVI (April 1, 1967), 14.

1935, Mrs. Snow studied philosophy at Yenching University, excelling in a course on Hegel. Helen and Edgar Snow intended to stay in China no longer than was necessary to produce knowledgeable books about the country. Mrs. Snow considered herself just a typical young American "willing to make a real effort to explore a new subject." [22]

By 1936, Chinese communism seemed the topic most in need of fresh exploration. In September, Mrs. Snow tried to join her spouse in Yenan. The Red Army's liaison officer in Sian, Liu Ting, informed her that it was too dangerous to attempt the trip and suggested that, in any event, Mr. Snow was expected to leave the Soviet area momentarily.[23] After her husband's return to Peiping, Helen Snow learned that a high-level conference of Communist leaders had been scheduled for May. This was a golden opportunity. Most of the CCP's top brass would be together at the same place and time.

For drama and suspense, Helen Foster Snow's entry into Communist China surpassed even that of her husband. On April 21, 1937, she left Peiping for Sian. Her reception in Sian was far from cordial. The trips made by Forman, Leaf, Keen, and her spouse had put the Chinese police on the alert. They were under orders to keep prying journalists away from Yenan. A captain from the Bureau of Public Safety forbade Mrs. Snow to leave the city limits. Even the Communist officials at Red Army headquarters in Sian were unwilling to help her. The Communists were engaged in delicate negotiations with Chiang Kai-shek and were therefore wary about contributing to an illegal escapade.[24]

If Helen Snow wanted to break the KMT blockade, she would have to do it on her own. There was no friendly

[22] Helen Foster Snow to the author, April 19, 1965; Snow, *Journey to the Beginning*, pp. 102–106, 119–123, 129–131, 138.

[23] Helen Foster Snow to the author, May 1, 1965.

[24] Wales, *My Yenan Notebooks*, pp. 1–10; *Inside Red China*, pp. 7, 10–11.

Tungpei officer to lead her to the borders of the beckoning land. Not the least of her problems was the fact that the name Snow had become infamous to the Sian authorities. The local missionaries were reluctant even to be seen with the wife of Edgar Snow. As Mrs. Snow wrote, "I was anathema, leprous." [25]

In breaking the news blockade, then, Mrs. Snow had to overcome obstacles of a greater magnitude than those which had faced her husband. A lesser spirit would have given up and returned to Peiping. Indeed, Mrs. Snow was at the point of despair when she luckily encountered a chivalrous young American who was willing to lend a helping hand. Kempton Fitch, who came from one of the oldest missionary families in China, was working in Sian for the Caltex Corporation. He introduced Mrs. Snow to a Scandinavian adventurer named Karl Efraim Hill.[26] The trio carefully devised a daring plan which involved a midnight flight from the Sian Guest House. Despite several harrowing mishaps, Mrs. Snow was able to elude the armed guards who had been posted outside the hotel. The unlikely was followed by the incredible, but the enterprising young lady eventually found herself being escorted by Fitch on the three-hour drive which separated Nationalist from Communist China. On April 30,

25 *Ibid.*, p. 10; *ibid.*, p. 8.
26 Mrs. Snow knew very little about Hill. She simply identifies him as a Scandinavian called "Effie." According to Philip J. Jaffe, however, Effie Hill was born in Inner Mongolia of Swedish missionary parents. Hill spoke Chinese, Mongolian, English, and German. He was, Jaffe recalled, an excellent driver and mechanic. Hill drove Mr. and Mrs. Jaffe, Owen Lattimore, and T. A. Bisson to Yenan in the summer of 1937. Jaffe to Benjamin J. Mandel, August 24, 1965. A copy of Jaffe's letter was forwarded to the author by Mr. Mandel, the Research Director for the United States Senate Internal Security Subcommittee. From 1933 to 1935 Hill served as a driver for the well-known Swedish scientist Sven Hedin on one of his expeditions to Sinkiang. See Sven Hedin, *The Silk Road* (trans. F. H. Lyon; London, 1938), p. 19. For information about Kempton Fitch see George A. Fitch, *My Eighty Years in China* (Taiwan, Republic of China, 1967), pp. 45, 89, 117.

1937, Helen Snow stood on Red soil. The combination of a difficult expedition to northwest China and the disquieting experience at Sian was too much for Mrs. Snow. It shattered her health for a number of years, and she has never fully recovered.[27]

Inside Red China, published under Mrs. Snow's pseudonym, Nym Wales, is the result of more than four months of close contact with Chinese Communists. When Helen Snow entered the Soviet regions in late April, the Communists were engaged in sensitive negotiations with Nanking. She left Yenan in September, just two weeks prior to the announcement of a united anti-Japanese front. Thus, she witnessed the historic transition by which the Red Army relinquished its old identity and became the Eighth Route Army. She spent most of the time between May and September in Yenan. By taking advantage of the high-level conference of CCP officials, she hoped to obtain the autobiographies of Communist leaders who had not been definitively sketched in *Red Star over China.* In a sense, then, *Inside Red China* can be classed as a companion volume to Edgar Snow's book.

The two authors approached their subject in a similar fashion. Like her husband, Mrs. Snow let the Chinese Communists speak for themselves and spent most of her time assiduously collecting their autobiographies. In this respect, the difference between the two books was one of degree rather than kind. Nevertheless, where Mr. Snow was the scholar-journalist, Mrs. Snow was more truly the scribe. Both *Red Star over China* and *Inside Red China* contain enormous amounts of historical material. In contrast to her husband, however, Mrs. Snow presented most of her sources in their raw form with little attempt at integrative analysis. Ac-

[27] Wales, *My Yenan Notebooks,* pp. 7–17; *Inside Red China,* pp. 15–25. Mrs. Snow contracted five kinds of dysentery during her trip to the Northwest. By the time she returned to Peiping, she had been ill for five months.

cordingly, *Inside Red China* might have appealed to specialists, but it was heavy going for the layman.[28]
One can carry the comparison further. In several respects, Mrs. Snow outdistanced her husband. *Inside Red China* was based on extensive interviews with practically every prominent Red leader. Helen Snow held conversations with Mao Tse-tung, Chu Teh, P'eng Teh-huai, and a host of lesser lights. At least in quantitative terms, Edgar Snow had been surpassed. Mrs. Snow also bettered her spouse in enthusiasm. At times her descriptions of China's Communists reach lyric proportions. She pictured the Red Army as an "incredible army of youth . . . all survivors of the fittest, the finest specimens of the human race that China has produced." The Communist trooper was equated with a medieval Galahad. The typical Red Knight was not merely intelligent, he was "precocious." Mrs. Snow even claimed that the Communist ethic had "actually taken the sting out of death" and had made the grave a "mark of victory." According to her, every Communist soldier would happily expire in the knowledge that his personal sacrifice brought the ultimate triumph of the Chinese revolution one step closer.[29] While Edgar Snow was essentially uncritical of the CCP, Helen Snow admired her Communist hosts with gay abandon.

The reception given *Inside Red China* by the periodical press fell considerably short of that which had greeted *Red Star over China*. Nevertheless, Mrs. Snow's account was generally well received. Rodney Gilbert and Owen Lattimore both emphasized that Mrs. Snow had been predisposed to ac-

[28] Mrs. Snow later philosophized on her inability to produce books which were popular and readable. It was the enormous difficulties encountered in securing the story, she reflected, which had led her to develop "an exaggerated sense of the value of every small detail and scrap of paper." After her experiences in 1937, she "was never able to make selections properly." History, she concluded, "became sacred to me." See Wales, *My Yenan Notebooks*, p. 19.

[29] Wales, *Inside Red China*, pp. 38–40, 48.

knowledge the Communists as China's finest. They added, however, that *Inside Red China* was a book worth reading.[30] T. A. Bisson was less cautious. He insisted that Helen Snow's volume was as indispensable to the student of Chinese communism as *Red Star over China*.[31]

Mrs. Snow had not been the only Westerner in Communist China during the summer of 1937. In June, a group of five drove into Yenan in "an ancient vintage Chevrolet, with makeshift fanbelts, ignition out of order, cranking very difficult, and radiator leaking." [32] Three of these, T. A. Bisson, Philip J. Jaffe, and Owen Lattimore, were members of the editorial board of the magazine *Amerasia*. Mrs. Agnes Jaffe, the wife of the managing editor of *Amerasia*, and Karl Efraim Hill, the Scandinavian who had assisted Helen Snow in her escape from Sian, completed the group. Hill had been hired to drive the Americans to Yenan.[33]

The *Amerasia* group had evaded the Nationalist blockade by employing an elaborate pretense. Mr. Jaffe acted the part of a rich American with a kidney disease who was going to the mountains for a cure. Lattimore, who spoke Chinese, was his interpreter. Bisson was just a friend who was going along for the ride. Since the Sian border officers believed Jaffe, it was a successful, if not unduly imaginative ruse.[34] After en-

[30] Rodney Gilbert, "With the Young Veterans of China's Army: Adventures of Two Westerners Among Y.M.C.A.-Minded Reds," *New York Herald Tribune Books*, February 19, 1939, 1–2; Owen Lattimore, review of *Inside Red China* in *Pacific Affairs*, XII (September 1939), 344–346.

[31] T. A. Bisson, "China at War," *Nation*, CXLVIII (February 25, 1939), 237–238.

[32] T. A. Bisson, Peiping, July 4, 1937, mimeographed letter to Raymond Leslie Buell, 893.00/14154, Department of State files. Buell, the president of the Foreign Policy Association, forwarded a copy of Bisson's letter to Dr. Stanley K. Hornbeck of the Department of State on July 23, 1937.

[33] Philip J. Jaffe to Benjamin J. Mandel, August 24, 1965.

[34] Jaffe, interview with the author, June 14, 1965; Owen Lattimore, conversation with the author, April 16, 1969.

during four days of flooded rivers, deeply pitted mountainous roads, and lice-infested Chinese hovels, the weary foreigners arrived in Yenan on June 21, 1937.
The warm reception in Yenan more than compensated for
the hazards of the road. Agnes Smedley cordially greeted the
Amerasia party at the gates of the city.[35] Bisson recalled later
that their three-day stay was a whirlwind of activity. "The
important Red leaders were all there, and placed themselves
entirely at our disposal in a steady round of interviews, discussions, dinners, lunches, inspection visits, posing for pictures, etc." [36] Mao Tse-tung, Chu Teh, and Chou En-lai
spent a number of hours in conversation with their honored
guests. A good time seems to have been had by all, and the
foreigners departed on June 24, favorably impressed by what
they had seen.
The spirit of Yenan infected Jaffe. "Even the dogs, the
most miserable of all living things in China," he rhapsodized, "were active and barking." He was particularly moved
by the cultural and educational progress which the Communists had fostered in Shensi, one of China's most backward
provinces.[37] Bisson's attention was riveted on the big political issue of the day, the possibility of a united front against
Japan. This Far Eastern authority for the Foreign Policy Association returned from Yenan convinced that the Communists were patriots determined to heal the breach which separated them from Nanking.[38]

[35] Jaffe, "China's Communists Told Me: A Specialist in Far Eastern Affairs Interviews the Leading Men of Red China in Their Home Territories," *New Masses*, XXV (October 12, 1937), 5. This is the feature article
of the October 12 issue of *New Masses*. Jaffe's essay is richly illustrated
with twenty-four photographs and a map.
[36] Bisson, Peiping, July 4, 1937, mimeographed letter to Buell.
[37] Jaffe, "China's Communists Told Me," 9–10. See also Jaffe, "The Far
East at the Crossroads," *Amerasia*, I (October 1937), 349–354.
[38] Bisson, *Japan in China* (New York, 1938), p. 195. This scholarly tome
grew out of Bisson's investigations in 1937. Bisson emphasizes the problem
of Sino-Japanese relations; China's Communists are given only brief con-

Like Bisson and Jaffe, Owen Lattimore was stirred by the charged atmosphere of Yenan. He was certain that the dynamic Chinese Communists were neither "bandits preying on society or condottieri aiming at power for the sake of power."[39] Lattimore perceptively noted, however, that he had not been in the Communist stronghold "long enough to make a close check between the facts as represented and the

_____

sideration. He was in China on a Rockefeller research fellowship granted him as a member of the staff of the Foreign Policy Association. His three-day stay in Yenan was only a minor interlude during several months of scholarly endeavor in the Far East. See also Bisson, "Mao Tse-tung Analyzes Nanking in Interview," *Amerasia*, I (October 1937), 360–365 and Bisson's testimony of March 29 and 31, 1952, in U.S. Senate, Committee on the Judiciary, Subcommittee on Internal Security, 82nd Cong., 1st and 2nd Sess., *Institute of Pacific Relations, Hearings* (Part 10, Washington, D.C., 1952), pp. 4212–4222.

[39] Owen Lattimore, "The Strongholds of Chinese Communism: A Journey to North Shensi," unpublished manuscript, 6. Lattimore wrote two essays, each six pages in length, shortly after his return from Yenan. The second was titled "The Present and Future of Chinese Communism: The Theory of the United Front." Copies of the two manuscript articles were included in the following dispatch: Frank P. Lockhart, Peiping, August 2, 1937, dispatch to the Secretary of State, 893.00/14179, Department of State files. Citations have been made directly to the manuscript essays.

In his testimony of March 4, 1952, before the Senate subcommittee which investigated the Institute of Pacific Relations, Lattimore said that he may have submitted one or two articles on his Yenan trip to the London *Times*. He could not, however, recall whether the *Times* had published this material. The writer has been unable to find evidence which would indicate that the *Times* printed anything by Lattimore which related to his experiences in 1937. It is unfortunate that Lattimore did not have copies of the essays in his files, as they would have corroborated much of the uncertain testimony which he presented before a skeptical Senate subcommittee. See U.S. Senate, *Institute of Pacific Relations, Hearings* (Part 10), pp. 3287–3292.

Lattimore briefly referred to his Yenan experience in the heated public correspondence which he exchanged with an irate victim of one of his book reviews. See "Comment and Correspondence," *Pacific Affairs*, X (December 1937), 450–459.

facts as they are." [40] This observation applies with equal validity to Lattimore's colleagues.

By one means or another, nearly a dozen "blockade runners" had contrived to have a firsthand encounter with Chinese Communists during the period between the Sian Incident and the establishment of a united front on September 22, 1937. The end product was a harvest of publicity favorable to the CCP. This early reporting trend was aptly summarized by R. L. Duffus in a review of *Inside Red China*. "Apparently it is almost impossible," Duffus wrote, "not to idealize these Chinese fighters for liberty." He thought that a balanced appraisal would have to mention the ruthless tactics employed against landlords and other opponents of communism. After all, the CCP did not hold its own "entirely by being kind." Duffus conceded, however, that as they emerged from the pages of *Inside Red China*, China's Communists were the most attractive revolutionaries of his time. [41] A final blow, if any was needed, had been dealt the bandit-remnant thesis. The writings of the blockade runners also reinforced, sometimes in exaggerated proportions, the favorable image of Chinese Communists which had been publicized widely in *Red Star over China*.

[40] Lattimore, "The Present and Future of Chinese Communism: The Theory of the United Front," unpub. manuscript, 893.00/14179, Department of State files, 2.

[41] R. L. Duffus, "Inside the China Called Red: An Uncommonly Interesting Report by Nym Wales, Whose Husband, Edgar Snow, Wrote 'Red Star over China,' " *New York Times Book Review*, July 23, 1939, 12.

[6]

The Open Door: 1937-1938

No outside observers were in Yenan when the Nationalists and Communists announced their intention to unite in resisting the Japanese invader. In the united-front statement of September 22, 1937, the CCP renounced the policy of overthrowing the KMT by force, declared an end to the program of land confiscation, and espoused the three principles of Sun Yat-sen. The Shensi Soviet was reorganized as the Shensi-Kansu-Ninghsia Border Area government (Shen-Kan-Ning), and the Red Army was redesignated the Eighth Route Army and placed under the nominal control of the Central government's Military Affairs Commission. On paper, at least, the CCP had been integrated.[1]

For their part, the Nationalists released many Communist political prisoners and agreed to subsidize a part of the Eighth Route Army. Neither side, however, had illusions about what the new coalition meant. The two parties knew that this second united front had been a shotgun marriage consummated under the pressure of a popular demand for a

[1] Conrad Brandt, Benjamin Schwartz, and John K. Fairbank, eds., *A Documentary History of Chinese Communism* (Cambridge, Mass., 1952), pp. 245–247. The "CCP's Public Statement on KMT-CCP Cooperation" was drafted on July 4, submitted to the Central Government on July 15, and published by the Kuomintang Central News Agency on September 22, 1937.

national stand against the Japanese.[2] With a decade of bitter hostility fresh in memory, as O. Edmund Clubb has observed, Communists and Nationalists alike could not help but have strong reservations about the partnership. While fighting the Japanese, both KMT and CCP "would give earnest thought to a future day of domestic reckoning."[3] The Communists did not even pretend to be abandoning their ultimate aims, and they stoutly maintained the administrative independence of their armed forces and border region bases.

Whatever their ultimate intentions, the Communists initially implemented the united-front agreement in a cooperative manner. Chiang Kai-shek was accorded great esteem in CCP propaganda, and the Communists professed a determination to struggle to the end at the side of the Central government. The Eighth Route Army did what it could to stem the relentless Japanese advance. At P'inghsingkuan Pass in eastern Shansi on September 25, 1937, Lin Piao's veterans ambushed and mauled the crack Japanese Fifth Division under General Itagaki Seishiro. Although this first major victory of the united front had little military importance, it did have considerable psychological significance. The battle gave a needed boost to Chinese morale and earned the Eighth Route Army valuable publicity. Wherever possible, the mobile forces of the Red Army supported Nationalist troops in combat engagements.[4]

The spirit of wartime unity reached its apex during the siege of Hankow. After Nanking fell to the Japanese in an

[2] Lyman P. Van Slyke, *Enemies and Friends: The United Front in Chinese Communist History* (Stanford, 1967), pp. 93–94; Jerome Ch'en, *Mao and the Chinese Revolution* (New York, 1967), p. 233.

[3] O. Edmund Clubb, *20th Century China* (New York and London, 1964), pp. 216–217.

[4] Van Slyke, *Enemies and Friends*, pp. 93–94; Samuel B. Griffith, II, *The Chinese People's Liberation Army* (New York, Toronto, London, and Sydney, 1967), pp. 63–65.

orgy of rape and plunder on December 12–13, 1937, the KMT transferred the seat of government to Hankow. Until the fall of this beleagured city in late October 1938, Communists and Nationalists sat in common council planning the prosecution of the war. The Central government authorized the publication of a Communist newspaper (the *Hsin Hua Jih Pao*), approved the formation of a second Communist army (the New Fourth Army), sanctioned the establishment of the Shansi-Chahar-Hopei Border Government (the Chin-Ch'a-Chi), appointed CCP officials to the National Military Council (Chou En-lai and Kuo Mo-jo), and granted their former adversaries membership in the newly created People's Political Council.[5] In Hankow in 1938 the united front developed, as a contemporary recalled, "as far as it ever would."[6]

Paradoxically, the defense of Hankow generated the first serious breach in the united front. A rancorous dispute erupted between the two parties over the question of how to respond to the Japanese assault on the city. The Communists advanced the slogan "Defend Wuhan to the death" and urged the arming of the masses for a Madrid-like, revolutionary stand. Chiang Kai-shek rejected the Communist proposal, ordered the Wuhan cities evacuated, and transferred his administrative capital to Chungking. From this time forward, KMT-CCP relations steadily deteriorated. Nonetheless, the period from the announcement of the united front on September 22, 1937, to the Japanese occupation of Hankow on October 25, 1938, can be described as an interlude of Chinese unity and collaboration.[7]

[5] Van Slyke, *Enemies and Friends*, p. 94; Ch'en, *Mao and the Chinese Revolution*, pp. 234–235; Theodore H. White and Annalee Jacoby, *Thunder Out of China* (New York, 1946), pp. 50–53.

[6] Paul Frillmann and Graham Peck, *China: The Remembered Life* (Boston, 1968), p. 19.

[7] Chalmers A. Johnson, *Present Nationalism and Communist Power: The Emergence of Revolutionary China, 1937–1945* (Stanford, 1962), pp.

During the cooperative phase of the united front, Hankow was more than the temporary capital of the Chinese nation. It was also a symbol and a mood. For a few months, this industrial center symbolized the determination of the Chinese people to put aside past differences and to meet the aggressor with all of the resources at their disposal. Hankow was also a mood of optimism and hope for the political future of China. Foreign observers were duly impressed by the apparent unity which bound Communist and Nationalist together. In 1938 there was, as one of them recalled, "really a united front. . . . It was possible to believe that the Chinese Communists had really subordinated themselves to the Government." [8]

The home of Bishop Logan H. Roots became a kind of united-front meeting place in Hankow. Roots was an Episcopalian cleric who, as a friend remarked, "loved all human beings quite indiscriminately." [9] Agnes Smedley affectionately called him "Comrade Bishop," others dubbed him the "Pink Bishop," and his residence was nicknamed the "Moscow-Heaven Axis." [10] All were welcome at Roots's dinner table, regardless of their political affiliations or reputations. Paul Frillmann, a Lutheran missionary and frequent guest, recalled that he had met "more kinds of people" than he

---

37–38; F. F. Liu, *A Military History of Modern China, 1924–49* (Princeton, 1956), pp. 197–202; White and Jacoby, *Thunder Out of China*, pp. 50–53.

[8] U.S. Senate, Subcommittee of the Committee on Foreign Relations, 81st Cong., 2nd Sess., *State Department Employee Loyalty Investigation, Hearings* (Part I, Washington, D.C., 1950), p. 785. Freda Utley made this statement on May 1, 1950. See also Utley, *Odyssey of a Liberal: Memoirs* (Washington, D.C., 1970), p. 211, and White and Jacoby, *Thunder Out of China*, p. 53.

[9] Ilona Ralf Sues, *Shark's Fins and Millet* (Boston, 1944), p. 55. See also Bishop Logan H. Roots, "To My China Friends: Reflections after Forty Years in China," *Amerasia*, II (May 1938), 168–170.

[10] Sues, *Shark's Fins and Millet*, pp. 174, 192; W. H. Auden and Christopher Isherwood, *Journey to a War* (New York, 1939), p. 52.

"had known existed."[11] Under the benign auspices of Bishop Roots, KMT officials and Western correspondents sipped tea with such Communist luminaries as Chou En-lai. If the "Moscow-Heaven Axis" was not to their liking, Western journalists could meet Chinese Communists simply by visiting the Hankow offices of either the Eighth Route Army or the *Hsin Hua Jih Pao.* Thus, for example, two English writers passed the evening of March 12, 1938, at Red Army headquarters engaged in friendly and informal conversation.[12] Israel Epstein, a correspondent for the United Press, spent some of his time in the buildings which housed the *Hsin Hua Jih Pao,* the Communist daily which was published at Hankow.[13] The nearly forty war correspondents who had congregated in Hankow to report on the defense of the city, then, had little difficulty establishing contact with Chinese Communists.[14] Their task was facilitated, moreover, by the presence of that ubiquitous American radical, Agnes Smedley.

Miss Smedley had arrived in Hankow on January 8, 1938, after a three-month trip with the Red Army in Shansi. While in Hankow, she served as an intermediary between the CCP and the foreign news and diplomatic communities. Miss Smedley was the channel through which foreigners obtained information about and contacts with Chinese Communists.[15] She was also instrumental in organizing the

[11] Frillmann and Peck, *China,* p. 15.

[12] Auden and Isherwood, *Journey to a War,* p. 61.

[13] I. Epstein, *The People's War* (London, 1939), p. 138. The *Hsin Hua Jih Pao* was edited by Chen Chia-kang, who also served as secretary to Chou En-lai.

[14] Anna Wang, *Ich kämpfte für Mao: Eine deutsche Frau erlebt die chinesische Revolution* (Hamburg, Germany, 1964), p. 201.

[15] U.S. Senate, Committee on the Judiciary, Subcommittee on Internal Security, 82nd Cong., 1st and 2nd Sess., *Institute of Pacific Relations, Hearings* (Part 14, Washington, D.C., 1952), p. 5469, testimony of John Paton Davies, Jr., August 10, 1951. See also Freda Utley, *China at War* (New York, 1939), pp. 73–77.

Northwestern Partisan Relief Committee (NPRC). The NPRC collected money and supplies for the Eighth Route Army. Spurred on by Agnes Smedley's driving energy, the NPRC accumulated $20,000 in Chinese currency and a respectable quantity of goods from the citizens of Hankow.

In February 1938, a goodwill delegation representing the NPRC journeyed to Eighth Route Army headquarters in Shansi. The spokesman for the group was Frances Roots, the daughter of the Episcopalian Bishop of Hankow. The party also included Judy Clark, a deaconess, John Foster and Charles Higgins, both American missionaries, and Ilona Ralf Sues, a Swiss writer. The Communists met their benefactors with an honor guard and held a mass meeting to celebrate the occasion. After presenting their substantial gift, most of these foreign humanitarians returned to Hankow.[16] Higgins and Miss Sues, however, proceeded directly from Shansi to Yenan. "The first thing we noticed," Miss Sues wrote of her initial impression of the Communist capital, "was that there was not a single beggar to be seen." [17] After interviewing Mao Tse-tung and other leaders, Higgins and Miss Sues went back to Hankow.

As the experience of the NPRC goodwill mission demonstrates, it was relatively easy in 1938 to make a trip to the Communist areas. The door was open to those willing to undertake the arduous trek to Yenan. Because of this situation, a large number of people from diverse backgrounds were able to have firsthand encounters with Chinese Communists. In addition to the NPRC group, two doctors, two scholars,

[16] Sues, *Shark's Fins and Millet*, pp. 193–194, 216–252. See also James M. Bertram, *Unconquered: Journal of a Year's Adventures Among the Fighting Peasants of North China* (New York, 1939), pp. 284–286. Bertram was at Eighth Route Army headquarters in Shansi when the goodwill mission arrived. John Foster returned to the Soviet regions in the summer of 1938. For a summary of his favorable impressions see *Foreign Relations of the United States: Diplomatic Papers, 1939*, III (Washington, D.C., 1955), pp. 142–144.

[17] Sues, *Shark's Fins and Millet*, p. 257.

and an American journalist were among those who made excursions to the guerrilla strongholds.

George Hatem was joined by two Canadian physicians in 1938. Dr. Norman Bethune, who had earned an enviable reputation as a thoracic surgeon before coming to China, literally worked himself to death trying to provide much-needed medical assistance to the Eighth Route Army. Bethune, a member of the Canadian Communist Party, left Hankow for Yenan in March, 1938. He spent most of his time with the mobile guerrilla bands of General Nieh Jung-chen in the mountains of Shansi and Hopei as medical adviser to the Chin-Ch'a-Chi. Until his death on November 12, 1939, Bethune labored tirelessly under the most primitive of conditions to save the lives of his Chinese comrades.[18] In the spring and summer of 1938, a fellow Canadian, Dr. Richard Brown, assisted Bethune.[19] After spending approximately three months with the Communist partisans, Brown returned to Hankow. Unlike Bethune, Brown was a medical missionary who despised the Russian brand of Bolshevism and its anti-Christian propaganda. However, as one of his acquaintances recalled, Brown had nothing but admiration for the Chinese Communists.[20] In addition to Hatem, Bethune, and Brown, about a half dozen other non-Chinese doctors ministered to the Red Army before the end of the Sino-Japanese War. An authoritative source listed seven physicians who had worked in guerrilla China prior to 1944.[21]

[18] Sydney Gordon and Ted Allan, *The Scalpel, the Sword: The Story of Dr. Norman Bethune* (London, 1954), pp. 136ff. See also Jonathan Spence, *To Change China: Western Advisers in China, 1620–1960* (Boston and Toronto, 1969), pp. 216–227; "Norman Bethune—Internationalist Fighter Imbued with Mao Tse-tung's Thought," *Peking Review*, Nos. 26–28 (June 28, July 5, July 12, 1968), 25–27, 27, 28.

[19] Gordon and Allan, *The Scalpel*, p. 158.

[20] Utley, *China at War*, p. 209.

[21] *In Guerrilla China: Report of China Defence League* (Chungking, 1943), *passim*. Madame Sun Yat-sen was the chairman of the China Defense League. This ostensibly nonpartisan group collected funds and sup-

J. Clayton Miller and George E. Taylor were both associated with Yenching University. Miller, an American student engaged in historical research, spent three weeks in the spring of 1938 with the Chinese guerrilla forces in central Hopei.[22] After witnessing the gloom and resignation that hung over Peiping, he was deeply impressed by the "new spirit" and "vital nationalism" of the Hopei partisans.[23] Miller was astonished to find that they had devised a comprehensive plan of military, political, economic, and social reforms. The mass educational program, he wrote, "did not allow even the most illiterate peasant to remain untouched."[24] Miller based his conclusions on personal observations and conversations with the Communist and Nationalist officials of Hopei who had united to drive the invader out of their province.

plies to aid the Communist guerrillas in their war against the Japanese. The doctors listed in this seventy-two page booklet were B. K. Basu (Indian), M. Frey (Austrian), Dwarkanath Kotnis (Indian), Ma Hai-Teh (American, pseudonym for George Hatem), Hans Mueller (German), I. Orlov (Russian), and Eva Sandberg (Swedish). Aside from their names, little additional information is given about these physicians. Kotnis, who joined the Chinese Communist Party, died in 1942. Mueller had been in the guerrilla regions since 1939. Basu was the chief surgeon of the International Peace Hospital in Yenan.

[22] J. Clayton Miller to the author, January 30, 1966. Mr. Miller, who was born in Ohio in 1909, earned an A.B. and M.A. in political science at Oberlin College. From 1930 to 1932, he taught at the Oberlin Shansi Memorial School near Taiku, Shansi. After studying at Yenching University in 1937 and 1938, he returned to the United States and enrolled in the Maxwell School of Public Administration at Syracuse University. Subsequently, Mr. Miller pursued a career as a management analyst for both private industrial corporations and various governmental agencies. He recalled that he was in the guerrilla area by April 22, 1938.

[23] Miller, "Japs Battle a Reborn China: Former Clevelander Tells of a New Government That is Functioning Smoothly within Nipponese Lines," *Cleveland Plain Dealer,* January 8, 1939, 1, 6.

[24] Miller, "The Chinese Still Rule North China: Political and Military Strategy of the Hopei-Shansi-Chahar Border Government," *Amerasia,* II (September 1938), 337.

From 1937 to 1939, Taylor held a position as tutor of European history and political science at Yenching University. In the summer of 1938, Taylor and a British colleague, Michael Lindsay, traveled in the Wutaishan region, which straddles the boundaries of Hopei and Shansi. Taylor talked with partisan leaders and examined a substantial number of guerrilla publications. He was favorably impressed by what he saw. The Communist-directed Border government, according to Taylor, had eliminated corruption, achieved harmonious relations with the people, instituted moderate economic and social reforms, and taken significant steps toward the development of democratically oriented mass organizations.[25]

In late December 1937, a "big, buxom, white-haired woman" with piercing blue eyes, "conservatively dressed in dark suits with white lace at the neck and black hats clacking with artificial fruit" arrived in Hankow.[26] After interviewing Madame Chiang Kai-shek and the Generalissimo, Anna Louise Strong left for the front. She spent ten days in January 1938 at Eighth Route Army headquarters in north Shansi, "sharing their meals and talking constantly with men and commanders." [27] By early February the fast-moving American woman had begun the long journey out of China.

The only thing startling about Anna Louise Strong's literary summation of her hurried trip to China was the intro-

---

[25] George E. Taylor, *The Struggle For North China* (New York, 1940), pp. 5, 104–117. See also the sworn statement of Michael Lindsay of June 3, 1952, in U.S. Senate, *Institute of Pacific Relations* (Part 14), p. 5368. Professor Taylor, who is a United States citizen, was born in England in 1905. He earned an undergraduate degree at the University of Birmingham in 1927 and was a Harvard-Yenching fellow in China from 1930 to 1932. Before going to Yenching University in 1937 as tutor in history and political science, he taught at the Central Political Institute in Nanking.

[26] Frillmann and Peck, *China*, p. 20.

[27] Anna Louise Strong, *One-Fifth of Mankind* (New York, 1938), p. 129. For an adequate summary of Miss Strong's trip in January 1938 to Eighth Route Army headquarters, see Strong, "Political Work of a Chinese Army," *Amerasia*, II (August 1938), 304–308.

duction. It was written, with best wishes, by Madame Chiang Kai-shek. But even Madame Chiang's blessing could not do much to improve *One-Fifth of Mankind*. A third-rate tract for the times, published in paperback, it went almost unnoticed in the periodical press. One reviewer was generous enough to say that Miss Strong was the daughter of a Congregationalist minister and that she possessed a firstrate mind.[28] The brief comment in the *New Republic* was more appropriate. *One-Fifth of Mankind* was, the *New Republic* observed, "admirably suited to those who read as they ride." [29]

Of the many Westerners who came into contact with the Chinese Communists in late 1937–1938, four are particularly noteworthy. The experiences of James M. Bertram, Agnes Smedley, Evans Fordyce Carlson, and Haldore Hanson are analogous in several respects. They all entered the Communist-controlled regions during the period when the united front functioned successfully. Their tours with the Eighth Route Army were of several months' duration, and, unlike Anna Louise Strong, they published substantial accounts detailing their experiences. Finally, they crossed paths in the course of their travels in guerrilla territory.

When Owen Lattimore was in Yenan in the summer of 1937, the Communists professed to welcome any and all foreigners to their stronghold. They seemed somewhat disappointed, moreover, that only Americans had chosen to take advantage of this open-door policy. The Communists hoped that other nationals, particularly the British, would visit their capital.[30] The first non-American journalist to avail himself of Yenan's hospitality was not long in coming.

[28] Edwin T. Buehrer, "Tracts For the Times," *Christian Century*, LV (December 7, 1938), 1504.

[29] "New Books: A Reader's List," *New Republic*, XCVII (January 4, 1939), 268.

[30] Owen Lattimore, "The Strongholds of Chinese Communism: A Journey to North Shensi," unpublished manuscript, 893.00/14179, Department of State files, 2–3.

James Bertram, a twenty-seven-year-old New Zealander, was in Tokyo when the Sino-Japanese War erupted. Without undue delay he returned to China, and in early September 1937, he left Japanese-occupied Peiping in the company of Edgar Snow and Teng Ying-ch'ao, the wife of Chou En-lai.[31] After smuggling Mrs. Chou through the Japanese lines as an amah, Bertram and Snow made their way to the Northwest. At Sian in mid-September there was a friendly reunion. Agnes Smedley was in the city convalescing from a back injury. Helen Snow had just returned from her long sojourn in Yenan. To the infinite relief of the local authorities, the Snows left Sian on September 23. Bertram and Miss Smedley, however, remained. Both were soon to take advantage of Yenan's policy of inviting the scrutiny of outside observers.[32]

Despite the formal announcement of the united front on September 22, the Sian authorities remained hostile toward the Communists. Fearing that the local police would forcibly deport him, Bertram vacated Sian concealed beneath some rice sacks in the rear of an Eighth Route Army truck. By October 13 he was in Yenan. He stayed there for nearly a month, during which time he held a series of interviews with Mao Tse-tung. Although he found it difficult to leave hospitable Yenan, in the first week of November he departed for the Shansi front. From November 1937 to February 1938, Bertram traveled with the Eighth Route Army. During his three-month stay in war-torn Shansi, he had conversations

[31] Bertram to the author, April 1965; Edgar Snow, *Journey to the Beginning* (New York, 1958), p. 188; *Red Star over China* (rev. and expanded ed., New York, 1968), p. 500. Mrs. Chou had been in Peiping convalescing from pulmonary tuberculosis when the Japanese occupation endangered her life.

[32] Bertram, *Unconquered*, pp. 33, 63–65, 77–79; Snow, *Journey to the Beginning*, pp. 188–192; Agnes Smedley, *China Fights Back: An American Woman with the Eighth Route Army* (London, 1939), pp. 24ff.; Smedley, *Battle Hymn of China* (New York, 1943), pp. 182–183; Nym Wales [Helen Foster Snow], *Inside Red China* (Garden City, New York, 1939), pp. 292ff.

with Chu Teh, Chou En-lai, P'eng Teh-huai, and Ho Lung. Bertram came out of the Shansi hills in February of 1938 filled with admiration for the valiant Communists who were organizing the people of North China to withstand the advances of a harsh invader.[33]

Unconquered: Journal of a Year's Adventures among the Fighting Peasants of North China is just what its title suggests—a collection of diary-like descriptions of the author's wanderings in wartime China. Bertram was appalled by Japanese ferocity, gratified by the simple friendliness of the Chinese people, and convinced that the dynamic Communists were infusing the masses with a new spirit of resistance and progressivism. He believed that while the Japanese might win every battle, China's awakened millions would triumph in the end. Naturally, the cadres of the Eighth Route Army would be in the vanguard of the Chinese liberation movement.

Bertram's book was received cordially but without much enthusiasm. Rodney Gilbert felt that *Unconquered* conveyed the atmosphere of a "co-educational scout jamboree." Although Gilbert did not care much for Bertram's predispositions, he concluded that the New Zealander had written an honest appraisal.[34] Owen Lattimore praised Bertram for accurate reporting, the *New York Times* found *Unconquered* interesting, and Victor A. Yakhontoff thought it was a useful study.[35] T. A. Bisson, however, rated Bertram's ef-

---

[33] Bertram, *Unconquered*, pp. 79, 84–86, 110, 125 136, *passim;* Bertram to the author, April 1965. Bertram held his first interview with Mao Tse-tung on October 13 and probably arrived in Yenan several days prior to that date.

[34] Rodney Gilbert, "With the Young Veterans of China's Army: Adventures of Two Westerners among Y.M.C.A.-Minded Reds," *New York Herald Tribune Books,* February 19, 1939, 2.

[35] Lattimore, review of *Unconquered* in *Pacific Affairs,* XII (June 1939), 208–209; "Unconquered China," *New York Times Book Review,* February 5, 1939, 12; Victor A. Yakhontoff, "China Can Win," *New Republic,* XCVIII (March 15, 1939), 172–173.

fort the "most effective piece of writing" which had come from the battle zones of China.[36] Bisson was alone in his adulation, as most reviewers remained unexcited about *Unconquered*.

On November 23, 1937, Bertram chanced upon Agnes Smedley in a small village in Shansi. She paused long enough to permit him to examine the manuscript of *China Fights Back* and then proceeded on her journey with the Eighth Route Army.[37] By October 16, 1937, she had sufficiently recovered from her back ailment to leave Sian for the North China front. Unlike Bertram, she did not proceed to Yenan; rather, she spent the months from October 1937 to January 1938 traveling with the roving headquarters of the Eighth Route Army in Shansi. These were among the happiest and most purposeful days of her life. She reveled in the title "friend of China" and referred to the Communist troops as "comrades." When the Communists expressed a concern about her personal safety and requested that she leave the battle zone, Agnes Smedley broke down and wept. "It seemed," she lamented, "I was bidding farewell to the very earth." [38] In January 1938, this disappointed woman went to Hankow where, as we have seen, she did her best to help the comrades still fighting on the Shansi front. Shortly before the conquest of Hankow, she would hasten off to rejoin the Communist warriors whose cause had come to absorb all of her energies.

China Fights Back is the diary of Miss Smedley's experiences from August 19, 1937, to January 9, 1938.[39] The

[36] T. A. Bisson, "China at War," *Nation*, CXLVIII (February 15, 1939), 237–238.
[37] Bertram, *Unconquered*, p. 171; Smedley, *China Fights Back*, pp. 195–198.
[38] Smedley, *China Fights Back*, p. 272.
[39] *China Fights Back* was first published in 1938 by the Vanguard Press of New York City. All citations, however, refer to the British edition published by Victor Gollancz in 1939.

manuscript was submitted to the publishers in the form of a rough draft, and the book is not conspicuous for literary craftsmanship. It is a badly organized autobiographical travelogue saturated with trivia. For example, the author includes a not particularly enlightening description of the amorous advances of her horse to an unnerved mare.[40] Furthermore, as one critic observed, the work is a "frankly biased account . . . written from the Communist point of view."[41]

Nonetheless, *China Fights Back* is based on extensive first-hand contact with the Eighth Route Army. As T. A. Bisson pointed out, "It is war reporting of the classic type, set down after long marches with fighting units behind enemy lines."[42] Also, as R. L. Duffus observed in his thoughtful review, Agnes Smedley's moving account had an unquestionable ring of sincerity. Despite misgivings about the tyranny of Marxism and Miss Smedley's emotional approach, Duffus was impressed by the images of Communist patriotism and liberalism conveyed by *China Fights Back*.[43] In a similar vein, Walter H. Mallory was so moved by Agnes Smedley's candor that he was inclined to overlook her obvious bias.[44] Finally, *China Fights Back* surpassed Miss Smedley's previous books in one important respect. While she was still the propagandist, she wrote now in a straightforward, factual manner that was more likely to convince readers than was her earlier fictional approach.

[40] Smedley, *China Fights Back,* p. 111.

[41] Walter H. Mallory, "China's Communist Front: Miss Smedley Tells Her Story with Candor and Sincerity, but with Obvious Partiality," *New York Herald Tribune Books,* July 24, 1938, 4. In 1938, Mallory was the Executive Director of the Council on Foreign Relations.

[42] Bisson, "With the Eighth Route Army," *Nation,* CXLVII (July 9, 1938), 48.

[43] R. L. Duffus, "The March of the Famous Eighth Route Army in China: Agnes Smedley Tells of Its Adventures in Extraordinarily Moving and Highly Informative Fashion," *New York Times Book Review,* July 10, 1938, 3, 17.

[44] Mallory, "China's Communist Front," 4.

At Eighth Route Army headquarters in south Shansi in mid-December, 1937, Chu Teh introduced Agnes Smedley to Captain Evans Fordyce Carlson of the United States Marine Corps.[45] Unlike Miss Smedley, this lanky officer was a newcomer to Red China. Yet, Carlson's encounter with China's Communists was to mark a milestone in foreign contacts with the CCP. He was the first outside military observer to scrutinize the operations of the Red Army. Furthermore, Carlson entered Communist territory under the auspices of the United States Navy and with the formal authorization of Chiang Kai-shek.

Evans Carlson was a Bible-quoting New Englander in the American Puritan tradition.[46] The son of a Congregationalist minister, he never finished high school, but he found a place for himself in the United States Army. Carlson joined up in 1912 and attained the rank of captain before resigning at the conclusion of the First World War. After giving civilian life an unsuccessful try, Carlson enlisted as a private in the Marines in 1922. In 1930 he gained some valuable experience—and the Navy Cross—by fighting against Augustino Sandino's guerrillas in Nicaragua. From 1927 to 1929 and again from 1933 to 1935, Carlson served as an intelligence officer in China.[47] He was, then, a professional sol-

[45] Smedley, *China Fights Back*, pp. 251–255; Evans Fordyce Carlson, *Twin Stars of China: A Behind-the-Scenes Story of China's Valiant Struggle for Existence by a U.S. Marine Who Lived and Moved with the People* (New York, 1940), pp. 68–69.

[46] Griffith, *The Chinese People's Liberation Army*, p. 255.

[47] Michael Blankfort, *The Big Yankee: The Life of Carlson of the Raiders* (Boston, 1947), pp. 81, 97, 162–169. The most valuable sections of Blankfort's biography are the lengthy citations from Carlson's diary and other private papers. Blankfort, who is primarily a dramatist, served under Major Carlson in the Marine Raiders during the Second World War. Although *The Big Yankee* is a hero-worshipping biography, it does contain much valuable information. The book abounds with artificial dialogue and unfootnoted citations. However, Evans F. Carlson read Blankfort's manuscript and confirmed the thoughts which were attributed to him by his admiring biographer.

dier who knew something about partisan warfare and who had spent a number of years in China prior to the outbreak of the Sino-Japanese War.

Despite his military background, Carlson did not fit many of the stereotypes of the professional soldier. One of his acquaintances characterized him as a "romantic," another as a principled moralist, and a third as a cultured military officer [48]; his biographer thought he could best be described as a "kind of Christian socialist." [49] During his wanderings with the Red Army in North China, he hoped to compare systematically the doctrines of Christianity with those espoused by the Chinese Communists.[50] Deeply religious, he was an avid reader of Ralph Waldo Emerson's *Essays* and of the New Testament. If Carlson was anything, he was a man "drunk with democracy." [51] Egalitarian democracy and sacrificial selflessness were his highest ideals.

Carlson was also a gregarious and impressionable person who formed opinions of others quickly and spontaneously. Shortly after being introduced to Chu Teh, the commander-in-chief of the Chinese Red Army, Carlson recorded in his diary: "Immediately and intuitively I felt that I had found a warm and generous friend, and a man who was a true leader of men." [52] Carlson got along well with most people and numbered individuals from many walks of life among his friends. A partial listing of his more important acquaintances would include Edgar Snow, Ambassador Nelson T. Johnson, and President Franklin D. Roosevelt.

[48] Utley, *China at War*, p. 211; Smedley, *Battle Hymn of China*, pp. 198–199; Haldore Hanson, *"Humane Endeavour": The Story of the China War* (New York and Toronto, 1939), p. 242. For other contemporary appraisals of Carlson see Sues, *Shark's Fins and Millet*, p. 302, and Bertram, *Beneath the Shadow: A New Zealander in the Far East, 1939–46* (New York, 1947), p. 56.

[49] Michael Blankfort to the author, October 19, 1964.

[50] Carlson, *Twin Stars of China*, p. 176.

[51] Blankfort, *The Big Yankee*, p. 360.

[52] *Ibid.*, p. 108.

In 1935, Captain Carlson was appointed second-in-command of the President's military guard at Warm Springs, Georgia. This fortuitous circumstance ultimately led to conversations between Roosevelt and Carlson in 1936, 1937, 1939, 1940, 1941, 1943, and 1944. One of the President's sons, James Roosevelt, served as Carlson's executive officer in the Second Marine Raider Battalion during World War II. The most significant product of Carlson's association with the President, however, consists of personal letters, many of them on the topic of China's Communists, which the marine wrote for the benefit of his commander-in-chief.[53] On July 15, 1937, just prior to his departure for the Far East, Carlson had an appointment with the President. Roosevelt asked Carlson to write him privately about what was going on in China. The President proposed that they keep this correspondence confidential.[54] From 1937 on, Carlson

[53] This correspondence is on deposit at the Franklin D. Roosevelt Library in Hyde Park, New York. It is located in the President's Personal File (PPF), 4951, Evans F. Carlson. Like other materials which the writer has examined in the Roosevelt papers, this collection reveals almost nothing about the President's thinking, but the very fact that the Carlson correspondence exists is of some importance. Carlson wrote frequently and extensively of his encounters with Chinese Communists. His letters were not addressed directly to the President but were channeled through the President's personal secretary, Miss Marguerite Le Hand. Nevertheless, they were intended for the eyes of Franklin D. Roosevelt. Miss Le Hand periodically acknowledged receipt of Carlson's reports, and she referred to the President's interest in them on several occasions. On November 27, 1937, after not hearing from Carlson in three weeks, Miss Le Hand wrote him expressing a desire to receive more information. In an undated memorandum to Miss Le Hand, probably written on April 26, 1938, Roosevelt requested that she write Carlson a cordial letter expressing his appreciation of the reports. Furthermore, Harold Ickes' account of a conversation with Roosevelt on March 4, 1938, clearly demonstrates that the President was reading Carlson's reports. See Harold L. Ickes, *The Secret Diary of Harold L. Ickes: The Inside Struggle, 1936–1939*, Vol. 2 (New York, 1954), pp. 327–328.

[54] Carlson to Miss Le Hand, August 14, 1937, Franklin D. Roosevelt papers.

regularly forwarded accounts of his experiences in China to the White House. As the President had requested, he kept these communications a closely guarded secret.[55]

While Carlson enjoyed his tour of duty at Warm Springs, he was also filled with nostalgia for the contemplative life of Peiping. As he wrote one of his friends, "I can think of nothing more interesting than to have access to a room full of dusty old records over which to pore and from which to glimpse here and there into the lives and thoughts of the men of ancient China." [56] In a subsequent letter to the same intimate, Carlson joyously gave notice that he would soon be returning to the Orient. He eagerly anticipated studying the language and customs of the Chinese people.[57] In August 1937 Carlson was back in China. He did not, however, have time to gratify his scholarly appetite. China was at war. The United States government now placed a premium on military observers, not cultural anthropologists. Admiral Harry E. Yarnell appointed Carlson an intelligence officer with the task of gathering information on the Sino-Japanese conflict.

It was as an official observer for the United States Navy that Carlson went to Communist China. His curiosity had been aroused by Edgar Snow's characterizations of the Communists. Carlson read a manuscript copy of *Red Star over China,* discussed the subject with its author, and decided to have a look for himself. Snow obtained Mao Tse-tung's acquiescence, Carlson's superiors gave their consent, and

[55] Carlson to Miss Le Hand, September 23, 1938, Roosevelt papers. The fact that Carlson corresponded secretly with the President has no particular significance. In his determination to hear a wide diversity of views, Roosevelt habitually sought information from sources outside the official channels of communication. He readily corresponded and talked with missionaries, newspapermen, and such wandering friends as Evans F. Carlson. See Arthur M. Schlesinger, Jr., "Franklin D. Roosevelt and Foreign Affairs," *New York Times Book Review,* July 6, 1969, 21.

[56] Carlson to Ambassador Johnson, January 26, 1936, Nelson T. Johnson papers, Library of Congress.

[57] Carlson to Johnson, February 21, 1937, Johnson papers.

Chiang Kai-shek put his stamp of approval on the proposed venture.[58] The ostensible purpose of the trip was to learn about Japanese methods of combatting guerrilla warfare.[59] On November 19, 1937, Carlson left Shanghai bound for Sian.

Carlson made two extended tours of the Communist regions. On the first, he proceeded directly to Eighth Route Army headquarters in Shansi. From December 1937 to February 1938, Carlson accompanied the Communist guerrillas in their forays behind Japanese lines. In fifty-one days, he traveled a thousand miles in Shansi and Hopei. It was an exhilarating experience. Carlson returned to Hankow on February 28, 1938, "feeling like an Olympic athlete." [60] His second undertaking was even more ambitious, involving a survey of the entire area from Inner Mongolia to the Shantung peninsula. Carlson arrived in Yenan on May 5, 1938. Ten days and two lengthy conversations with Mao Tse-tung later, he departed for the front. When he returned to Hankow on August 7, 1938, Carlson could boast that he had traveled "nearly fifteen hundred miles across north China, and thrice through the Japanese lines." [61] This expedition had taken the American observer into the provinces of Shensi, Suiyuan, Shansi, Hopei, and Shantung.

After this three-month journey in North China, Carlson was so excited that he could not, as one newspaperman wrote, "keep what he had seen to himself." [62] He had been to Valhalla and wanted to tell the world about it. He exceeded the limits of his diplomatic position by granting extensive interviews to the colony of American and European reporters who had gathered in Hankow. Unsparing in his praise of Communist military and political institutions, Carl-

---

[58] Snow, *Journey to the Beginning*, p. 196; Carlson, *Twin Stars of China*, pp. 33–58; Blankfort, *The Big Yankee*, pp. 188–194.

[59] Carlson to Miss Le Hand, November 1, 1937, Roosevelt papers.

[60] Carlson to Miss Le Hand, March 4, 1938, Roosevelt papers.

[61] Carlson, *Twin Stars of China*, p. 226.

[62] Epstein, *The People's War*, p. 200.

son astonished the journalists by answering all the questions put to him and by allowing his name to be mentioned in their dispatches.[63] On September 17, 1938, Carlson's superiors informed him that he would be held strictly accountable for these activities. Although Agnes Smedley and others urged him to exercise more discretion, the talkative marine impulsively resigned from the Corps.[64] "I wished to be free to speak and write," Carlson explained, "in accordance with my convictions." [65] Toward the end of December 1938, he was back in the United States. Driven by his conscience, Carlson spoke and wrote "like a man possessed." [66]

The ex-marine delivered orations before public audiences, contributed articles to several magazines, and published two books. The first, *The Chinese Army,* was a mediocre technical treatise which went almost unnoticed in the general press.[67] Carlson's subsequent volume, *Twin Stars of China,* aroused a good deal of interest.[68] R. L. Duffus was somewhat incredulous at the spectacle of a leatherneck who spoke in ecstatic terms of a Red utopia. Carlson's Communists, Duffus observed, seemed more like "old fashioned" American minutemen than Bolshevik or Nazi totalitarians.[69] Rodney Gilbert found it difficult to accept entirely the marine's view of

[63] Wang, *Ich kämpfte für Mao,* pp. 201–204.

[64] *Ibid.,* p. 203.

[65] Blankfort, *The Big Yankee,* p. 255. The quotation is from Carlson's diary entry of September 19, 1938. See also Carlson to Miss Le Hand, September 23, 1938, Roosevelt papers.

[66] Blankfort, *The Big Yankee,* p. 269.

[67] Carlson, *The Chinese Army: Its Organization and Military Efficiency* (New York, 1940).

[68] Carlson sent copies of his books and articles to the White House. On one occasion, the President forwarded a Carlson essay to Secretary of State Cordell Hull with the comment "to read and return." See President Roosevelt, memorandum for the Secretary of State, December 4, 1939, Roosevelt papers.

[69] Duffus, "An American Marine Reports on China: After Wide Investigation He Expresses High Hope for Democracy There," *New York Times Book Review,* September 22, 1940, 4, 34.

the Reds as selfless patriots and benevolent democrats. None-theless, Gilbert rated *Twin Stars of China* above all competi-tors when it came to an analysis of the military aspects of the Sino-Japanese conflict.[70] Freda Utley, a British writer who had met Carlson in Hankow, was alone in her carping criti-cism of *Twin Stars of China*. Carlson's military judgments, she wrote, "would appear to be as penetrating and revealing as his political judgments are naïve." To imply that Mao Tse-tung was a liberal, to ignore the role of the Comintern, and to misrepresent the tactical nature of the CCP's moder-ate policies were, she thought, shortsighted absurdities. Carl-son's writing reflected, Freda Utley concluded, a "complete ignorance" of Marxist doctrine and the history of the Chinese Communist Party.[71]

In July, 1938, at Fuping in western Hopei, Carlson en-countered a fellow American, Haldore Hanson,[72] who was the fourth and last Westerner to make an extensive investi-gation of the Communist regions during the days of KMT-CCP cordiality. In one important respect, Hanson differed from those who had preceded him into the guerrilla regions of North China: he was more objective than Bertram, Carl-son, or Agnes Smedley. If this trio can be said to represent something approaching romantic intoxication, Hanson sym-bolized realistic equanimity. Hanson consciously recognized the factor of human bias and consistently tried to see both sides of any particular issue.

A major in history and political science, Hanson gradu-ated from Carleton College during the depression. Since Phi Beta Kappa keys "were hanging in most pawn shops and Ph.D.'s were mowing lawns at twenty cents an hour," he de-

---

[70] Gilbert, "When the Japanese Came," *New York Herald Tribune Books,* October 27, 1940, 22.

[71] Utley, "Sir Galahad in China," *Saturday Review of Literature,* XXII (October 5, 1940), 13.

[72] Carlson, *Twin Stars of China,* p. 234; Hanson, "*Humane Endeav-our,*" pp. 242–243.

cided to make his pot of gold in the Far East. Although he had to spend time in the brig as a stowaway on a Japanese liner, the young adventurer managed to reach the Orient in the summer of 1934. From 1934 to 1938, Hanson tried his hand at a number of vocations. He worked as a secretary for a retired Chinese official, taught English at a Chinese college, and finally launched himself on a career as a free-lance writer. When the Sino-Japanese War broke out, Hanson joined the staff of the Associated Press in Peiping.[73]

Prior to 1937, Hanson had neither written about the Chinese Communists nor had any contact with them.[74] He admittedly had little theoretical understanding of communism, but he had known two American students who were Marxists and he respected their maturity and encyclopedic knowledge. He was, moreover, indignant at the poverty which crushed the Chinese masses and sympathetic to the humanitarian goals professed by the CCP.[75] On the other side, his experiences with the Nanking regime had been unsatisfactory. Chiang Kai-shek's White Terror was much in evidence when Hanson first arrived in China, and three of his Chinese students at Peiping's Commercial College disappeared into one of the KMT's prisons. This incident left an unpleasant taste in Hanson's mouth.[76] Hanson's experiences and assumptions, then, predisposed him toward antipathy for the KMT and empathy for the CCP. Like most Americans, he favored the underdog. Nevertheless, he had the ability to stand above the battle and view Chinese internal developments from the outside. He never did, like so many others, bubble over with enthusiasm for the Eighth Route

---

[73] Hanson, *"Humane Endeavour,"* pp. 3–41.

[74] U.S. Senate, *State Department Employee Loyalty Investigation* (Part 1), pp. 345–348. Hanson gave his testimony on March 28, 1950, specifically in response to some accusations made by Senator Joseph R. McCarthy.

[75] Hanson, *"Humane Endeavour,"* pp. 30–32, 303.

[76] *Ibid.,* p. 30.

Army. When he met the Chinese Communists, he was impressed but not overwhelmed.

In March 1938, Hanson was sought out by a guerrilla intelligence officer who was admittedly seeking publicity for his cause. After listening to tales of partisan resistance behind enemy lines, the skeptical journalist decided to have a look for himself. In the company of this Chinese agent, Hanson left Peiping and bicycled into the Hopei countryside. After two weeks in guerrilla territory, the American returned to Peiping. He was no longer dubious about the existence of a dynamic politico-military resistance movement in the rural areas of central Hopei. In May, Hanson's employers gave their consent to a more extended tour of the Chinese hinterlands, and, beginning in the summer of 1938, he spent approximately two and a half months traveling with the Eighth Route Army in Hopei, Shansi, and Shensi. He was also able to interview Mao Tse-tung in Yenan. He left the border regions in the fall of 1938 with one overriding conviction about China's Communists. "They were," he wrote, "fighting against Japan more wholeheartedly than any other group in China." After scrutinizing Chiang Kai-shek's new stronghold in western China, Hanson returned to the United States in early 1939.[77]

Hanson's autobiographical account of the China war, *"Humane Endeavour,"* was his first book. It did not, according to Hanson, "sell very well." [78] Nonetheless, the skillfully written volume was warmly received by contemporaries. Nathaniel Peffer felt that Hanson's work excelled all others as an epic description of the Sino-Japanese conflict.[79] Two

[77] *Ibid.,* pp. 217ff., the quotation is from page 313; Hanson, "The People behind the Chinese Guerrillas," *Pacific Affairs,* XI (September 1938), 285–298.

[78] U.S. Senate, *State Department Employee Loyalty Investigation* (Part 1), p. 350.

[79] Nathaniel Peffer, "The China at War and the China behind the Lines: New Books by Freda Utley and Haldore Hanson That Complement Each Other," *New York Times Book Review,* December 24, 1939, 5.

other reviewers evaluated *"Humane Endeavour"* as one of the most informative reports on China to appear in print.[80] Hanson's effort was, indeed, an articulate and substantial appraisal of Chinese affairs.

On March 12, 1938, two British writers declined an invitation to observe the Eighth Route Army on the grounds that its story had already been well-reported by numerous journalists. W. H. Auden and Christopher Isherwood even passed through Sian without making an effort to visit Yenan.[81] Such indifference would have been inconceivable only a year earlier, but by the spring of 1938 the CCP had ceased to be an unknown quantity in the remote hinterlands of China. Beginning in late 1937, what had been a trickle of furtive encounters with China's Communists had broadened into a torrent of open confrontations. The mysterious had become the commonplace.

In retrospect, the months from September 1937 to October 1938 marked the high tide of both the united front and of foreign contact with the Chinese Communists. Encouraged by the political situation and the open-door policy of Yenan, large numbers of Americans and Europeans were able either to visit the Communist areas or to converse freely with CCP representatives in Hankow. The result was an unprecedented stream of firsthand information on the Chinese Communist movement and a new harvest of publicity favorable to the CCP.

[80] Gilbert, "A Minnesota Boy Goes to Japan and to China: Mr. Hanson Ventured Behind the Guns and Saw the Legendary Escapades of the Guerrillas," *New York Herald Tribune Books,* January 21, 1940, 6; Maxwell S. Stewart, "War-torn China," *Nation,* CL (January 27, 1940), 105).
[81] Auden and Isherwood, *Journey to a War,* p. 61.

[7]

Closing the Door: 1939

The years 1939–1944 in China were troubled ones. "The quality of China-At-War," an eyewitness wrote, "was one of total confusion." [1] Contributing importantly to this disarray was uncertainty over KMT-CCP relations. During most of the period, there were really three wars in progress simultaneously. Both the Nationalists and Communists fought the Japanese, and they also fought each other. While a semblance of internal unity was maintained in China throughout the Sino-Japanese War, by 1941 the term "united front" had become meaningless.

The tensions between the two Chinese parties had never been far below the surface. Even before the subjugation of Hankow by the Japanese in October 1938, they had begun to come into the open. In August several Communist organizations were dissolved by the Wuhan Garrison headquarters. The Communists protested strongly. This was, as the American consul-general in Hankow observed, "the first public split in the united front." [2] The Central government, opposing the Communist plan to defend the Wuhan area, went so

[1] Theodore H. White and Annalee Jacoby, *Thunder Out of China* (New York, 1961), p. v. This remark was made by White in the introduction to the paperback edition of *Thunder Out of China*.

[2] Paul R. Josselyn, Hankow, August 21, 1938, telegram to the Secretary of State, 893.00/1100, Department of State files.

far as to prohibit the organization of first-aid corps for service at the front.[3] Subsequent developments were even more ominous.

KMT-CCP relations after 1938 were characterized by a steady deterioration in the united front. With the conquest of Hankow, Chiang Kai-shek was compelled to relocate the nation's capital in Chungking. By 1939, however, the Japanese offensive had ground to a halt, and a military stalemate had developed. The *raison d'être* for the unholy union between the Communists and Nationalists had been defense against an aggressive invader. "When the attack stopped," as Theodore H. White and Annalee Jacoby remarked, "the union began to fall apart." [4]

As early as April 1938, there was an armed clash between Nationalist and Communist troops. In 1939 such occurrences became commonplace; by the end of 1940 they were epidemic. As the united front disintegrated, the Central government gradually re-established its blockade of the Communist areas. By the summer of 1939, a stringent military blockade had been imposed on the Shen-Kan-Ning. In the winter of 1939–1940, the Nationalists launched an offensive against the outskirts of the Border Region. Thereafter, blockhouses were erected, 200,000 KMT troops were stationed around the Shen-Kan-Ning, and all economic aid to the Communists was suspended. Then, in early 1941, with the New Fourth Army Incident, the two parties came perilously close to open civil war.[5]

[3] *Foreign Relations of the United States: Diplomatic Papers, 1938,* III (Washington, D.C., 1954), p. 262.

[4] White and Jacoby, *Thunder Out of China* (New York, 1946), pp. 72–73.

[5] Chalmers A. Johnson, *Peasant Nationalism and Communist Power: The Emergence of Revolutionary China, 1937–1945* (Stanford, 1962), pp. 117–122; Anna Louise Strong, "The Kuomintang-Communist Crisis in China," *Amerasia,* V (March 1941), 11–23; Frederick V. Field, "Are Chinese Again Fighting Chinese?" *ibid.,* III (September 1939), 315–319; Jerome Ch'en, *Mao and the Chinese Revolution* (New

If Hankow was the apogee of the united front, the New Fourth Army Incident was its nadir. In retrospect, Lin Piao called it the "gravest lesson" of the Sino-Japanese War.[6] In early January 1941, the headquarters unit of the New Fourth Army clashed with Nationalist troops in south Anhwei. Both sides suffered thousands of casualties, but the Communist detachment was nearly annihilated. Yeh T'ing, the commander of the New Fourth, was taken prisoner. His chief of staff was killed. Chungking accused the New Fourth Army of a breach of military discipline and demanded its dissolution. Yenan, labeling the event a treacherous ambush by depraved militarists, responded by reconstituting the New Fourth Army under the command of Ch'en Yi. While both sides recoiled somewhat from the events of January 1941, and there was no further civil strife on such a large scale until after the Japanese had been defeated, the possibility of any real KMT-CCP collaboration in the future had greatly diminished. After 1941, KMT-CCP relations did not get perceptibly worse, but neither did they improve.[7] The united front was preserved in name only. In fact, as Chalmers A. Johnson wrote, it existed solely as a "poorly observed truce."[8]

Underlying KMT-CCP friction was the phenomenal expansion of Communist power. In 1937 the strength of the Red Army was approximately 90,000 men, and the Shen-Kan-Ning incorporated possibly one and a half million peo-

York, 1967), pp. 203–205, 234–236; Lyman P. Van Slyke, *Enemies and Friends: The United Front in Chinese Communist History* (Stanford, 1967), pp. 95–96; Samuel B. Griffith, II, *The Chinese People's Liberation Army* (New York, Toronto, London, and Sydney, 1967), p. 69.

[6] Lin Piao, "Long Live the Victory of People's War," in *China after Mao*, by A. Doak Barnett (Princeton, 1967), p. 212.

[7] Stuart Schram, *Mao Tse-tung* (New York, 1966), p. 201; Ch'en, *Mao and the Chinese Revolution*, p. 252; White and Jacoby, *Thunder Out of China*, pp. 75–76; Van Slyke, *Enemies and Friends*, p. 96.

[8] Johnson, *Peasant Nationalism and Communist Power*, p. 138.

ple. With the outbreak of the Sino-Japanese conflict, Communist cadres threw themselves with fanatical zeal into the job of organizing the apathetic Chinese peasantry. They established a number of guerrilla bases, most of which were located in the Japanese-occupied regions of North China. By the end of the war in 1945, there were nineteen Communist-dominated "Liberated Areas" with a population of about 90,000,000. Furthermore, the Eighth Route Army had increased tenfold, to 900,000 troops. These frontline regulars were backed up by a militia of some two millions.[9] As White and Jacoby wrote, the Chinese Communists had "exploded rather than expanded."[10] The extraordinary growth of Communist power forms the background to the KMT blockade of the Shen-Kan-Ning. Wherever possible, the Central government labored to contain the rampaging spiral of Red aggrandizement.

The degree of foreign access to the Communist areas depended on the vagaries of Chinese politics. As hostility mounted between Chungking and Yenan, it became increasingly difficult for foreigners to establish contacts with the Chinese Communists. In this respect, 1939 was the year of transition. It was still possible to enter the Border Regions from Nationalist territory during most of that year. But as one reporter recalled, 1939 was the "last year of an effective united front between Kuomintang and Communist."[11]

At least nine foreigners traveled in the Communist re-

[9] For varying statistical estimates, see John Gittings, *The Role of the Chinese Army* (London, New York, and Toronto, 1967), pp. 59–61, 303; Johnson, *Peasant Nationalism and Communist Power*, pp. 73–77; Ch'en, *Mao and the Chinese Revolution*, pp. 246, 250, 252, 255; Lin Piao, "Long Live the Victory of People's War," pp. 219, 221–222; John King Fairbank, *The United States and China* (rev. ed., New York, 1958), p. 235; O. Edmund Clubb, *20th Century China* (New York and London, 1964), pp. 253–254.

[10] White and Jacoby, *Thunder Out of China*, p. 199.

[11] James M. Bertram, *Beneath the Shadow: A New Zealander in the Far East, 1939–46* (New York, 1947), p. 30.

gions during 1939. Two of them visited the New Fourth Army in central China. Seven others toured Eighth Route Army territory in either the Shen-Kan-Ning or Chin-Ch'a-Chi Border Regions. These trips to the guerrilla strongholds varied in length of time from a few days to more than a year. Collectively, they represent the ebb tide which followed the deluge of reportorial encounters with the Chinese Communists during the early months of the united front.

For better than two years, Agnes Smedley wandered through the rural areas of central China. She spent much of the time with the New Fourth Army. While in Hankow, she joined the Red Cross Medical Corps and secured a position as special correspondent for the *Manchester Guardian*. When the Japanese occupied the Wuhan cities, she moved south to Changsha. On October 29, 1938, she made her way to the areas controlled by the New Fourth Army in the lower Yangtze region. From late 1938 to the spring of 1941, she roamed through central China, giving lectures on morale to dispirited Nationalist and Communist soldiers and trying her best to improve the primitive Chinese medical services. Ravaged by malaria and malnutrition, she was finally compelled to go to a Chungking hospital in June 1941. From Chungking she proceeded to Hong Kong. Unable to get through the KMT lines to rejoin the Communist partisans, she decided to return to the United States. After twenty-two years of almost uninterrupted absence, America was like another planet to this old China hand.[12] Early in 1950, after several unsuccessful attempts to return to her beloved China, Agnes Smedley died a very poor woman in Great Britain.[13]

[12] Agnes Smedley, *Battle Hymn of China* (New York, 1943), pp. 220, 236ff.

[13] Smedley, *The Great Road: The Life and Times of Chu Teh* (New York, 1956), p. ix, publisher's foreword; Edgar Snow to the author, August 23, 1964; Freda Utley, *Odyssey of a Liberal: Memoirs* (Washington, D.C., 1970), pp. 204, 209.

Battle Hymn of China, her account of her experiences from 1938 to 1941, was the best of her many books. While reviewers were generally critical of her emotional intemperance, they spoke favorably of her apparent sincerity and honesty.[14] As was to be expected, she described the New Fourth Army as "the most effective and intellectually enlightened military force in the enemy rear." [15] She was, then, still the partisan. The object of her partisanship, however, was more than the Chinese Communists. It was all of China, and she reserved her bitterest diatribes for the Japanese. While a strain of muted criticism against the KMT runs through the book, she does not hesitate to praise individual Nationalist detachments for their contribution to the war effort. *Battle Hymn of China* is a more polished piece of writing than any of her earlier works. Autobiographical in structure, it is based on extensive contact with the guerrilla cadres of the New Fourth Army, and it is clearly and sometimes vividly written.

The identity of the second foreigner who spent time with the New Fourth Army in 1939 is something of a mystery. During the spring of 1939 and again in the summer of 1941, a German writer of decidedly radical convictions visited the Communist guerrillas behind Japanese lines in central China. This particular individual chose to sign his articles with the pseudonym "Asiaticus." He has been identified by contemporaries as either an ex-Communist or a bona fide member of the German Communist Party. His real name

[14] For example, see Ralph Bates, "Here Is China," *Nation,* CLVII (October 2, 1943), 383–385; Chen Yih, "Agnes Smedley's Stories of China," *New York Times Book Review,* September 5, 1943, 3; Malcolm Cowley, " 'Tell Your Countrymen,' " *New Republic,* CIX (September 13, 1943), 366–367; Clifton Fadiman, "Books: Everyman's Guide to Tokyo," *New Yorker,* XIX (September 11, 1943), 84–85; Mark Gayn, "Thirteen Years in China," *Saturday Review of Literature,* XXVI (September 18, 1943), 22.

[15] Smedley, *Battle Hymn of China,* p. 259.

supposedly was either Heinz Shippe or Shipper, or Heinz Moeller, or Hans Mueller.[16] The only Westerner who seems to have known "Asiaticus" personally was Karl August Witt-fogel, a professor of Chinese history, who met him in Shang-hai in 1937. "Asiaticus" was, Wittfogel recalled, Heinz Moeller, an important figure in the German Communist Party.[17] According to Philip Jaffe, "Asiaticus" was killed, probably in 1941, on one of his periodic trips between Shanghai and the New Fourth Army base.[18]

Whatever his true identity, "Asiaticus" wrote a series of articles based on his eyewitness observations of the New Fourth Army.[19] Probably entering the partisan regions of Anhwei from Shanghai, he was able to observe the guerrillas in action and to talk with leading Communist figures like Yeh T'ing and Ch'en Yi. He described the New Fourth Army as a disciplined, popular, and self-sacrificing group of heroic patriots.[20] His articles bristle with tirades against so-called Fascist elements in the KMT and are cluttered with glowing generalizations about the stalwart cadres of the New Fourth.

[16] Edgar Snow, *Random Notes on Red China, 1936–1945* (Cambridge, Mass., 1957), pp. 20–22; U.S. Senate, Committee on the Judiciary, Subcommittee on Internal Security, 82nd Cong., 1st and 2nd Sess., *Institute of Pacific Relations, Hearings* (Part 9, Washington, D.C., 1952), p. 3132, testimony of Owen Lattimore.

[17] U.S. Senate, *Institute of Pacific Relations* (Part I), p. 308. Professor Wittfogel gave his testimony on August 7, 1951.

[18] Philip J. Jaffe, interview with the author, June 14, 1965.

[19] Asiaticus," "Chou En-lai on the New Stage of the Anti-Japanese War," *Amerasia*, III (June 1939), 184–190; "The Yangtze Triangle Guerrilla War," *ibid.* (August 1939), 275–281; "The Fascist Axis vs. the United Front in China," *ibid.*, IV (February 1941), 543–546; "Autobiography of General Yeh Ting," *ibid.*, V (March 1941), 24–29; "China's Internal Friction Aids Japan," *ibid.* (May 1941), 118–122; "New Fourth Army Area Revisited," *ibid.* (September 1941), 287–294; "Behind the Japanese Lines in Central Asia," *ibid.* (October 1941), 355–360.

[20] "Asiaticus," "The Yangtze Triangle Guerrilla War," 278.

As the experience of "Asiaticus" suggests, one way to establish contact with Chinese Communists was simply to walk out of Japanese-occupied cities into the surrounding countryside. This was true especially in North China, where the rural areas largely belonged to the Eighth Route Army. Thus, in the summer of 1939 Ralph Lapwood and Michael Lindsay entered the Chin-Ch'a-Chi from Peiping. Lindsay and Lapwood were British nationals who taught at Yenching University. Lapwood, a Christian missionary who had been in China since 1932, was on his way to Sian. Before reaching his destination, Lapwood traveled for three months and a thousand miles through territory which was under the control of the Eighth Route Army. In guerrilla China, he found democratically elected local governments, incorruptible officials, and spirited mass organizations. Above all, the British missionary was impressed by the high morale and idealism of the Communist soldiers.[21]

While Lapwood did not get to Yenan, most of the foreign traffic in 1939 was directed to the Communist capital. Yenan was still the Red mecca, the center of attraction to which Westerners naturally gravitated. In the spring of 1939 a party of three made the trek to Yenan. They examined Communist institutions and held an interview with Mao Tsetung. The group was made up of a university professor, a medical missionary, and a journalist. Andrew T. Roy was a young American teacher who had taught at the University of Nanking. Dr. Robert Brown and Joy Homer were the other members of this inquisitive band of foreigners. Miss Homer bequeathed to posterity a published account of her encounter with China's Communists.[22]

[21] Ralph and Nancy Lapwood, *Through the Chinese Revolution* (London, 1954), pp. 24, 27, 31, 33. For biographical information on Michael Lindsay see below, pp. 131, 133–135.

[22] Joy Homer, *Dawn Watch in China* (Boston, 1941). For a brief description of Roy's favorable impressions of Yenan, see *Foreign Relations of the United States: Diplomatic Papers, 1939*, III (Washington, D.C., 1955), pp. 189–190.

Joy Homer had come to China as press correspondent for the Interdenominational Church Committee for China Relief (ICC). The purpose of her assignment was to promote the ICC's fund-raising program by gathering information and photographs which were to be published in the United States. This was Miss Homer's first trip to China, and she made the most of it. From December 1938 to November 1939, she traveled widely in China. It was love at first sight. In Chungking, Miss Homer was, as she phrased it, "almost annihilated . . . with kindness." The KMT rolled out the red carpet for their American guest. Chungking's culinary hospitality was of such proportions that she was in a condition of "perpetual indigestion." In addition to undergoing innumerable four-and-a-half-hour banquets replete with exotic food and endearing companionship, she was freely granted interviews with nearly every prominent figure in the Nationalist government. The ICC's press correspondent basked in the attention that the KMT showered upon her. She had been treated like a head of state on tour, and she appreciated it. Her descriptions of the Chungking regime and its leaders reach the heights of romantic rhapsodizing. All that Chiang Kai-shek had to do was to pass by on the road near where this impressionable Yankee was standing, and she was immediately talking about his "electric and almost chilling presence." [23]

Prior to her encounter with Chinese Communists, then, Joy Homer was emphatically pro-KMT. Beyond this, her assumptions and attitudes were decidedly anti-Communist. She fully expected to find sinister Russian agents and hardened Chinese Bolsheviks in Yenan. She was frankly disappointed when she found neither. Her narrative is scattered with telltale words and phrases like "surprisingly" and "in spite of ourselves." The only Russian she encountered in Yenan was, disappointingly enough, a "homesick" photogra-

---

[23] Homer, *Dawn Watch in China,* pp. 4, 73–78.

pher who seemed quite harmless. She concluded that the Chinese Reds were the "victims of a host of popular fallacies." Contrary to what Joy Homer had assumed, they were young, enthusiastic, efficient, patriotic, and even "lovable." Her final assessment was that they were simply "good human material." [24]

The contemporary reviews of Joy Homer's truly delightful account of a year's journey through the interior of China were uninspired summaries. If there was any consensus in these essays, it was that she had written a charming but unduly optimistic travelogue. T. A. Bisson thought that *Dawn Watch in China* was a "little too lyrical," but he enjoyed reading it.[25] Another uncritical critic concluded that it was just a wonderful book.[26] Helen Snow's only relevant criticism of Joy Homer's work was that it was much too "romanticized." [27]

In the summer of 1939, George A. Fitch spent three days in Yenan. An ordained Presbyterian minister and strong supporter of Chiang Kai-shek, Fitch was a veteran of more than thirty years experience in China as an official of the International Committee of the Y.M.C.A.[28] His trip to the Shen-Kan-Ning was made for the specific purpose of refuting

[24] *Ibid.,* pp. 226, 228, 241.

[25] T.A. Bisson, "New Dimensions in China," *Saturday Review of Literature,* XXIII (April 26, 1941), 16.

[26] Elsie McCormick, "Beneath the Bombs in China: An American Girl Reports on Her Extensive Travels," *New York Herald Tribune Books,* April 13, 1941, 7.

[27] Nym Wales [Helen Foster Snow], "China Station," *New Republic,* CV (September 8, 1941), 316.

[28] It was George A. Fitch's son, Kempton Fitch, who helped Helen Snow enter the Communist regions from Sian in 1937. During the 1950's, both George A. Fitch and his wife, Geraldine Fitch, were leading figures in such prominent pro-Nationalist organizations as the Committee to Defend America by Aiding Anti-Communist China and the American China Policy Association. See Ross Y. Koen, *The China Lobby in American Politics* (New York, 1960), pp. 59–60.

the "flood of malicious propaganda" to the effect that the Chinese Reds were disloyal to the Generalissimo. After talking with Mao Tse-tung and Chou En-lai, Fitch had not the least doubt of their "absolute patriotism and loyalty to Chiang Kai-shek." [29]

In the fall of 1939, James Bertram almost paid another visit to Yenan. After his trip to the Soviet regions in 1937–1938, he had spent most of his time working for Madame Sun Yat-sen's China Defense League. In the summer of 1939, he was placed in charge of a relief convoy from the China Defense League to the Eighth Route Army. By early September he had guided his caravan of twenty-three vehicles—which were loaded with medical supplies—to Sian. At the Guest House, Bertram encountered an old friend who was also en route to Yenan, Edgar Snow. Upon hearing news of the outbreak of the European conflagration, Bertram decided to return to New Zealand and see if there was a place for him in the struggle against fascism. After failing to secure an appointment as war correspondent with the New Zealand Expeditionary Force, Bertram went back to work for the China Defense League. Subsequently, he served for a short time as press attaché in the British Embassy at Chungking, was taken captive in the battle for Hong Kong, and spent the war years in Japanese prison camps. In the meantime, Snow had made the trip to Yenan which Bertram had sacrificed.[30]

[29] George A. Fitch, "China's Northwest Life-Line," *Amerasia,* IV (September 1940), 301, 305. In his memoirs, Fitch remembered Chinese communism as a "diabolical octopus" and the Shen-Kan-Ning as a virtual "slave state." He does not explain the absence of such harsh descriptions in the article he wrote for *Amerasia* in 1940. See Fitch, *My Eighty Years in China* (Taiwan, Republic of China, 1967), pp. 144–160.

[30] Bertram, *Beneath the Shadow,* pp. 7ff. See also Bertram's *Return to China* (London and Melbourne, 1957). This is largely an account of Bertram's visit to Communist China in 1956. However, he also includes some scattered biographical reminiscences in this volume.

By the time Snow tried to enter Communist territory in mid-September 1939, a tight blockade had been established along the borders of the Shen-Kan-Ning. Large numbers of the KMT's best troops, under the command of generals Hu Tsung-nan and Chiang T'ing-wen, controlled the roads leading to Yenan. Snow anticipated the problem. He had secured letters from T. V. Soong, the Generalissimo's brother-in-law, to generals Hu and Chiang and was traveling as a delegate of a recognized wartime organization, the Chinese Industrial Cooperatives (Indusco). Snow's official mission was to inspect the Indusco depot at Yenan. He successfully negotiated the Sian crossing and spent approximately ten days in Yenan. During this time, he had two formal interviews with Mao Tse-tung on September 25 and 26. Probably in early October, Snow returned to the KMT's domain. This proved to be Snow's last direct encounter with China's Communists until 1960.[31]

Snow found the Shen-Kan-Ning Border government little different from its Soviet-style predecessor. Since his visit of 1936, the CCP's organizations and policies had been embellished with new names. The institutions and programs, however, had not been altered in any fundamental manner. Land redistribution had been suspended and the gentry could now vote. In spite of the extended franchise, the numerical strength of the Communist-directed peasantry meant that the decision-making machinery was still in the control of the CCP. In short, save for the nomenclature, Snow was quite at home with the Yenan regime of 1939. Furthermore, as in 1936, Snow was impressed by the invincible spirit of the Red Army and the progressive character of the Communist administration of the Shen-Kan-Ning. In one important

[31] Snow, *The Battle for Asia* (New York, 1941), pp. 259–265; *Journey to the Beginning* (New York, 1958), pp. 230–231; *Random Notes on Red China*, pp. 69, 72; "The Chinese Communists and Wars on Two Continents: Interviews with Mao Tse-tung," *China Weekly Review*, XCI (January 13, 20, 1940), 244–246, 277–280.

respect, the situation had changed. Snow pointed out that by 1939, Communist power, in the form of partisan bases, had increased sixfold during the last three years.[32]

Robert Gale Woolbert best summarized *The Battle for Asia* in his two sentence annotation in *Foreign Affairs.* Snow, Woolbert wrote, "devoted much of his space and sympathies to the Chinese Communists." [33] But Snow also filled many of his pages with unflattering remarks about the KMT. While Snow's volume generally describes events in the Far East after 1937, it focuses on the problem of Chinese internal affairs. In this respect, as one reviewer observed, Snow's comments on the KMT were like "douches of acid." [34] *The Battle for Asia* was the first account of the Sino-Japanese War sharply to criticize the domestic policies of the Chungking regime and clearly to draw attention to the problem of KMT-CCP discord. Chiang Kai-shek's government is characterized as an autocratic, semifeudal dictatorship.[35] Woolbert's brief description of *The Battle for Asia* was accurate, but he was describing only one side of a two-edged sword.

The Battle for Asia was widely and favorably reviewed by contemporaries. T. A. Bisson felt that parts of it should be "required reading." [36] Paul Hutchinson, the managing editor of the *Christian Century*, went even further. He did not believe that any American should have a right to discuss publicly the Far Eastern policy of the United States until he had read Snow's brilliant study.[37] While William Henry Chamberlin thought that the lenses in Snow's glasses were "mildly pink," he concluded that this slight case of dichro-

[32] Snow, *The Battle for Asia*, pp. 317–320, 335–341, 351.

[33] Robert Gale Woolbert, review of *The Battle for Asia* in *Foreign Affairs,* XIX (July 1941), 883–884.

[34] Bisson, "The Struggle for the East," *New Republic,* CIV (April 14, 1941), 506–507.

[35] Snow, *The Battle for Asia*, pp. 116, 212–215, 238.

[36] Bisson, "The Struggle For the East," 506.

[37] Paul Hutchinson, "Asiatic Battlefront," *Christian Century,* LVIII (April 2, 1941), 460.

matism was only a minor blemish in what was one of the most important accounts of Chinese affairs.[38] The *Saturday Review of Literature* carried Snow's picture on its cover for March 1, 1941. Miles Vaughn, a former Far Eastern correspondent for the United Press, praised Snow as "probably the best informed of any American on the Chinese Communist Party."[39]

There was, however, one serious dissenter. Freda Utley had a few words of approbation for *The Battle for Asia,* but her commentary was basically a critique of Snow's assumptions and point of view. Her fundamental complaint was that Snow was politically naïve and did not adequately understand the nature of communism. Her own experiences in the U.S.S.R. had led her to mistrust Communist professions of liberalism. Since the Chinese Reds were, according to her, under the discipline of the Comintern, one could not trust them in either the short or the long run. Because Snow had never been to the Soviet Union, and because he viewed Bolshevism through the eyes of the "as-yet-uncorrupted" Chinese Reds, he was "one of those Communist sympathizers who is essentially a liberal and a humanitarian but who . . . is not yet disillusioned."[40]

[38] William Henry Chamberlin, "Asiatic War," *Current History and Forum,* LII (April 1941), 56–57.

[39] Miles Vaughn, "The Inner Drama of China," *Saturday Review of Literature,* XXIII (March 1, 1941), 5. For other favorable reviews see Joseph Barnes, review of *The Battle for Asia* in *Pacific Affairs,* XIV (June 1941), 222–226; Clifton Fadiman, "Books: Boston and Maine —Light on Asia," *New Yorker,* XVII (February 22, 1941), 68, 70–71; Rodney Gilbert, "The Cities, People and Revolution in China: Edgar Snow Writes a Lively and Discerning Travelogue, Then Risks Bold Prophecy," *New York Herald Tribune Books,* February 23, 1941, 3; Maxwell S. Stewart, "China in Travail," *Nation,* CLIII (February 22, 1941), 215–217.

[40] Utley, "A Terse, Authentic Report of the Terror in China: Edgar Snow Writes That the 'Deliberate Degradation of Man Has Been Thoroughly Systematized by the Japanese Army,'" *New York Times Book Review,* March 9, 1941, 9. For biographical information on Freda Utley see below, pp. 241–243.

Not long after Snow left Yenan, the Nationalists further tightened their blockade of the Shen-Kan-Ning. By early 1940, Westerners—of any profession—were generally not permitted to enter the Border Regions. This policy of exclusion was dictated by the logic of Chinese politics and the past performance of Western journalists who invariably returned from Yenan to write reports favorable to the CCP. The strengthened KMT blockade would prove to be so effective that for nearly four years Chinese Communists would be, for all practical purposes, isolated from contact with the West.

[8]

The News Blockade
Reimposed: 1939-1944

Edgar Snow's trip to Yenan in 1939 turned out to be the last made by any foreign journalist until the summer of 1944. With very few exceptions, Chungking was able to close the door to firsthand encounters with Chinese Communists. The Nationalists, however, were not able to maintain, as they had from 1928 to 1936, a complete vacuum of Western contacts with the CCP. Chungking could do nothing to prevent an individual from entering the Communist areas from some point in Japanese-occupied China. Furthermore, it was possible, though not politic, for an outsider to speak with a Communist official in Chungking. Throughout the war years, the Central government allowed the CCP to operate a liaison office and newspaper in the nation's capital.

Chou En-lai was the resident Communist liaison officer in Chungking. This skillful diplomat was, as one old China hand recalled, a gold mine for gossip about Chiang Kai-shek and the KMT.[1] If a newspaperman was so inclined, he could arrange an interview with the amiable Chou; but the Nationalist authorities frowned on any such tête-à-tête. Hollington K. Tong, the Vice-Minister of Information, told a corre-

---

[1] A. T. Steele, *The American People and China* (New York, Toronto, and London, 1966), p. 46.

spondent for the *Christian Science Monitor* that anyone who
attended a press conference conducted by the Communists
was "an enemy of China." [2] If a reporter became too indis-
creet, he could lose his cable privileges, find it difficult to
obtain information from official sources, or undergo any
number of other trying inconveniences. Nonetheless, some
Western journalists were willing to run these risks.

In December 1940, Anna Louise Strong made her fourth
trip to China, flying from Moscow to Chungking. She stayed
in the Chinese capital just long enough to collect a file of
materials from Chou En-lai on the problem of KMT-CCP
relations.[3] On the strength of these documents, she published an historical sketch of disputes between the two parties. The apparent purpose of her article was to bypass the
Nationalist censorship and bring the threatening Chinese internal situation to the attention of Americans. She wrote of
the undemocratic character of the Chungking regime, of the
senseless blockade of the Border Regions, and of a series of
ominous armed clashes between Communist and Nationalist
forces. She concluded her one-sided account of China's domestic imbroglio by warning of the grave possibility of
"widespread civil war." [4]

Like Anna Louise Strong, Robert W. Barnett and Vincent
Sheean were able to obtain unusually outspoken appraisals
by talking with Chou En-lai. Barnett, a staff member of the
Institute of Pacific Relations, was in Chungking from Febru-
ary 18 to March 2, 1941. Chou told him that the basis of
KMT-CCP cooperation had been "shattered" by the New
Fourth Army Incident and spoke of open civil war as a real

---

[2] Gunther Stein, *The Challenge of Red China* (New York and London, 1945), p. 20.

[3] Philip J. Jaffe, "The Strange Case of Anna Louise Strong," *Survey*,
LIII (October 1964), 131.

[4] Anna Louise Strong, "The Kuomintang-Communist Crisis in
China," *Amerasia*, V (March 1941), 11–23.

possibility.[5] Although Sheean was in Chungking for less than a week in November 1941, he learned that despite "bland assurances" to the contrary, KMT-CCP hostility was deeply entrenched. Sheean, whose animosity toward the KMT had not lessened since 1927, believed that the united front had "ceased to exist." [6]

Ernest Hemingway also went to China in 1941. Before he left the United States, he talked with Harry Dexter White of the Treasury Department. White asked Hemingway to investigate KMT-CCP relations and report his findings to the Secretary of the Treasury, Henry Morgenthau, Jr. On July 30, 1941, after his return from China, Hemingway wrote Secretary Morgenthau a detailed letter on Nationalist-Communist tensions.[7] Because of the atypical nature of Hemingway's assessment, this letter merits consideration in some detail.

Like other foreign journalists, Hemingway was impressed by Chou En-lai's intelligence and "enormous charm." After talking with Chou and certain KMT leaders, he concluded that the mutual bitterness of the two parties could scarcely be exaggerated. The Nationalists, he wrote, regarded the Japanese as only a " 'SKIN DISEASE' " but the Chinese Reds as a " 'HEART DISEASE.' " The unusual aspect of Hemingway's appraisal is that he found himself in substantial agreement with the Nationalist diagnosis of the Red disease and not with that of Chou En-lai.[8]

[5] Robert W. Barnett, "An Interview With Chou En-lai," *Amerasia*, V (May 1941), 123–127. See also Barnett, "China's Expectations," *ibid.* (June 1941), 163–166.

[6] Vincent Sheean, *Between the Thunder and the Sun* (New York, 1943), pp. 343–349, 639–640.

[7] U.S. Senate, Committee on the Judiciary, Subcommittee on Internal Security, 89th Cong., 1st Sess., *Morgenthau Diary: China*, II (Washington, D.C., 1965), pp. 457–458. For a brief comment on Hemingway's trip to China see "Chungking Mecca for Well-Known Writers," *China Weekly Review*, XCVI (May 10, 1941), 314.

[8] U.S. Senate, *Morgenthau Diary*, II, p. 458.

Hemingway's approach to Chinese communism was colored by his experiences during the Spanish Civil War. He reasoned that the Chinese Communists would try to extend their territorial base without regard to commitments "they may accept on paper." The only possibility he could see of avoiding war between the KMT and CCP was an agreement, to be negotiated with the U.S.S.R. by the Chungking government, partitioning China into separate areas of Communist and Nationalist control. Hemingway went on to caution against wholehearted acceptance of the CCP's version of events. By catering to journalists of the caliber of Edgar Snow, he explained, the Communists had gained superb publicity and Americans had acquired an extravagant idea of the Eighth Route Army's role in the struggle against the Japanese. While Hemingway criticized Chiang Kai-shek for distorting facts and the KMT for its reactionary policies, he emphasized the tactical nature of CCP propaganda. He recalled the lessons he had learned in Spain and suggested that Communists "always try to give the impression that they are the only ones who really fight." Unfortunately, Hemingway kept his remarks confidential. One of America's most influential writers purposely refrained from publishing anything which might lead to a worsening of Chinese internal affairs.[9]

Ernest Hemingway's evaluation was very unusual in that it was essentially anti-Communist. Far more typical were those who, like Anna Louise Strong, Barnett, and Sheean, ac-

[9] *Ibid.*, pp. 458–461. Hollington K. Tong, the Chinese Vice-Minister of Information, wrote an interesting assessment of Hemingway. Tong wrote: "Not all the foreign correspondents accepted unreservedly the Communists' version of this New Fourth Army showdown or of later clashes. The conversations I had with Ernest Hemingway, when he was in China in 1941 convinced me that he was an impartial and fair observer. . . . His experiences in Spain had given him a background against which he could more impartially judge our situations than many others." See Hollington K. Tong, *Dateline—China: The Beginning of China's Press Relations with the World* (New York, 1950), p. 151.

cepted the Communist version of the disintegration of
Chinese unity. It is small wonder, then, that Nationalist officials discouraged meetings with Chou En-lai. This persuasive diplomat knew how to gain valuable publicity for his
cause. The skill of the Chinese Communists in presenting
their case also helps to explain why inquisitive reporters
were not allowed to travel from Chungking to Yenan.

Without exception, foreign correspondents were prohibited by the Nationalist government from visiting Communist
areas. Yenan and its environs were off limits. Throughout
the period from 1940 to the summer of 1944, there is only
one verifiable instance of a Westerner who "legally" entered
the Shen-Kan-Ning, and he was not a reporter but a missionary for the Presbyterian Board of Foreign Missions.

Stanton Lautenschlager was born in Canada, received his
college education in the United States, and was sent to
China in 1920. Like many other ministers of the Gospel,
Lautenschlager taught at various Chinese Christian colleges.
After 1937, he was employed as an instructor of English and
political science at Cheeloo University, Chengtu, Szechuan.
In the fall of 1940, he traveled in northwest China. From
November 10–18, he was in the Communist areas, even con-
triving to spend five days in Yenan. During this time, Lautenschlager held long conversations with Chu Teh and other
Communist leaders.[10] Although he does not explain how he
came to visit the Shen-Kan-Ning, the trip was probably made
with the knowledge and consent of the Nationalist authorities.

[10] Stanton Lautenschlager, *Far West in China* (New York, 1941),
foreword, n.p., pp. 1ff. This is a forty-eight-page pamphlet, about half
of which is devoted to Lautenschlager's encounter with the Chinese
Communists. Lautenschlager's *With Chinese Communists* (London,
1941) is a reprint of the relevant sections of *Far West in China* for the
World Issues Pamphlets series. For additional information on Lautenschlager's trip to the Communist regions in 1940 see Nelson T.
Johnson, Chungking, March 6, 1941, dispatch to the Secretary of State,
893.00/14680, Department of State files.

Initially ill at ease in a land "said to be ruled by people who did not believe in God," the Presbyterian missionary found himself treated as an honored guest. The people of the Border Regions were happy, healthy, and eminently friendly. All of Lautenschlager's expenses were paid for by his Communist hosts. He was even permitted to preach a few sermons, in private, to certain Communist dignitaries. After one particularly moving session with the secretary-general of the Border government, Lautenschlager felt that a mutual understanding had been reached. Before he left Yenan, Chu Teh told him that he could return and establish a parish on any site that was deemed suitable. The minister happily concluded that he had encountered a "welcome so great that it seems to me a new open door for the church." [11]

Lautenschlager's account of his visit to the Shen-Kan-Ning is notable in one respect. In contrast to most other observers, he chose to focus his attention on the sometimes trivial but always interesting socioeconomic realities of everyday existence. Family life seemed to him normal and unexceptional, the peasants were comfortably dressed and well fed, not one beggar roamed the streets of Yenan, workers were adequately paid and there was no unemployment, class distinctions were unknown, educational privileges had been extended greatly, and babies were fat and healthy. Above all, the people of the Border Regions embodied the spirit of youth. They were, according to Lautenschlager, young both in age and in élan. [12]

After Lautenschlager's visit, no foreigner traversed KMT territory to the Shen-Kan-Ning until the summer of 1944. A handful of Westerners, however, did enter the Chin-Ch'a-Chi from Japanese-occupied China after 1940. None of them were journalists, and their presence in the Communist areas can be attributed largely to fortuitous circumstances. While very little of what they saw was recorded in print, their en-

[11] Lautenschlager, *Far West in China,* foreword, n.p., pp. 7–8, 23–24.
[12] *Ibid.,* pp. 10–18.

counters with China's Communists are not insignificant. They provide an element of historical continuity in foreign contacts with the CCP. Furthermore, at a time when the KMT blockade was extraordinarily effective, the meager accounts that were published by several of these foreigners did offer the outside world at least some firsthand information on the Chinese Communist movement.

Michael Lindsay was no stranger to the Chinese Communists. In the summer of 1938 and again in the summer of 1939, he had accompanied, respectively, George E. Taylor and Ralph Lapwood to the Chin-Ch'a-Chi. When Lindsay heard news that the Japanese had bombed Pearl Harbor, he decided that it was an auspicious moment to make another visit to that part of China which was controlled by the Eighth Route Army. In the company of his Chinese wife, Li Hsiao-li, and two British colleagues from Yenching University, Claire and William Band, Lindsay left Peiping as expeditiously as was feasible. The foursome drove out of the city, parked their automobile, and walked into the hills. Within a short time, friendly villagers put them in contact with the partisans. From December 1941 on, they were under the protection of the Eighth Route Army.[13]

Lindsay was on familiar ground when he rejoined his guerrilla friends. He had been among the most active Westerners in Peiping in securing material assistance for the Chinese partisans. The Bands were something else again. Of all the foreigners who entered the Communist areas, they were the most out of place. Since 1939, they had been en-

[13] U.S. Senate, Committee on the Judiciary, Subcommittee on Internal Security, 82nd Cong., 1st and 2nd Sess., *Institute of Pacific Relations, Hearings* (Part 14, Washington, D.C., 1952), pp. 5368–5370, sworn statement of Michael Lindsay of June 3, 1952; Claire and William Band, *Dragon Fangs: Two Years with Chinese Guerrillas* (London, 1947), pp. 10–11. The American edition of the Bands's volume is titled *Two Years with Chinese Communists* (New Haven, Conn., 1948).

gaged in research in physics and mathematics at Yenching University. Both were very bourgeois, essentially apolitical, refined, and unadventurous—perhaps the classic professorial stereotype. The Bands felt much more at home in the decorous atmosphere of Peiping than they did in rural China. The few obscure political notions which they did possess were unsympathetic to radicalism in general and communism in particular. The Bands were, in short, misfits in Communist China. Nonetheless, all things considered, they rather enjoyed their lengthy stay in the Chin-Ch'a-Chi.[14]

For more than two years, the Bands leisurely wandered about guerrilla China taking in the sights, inspecting various institutions, talking with Communist officials, and sporadically teaching mathematics and physics to eager Chinese students. They were treated with circumspection. When the Communists discovered that their initially dissatisfied English guests yearned for privacy and exotic food, they amply provided them with both. A typical comment about the Bands' culinary experience reads: "During the week we were in Paoteh we feasted on the fat of the land." They characterized their stay in Yenan as "an exceedingly enjoyable three months of interviews, entertainments and visits." Yet, the Bands remained habitually suspicious of the intentions of the CCP.[15]

By May 1943, they felt that they had outlived their welcome. They were, also, concerned over unsanitary conditions, apprehensive about the possibility of contracting a disease, and somewhat embarrassed at accepting so much hospitality in return for so little service. These misrouted tourists requested that they be sent through the Communist lines to Nationalist China. It took some doing and not a little time, but in early January 1944 the Bands left Yenan for Chungking. The hospitable Communists persuaded them to accept $5,000 in Chinese national currency to help pay their

[14] Claire and William Band, *Dragon Fangs,* pp. 8–10, 76–78.
[15] *Ibid.,* pp. 209–210, 236, 264.

travel expenses. With KMT machine guns facing them and CCP rifles behind them, the Bands warily crossed the no man's land between Nationalist and Communist China. They were understandably relieved when the Nationalist pillboxes had been passed, and they were safely in the more familiar "old world atmosphere of class distinctions and private enterprise." [16]

Claire and William Band summarized their encounter with China's Communists in the following words: "For our part we had been jerked down off our balcony seat, pushed out of the professorial chair, and forced against our inclinations, among a virile people on the rough mountain trails of real life. It has been a revelation to us." It had, indeed, been an informative experience for the two British academicians. Over a two-year period, they had walked more than 1,000 miles from Peiping to Yenan in the company of the Eighth Route Army. On the whole, this extensive contact eventuated in favorable impressions. During their entire stay in the Border Regions, the Bands emphasized, they had not been bothered by a drunken or disorderly Communist trooper. "In all our experience," they wrote, "we have never seen a more spartan group than the Communist Armies." Furthermore, given the Chinese tradition of peasant-soldier hostility, these British scholars were astonished to find that the prevalent civilian-military relationship was one of cordiality and cooperation. Finally, the Bands were struck by the spectacular progress of the CCP in developing effective, democratic government.[17]

Michael Lindsay spent more time in the Communist-controlled regions of China than any of the other foreigners who visited these areas between 1936 and 1945.[18] He did not

[16] *Ibid.*, pp. 180–183, 224, 268–271, 278.

[17] *Ibid.*, pp. 112, 122–123, 133, 332–333, 340.

[18] I am here excluding persons like Otto Braun and George Hatem, who made the Border Region their permanent place of residence, and who for all practical purposes can be considered part of the Communist regime.

leave Red China until November 1945—that is, until after the conclusion of the war. Lindsay spent most of his four years in the Border Regions working as a specialist in radio technology. In 1943, he was officially appointed adviser to the Communications Department of the Shansi-Chahar-Hopei Military District. In the spring of 1944 he moved from the Chin-Ch'a-Chi to Yenan, where he designed a powerful radio transmitter and assisted the CCP's New China News Agency with its English-language service.[19] Lindsay was, then, in an advantageous position to evaluate the nature of the Chinese Communist movement. It would be difficult to duplicate his extensive firsthand contact with the Chinese Reds.

During the period from 1940–1944, Lindsay was one of the few who provided the outside world with a published account of his impressions. G. Martel Hall, an American citizen who traveled from Peiping through the Chin-Ch'a-Chi en route to Chungking, brought out a lengthy memorandum which had been prepared by Lindsay.[20] Eventually, Lindsay's report became the object of a special issue of the magazine *Amerasia* and was also reproduced in pamphlet form.[21] His essay thus became the first comprehensive eyewitness analysis of the Border Regions to appear in print since Edgar Snow's *The Battle for Asia.*

On the whole, the military, political, economic, and social progress which had taken place under the auspices of the Eighth Route Army favorably impressed Lindsay. The Japanese held most of the railroad lines and administrative centers of North China; the countryside belonged to the guerril-

[19] U.S. Senate, *Institute of Pacific Relations* (Part 14), pp. 5369–5370.

[20] John Carter Vincent, Chungking, April 2, 1943, dispatch to the Secretary of State, 893.00/14996, Department of State files.

[21] Michael Lindsay, "The North China Front: A Study of Chinese Guerrillas in Action," *Amerasia*, VIII (March 31 and April 14, 1944), 100–110, 117–125; Lindsay, *North China Front* (London [1944]). This pamphlet, which was published by the China Campaign Committee, is a reprint of the essays which first appeared in *Amerasia*.

las. By sapping Japanese manpower and hindering the exploitation of Chinese resources, the partisans were making an important contribution to the war effort. Furthermore, active guerrilla cadres had mobilized the peasantry into "democratic" mass organizations. Border Region political institutions were the product of universal suffrage, and the Communists voluntarily limited themselves to one-third of any particular elective body. Education, on both the elementary and adult levels, was strongly encouraged. Economically, progressive taxes had been introduced and hopeful beginnings had been made in industrial and agricultural development. Most notably, corruption in government had been almost completely eliminated. In sum, Lindsay found a record of military, political, social, and economic progress which was "quite impressive considering the difficulties of the situation." Since 1937, the northern provinces had been transformed "from one of the most backward to one of the most progressive areas of China." [22]

The sojourns of the Lindsays and the Bands in the Border Regions were for a protracted length of time. The additional half dozen Westerners who in 1942 and 1943 followed them into the Chin-Ch'a-Chi were merely temporary wards of the Eighth Route Army, people en route to Chungking. For example, a Dutch engineer by the name of Carl Brondgeest escaped from Peiping in 1942 and traveled quickly through the Chin-Ch'a-Chi. Before joining the Dutch navy, Brondgeest gave a verbal report to the China Aid Council praising the Border Region authorities for their patriotism and progressive social and economic programs.[23] More important were the observations of G. Martel Hall, George Uhlmann, and Gustav Soderbom.

[22] Lindsay, "The North China Front," 101–102, 105–107, 117–118, 120–125.

[23] "China's International Peace Hospitals," *Far Eastern Survey*, XII (April 19, 1943), 79–80; *In Guerrilla China: Report of China Defence League* (Chungking, 1943), p. 69.

G. Martel Hall, the man who carried Michael Lindsay's memorandum out of the Chin-Ch'a-Chi, left Peiping on May 21, 1942. Some eight months later, on January 26, 1943, he arrived in Chungking. Unlike the foreigners who had preceded him to the Communist strongholds, Hall was a businessman. An American citizen who had been associated with the National City Bank of Peiping, he had, as he readily admitted, "suffered from a strong prejudice against those *so-called* communists." [24] His face-to-face contact with the Chinese Reds caused him to change his attitude.

During his trek through the provinces of Hopei, Shansi, and Shensi, Hall was permitted to "wander about at will, dropping in here and calling there with no guide unless requested." He was surprised to learn that, in spite of numerous Japanese blockhouses, the countryside was relatively free from their control. Hall further observed that the Eighth Route Army was successfully waging "incessant warfare" against the invader. He attributed the high morale and effectiveness of the Red Army to the close cooperation which existed between the civilian and military branches of guerrilla society. Hall saw neither bandit nor beggar in the Communist areas. The people were, he concluded, well fed and clothed, they were making a genuinely patriotic effort to defeat the enemy, and their government was the "most nearly democratic" that he had found in China.[25]

In the spring of 1942, the Eighth Route Army assisted two

[24] Vincent, Chungking, March 15, 1943, dispatch to the Secretary of State, 893.00/14981, Department of State files. At the request of the American Embassy in Chungking, Hall provided the Department of State with a written report summarizing his observations of the Communist-controlled areas. All quotations are from this report. It was forwarded to the Department by Vincent in the dispatch cited above. Hall's memorandum is dated March 4, 1943. The emphasis of "so-called" is Hall's.

[25] *Ibid.* For a brief summary of Hall's observations see *Foreign Relations of the United States: Diplomatic Papers, 1943. China* (Washington, D.C., 1957), pp. 203–204.

French military officers, lieutenants Uhlmann and D'Anjou, to escape from Peiping through the Border Regions to Chungking. George Uhlmann, who left a published record of his most persuasive encounter with the Chinese Communists, had served in the French Navy and Consular Service at Peiping. Both Uhlmann and D'Anjou went to Chungking in order to join the Free Fighting French Forces.[26]

Uhlmann's account glows with enthusiasm for the Chinese Communists. The lieutenant's attention was, understandably, focused on the Red Army. Uhlmann was particularly moved by the fighting spirit and comradely *élan* which prevailed throughout the ranks of the Eighth Route Army. Like pesky mosquitoes, he analogized, the Communist guerrillas continuously and effectively stung the lumbering Japanese elephant. Moreover, the Chinese Communists had roused the slumbering peasantry to the ideals of popular nationalism, economic progress, and democratic self-rule.[27]

In 1943, two foreigners traveled in the Communist areas. Gustav Soderbom was a Swedish trader of many years' residence in Peiping and Inner Mongolia. In the company of Daniel De Lille, a French national, Soderbom left Peiping on April 19. After being escorted by the guerrillas through the Chin-Ch'a-Chi, Soderbom arrived in Yenan on July 3. He remained in the Communist capital until August 3, at which time he proceeded to Sian. While in Sian awaiting permission to continue to Chungking, Soderbom held a conversation with a United States Foreign Service officer.[28]

Like other Westerners, Soderbom was struck by the high morale of the Red Army, the cordial relations prevailing be-

---

[26] Lieutenant George Uhlmann, "Land of Five Withouts," *Far Eastern Survey,* XII (May 3, 1943), 86–89; *In Guerrilla China,* p. 69.

[27] Uhlmann, "Land of Five Withouts," 86–88.

[28] Everett F. Drumright, Sian, August 16, 1943, memorandum of conversation with Mr. Gustav Soderbom, 893.00/15134, Department of State files. The conversation between Drumright and Soderbom was held on August 12, 1943.

tween the guerrillas and the civilian populace, and the adequate level of economic well-being which characterized life in the Border Regions. Unlike other firsthand observers, Soderbom charged that large crops of the opium poppy were being produced in Shansi to bolster Communist finances. He also asserted that because of a deficiency in military materiel the Eighth Route Army was relatively passive when it came to engaging the Japanese. On the whole, however, the Swedish merchant was more favorable than critical in assessing the Communists.[29] Soderbom and De Lille seem to have been the only outside observers who traveled through the Border Regions in 1943.

From 1940 to 1944, then, the Nationalist blockade prevented all but a handful of foreigners from gaining firsthand information about the Chinese Communist movement. None of those who entered the Communist areas were professional writers or journalists who had set out expressly to provide the outside world with reports on the CCP. The consequence was a serious deficiency in knowledge of what Chinese Communists were thinking and doing.

The phenomenal expansion of Communist power behind Japanese lines took place in a reportorial vacuum comparable to the days before 1936. Nothing was known about such important developments as the *Cheng Feng,* or ideological rectification campaign, of 1942.[30] Incredible as it may seem, all of the eyewitness information on the Chinese Communists available to the reading public from 1940 to 1944 was contained in Lautenschlager's pamphlet, Lindsay's essay, Brondgeest's oral report, and Uhlmann's article.

It is highly improbable that the few reports which filtered through the KMT blockade made much of an impact in most foreign quarters. While a writer like Edgar Snow was

[29] *Ibid.* See also *Foreign Relations of the United States, 1943: China,* pp. 315, 325–327.

[30] On the *Cheng Feng* movement see Boyd Compton, *Mao's China: Party Reform Documents, 1942–44* (Seattle, 1952).

aware of Lindsay's article and had spoken personally with Hall, he had little else to go on. Snow's glib statement that the several foreigners who had escaped the Japanese from Peiping had "given fairly complete pictures" of the Border Regions is difficult to understand.[31] His slender account of developments in Red China after the outbreak of the Second World War certainly does not demonstrate an authoritative command of the subject. Snow was closer to the truth when he observed, in the same book, that virtually all news of the Eighth Route Army had been banned by the KMT since 1939.[32]

Although G. Martel Hall published nothing about his trip through the Communist areas, his views probably were more influential than those of any other firsthand observer in the years from 1940 to 1944. He discussed his experiences with Edgar Snow and Vice-President Henry A. Wallace, both of whom were impressed. During a conversation with Chiang Kai-shek on June 22, 1944, Wallace referred to Hall's high praise of the Chinese Communists. Chiang impugned Hall's ideas with the assertion that, like Evans F. Carlson and "many other Americans," he was "under the influence of Communist propaganda." [33] It is unlikely that the Vice-President accepted Chiang's simplistic formula for explaining why outsiders responded to Chinese Communists as they did.

Aside from the written and oral reports of a few firsthand observers, the only other major source for information on the CCP from 1940 to 1944 was in Chungking, where Chou En-lai or some other Communist spokesman was usually on duty. For reasons which were discussed earlier, even this source of information seems to have been used sparingly by Western newsmen. Significantly, Anna Louise Strong, Rob-

[31] Snow, *People on Our Side* (New York, 1944), p. 293.
[32] *Ibid.*, p. 288.
[33] *United States Relations With China: With Special Reference to the Period 1944–1949* (Washington, D.C., 1949), p. 553.

ert W. Barnett, and Vincent Sheean were temporary visitors to Chungking. These itinerant writers could afford the risks involved in interviewing Chou and giving a frank appraisal of Chinese affairs. What did they have to lose? On the other side, the accredited foreign reporters in China had careers to consider. They were the primary objects of the heavy-handed censorship which prevailed in KMT China during the war years.

[9]

The Censorship: 1937-1944

The Chinese government was, as Ambassador Clarence E. Gauss reported, "supersensitive" to criticism.[1] He thought that an inability to accept disparaging comments was common to all Chinese and to Chiang Kai-shek in particular.[2] If Chiang can be considered typical, Ambassador Gauss had formulated a convincing generalization. When Vice-President Henry A. Wallace visited Chungking in the summer of 1944, Chiang seized the opportunity to protest American press criticism and urge that it be stopped.[3] A few months later, the Generalissimo became so incensed over an article in *Collier's* magazine that he asked the commanding general of the United States forces in the China Theater to issue a public refutation.[4]

---

[1] *Foreign Relations of the United States: Diplomatic Papers, 1942. China* (Washington, D.C., 1956), p. 157.

[2] *Foreign Relations of the United States: Diplomatic Papers, 1944. China* (Washington, D.C., 1967), pp. 648–649.

[3] *United States Relations With China: With Special Reference to the Period 1944–1949* (Washington, D.C., 1949), p. 552.

[4] General Albert C. Wedemeyer, January 14, 1945, telegram to General George C. Marshall, Patrick J. Hurley papers. The article in question was Mark Gayn's "Crisis in China," *Collier's*, CXIV (October 28, 1944), 17–18, 44. It probably was no accident that when General Wedemeyer took the unusual step of granting an interview in which he sharply refuted current criticisms of the Central government, he chose

Before 1943, even Chiang Kai-shek had little reason to complain about the American press, given the pro-Chinese euphoria that had prevailed in the United States since 1937.[5] This period has been characterized aptly as the "Age of Admiration," a time when highly sympathetic images of China saturated the American news media.[6] Impressed by the gallant Chinese stand against the Japanese invasion, *Time* magazine named the Generalissimo and Madame Chiang Kai-shek "Man and Woman of the Year" for 1937.[7] With the attack on Pearl Harbor in 1941 the Chinese became heroic allies in the world-wide defense of freedom. American enthusiasm for the Chungking regime peaked in 1943, when Madame Chiang made a widely publicized trip to the United States. She addressed both houses of Congress and received a standing ovation in the Senate.[8]

China had always looked rather different from the inside. To American correspondents in that war-torn nation, the pro-Chinese euphoria prevailing in the United States seemed unreal.[9] Instead of sacrificial and massive resistance to the common enemy, firsthand observers found military lethargy, rampant corruption, and civil strife. Individuals like Edgar Snow had tried to express the alarm of those who viewed China from the inside as early as 1941, but such efforts were rare. Prior to 1943, even those most disillusioned with the

---

Collier's as his public outlet. See Lt. Gen. Albert C. Wedemeyer, as told to George Creel, "Don't Count China Out," *Collier's*, CXVI (July 7, 1945), 24–25, 46.

[5] A. T. Steele, *The American People and China* (New York, Toronto, and London, 1966), p. 23.

[6] Harold R. Isaacs, *Scratches on Our Minds: American Images of China and India* (New York, 1962), p. 164.

[7] Felix Greene, *A Curtain of Ignorance: How the American Public Has Been Misinformed About China* (Garden City, N.Y., 1964), pp. 14–15.

[8] Isaacs, *Scratches on Our Minds*, pp. 174–175.

[9] Steele, *The American People and China*, p. 23.

KMT muted their criticism in public. Whatever they might think of the Central government, Western reporters were reluctant to aggravate KMT-CCP relations or to write anything that might benefit the Japanese. " 'Bad news about China is good news for Japan,' " Snow explained, "was the thought that kept the most conscientious correspondents from spilling the most damaging facts about the Kuomintang." [10]

One of the peculiarities of foreign reporting from 1937 to 1943 is that it was united-front reporting. People who knew better provided the public with a distorted perspective on such crucial issues as that of KMT-CCP relations by avoiding a candid analysis of Chinese realities. There were exceptions to the rule, but the evidence indicates that long-standing detractors of the Central government did not tell, as they saw it, the whole truth. Some of them even wrote panegyrics about the KMT.

In 1935, Anna Louise Strong had contemptuously characterized Chiang Kai-shek as a militaristic traitor to the Chinese nation.[11] Three years later, she depicted the Generalissimo as China's George Washington, a valiant defender of freedom.[12] Even that redoubtable champion of the Chinese Communists, Agnes Smedley, uncharacteristically suppressed her real feelings in public after 1937. In private, as one of her acquaintances recalled, hatred for the Chungking regime "kept oozing out of her. . . . Whenever she pronounced the word 'Kuomintang' it sounded like swearing." [13] In 1939, however, when she wrote *China Fights Back*, Miss Smedley not only abstained from her usual invectives against the Nationalists but even had a few good words for the patriotic

[10] Edgar Snow, *Journey to the Beginning* (New York, 1958), p. 225.

[11] Anna Louise Strong, *China's Millions: The Revolutionary Struggles from 1927 to 1935* (New York, 1935), p. 428.

[12] Strong, *One-Fifth of Mankind* (New York, 1938), p. 9.

[13] Ilona Ralf Sues, *Shark's Fins and Millet* (Boston, 1944), p. 191.

spirit of the Generalissimo's legions.[14] With China fighting to survive, she explained in 1943, it was "not polite" to write the truth about Nationalist officials.[15]

Despite the self-imposed censorship of most foreign correspondents, it was only a matter of time before the view from inside China reverberated in the United States. In 1943, dissonant voices began to disrupt the common litany of praise for all things Chinese. In that year, Vincent Sheean took exception with the American tendency to see only the brighter side of Chiang Kai-shek's China. Sheean flailed the Generalissimo as a ruthless opportunist, criticized the Central government for corruption and insensitivity to the literally starving Chinese people, condemned the Kuomintang Party as a "fossilized" relic, and wondered aloud why Nationalist concentration camps were so overcrowded.[16] More important than Sheean's bitter dissent was what one concerned State Department official described as the "small flood" of critical articles which made their appearance in the American press in 1943.[17]

The Nationalist government was particularly disturbed by the writings of four American authors. The first, Pearl Buck, was renowned as a friend of China. Writing shortly after Madame Chiang Kai-shek's highly successful trip, Mrs. Buck deplored the tendency of Americans to respond to such events with emotional sentimentality. Predicting ultimate disillusionment, she called for more common sense in thinking about China. That nation, Mrs. Buck warned, "is ill." She feared that antidemocratic elements were gaining ascendancy

[14] For example, see Agnes Smedley, *China Fights Back: An American Woman with the Eighth Route Army* (London, 1939), p. 18.

[15] Smedley, *Battle Hymn of China* (New York, 1943), p. 185.

[16] Vincent Sheean, *Between the Thunder and the Sun* (New York, 1943), pp. 343–349.

[17] *Foreign Relations of the United States: Diplomatic Papers, 1943. China* (Washington, D.C., 1957), p. 98.

in the Central government. This meant military immobility, increased friction with Chinese Communists, corruption in high places, and the suppression of free speech. Mrs. Buck placed the blame for the growing rot in Chungking on the low priority the United States accorded the China Theater and on the reactionary men around Chiang Kai-shek. She still regarded the Generalissimo himself as a great leader, the living symbol of Chinese unity.[18]

A spokesman for the KMT thought that the second of these American authors, T. A. Bisson, had swallowed the Communist line "hook, line and sinker." [19] In an article in *Far Eastern Survey*, a magazine published by the American Council of the Institute of Pacific Relations, Bisson heralded the emergence of "two Chinas": a "feudal" KMT China and a "democratic" CCP China. Chinese Communists were mobilizing the masses and inflicting heavy casualties on the Japanese. Chinese Nationalists were decreasing their military effort and neglecting needed economic and political reforms. While more categorical in his denunciations than Mrs. Buck, Bisson also praised Chiang Kai-shek's government for long years of resistance to Japan with very little help from the United States.[20]

The comments of the third American author generated

[18] Pearl S. Buck, "A Warning About China: A Great Friend of the Chinese People Points to Dangers That May Lose Us a Valuable Ally," *Life*, XIV (May 10, 1943), 53–54, 56.

[19] C. L. Hsia, "Letters to the Editor," *Far Eastern Survey*, XII (August 11, 1943), 158–159. Dr. Hsia was a member of the China Council of the Institute of Pacific Relations.

[20] T. A. Bisson, "China's Part in a Coalition War," *ibid.* (July 14, 1943), 135–141. In a private letter, Stanley K. Hornbeck criticized Bisson's "two Chinas" concept as an oversimplification. He also thought that the use of the highly misleading word "feudal" was bound to irritate the Chinese and confuse Westerners. See Stanley K. Hornbeck to Edward C. Carter, August 1, 1943, Hornbeck papers, Stanford University.

more excitement in Chungking than those of the other critics. Hanson W. Baldwin, the influential military editor of
the *New York Times,* suggested that China had been over-
sold to Americans by missionaries and motion pictures.
Nearly worthless Chinese military communiqués also had
fostered a China myth by inflating skirmishes into battles.
Baldwin asserted flatly that the military situation in China,
more a "geographer's expression" than a nation, was bad,
had been bad for two years, and probably would get worse.
He warned that the "main burden of victory" would of necessity fall to American arms. Poorly officered Chinese
troops could not be counted on to expel the invader from
their midst. Baldwin did not, however, write off the Chinese
armies. Inspired by Chiang Kai-shek's unshakable spirit, the
Chinese were making an important contribution by forcing
the Japanese to commit men and resources to the occupation
of China.[21]

Nathaniel Peffer, the fourth American author, wrote an
essay that elicited a sympathetic response from Secretary of
State Cordell Hull. Unlike the Chinese Nationalists, Hull
did not feel that Peffer's remarks were overdrawn or unfair
to China.[22] Peffer did write that Americans had made fools
of themselves by hailing Madame Chiang Kai-shek as a "lat-
ter-day composite of Plato and Joan of Arc." He also depre-
ciated the idealization of China as a Jeffersonian democracy
led by selfless statesmen. On the other side, Peffer spoke out
against the "stream of bearish and deprecatory" reports
which were beginning to have an impact in Washington. It
was being whispered, he observed, that the Chungking regime was a vilely corrupt Fascist dictatorship more concerned with destroying Chinese communism than with fighting Japanese militarism. He thought that such judgments

[21] Hanson W. Baldwin, "Review of the Chinese Situation," *New York Times,* July 20, 1943, 7; "Too Much Wishful Thinking about China," *Reader's Digest,* XLIII (August 1943), 63–67.

[22] *Foreign Relations of the United States, 1943: China,* p. 183.

were "as far from the truth" as the romantic China myth which had been fabricated after Pearl Harbor.[23]

China, Peffer suggested, had to be understood in terms of its own past and cultural traditions. To judge Chungking by Western standards would be unfair. While corruption, military inefficiency, official callousness, and undemocratic tendencies might be shocking to Americans, a certain amount of such behavior was normal to China. Many of those who now condemned the Chinese did not know enough for long enough to have a meaningful perspective. To avoid tragic misunderstandings on both sides, Peffer advised his countrymen not to leap to conclusions but to suspend judgment and to exercise tact and patience.[24] Implicitly criticizing the writings of such individuals as Hanson Baldwin, Nathaniel Peffer had in effect made an appeal for more balance in American reporting on China.

Neither Americans nor Chinese paid much heed to Peffer's plea for reciprocal tolerance. What Clarence Gauss described in 1943 as a comparatively mild tendency to criticize the favorable image of China that had been presented to the American public quickly assumed larger proportions.[25] Western reporting on Chiang Kai-shek's government grew increasingly strident, reaching a crescendo of outrage with the recall of General Joseph W. Stilwell in October of 1944.[26] As for the Chinese, it was indicative of their response to criticism that even Peffer's restrained analysis angered KMT officials. Mrs. Buck's relatively mild evaluation also engendered much hostility. At a news conference on July 28, 1943, a spokesman for the Central government heatedly de-

[23] Nathaniel Peffer, "Our Distorted View of China," *New York Times Magazine*, November 7, 1943, 7.

[24] *Ibid.*, 7, 40–41.

[25] Clarence E. Gauss to Hornbeck, September 4, 1943, Hornbeck papers.

[26] Steele, *The American People and China*, pp. 23–24, 28–30; Isaacs, *Scratches on Our Minds*, pp. 187–188.

nounced Bisson's "two Chinas" idea as false and malicious. But it was Hanson Baldwin who caused the most resentment. Nationalist leaders were irritated by the charge that their military communiqués were unreliable and shocked at Baldwin's use of "geographer's expression," a phrase that was associated with Japanese propaganda.[27]

The overall Chinese reaction to American press criticism was, as a Foreign Service officer reported, "little short of fantastic." [28] A special meeting of KMT party heads and cabinet ministers was held to discuss the problem. Fearing that press criticism would have an adverse effect on relations with the Central government, the chargé d'affaires of the United States at Chungking urged his superiors in Washington to issue a statement discounting unfavorable comments on China.[29] While such a proclamation was not forthcoming, Secretary Hull did bring Hanson Baldwin's remarks to the attention of the Secretary of War, Henry L. Stimson. Referring to the unhappy ramifications of such writings, Hull suggested that United States military personnel might have leaked statements to Baldwin. Although Stimson doubted that American officers had been providing Baldwin with information, he did promise to investigate and to take steps to guard against embarrassments in the future.[30] For its part, the Department of State engaged in some discreet diplomacy with the representatives of the press. Emphasizing the delicacy of the situation, State Department officials told Robert W. Martin of *Time-Life* that it would be desirable to avoid unbalanced reporting on China.[31]

[27] *Foreign Relations of the United States, 1943: China*, pp. 82, 87, 146, 149, 182–183.

[28] George Atcheson, Jr., Chungking, September 7, 1943, dispatch to the Secretary of State, 893.00/15135, Department of State files. See also John F. Melby, *The Mandate of Heaven: Record of a Civil War, China, 1945–49* (London, 1968), p. 88.

[29] *Foreign Relations of the United States, 1943: China*, pp. 87–89.

[30] *Ibid.*, pp. 102–104, 126–127.

[31] Edwin F. Stanton, Washington, December 30, 1943, memorandum of a conversation, 893.00/15233, Department of State files.

Press criticism of the Central government had, as Nathaniel Peffer warned, poisoned Sino-American relations. Some Americans, including Ambassador Gauss and Secretary Hull, felt that public criticism of the KMT was good. It would, they thought, spur Chungking to undertake sorely needed reforms.[32] Gauss even imagined that the sobering effect of press criticism would help to improve Chinese-American relations.[33] This was not the view of the government of Chiang Kai-shek. Wei Tao-ming, the Chinese Ambassador to the United States, tried to explain the almost hysterical reaction of his government to unfavorable publicity. In a conversation in May 1944 with John Carter Vincent, the Chief of the Division of Chinese Affairs, Ambassador Wei stated that press criticism was damaging to Sino-American friendship because "face" was a matter of great importance to Nationalist officials.[34]

In traditional Chinese thought, "face," or moral prestige, was one of the ingredients necessary to the maintenance of power. Power depended partly on prestige. A leader's influence over the people was believed to be contingent on his right conduct in office. Virtuous behavior provided an ethical sanction for the exercise of authority. Improper conduct, on the other side, undermined the moral prestige and hence the influence of a government. So important was the loss of "face" that it might set in motion a course of events culminating in the downfall of a regime. In more poetic terms, a ruler whose moral worth had been discredited could anticipate that the Mandate of Heaven might pass into more deserving hands.[35]

The concept of "government by goodness" conditioned

---

[32] *Foreign Relations of the United States, 1944: China,* pp. 594, 894.

[33] Gauss to Hornbeck, September 4, 1943, Hornbeck papers.

[34] *Foreign Relations of the United States, 1944: China,* p. 413.

[35] John King Fairbank, *The United States and China* (rev. ed., New York, 1958), pp. 56–57, 84, 223–225; Fairbank, *China: The People's Middle Kingdom and the U.S.A.* (Cambridge, Mass., 1967), pp. 61, 78; Melby, *The Mandate of Heaven,* pp. 4–5.

the Chinese response to criticism. In Nationalist China, as well as in ancient China, critics spoke out at their own risk.[36] Historically conditioned to think less in institutional than in personal terms, Chinese Nationalists did not distinguish between policies and people.[37] Thus, while Hanson Baldwin and T. A. Bisson both praised Chiang Kai-shek and condemned only Chinese military and economic programs, the Generalissimo could not help but take their comments as a personal affront. Since the Confucian idea of government by moral men had significant political implications, such criticism was by its very nature subversive. It questioned the basis of political success, the virtuous conduct of a ruler. Critics, as John K. Fairbank has observed, were "seen as enemies," for they discredited the holders of power and tore down the prestige by which that power was partially sustained.[38] While Chinese certainly had no monopoly on sensitivity to criticism, it had a greater import for them than it did for Westerners.

The most direct way to sustain "face" was to suppress criticism. Accordingly, Chungking's control of the press, both foreign and domestic, was, as one journalist recalled, "quite ruthless." [39] For example, the *Hsin Hua Jih Pao,* the Communist daily published in Chungking, was heavily censored.[40] In its dealings with the foreign press, the Chinese government showed an equal determination to prevent disa-

[36] Fairbank, *China,* p. 78. See also Charles O. Hucker, *The Censorial System of Ming China* (Stanford, 1966), pp. 66–108.

[37] James E. Sheridan, *Chinese Warlord: The Career of Feng Yü-hsiang* (Stanford, 1966), pp. 283–286.

[38] Fairbank, *China,* p. 124.

[39] Eric Sevareid, "Censors in the Saddle," *Nation,* CLV (April 14, 1945), 415.

[40] Lyman P. Van Slyke, *Enemies and Friends: The United Front in Chinese Communist History* (Stanford, 1967), p. 154. See also *Foreign Relations of the United States, 1942: China,* p. 201 and *Foreign Relations of the United States: Diplomatic Papers, 1945. The Far East and China* (Washington, D.C., 1969), p. 412.

greeable reports from finding their way into print. The vice-minister of information served as chief censor of the dispatches written by Western correspondents. He operated under a set of regulations which prohibited the publication of anything contrary to the "highest principles" of the nation, of anything which was prejudicial to the "interests of the Republic," of anything which disturbed the domestic tranquility, and of anything which was harmful to Chinese relations with "friendly Powers." [41] Under these broad guidelines, the vice-minister had considerable latitude in censoring the communiqués of foreign newsmen.

The Chinese authorities were more sensitive to the topic of KMT-CCP relations than to any other. "We were never permitted," an indignant correspondent recalled, "to say a word about the Communists in any of our dispatches—except perhaps to quote the Generalissimo and other high government officials." [42] Dr. H. H. Chang, the vice-minister of information, followed a policy of expunging any mention of Chinese Communists from the dispatches of Western newsmen. Chang became so habituated to this *modus operandi* that he made an incredible blunder in September 1937. When foreign correspondents quoted the KMT's Central News Agency and an official Nanking statement on the formation of the united front, Chang viewed the story as just another reference to the Chinese Reds and therefore killed the report! Chang later explained that after emasculating so many previous allusions to the Chinese Communists, he figured that he might as well table this one also.[43] That, of course, ended his career as vice-minister of information.

---

[41] Hollington K. Tong, *Dateline—China: The Beginning of China's Press Relations with the World* (New York, 1950), pp. 251–252. This volume was first published in China under the title *China and the World Press* ([Nanking?], [1948?]).

[42] Harrison Forman, *Report from Red China* (New York, 1945), p. 1. See also *Foreign Relations of the United States, 1943: China*, p. 64.

[43] Tong, *Dateline—China*, p. 9.

From 1937 to 1945 the unenviable responsibility for overseeing the foreign press community fell on the shoulders of Hollington K. Tong. Dr. Chang's successor was what might be called an "Americanized" Chinese, a man torn between the values of two civilizations. As a graduate of Edgar Snow's alma mater, the University of Missouri, and the Columbia School of Journalism, Tong had embraced the liberal ideals of the west. Since his education in the United States, Tong wrote, "in the bracing atmosphere of free democratic institutions, I have unquestioningly regarded free speech and a free press as the intrinsic qualities of a genuine democratic state." [44] This man found himself in the uncomfortable position of being compelled, against his assumptions and inclinations, to blue-pencil ruthlessly American and European reports on the Chinese situation. In 1950, Tong authored one of the more remarkable laments of the recent past. *Dateline —China,* the story of China's press relations with the West, is a fascinating reminiscence of Tong's personal quandary, a revealing commentary on reporting on the Chinese Communists, and a candid account of the oppressive character of the KMT news censorship.

For a time, Tong was able to perform his responsibilities with little difficulty. During the early days of the united front, China received favorable publicity abroad and the new vice-minister took comfort in the knowledge that foreign reporters had few complaints about his handling of the censorship problem. In Hankow in 1938, Tong received the full co-operation of Chou En-lai in the effort to maintain cordial relations with the press. "Never at any period of the war," the vice-minister recalled, "did our work run so smoothly." Significantly, Tong dates the beginning of serious criticism of the KMT and of his troubles with Western correspondents to the breakdown of the united front. The "greatest stumbling block to a good press on China abroad," he wrote, was "the Communist problem." [45]

[44] *Ibid.*, p. 258.
[45] *Ibid.*, pp. 51, 146.

After the fall of Hankow, Chungking, as Tong delicately phrased it, "pursued a policy of studied reticence on the Communist controversy." [46] That is, the KMT supplemented its blockade of the Shen-Kan-Ning with an energetic news censorship. Tong found himself obliged to subject the communiqués of Western correspondents to a scrutiny not unworthy of that of his unlamented predecessor. At times this censorship was so rigorous that it approximated a blackout of information on the Chinese Communist movement. Particularly after the New Fourth Army Incident, the KMT news blockade on the subject of Chinese communism became exceedingly rigid. The Nationalist authorities, Tong admitted, "now fell into the bad publicity habit of indiscriminate denial of all news published abroad about the Communists." [47] Questions about KMT-CCP frictions were met with the assertion that this was a local problem, not a subject to be publicized abroad.[48] Even the existence of the military blockade of the Communist areas, a matter of common knowledge, was categorically denied by Tong's superiors.[49]

Bland denials and strict censorship policies drove Western journalists, as one of them recalled, "almost to the point of desperation." [50] A central theme in *Dateline—China* is the swelling tide of reportorial acrimony from 1939 to 1944. By the summer of 1941, the accumulation of grievances had heated tempers to the boiling point. In a memorandum to the Generalissimo of June 14, 1941, seven journalists representing some of the world's most prominent news-gathering agencies remonstrated against the highhanded manner of

[46] *Ibid.,* p. 146.

[47] *Ibid.,* p. 155.

[48] *Foreign Relations of the United States, 1944: China,* p. 350.

[49] *Ibid.,* pp. 344, 349–350.

[50] U.S. Senate, Subcommittee of the Committee on Foreign Relations, 81st Cong., 2nd Sess., *State Department Employee Loyalty Investigation, Hearings* (Part 2, Washington, D.C., 1950), p. 2144; letter of Theodore H. White, Paris, May 2, 1950, to the chairman of the Loyalty-Security Board.

KMT authorities.[51] The manifold injustices they listed fell into three categories: censorship, inadequate press facilities, and surveillance. Most important were the problems of surveillance and censorship. The correspondents objected to being constantly spied upon by agents of the Chinese secret police and confessed resentment at such "fascist" practices. As for the censorship, the seven complained that it was inconsistently applied and unduly severe. "News that can be dispatched abroad one day," they observed, "is prohibited the next day, and vice versa." These experienced correspondents disliked being compelled to write their reports to conform to the whims of capricious bureaucrats.[52]

Despite the protest, the situation showed little sign of improvement. If anything, matters got worse. In the summer of 1943, Chang Tao-fan, the minister of information, spent three and a half hours persuading the correspondent for the *New York Times* to withdraw a dispatch on KMT-CCP relations.[53] At about the same time, Gunther Stein became the object of a rather perverse retaliation against T. A. Bisson's article on the "two Chinas." Since Stein was correspondent for both the *Christian Science Monitor* and the Institute of

[51] Clarence E. Gauss, Chungking, June 30, 1941, dispatch to the Secretary of State, 811.91293/292, Department of State files. A copy of the memorandum is enclosed with this dispatch. It was signed by Spencer S. Moosa (Associated Press), J. Melville Jacoby (*Time-Life*), James L. Stewart (*New York Herald Tribune*), F. Tillman Durdin (*New York Times*), Thomas Chao (Reuters), Leslie L. Smith (London *Times*), and F. McCracken Fisher (United Press).

[52] *Ibid.* In the dispatch which accompanied the memorandum, Ambassador Gauss wrote that press conditions in China had been accurately portrayed by the frustrated American and British journalists. After a fact-finding mission to China undertaken at the request of President Roosevelt, Representative Michael J. Mansfield of Montana reported on January 3, 1945, that the "worst censorship in the world is located in Chungking and there is one detective assigned to every ten foreigners." See *Foreign Relations of the United States: Diplomatic Papers, 1945: The Far East and China*, p. 12.

[53] *Foreign Relations of the United States, 1943: China*, pp. 290–291.

Pacific Relations, the Nationalists had a means of retribution. Stein's privilege of using the radio facilities of the Chinese government in order to transmit messages was revoked.[54] This action constituted a rather roundabout way of protesting Bisson's critique, but it was illustrative of the character of the KMT news blackout. With the reporter for the *New York Times,* the Nationalists employed persuasion; with the correspondent for the Institute of Pacific Relations, they used coercion. In both instances, the displeasure of the Chinese authorities had been aroused by efforts to discuss a forbidden subject, the problem of KMT-CCP relations.

By 1944, Western newsmen had, as Hollington K. Tong wrote, become so exasperated that their resentment manifested itself "in open and organized resistance." On April 18, 1944, they petitioned the Generalissimo to take "early action" to liberalize Chinese press policies. With the notable exception of the *Tass* reporters, the document was signed by all the foreign war correspondents accredited to the Chinese government. The irate journalists complained of being thwarted in writing news that implied criticism of the Chungking regime, that revealed the "full gravity" of the Chinese economic situation, that disclosed "tenseness" in KMT-CCP relations, that questioned the Nationalist military apparatus, and that referred to anything other than the "most formal" aspects of Chinese foreign affairs. They also charged that the meaning of many dispatches had been distorted by unjust deletions.[55]

Hollington Tong sympathized with the plight of Western newsmen and advocated a more liberal policy toward the foreign press. But the vice-minister was, as he once remarked, "up against the stronger elements in the government." The notion that a publication should present more than one side of the picture was abhorrent to KMT politicians. Accus-

[54] *Ibid.,* p. 79. See also Tong, *Dateline—China,* pp. 204–206.
[55] Tong, *Dateline—China,* pp. 248–250. Tong quotes in full the petition of April 18.

tomed to the tradition of a controlled press, Nationalist leaders never acquired a clear conception of the meaning or importance of free speech. The task of facilitating relations with the foreign press community was, Tong wrote, "vastly complicated" by the attitude of his superiors. All through his years in the Ministry of Information, Tong faced the "continuing problem of Chinese incomprehension of American journalistic methods and standards." [56]

Western correspondents found Chinese methods and standards equally incomprehensible. Since the KMT did not allow criticism by Chinese newsmen, Ambassador Gauss saw no reason why foreign journalists could expect to be treated differently.[57] But American reporters of the 1930's and 1940's were reared in the tradition of "publish and be damned." Conceiving themselves to be self-appointed guardians of the truth, they believed in reporting the facts, however painful.[58] Assuming that the press must be free, they tended to equate censorship with an absence of democracy.[59] Although there were few complaints by the Russian journalists, those accustomed to freedom of the press chafed under the heavy restrictions imposed by the Central government.

The dissatisfaction was, of course, mutual. If Chinese Nationalists showed scant regard for the strongly held Western value of freedom of the press, foreign reporters often were insensitive to the Chinese concern for "face." Some of the acrimony might have been reduced had Western journalists

[56] *Ibid.*, pp. 8–9, 150.

[57] *Foreign Relations of the United States, 1944: China*, p. 406.

[58] James Reston, *The Artillery of the Press: Its Influence on American Foreign Policy* (New York and Evanston, 1966), pp. ix, 3–6, 9.

[59] For some perceptive comments on the differing assumptions of Americans and Chinese about freedom of the press, see the remarks by Floyd Taylor and Liu Chieh in *Foreign Relations of the United States, 1944: China*, pp. 107–108, 129–130. Taylor was an American journalist who worked for the Chinese Ministry of Information. Liu Chieh was the Minister-Counselor of the Chinese Embassy in Washington.

been more prudent in their choice of words and less eager to rush their stories into print. On the other side, the Chinese might have reduced tensions by relaxing the censorship and placing more trust in the discretion of foreign correspondents. The result could have been less bitterness and more understanding in Sino-American relations. In retrospect, however, such speculations may be nothing more than wishful thinking. So few on either side were willing to compromise that it seems that Western reporters and Chinese Nationalists were locked in a genuine cultural conflict. Upholding the Mandate of Heaven dictated one set of ethical imperatives, the freedom of the press another.

[10]

Press Party to the Northwest: 1944-1945

While KMT officials ignored pleas for a relaxation of the censorship, the amiable Communists openly invited the scrutiny of outside observers. As Nelson T. Johnson wrote, the representatives of the American press were courted by the Chinese Communists.[1] Western newsmen were told that they would be welcome at Yenan and given advance guarantees of freedom of investigation and movement.[2] Because of travel restrictions imposed in 1939, none of the regular war correspondents assigned to Chungking knew much about the Communist areas at first hand. But they were intensely interested. The few travelers who trickled through the KMT blockade, as the president of the Foreign Correspondents' Club recalled, "took on the proportions of men from Mars." Individuals like G. Martel Hall and Gustav Soderbom were "interviewed until exhausted."[3]

Many reporters applied for permission to visit the Border

[1] Nelson T. Johnson to Stanley K. Hornbeck, January 16, 1941, Hornbeck papers, Stanford University.

[2] *Foreign Relations of the United States: Diplomatic Papers, 1944. China* (Washington, D.C., 1967), pp. 352–353, 408.

[3] Brooks Atkinson, "Critic at Large: Publications of State Department Papers on China of 1943 Evokes Reflections," *New York Times*, April 10, 1962, 40.

Regions. The Nationalists never flatly rejected these applications, but they advanced one pretense after another to explain the inadvisability of a trip to the Communist areas. As the vice-minister of information expressed it, a "policy of discouragement of visits to the Northwest had been adopted." [4] Indeed, it has been reported that the vice-minister, possibly in an unguarded moment, told a foreign newsman that correspondents were prohibited from investigating Red China because those who had been there had returned only to write favorable reports.[5] Then, a newly appointed minister of information, Liang Han-chao, made a fatal slip of the tongue.

At one of his first press conferences in November of 1943, Liang gave an off-hand "yes" to Harrison Forman's request for permission to travel to Yenan. Before Liang was fully aware of the tempest he had stirred up, other foreign correspondents were demanding authorization to visit the blockaded regions. Liang's news conferences degenerated into what Tong called the "battle of the alley." Tempers flared as a sobered Liang matched wits with his charges. A "veritable feud," Tong confessed, had broken out between the Ministry of Information and the foreign press community. The journalists seized the opportunity presented by Liang's commitment to air their encrusted grievances. As Tong wrote, "issues" had "come to a head" over the question of access to Yenan.[6]

At the conclusion of a spirited press conference on February 16, 1944, a group of correspondents, led by Brooks Atkinson of the *New York Times,* handed Liang a formal re-

[4] Hollington K. Tong, *Dateline—China: The Beginning of China's Press Relations With the World* (New York, 1950), p. 242. See also *Foreign Relations of the United States, 1944: China,* p. 43.

[5] U.S. Senate, Committee on the Judiciary, Subcommittee on Internal Security, 89th Cong., 1st Sess., *Morgenthau Diary: China,* II (Washington, D.C., 1965), p. 1076.

[6] Tong, *Dateline—China,* pp. 242–243.

quest petitioning Chiang Kai-shek for authorization to go to Yenan.[7] Much to their surprise, the correspondents were informed on February 23 that the Generalissimo had given his assent. The jubilant reporters felt that persistent questioning had forced the decision. Others conjectured that Chiang believed his own propaganda. According to this theory, high KMT officials thought that conditions in the Border Regions were so bad that the dispatches of Western journalists would debunk Communist claims.[8] Hollington Tong's explanation supports that of the newsmen. The movement for a trip to Yenan, he wrote, "had gone so far that the Generalissimo had no other alternative but to agree." [9]

Whatever their reasons might have been, the Nationalists could impose certain stipulations. On March 1, the journalists were informed that those making the trip would be required to first investigate the non-Communist areas of the Northwest, would have to stay in the Communist regions for a minimum of three months, and would have to submit their reports to the Ministry of Information for censorship.[10] The group would have to include Chinese newsmen and would be jointly headed by Hsieh Pao-chao of the Legislative Yuan and Teng Yu-teh of the Ministry of Information.[11] These precautions did not seem sufficient to Tong. Floyd Taylor, an American journalist who worked for the Ministry of Information, was asked to become a member of the press party. It was hoped that he would write articles to offset dispatches

[7] *Foreign Relations of the United States, 1944: China,* pp. 349–350. For a detailed and absorbing report on the press conference of February 16 see U.S. Senate, *Morgenthau Diary,* II, pp. 1068–1075.

[8] *Foreign Relations of the United States, 1944: China,* pp. 365–366.

[9] Tong, *Dateline—China,* p. 242.

[10] *Foreign Relations of the United States, 1944: China,* p. 372; Harrison Forman, *Report from Red China* (New York, 1945), pp. 1–3; Gunther Stein, *The Challenge of Red China* (New York and London, 1945), pp. 24–28.

[11] *Foreign Relations of the United States, 1944: China,* p. 420; Tong, *Dateline—China,* p. 244.

unfavorable to the KMT and pro-Communist in orientation. Taylor prudently declined the offer.[12]

Maurice Votaw, another American employee of the Ministry of Information, was more responsive to the idea of making a trip to Yenan. Whether or not he was acting in collusion with the Chinese government is unknown, but Votaw did have the reputation of being a "Kuomintang stooge." Formerly chairman of the department of journalism at St. John University in Shanghai, Votaw had joined Tong's staff sometime after 1937 and had been placed in charge of the management of the Chungking Press Hostel. Votaw's inclusion in the group as the representative for the Associated Press raised a storm of protest. The other foreign correspondents insisted that an influential news agency like the AP should be represented by an impartial observer. One journalist felt so strongly about the matter that he threatened to expose Votaw's connections. Informing his government of the attitude of the press community, Ambassador Clarence E. Gauss agreed with their assessment of the need for unbiased reporting and advised the Department of State discreetly to inform the AP officials in Washington of the problem. This was done, and Votaw's appointment was canceled.[13]

Votaw made the journey to Yenan, as correspondent for the *Toronto Daily Star* and the *Baltimore Sun*. The AP assignment was given to Gunther Stein, who also represented the *Christian Science Monitor* and the London *News-Chronicle*. The other Western journalists involved were Harrison Forman, Israel Epstein, Father Cormac Shanahan, and N. Protsenko. Forman represented the *New York Herald Tribune*, the London *Times*, and the United Press; Epstein, who was normally retained by Allied Labor News, the *New York Times*, *Time* magazine, and the Sydney *Morning Herald*;

[12] *Foreign Relations of the United States, 1944: China*, p. 1127.

[13] Tong, *Dateline—China*, pp. 101–102, 231; *Foreign Relations of the United States, 1944: China*, pp. 389–390, 392, 395.

Shanahan the *China Correspondent* and various other Catholic publications; Protsenko the *Tass* News Agency. In addition to these six foreign reporters, the press party included nine Chinese newsmen, two Chinese employees of Tong's office, and the two Chinese officials who had been named to lead the expedition.[14]

The handful of journalists who departed from Chungking on May 17, 1944, was officially designated the "Press Party to the Northwest." After spending several weeks in Sian and its environs, the Press Party proceeded on to Red China. The group divided in mid-July. Shanahan and the Chinese newsmen returned to Chungking, but the other foreign correspondents stayed in the Communist areas until October. Two additional Western reporters were granted permission to travel to Yenan. In the fall of 1944, Brooks Atkinson of the *New York Times* and Theodore H. White of *Time-Life* paid brief visits to the Communist capital. Thus, for the first time since Edgar Snow's interviews with Mao Tse-tung in 1939, foreign correspondents were allowed to observe the Chinese Communist movement at first hand.

That earlier trip by Edgar Snow had not been forgotten. Some Chinese speculated that the consequence of authorizing the Press Party might be that the KMT would have to cope with "eleven Edgar Snows" instead of one.[15] In actuality only eight foreign reporters were able to meet with Chinese

[14] *Foreign Relations of the United States, 1944: China*, p. 424; Tong, *Dateline—China*, p. 244. The Chinese correspondents involved were Kung Chao-kai (*Ta Kung Pao*), C. Y. Hsu and Yang Chia-yung (Central News Agency), Chang Wen-po (*Central Daily News*), Hsieh Shuang-chiu (*Sao Tang Pao*), Chow Peng-yuan (*Kuo Min Kung Pao*), Chao Chao-kou (*Sin Min Pao*), Chin Tung-ping (*Commercial Daily News*), Chao Ping-lang (*China Times*). All of the newspapers cited above were published in Chungking. Jimmy Wei and Frank Tao were the Chinese employees of Tong's office. For a summary of C. Y. Hsu's observations on his Yenan experience, see *Foreign Relations of the United States, 1944: China*, pp. 571–572.

[15] *Foreign Relations of the United States, 1944: China*, pp. 366–367.

Communists in 1944, not eleven. With few exceptions, however, they did form impressions similar to those of Snow. As A. T. Steele wrote, these new visitors to Yenan "wired home reams of copy, most of it friendly." [16]

Israel Epstein did, indeed, wire home reams of copy, all of it friendly.[17] Cormac Shanahan wired home very little, nearly all of it unfriendly.[18] Maurice Votaw did not wire home anything, possibly because what he had to say would not have seemed friendly to his employers. In a news broadcast from Yenan, monitored by the United States Office of War Information in Chungking, Votaw praised the Communists for their military prowess and marveled at the close cooperation between the Eighth Route Army and the people.[19] But of the half-dozen Western reporters in the Press Party, only Gunther Stein and Harrison Forman published detailed accounts of their observations.

Both Forman and Stein were professional journalists with

[16] A. T. Steele, *The American People and China* (New York, Toronto, and London, 1966), p. 25.

[17] The following unsigned dispatches probably were written by Epstein: "Communist Army in China is Strong," *New York Times,* July 1, 1944, 6; "China Communists Confer With Rich," *ibid.,* August 6, 1944, 19; "No Opium Poppies on Way to Yenan," *ibid.,* August 14, 1944, 5; "China Communists From All Classes," *ibid.,* August 20, 1944, 23. For a signed essay by Epstein see "Light on the Chinese Puzzle," *Labour Monthly,* XXVII (June 1945), 173–178. Epstein, who was born in Poland and had visited the United States, was a person without nationality. He became a Chinese citizen sometime after the Second World War and was employed as an editor by the Foreign Languages Press in Peking until his arrest by the Chinese authorities in 1968. See "American Purged by Chinese Reds," *New York Times,* May 1, 1968, 15.

[18] For example, see Cormac Shanahan, "China's Communist Puzzle," *China Monthly,* VI (June 1945), 9–12.

[19] F. McCracken Fisher, October 28, 1944, to Patrick J. Hurley, Patrick J. Hurley papers. Fisher, the head of the OWI in China, enclosed with this letter excerpts from various Yenan broadcasts. See also U.S. Senate, Committee on the Judiciary, Subcommittee on Internal Security, *The Amerasia Papers: A Clue to the Catastrophe of China,* II (Washington, D.C., 1970), pp. 1114–1117.

considerable experience in the Far East. During his career as photographer, explorer, and war correspondent, Forman had worked for a large number of news agencies, including the *New York Times* and the National Broadcasting Company. Because of his trip in 1937, he was the only foreign member of the Press Party with previous firsthand knowledge of the Communist areas. A naturalized British citizen of German origin, Stein specialized in the analysis of economic affairs. He had first come to China in 1932 and was known to have unusually good connections with important Nationalist leaders like T. V. Soong, the Generalissimo's brother-in-law. From 1939 to 1944 Stein was the Chungking agent for the *Christian Science Monitor* and also reported the news for the Manchester *Guardian* and the London *News-Chronicle*. In addition to a lengthy exposure to China, Stein had spent more than a year in Moscow as a correspondent for the *Berliner Tageblatt*. This gave him a comparative perspective on Chinese communism not available to most foreign journalists.[20]

As had been stipulated, the Press Party examined the non-Communist regions of the Northwest before proceeding to Yenan. If the purpose of this detour had been to impress foreign correspondents favorably prior to their encounter with Chinese Communists, the Ministry of Information had miscalculated. The members of the Press Party were handled, Stein wrote, as if they were "royalty from potentially hostile nations." Banquets, speeches, and staged popular demonstrations did not convince Stein that he had seen a new and better China. He described Sian as a "grim bastion" of antiliberalism and was soon even "getting a bit homesick"

[20] Forman, *Report from Red China*, p. 3; Stein, *The Challenge of Red China*, pp. 10–19, 28; F. W. Deakin and G. R. Storry, *The Case of Richard Sorge* (New York, 1966), p. 342; U.S. Senate, Subcommittee of the Committee on Foreign Relations, 81st Cong., 2nd Sess., *State Department Employee Loyalty Investigation, Hearings* (Part 2, Washington, D.C., 1950), p. 2074.

for the stuffy atmosphere of Chungking. Like Stein, Forman felt uncomfortable while in Sian. He complained of being followed by plainclothesmen. Nonetheless, Stein and Forman had been thoroughly indoctrinated by their Nationalist hosts before they reached the Communist strongholds. They were told that the Reds cultivated the opium poppy, displayed anti-KMT banners, avoided fighting the Japanese, and ruled the peasants by such heavy-handed totalitarian means as secret police and concentration camps.[21]

The questions which Forman and Stein asked about Chinese Communists were influenced by the KMT's accusations. Their approach to the subject of Chinese communism was, in short, polemical. As Forman put it: "Were the Communists really as bad as they were painted by the Government authorities?" [22] Stein spent four and a half months in Yenan finding answers to such queries. Forman not only investigated conditions in the capital, he also traveled behind enemy lines with the Eighth Route Army in the Shansi-Suiyuan Anti-Japanese Base. On nearly every count, Stein and Forman found little evidence to support KMT allegations.

Contrary to what they had been led to expect, neither Stein nor Forman found the slightest trace of opium cultivation in the Border Regions. As to Communist military inactivity, Forman personally witnessed separate guerrilla assaults on Fenyang and Lofan. Although Stein never ventured into the front areas, he was inclined to accept Communist battle statistics and claims. Both correspondents em-

[21] Stein, *The Challenge of Red China,* pp. 30, 38; Forman, *Report from Red China,* p. 4.

[22] Forman, *Report from Red China,* p. 2. At times, KMT propaganda went to absurd extremes. Hugh Deane, a correspondent for the *Christian Science Monitor,* recounted a story, carried in the Nationalist-controlled press in 1941, which suggested that Mao Tse-tung smoked $1,000 worth of Moscow-imported cigars a month and had deflowered a virgin in each village the Red Army passed through on the Long March. See Hugh Deane, "Political Reaction in Kuomintang China," *Amerasia,* V (July 1941), 212.

phatically rejected the KMT's imputations of Red totalitarianism. Forman characterized the Border regime's political
system as "representative democracy," and Stein concluded
that the CCP had sponsored the development of "genuine
local self-government." On the count of anti-Nationalist agi-
tation, however, they did find substantiating evidence. Only
a few propaganda placards were visible to the naked eye, but
Communist officials verbally peppered the KMT with
charges of fascism and banditry.[23] Nevertheless, the general
impressions which Forman and Stein derived from their observations of Communist China were contrary to the dreary
picture projected by Chinese Nationalists.

Five months in the Border Regions left no doubt in Forman's mind that KMT propaganda was untrue. Feeling
strongly that something should be done, while still in Yenan
Forman publicly vowed to speak out to "the whole
world." [24] Once back in Chungking, Forman found the Ministry of Information to be uncooperative. In a letter to General Patrick J. Hurley, President Roosevelt's special envoy to
China, Forman complained of being "hogtied and gagged"
by the Chinese censorship. Anticipating that the President's
agent would be returning to Washington soon, Forman
asked Hurley's permission to go along on the same flight.
Forman wanted, he explained, to tell the "folks back home"
of what the Communists had accomplished.[25] Since Hurley
stayed on in Chungking to replace Clarence E. Gauss as
United States Ambassador to China, Forman had to find another means of transportation. Nonetheless, by 1945 the impatient reporter was back in America.

Forman wasted little time in making his views known.
He told the American people that the Communists had

[23] Forman, *Report from Red China*, pp. 10, 56, 101, 130, 168, 184,
230–238; Stein, *The Challenge of Red China*, pp. 75, 125–127, 247,
335.
[24] Fisher to Hurley, October 28, 1944.
[25] Forman, Chungking, October 27, 1944, to Hurley, Hurley papers.

"achieved a miracle in China—the respect and cooperation of the people." [26] Forman's account of that miracle, *Report from Red China*, is saturated with such comments, but the importance of the book goes far beyond its highly favorable appraisal of the Chinese Communist movement. Like Edgar Snow's principal volume, *Report from Red China* had, as one reviewer exclaimed, broken an "ironclad blockade" of several years' duration.[27] Forman had been the first member of the Press Party to get his story into print, and contemporaries were quick to hail it as an authoritative eyewitness testimonial.[28]

The fervor with which *Report from Red China* was received in the general press was out of proportion to the book's merits. As far as journalistic productions are concerned, this hastily written volume is neither unusual nor particularly incisive. More importantly, in some respects *Report from Red China* is misleading. Among both Chinese and Western journalists, Forman had a reputation for sensationalism and factual carelessness. Michael Lindsay, who helped the Press Party in Yenan, thought that Forman had paid little attention to getting the facts straight and had filed dispatches containing "stupid inaccuracies." [29]

Some of the statements in *Report from Red China* seem to

[26] Forman, *Report from Red China*, p. 213.

[27] Maxwell S. Stewart, "The Chinese Communists," *Nation*, CLX (March 24, 1945), 338.

[28] For the laudatory comments of contemporary reviewers see Owen Lattimore, "Report from Red China," *Atlantic Monthly*, CLXXV (April 1945), 133; Agnes Smedley, "Red China in the News," *New Republic*, CXII (March 12, 1945), 363–364; Edgar Snow, "The Kuomintang and the Question of Chinese Communism," *New York Times Book Review*, March 11, 1945, 3, 20; Richard Watts, Jr., "Inner War," *Saturday Review of Literature*, XXVIII (March 10, 1945), 9–10, 31.

[29] U.S. Senate, *Morgenthau Diary: China*, II, p. 1330. See also Tong, *Dateline—China*, p. 245, and the testimony of John S. Service in U.S. Senate, *State Department Employee Loyalty Investigation, Hearings* (Part 2), p. 2011. In an interview with the author on January 11, 1966, Philip Jaffe assessed Forman as an unreliable reporter.

bear out Lindsay's observations. For example, Forman depicts Mao Tse-tung as a revisionist who had disavowed communism. He quotes Mao as having no plan to establish the dictatorship of the proletariat and even suggests that Chou En-lai was a true believer whose ideas were at odds with those of the CCP leader.[30] These amazing revelations are not only at variance with the findings of the other members of the Press Party, they also have no parallel in the entire corpus of firsthand analyses of the Chinese Communist movement to 1945. Yet, Forman's random observations were not without value. At the very least, *Report from Red China* informed the outside world that five years of military and news blockade had failed to lessen the appeal of the Eighth Route Army.

In terms of acclaim, the reviews of Stein's volume rivaled those of Forman's work. Nathaniel Peffer, for example, called *The Challenge of Red China* "the most comprehensive account to date of one of the most interesting spots on the globe." [31] Stein's book was more deserving of such comments than Forman's. While *The Challenge of Red China* is too rambling and lacks artistry, Stein provides the reader with much factual data. He minimizes himself and approaches the subject in a methodical, empirical manner. Stein was, a Foreign Service officer testified, a person of "Germanic thoroughness" and "by far the most assiduous of the correspondents." [32] In contrast to Forman, moreover, Stein was not uncritical. *The Challenge of Red China* is a more substantial and less impressionistic firsthand account

[30] Forman, *Report from Red China*, pp. 179–180.

[31] Nathaniel Peffer, "Contrasting Yenan and Chungking," *New York Times Book Review*, October 28, 1945, 4. For other enthusiastic reviews see Andrew Roth, "Yenan," *Nation*, CLXI (November 24, 1945), 556; Watts, "Spotlight on the Far East," *New Republic*, CXIII (December 24, 1945), 874.

[32] U.S. Senate, *State Department Employee Loyalty Investigation, Hearings* (Part 2), p. 2073, testimony of John S. Service.

than *Report from Red China.* Nevertheless, Stein's major conclusion was similar to that of Forman. Both men felt that they had seen something almost too good to be true: a new, a better China.

Father Cormac Shanahan, who had come to China as a missionary in 1926, disagreed with Forman and Stein. This Roman Catholic priest's views occupy a special niche in the Western literature on the Chinese Communist movement. Shanahan's encounter with the CCP was anything but persuading. As correspondent for the *Sign* and the *Catholic Monthly* and editor of the *China Correspondent,* his press credentials were in order. Shanahan, however, did not go to the Border Regions simply to gain information about China's Communists. He also hoped to ascertain the status of Catholic communicants and to obtain permission to reopen the Catholic missions situated in Communist territory. Although he succeeded in negotiating an accord with the Communist officials, Chou En-lai refused to ratify the agreement. Shanahan was not particularly happy about this turn of events. His writings also may have been influenced by the fact that the Chinese government subsidized the *China Correspondent.* Perhaps most important was Shanahan's fundamental anticommunism. He admitted to a predisposition against communism as a priest of the Catholic Church.[33]

The only kind remark which Shanahan made in public about Chinese Communists was that they had "fighting spirit." He quickly added, however, that gangsters also possessed a martial *élan.* Shanahan contended that the Reds had

[33] *Foreign Relations of the United States, 1944: China,* p. 482; Cormac Shanahan, "The Challenge of Gunther Stein," *China Monthly,* VII (February 1946), 65. Shanahan's article is a hostile review of Stein's *The Challenge of Red China.* In his book, Stein stated that Shanahan had obtained the desired permission. See Stein, *The Challenge of Red China,* p. 239. According to Ambassador Gauss, Shanahan was replaced as editor of the *China Correspondent* because of his "violent antipathy to the Chinese Communists." See U.S. Senate, *The Amerasia Papers,* I, pp. 497–498.

been under orders since 1939 to refrain from engaging the Japanese. According to him, the KMT was shouldering the military burden in China, not the CCP. Shanahan asserted that the Communists would not even trust the peasants with guns but allowed them to carry only "short spears." This was understandable, he wrote, as the masses dreaded their Communist masters "even as they hate the Japs." The Shen-Kan-Ning was a police state. Its inhabitants were strictly regimented and kept in line by a massive spy system. Arrests were made *"on mere suspicion,"* and individuals were *"held without court trial until they confess."* Shanahan certainly found no evidence of democracy in Yenan. Government officials were hand picked, policies were dictated by the party, and voting was a "mere formality." In Shanahan's estimation, the Communists were usurpers maintaining their position by an indiscriminate abuse of power. He succinctly described the Communist formula for political ascendancy. The Reds, he said, gained leadership over the people by assassinating local magistrates and driving off KMT army remnants. As Shanahan saw it, the proper solution to the Communist problem was the CCP's submission to Chiang Kai-shek. As for Red recalcitrance toward Chungking, Shanahan judged this to be a "small affair." Without outside assistance, the CCP could not interfere seriously with the progress China was "bound to make after the war." [34]

Compared with the observations of such journalists as Gunther Stein and Harrison Forman, it seems that Shanahan was describing another planet. The marked divergence of his views from those of other Occidentals who had face-to-face encounters with Chinese Communists is graphically illustrated by his appraisal of their writings. Shanahan dismissed Stein's *The Challenge of Red China* as the work of a "crusader and special pleader for the Chinese Communists." [35]

[34] Shanahan, "China's Communist Puzzle," *China Monthly*, VI (June 1945), 9–12. The underscoring is Shanahan's.
[35] Shanahan, "The Challenge of Gunther Stein," 65.

He also downgraded the ideas of Forman, Owen Lattimore, and Edgar Snow and insinuated that they were Communist propagandists.[36] In private, Shanahan was less severe. While still maintaining that the Chinese Reds were Communist totalitarians, he did not hesitate to praise them for specific achievements. He was impressed favorably by the Eighth Route Army and by the agricultural and industrial programs of the Yenan regime.[37]

In October 1944, Gunther Stein left Yenan for Chungking in the company of Brooks Atkinson.[38] Atkinson had been told lurid stories about the "depraved villanies" of Chinese Communists in Chungking. He was prepared for just about anything when he first set foot on Red soil. Although he spent only a fortnight in Yenan, Atkinson saw enough to be convinced of the absurdity of KMT propaganda. Atkinson jested that he was astonished to find that Chinese Communists "had two eyes, two ears, two arms and two legs, like most human beings." They did not appear to be any more ferocious "than ordinary persons; no more evil was written on their faces." In fact, the people inhabiting the Border Regions seemed to be happier and healthier than those in other sections of China.[39] As with Stein and Forman, Atkinson had been preconditioned by Nationalist allegations to look for the nefarious where it apparently did not exist.

In the fall of 1944 another American correspondent flew from Chungking to Yenan. Theodore H. White of *Time-*

[36] Shanahan, "False Solution in Asia," *China Monthly*, VI (December 1945), 22–24, 26. This book review is primarily devoted to a critique of Lattimore's "insidious" *Solution in Asia* (Boston, 1945).

[37] *Foreign Relations of the United States, 1944: China*, p. 483. See also U.S. Senate, *The Amerasia Papers*, I, pp. 667–672.

[38] Stein, *The Challenge of Red China*, p. 460.

[39] Brooks Atkinson, "Yenan Is Well Fed With Big Harvest," *New York Times*, September 25, 1944, 9. See also Atkinson's delightful vignette on everyday life in Yenan: "Yenan, A Chinese Wonderland on 3 Kinds of Time, Has One Clock," *New York Times*, October 6, 1944, 12.

Life spent only a few weeks in the Communist capital trying to obtain firsthand knowledge of the CCP. Like those who had preceded him, White was curious to discover whether the KMT's version of Communist behavior squared with the facts. It did not. He soon discarded the thesis that the Red Army was not fighting the Japanese. This contention was, he wrote, "fantastically incorrect." Furthermore, White could unearth no evidence of a totalitarian apparatus.[40] The impressions he carried away from his brief sojourn in the Shen-Kan-Ning bore little relationship to the KMT's hostile stereotypes. White concluded that the Communist government had a solid base of mass support, that its policies were reformist in nature, and that its claims of employing democratic methods were "unquestionably true."[41]

As White's appraisal suggests, Nationalist propaganda was counterproductive. Indeed, the entire range of Chungking's press policies, some of which Ambassador Gauss thought represented "near-stupidity," worked to the advantage of China's Communists.[42] Almost by default, Chinese Nationalists placed Chinese Communists in the enviable position of championing freedom of the press. The CCP took full advantage of the opportunity presented. No dispatch was ever tampered with by a Communist official. Reporters, and even some Foreign Service officers, made a point of the fact that there was no censorship whatever in Yenan.[43] A primary factor in the KMT's poor foreign press, as Tong admitted, was the combination of Communist skill and Nationalist blunders in handling the problems of censorship and propaganda.[44] Nonpartisan observers, Theodore White wrote in

[40] Theodore H. White and Annalee Jacoby, *Thunder Out of China* (New York, 1946), pp. 210, 232.

[41] White, "Inside Red China," *Life*, XVII (December 18, 1944), 39–40, 46.

[42] *Foreign Relations of the United States, 1944: China*, p. 406.

[43] For example, see White and Jacoby, *Thunder Out of China*, p. 233, and *Foreign Relations of the United States, 1944: China*, p. 520.

[44] Tong, *Dateline—China*, p. 146.

an apologetic post-mortem, naturally inclined to favor the side which invited freedom of investigation and movement.[45]

Chinese Nationalists had hoped that their liberality in authorizing the Press Party would have a good-will effect.[46] This illusion was shattered as soon as the dispatches filed from Yenan had been digested in the Ministry of Information. The result was, as Tong recalled, "an extremely bad reaction." Convinced that retracting the ban on travel had been an error, Chungking reimposed its news blockade of the Shen-Kan-Ning in October 1944. Even Tong favored reviving the prohibition of visits to Yenan. It was far better, he explained, to refuse permission outright than to allow reporters to go to the Communist areas "and then apply wholesale censorship to their dispatches." [47]

As Tong's comment suggests, the Chinese government had added insult to injury by responding in character to the deluge of dispatches weighted in favor of the CCP. The vice-minister was directed to deal with the problem more ruthlessly than he personally thought necessary.[48] Reports filed from Yenan were subjected to prolonged delays before clearance and censored mercilessly. Most of the dispatches were reduced to a few innocuous generalizations. So thorough were the Chinese censors that the emasculated reports of the Press Party have little value to the present-day scholar as sources of information on the Chinese Communist movement.

Western correspondents also responded in character. They objected bitterly to the renewed news blackout.[49] When appeals to freedom of the press went unheeded by the Chinese

[45] White and Jacoby, *Thunder Out of China* (New York, 1961), p. 213n.

[46] Tong, *Dateline—China,* p. 248.

[47] *Ibid.,* pp. 247–248.

[48] *Ibid.,* p. 247.

[49] "Correspondents Complain to Chinese on Censorship," *New York Times,* October 12, 1944, 16.

government, the frustrated journalists began leaving Chungking for places where they could express their views freely. After having two of four dispatches filed between September 30 and October 9 killed in toto by the Ministry of Information, Brooks Atkinson returned to the United States. As Harrison Forman had before him, Atkinson left China for the specific purpose of circumventing the Nationalist censorship.[50] It became a "regular routine," Tong observed, for journalists to go to the United States and vent their pent-up anger in books and articles critical of the KMT.[51] Many Western reporters simply saw no alternative to flight. By 1945 the Central government had become unbending in its determination to control the press.

The depth of Chungking's resolve to still the voices of dissent can be seen in the Isaacs case. Harold R. Isaacs of *Newsweek* magazine was refused re-entry into China for writing articles unfavorable to the Nationalist government.[52] After a year in the China-Burma-India Theater, Isaacs had returned to the United States and published articles critical of the KMT. His contribution to the April 23, 1945, issue of *Newsweek* was particularly searing. Isaacs characterized the Central government as a "semi-medieval tyranny" alienated from the Chinese people and quickly losing its grip on reality. Chinese Communists, by contrast, had gained mass support and even allowed a small degree of self-government.[53]

Upon learning that Isaacs was planning to return to Chungking, T. V. Soong instructed the Chinese Embassy in Washington to refuse a visa. Soong acted in the belief that

[50] U.S. Senate, *State Department Employee Loyalty Investigation, Hearings* (Part 2), p. 2420. Atkinson gave his testimony on June 8, 1950. See also Tong, *Dateline—China*, pp. 247–248.

[51] Tong, *Dateline—China*, pp. 218–219.

[52] Tillman Durdin, "Second U.S. Writer Barred by Chinese," *New York Times*, July 23, 1945, 3.

[53] Harold Isaacs, "China: Today's Bitter Fiasco, Tomorrow's Sure Battleground and a Problem That Must Be Solved Before World Peace Is Won," *Newsweek*, XXV (April 23, 1945), 60–61.

Isaacs was responsibile for articles in *Newsweek* critical of the KMT.[54] Fearing that the Isaacs case would have an adverse impact on public opinion in America, "where freedom of press is considered important," the Department of State instructed Ambassador Patrick J. Hurley to discuss the matter with the Chinese authorities. Hurley was to stress the "broad implications" of the Chinese action.[55] In a memorandum of August 8, 1945, K. C. Wu, the acting minister of foreign affairs, blandly maintained that freedom of the press was not at issue. Rather, Wu contended, Isaacs had conspired to "undermine the authority" of the Chinese government during his stay in China.[56] In a plainly worded dispatch, the Secretary of State told Hurley to ask for specific evidence documenting the serious charge that had been made. Arguing that the time was not opportune, Hurley declined to press the matter.[57]

Ambassador Hurley had never shown much enthusiasm for intervening in behalf of American correspondents. In part, this may have been because he had at his disposal reports from United States military attachés accusing journalists like Isaacs and White of being "professional" Communists. From the same source, Hurley was aware that foreign correspondents made no secret of their low opinion of his abilities.[58] Since Hurley was nearly as sensitive to criticism as Chiang Kai-shek, this information probably did not further his zeal for upholding freedom of the press.

[54] C. C. Chien, Chungking, May 7, 1945, to Hurley, Hurley papers. Chien was an official in the Ministry of Economic Affairs.

[55] *Foreign Relations of the United States: Diplomatic Papers, 1945. The Far East and China* (Washington, D.C., 1969), p. 1476.

[56] *Ibid.*, pp. 1479–1480.

[57] *Ibid.*, pp. 1481–1482.

[58] Captain Henry T. Jarrell, Chungking, August 1, 1945, memoranda for the Ambassador, Hurley papers. In later years, Hurley accused Theodore H. White and Edgar Snow of being pro-Communist liars. See Hurley, June 11, 1947, to Ben S. Hibbs, and Hurley, February 29, 1948, to Hollington K. Tong, Hurley papers.

As early as November 1944, Hurley had concluded that correspondents like Theodore White were an impediment to the successful implementation of American foreign policy. Hurley took the position that comments unfavorable to our Chinese ally endangered the objective of supporting the government of Chiang Kai-shek.[59] In a letter to Congressman Joseph W. Martin, Jr., the Ambassador implied that press reports hostile to the KMT were "false propaganda." In 1945, feeling strongly that people in the United States should know the "truth about China," Hurley concocted a fantastic scheme to blunt American press criticism.[60] On August 1, he requested permission to invite Henry Luce to come to Chungking. This proposal had the approval of General Albert C. Wedemeyer, T. V. Soong, and Chiang Kai-shek. The consensus was that Luce's "constructive" attitude would provide a healthy contrast to the carping of the *Time-Life* war correspondents in China. The Secretary of State was less than enthusiastic about Hurley's idea. James F. Byrnes did not think that it would be appropriate for an official of the United States government to sponsor an American publisher's visit to a foreign country. The Department of State, the Secretary warned, did not want to be charged with favoritism.[61]

Hurley professed a dedication to the principle of freedom of the press and an opposition to censorship, "except on grounds of military necessity." [62] The Ambassador also claimed that there was "considerable freedom of speech and press" in Nationalist China. After all, he reasoned, did not

[59] *Foreign Relations of the United States, 1944: China*, pp. 673–674; Ellis O. Briggs, Chungking, June 15, 1945, memorandum of a conversation, Hurley papers. See also *Foreign Relations of the United States, 1945: The Far East and China*, pp. 109–110.

[60] Hurley, Chungking, July 2, 1945, to Joseph W. Martin, Jr., Hurley papers.

[61] *Foreign Relations of the United States, 1945: The Far East and China*, pp. 142–143, 147–148.

[62] *Ibid.*, p. 116.

the Chinese government permit the Communists to publish a newspaper in Chungking? [63] The assertion that the KMT allowed a free press scarcely requires refutation. Even the Chinese vice-minister of information did not try to defend such an untenable proposition. So meticulous was Chinese control of the press that criticisms of Ambassador Hurley were not allowed.[64]

Two *Time-Life* correspondents once accused Hurley of having an enormous fear of the press.[65] While the charge may be extreme, it is clear that the Ambassador strongly disliked public criticism either of himself or of the Chinese government. In practical terms, this meant that American reporters lacked a forceful advocate of their interests in the United States Embassy at Chungking. It is small wonder that after men like Harold Isaacs had spoken their minds, they found the door to China closed. Having learned its lesson, the Chinese government was determined to control the press. In this resolve, Chinese Nationalists had the tacit cooperation of the leading representative of the United States government in China. At a press conference on April 28, 1945, Hurley told the assembled newsmen that he submitted himself completely to censorship by both the American military and the Chinese.[66] In the light of this attitude, it is only mildly surprising that the Department of State found it necessary to remind Ambassador Hurley that his country was a proponent of freedom of the press.[67]

The trips of White and Atkinson represented the termination of Western reportorial encounters with Chinese Communists prior to the end of the Second World War. Their

[63] *Ibid.*, p. 427.
[64] White and Jacoby, *Thunder Out of China* (New York, 1946), p. 249.
[65] *Ibid.*
[66] *Foreign Relations of the United States, 1945: The Far East and China*, p. 378.
[67] *Ibid.*, p. 1478.

applications to visit Yenan had been authorized in September 1944, but in October of the same year similar applications requested by a group of foreign correspondents were denied.[68] By October, the emasculated pro-Yenan reports of the Press Party to the Northwest had begun to appear in the American press and the Central government had determined to prevent any further contacts with Chinese Communists. This time Chungking did not waver in its resolve. As late as August 9, 1945, as the war drew to a close, foreign journalists were asking General Wedemeyer to use his good offices to get the restrictions lifted on access to the Communist areas.[69]

From 1939 to 1944, the Chinese government had held Western correspondents on a short leash. Their travel requests were pigeonholed, their dispatches were censored. A few reports, by such fortuitous visitors to the Border Regions as Michael Lindsay, had managed to seep through the KMT's news blackout. These reports, however, were hardly more than flickering candles in the midst of a great darkness. For five years Red China had been an "unfathomable mystery" to most journalists.[70] The news blockade was not truly breached until the Nationalists authorized the Press Party to the Northwest. In a sense, the trip of the Press Party was an event comparable to Edgar Snow's journey of 1936. Both of these penetrations of the blockade marked the end to years of enforced silence and factual ignorance on the subject of Chinese communism. The writings of foreign correspondents in 1944–1945 offered something that had been missing for far too long, authoritative information on the CCP.

[68] Tong, *Dateline—China,* p. 247; Walter G. Rundel, Chungking, October 27, 1944, to Major Albert W. Bloom, and Bloom, Chungking, October 28, 1944, to Hurley, Hurley papers. The correspondents desiring permission to go to Yenan were Rundel of the United Press, Clyde Farnsworth of the Associated Press, Fritz Opper of the American Broadcasting Company, and Harold Isaacs of *Newsweek* magazine.

[69] Stenographic transcript of a press conference held by General Wedemeyer, Chungking, August 10, 1945, Hurley papers.

[70] Atkinson, "Critic at Large," 40.

The renewal of the news blockade in the fall of 1944 merely compounded the damage already done by the press policies of the Chinese government, Chungking's temporary relaxation of control over the press had come too late, had been implemented too reluctantly, and had been withdrawn too soon. A repentant vice-minister rued the whole affair as it had resulted in "distinct harm to China's name abroad." [71] The vice-minister might have added that the main beneficiary of Chungking's short-lived appeasement of Western journalists was the CCP.

[71] Tong, *Dateline—China*, p. 248.

★ PART III

IMAGE AND REALITY:
THE CHINESE COMMUNISTS
IN WESTERN LITERATURE

[11]

Superior Human Beings

A striking feature of the Western literature on Chinese communism is its uniformity. The reports made by Americans and Europeans who traveled in the Communist areas between 1937 and 1945 are remarkably similar in tone and content. So much so, in fact, that the literary representation of the Chinese Communist movement can be dealt with topically, with minimal attention to chronology and changes over the course of time.

The foreigners who investigated the Border Regions shared an interest in gaining insight into six aspects of the Chinese Communist movement. They were concerned about the CCP's leadership, military apparatus, domestic program, relationship to the Kuomintang, connections with the Soviet Union, and revolutionary commitment. Although individuals phrased their inquiries in a variety of ways, their questions can be summarized as follows. What kind of men were the leaders of the CCP? What accounted for the Red Army's remarkable record of tenacity and survival? How did the Communist regimes govern the peasant masses living under their rule? What was the nature of the CCP's commitment to the united front with the KMT? Were Chinese Communists tools of Moscow? Were they bona fide Marxists? Many of these queries overlapped and were interconnected with one another. Most of them were formulated with the KMT's negative and denunciatory propaganda in mind. They were asked with subtle variations, at different times, and by heterogeneous individuals. Nevertheless, the answers given were analogous to the extent that they eventuated in a widely shared imagery of the Chinese Communist movement.

The Communist leaders made a lasting impression on their Western guests. While nearly every CCP official of any prominence became the object of one or another reporter's curiosity, Mao Tse-tung and Chu Teh were the center of attraction. As T. A. Bisson wrote, Mao was "overwhelmingly impressive" and Chu "almost equally impressive." [1] Mao was a correspondent's delight, casual in his manner, generous with his time, and masterful in his conversation. This chain-smoking Hunanese normally scheduled his interviews, which were conducted in the rustic atmosphere of a loess cave, for late in the evening. They continued until two or three in the morning, when a blear-eyed but satiated newsman would take leave of his unwearied host. While Chu Teh's style was considerably different from Mao's, his demeanor was equally arresting. This soft-spoken and retiring warrior had less time to spend away from his responsibilities as commander-in-chief of the Red Army, but it was never too difficult to arrange a meeting with him. Chu's trademark was an engaging smile, a friendly handshake, and the open-faced simplicity of an undevious man. He might drop in at any time bearing such gifts as a bag of peanuts and self-effacingly inquire whether the foreign guest might want to ask him some questions. Such an approach seldom failed to warm the heart of even the most hardened journalist.

Evans F. Carlson came to love Chu Teh "as he loved no other man except his father." [2] The American marine could scarcely find words adequate to express his admiration for

[1] T. A. Bisson, Peiping, July 4, 1937, mimeographed letter to Raymond Leslie Buell, 893.00/14154, Department of State files.

[2] Michael Blankfort, *The Big Yankee: The Life of Carlson of the Raiders* (Boston, 1947), p. 199.

the Red general. Chu Teh possessed, in Carlson's estimation, "the kindliness of a Robert E. Lee, the humility of an Abraham Lincoln, and the tenacity of a U. S. Grant." [3] Agnes Smedley rivaled Carlson in her adulation of the Communist commander-in-chief. She preferred him to all others and composed a biography extolling his virtues. [4] Chu Teh struck Helen Snow as the most nonmilitary soldier she had ever encountered. He was, according to her, benevolent, soft-spoken, and unaffectedly democratic in his mannerisms. Above all, she wrote, Chu was "modest, even to the point of self-effacement." [5] Harrison Forman thought that the "roly-poly" Communist general resembled "a fatherly old cowpuncher." [6] Anna Louise Strong visualized Chu as "a kindly, simple, farmer-like person." [7] While the commandant of the Red Army impressed Bertram as a person of "iron resolution," this unassuming warrior hardly seemed to be the material from which revolutionaries are made. Bertram described Chu as an "ugly little man with a gentle manner and disarming smile." [8]

Only the Bands had second thoughts about General Chu. They depicted him as a pock-marked bulldog of a man who resembled a "hard-boiled old bandit." Nevertheless, they added, he behaved like a gentleman. [9] Chu Teh certainly did not impress other foreigners as being a brigand or a hard-

[3] Evans Fordyce Carlson, *Twin Stars of China: A Behind-the-Scenes Story of China's Valiant Struggle for Existence by a U.S. Marine Who Lived and Moved with the People* (New York, 1940), p. 66.

[4] Agnes Smedley, *The Great Road: The Life and Times of Chu Teh* (New York, 1956), *passim.*

[5] Nym Wales [Helen Foster Snow], *Inside Red China* (Garden City, New York, 1939), p. 110.

[6] Harrison Forman, *Report from Red China* (New York, 1945), p. 97.

[7] Anna Louise Strong, *One-Fifth of Mankind* (New York, 1938), p. 127.

[8] James Bertram, *Unconquered: Journal of a Year's Adventures among the Fighting Peasants of North China* (New York, 1939), p. 160.

[9] Claire and William Band, *Dragon Fangs: Two Years with Chinese Guerrillas* (London, 1947), p. 242.

ened Bolshevik. As Ralph Lapwood observed, Chu "was entirely different from one's picture of a ruthless rebel leader." [10] Indeed, this most unlikely soldier projected an almost pastoral image.

The charismatic force of Mao Tse-tung is truly astonishing. Through the writings of Americans and Europeans, Mao became a legend in his own time. To Edgar Snow, Mao was the prophet in a cave. Despite Mao's apparent nonchalance, Snow was captivated by the imaginative Communist leader's "native shrewdness." Snow felt a "certain force of destiny . . . a kind of solid elemental vitality." [11] Mao was, moreover, as Snow and others observed, "good company." [12] Helen Snow emerged from Mao's darkened cavern with memories of an "Olympian figure" who made pronouncements like a "Delphian oracle." [13] Evans F. Carlson told Haldore Hanson that Mao Tse-tung was the "most selfless man" he had ever encountered, "a social dreamer, a genius living fifty years ahead of his time." [14] Not long after his conversation with Carlson, Hanson too reached Yenan and held an interview with Mao. Like Carlson, Hanson concluded that he was an unpretentious, "completely selfless man." Hanson suggested that, next to Stalin, Mao Tse-tung was "the most powerful Marxian thinker and leader in world politics." [15] In a similar vein, James Bertram dubbed him the "Chinese Lenin," describing him as having "incomparably the coolest and most balanced mind" in China. Bertram was aware that he had been in the presence of "an immense intellectual force, a brain moving easily and surely along orderly lines of

[10] Ralph and Nancy Lapwood, *Through the Chinese Revolution* (London, 1954), p. 31.

[11] Edgar Snow, *Red Star over China* (New York, 1961), pp. 71, 74.

[12] Snow, *Journey to the Beginning* (New York, 1958), p. 167.

[13] Wales, *Inside Red China,* p. 277.

[14] Haldore Hanson, *"Humane Endeavour": The Story of the China War* (New York and Toronto, 1939), pp. 170–171.

[15] *Ibid.,* pp. 303–305.

thought." The only vices which the New Zealander could find in the Chinese Lenin were his inordinate love of red peppers and his partiality for tobacco.[16]

On a more prosaic level, Gunther Stein characterized Mao as a "broad, full-blooded peasant-intellectual in baggy pants." [17] Joy Homer depicted the chairman of the CCP as a rather humorous and "boyish looking" individual. She recognized, however, that his mind was as "sharp and flexible as steel." [18] The Chinese Lenin's "exotic personality" fascinated Earl H. Leaf. He was attracted by Mao's gentle manner, laughing eyes, sense of humor, directness of speech, and democratic behavior. "Far from being a fanatic on the subject of communism, Mao will sit up with anyone far into the night discussing any subject from lipstick to Leninism and displaying a remarkable knowledge of world and current events." [19] When Ilona Ralf Sues met the Red leader she felt that she had caught "a fleeting glimpse of eternity." She became almost mystical about Mao. He was, she wrote, "the Chinese nation incarnate," a man who was at once peasant, philosopher, poet, statesman, and revolutionary. Moreover, she rhapsodized, he possessed "the most wonderful face I have ever seen." [20]

One of the few people to record an unfavorable impression of Mao Tse-tung was, strangely enough, Agnes Smedley. When she first met the Chinese Lenin, she was "repelled by the feminine in him." She described his presence as "tall" and "forbidding," his face as "dark" and "inscrutable," his hands and mouth as "feminine." "Whatever else he might

[16] Bertram, *Unconquered*, pp. 106–108.

[17] Gunther Stein, *The Challenge of Red China* (New York and London, 1945), p. 4.

[18] Joy Homer, *Dawn Watch in China* (Boston, 1941), p. 235.

[19] Earl H. Leaf, "Mao Tse-tung's Life Is Thrilling, Hectic Story; Has Become Almost Legend to Chinese During 10 Years," *North China Star*, June 5, 1937, 1, 8.

[20] Ilona Ralf Sues, *Shark's Fins and Millet* (Boston, 1944), pp. 283–284.

be," she concluded, "he was an aesthete." [21] But Agnes Smedley's was a minority view. To most foreign observers, Mao Tse-tung was not, as his detractors alleged, effeminate, fanatical, or extremist. Rather, Mao was the Voltaire of the Chinese revolution, a superior being of penetrating intelligence and monumental genius. He was, as Victor Keen wrote, "the Chinese Stalin"—an impressive leader who could compose with equal facility bluntly phrased political manifestoes or classical Chinese essays.[22]

While it would be cumbersome to detail the reaction to all of the other Communist luminaries, it is possible to sketch the American response to several of their number who projected fairly distinct images. Chou En-lai was the perfect diplomat, suave in his manner and adroit in dealing with people. Thus, for example, Freda Utley remembered Chou as a charming, intelligent, "most persuasive" human being who probably "made more converts to the Chinese Communist cause than any other man living." [23] General P'eng Teh-huai was the Puritan of the Eighth Route Army, moral, spartan, and competent. Helen Snow categorized P'eng as "quite a typical Cromwellian Ironsides type." [24] General Ho Lung was the Robin Hood of the Red Army, a blustering individual who always lived up to his colorful reputation. He challenged Haldore Hanson to a horse race, with the horse as the prize. This engaging Communist was, Hanson reflected, "a comical braggart, a living picture of Rhett Butler from the pages of *Gone with the Wind,* a great storyteller, an ardent cigar smoker, and above all, a lover of

[21] Smedley, *Battle Hymn of China* (New York, 1943), pp. 168–169.

[22] Victor Keen, "Chinese Soviet's Youthful Army a Merger of Private Battalions," *New York Herald Tribune,* June 6, 1937, II, 5.

[23] Freda Utley, *The China Story* (Chicago, 1951), p. 105. See also Smedley, *Battle Hymn of China,* p. 173.

[24] Wales, *My Yenan Notebooks* (Madison, Connecticut, 1961), p. 6. See also *Inside Red China,* pp. 30–31.

horses." [25] Lin Piao, the hero of P'inghsingkuan Pass, was viewed as the embodiment of military virtue, of imaginativeness and daring. Edgar Snow called General Lin "the most talented young officer" serving under Chu Teh.[26] Finally, the leading military officer in the Chin-Ch'a-Chi, General Nieh Jung-chen, was the refined professional soldier. Hanson designated this cultured and able warrior "the best dressed man in the Eighth Route Army." [27]

What kind of men, then, were the leaders of the CCP? Those who met them were impressed by their dynamism, intelligence, dedication, and cordiality. But perhaps the more important question is what kind of people they were not. Only Ho Lung bore a resemblance to the bandit stereotype, and most foreigners found it difficult to take him too seriously. Above all, these Communists were not hewn from the same rock. They did not project the classic Leninist image of a monolithic, conspiratorial, secretive band of ruthless revolutionaries. They did not, by any stretch of the imagination, resemble the hard-core conspirators delineated in Lenin's *What Is to Be Done?* These Chinese Communists, to paraphrase Brooks Atkinson, seemed like human beings, and some of them superior types at that!

In retrospect, it seems that firsthand observers underestimated the solidarity and ruthlessness of Chinese Communists in general, and that they overestimated the originality of Mao Tse-tung in particular. While Mao was a great strategist and tactician of guerrilla warfare, as a creative dialectician his thought before 1945 did not even rise to the level of Stalin's arid theorizing. As Arthur A. Cohen wrote, Mao at-

[25] Hanson, *"Humane Endeavour,"* p. 285.
[26] Snow, "The Man Alongside Mao: Deputy Lin Piao's Thoughts and Career," *New Republic,* CLV (December 3, 1966), 16. See also Smedley, *China Fights Back: An American Woman With the Eighth Route Army* (London, 1939), p. 118.
[27] Hanson, *"Humane Endeavour,"* p. 285.

tained no genuine distinction as a theory maker "unless 'theory' is taken to mean political stratagems rather than basic abstract principles." [28] It would, of course, be too one-sided to maintain that Mao Tse-tung made no contributions to Marxist philosophy. But Mao only began his study of dialectics in earnest in 1936, and it was not until the 1950's that he began to devise a distinctly Chinese variant of Marxism and to make original contributions to Leninism.[29] On the more positive side, firsthand reporters had perceived accurately the dynamism and dedication of the leaders of the Chinese Communist Party.

[28] Arthur A. Cohen, *The Communism of Mao Tse-tung* (Chicago and London, 1964), p. 189. See also Gabriel Kolko, *The Politics of War: The World and United States Foreign Policy, 1943–1945* (New York, 1968), pp. 240–242.

[29] Stuart R. Schram, *The Political Thought of Mao Tse-tung* (rev. and enlarged ed., New York, Washington, and London, 1969), pp. 87–88, 100–101, 134–138.

[12]

Prince Valiant
in Straw Sandals

The battle for P'inghsingkuan Pass in September 1937 was the first and only time during the Sino-Japanese War that the Eighth Route Army committed an entire division to formal combat. After the action at P'inghsingkuan, the Communists emphasized guerrilla warfare and the mobilization of the peasants. Aside from the "Hundred Regiments Offensive" of 1940 against the Japanese-controlled railway system in North China, the Red Army undertook no major military operations from 1938 to 1945. Like the KMT, the CCP carefully husbanded its divisions for the anticipated postwar struggle for power in China.[1]

In 1945, General Chu Teh implied that the Eighth Route Army had borne the brunt of the fighting against Japan. Chu boasted that his soldiers had with "unparalleled heroism" won "victory after victory," while Nationalist troops had followed a "defeatist strategy" of "mass retreat." In fact, as Samuel B. Griffith wrote, the three Chinese divisions under General Stilwell in Burma inflicted more damage on the Japanese in two years than the guerrilla operations of the Communists had in eight. As much a political as a military institution, the Red Army devoted more energy to

[1] Samuel B. Griffith, II, *The Chinese People's Liberation Army* (New York, Toronto, London, and Sydney, 1967), pp. 63–74.

indoctrinating Chinese peasants than it did to killing Japanese soldiers.[2]

Mesmerized by the novelty—or as Theodore H. White wrote, the "epic grandeur"—of massive guerrilla warfare, Western correspondents tended to accept the exaggerated military claims of the CCP.[3] They did not, however, underestimate the ideological and political role of the Chinese Red Army. Firsthand observers were nearly unanimous in drawing attention to the political character of the Communist military apparatus, and they were as impressed by the rank and file of the Eighth Route Army as they had been by the leaders of the CCP.

Not long after Edgar Snow had set foot on Communist territory, he came across a Red trooper. It was admiration at first glance. Snow took an immediate liking to this "honest-looking youth." Subsequent contacts did not alter the initial impression. These Communist warriors did not bear any resemblance to the semicomical soldiers of Chinese lore, those pawns in a chess game wherein the decisive moves were made by means of "silver bullets" or bribery. Rather, Snow contended, these were determined, principled, uncompromising fighters. Instead of being passive, the legions of the Red Army were the embodiment of positive dynamism. Snow observed that they sang constantly, were spontaneous in their behavior, and that their polished discipline "seemed almost entirely self-imposed." The typical Red paladin was about nineteen years old, literate, and, Snow claimed, a virgin. Snow noticed, moreover, that social and economic egalitarianism pervaded the ranks of this spirited military force. Informality characterized the relations between officers and men. There was little difference between the way a general and a private ate, dressed, or was quartered. Finally, the Eighth Route Army was, according to Snow, "the only politi-

[2] *Ibid.*, pp. 75–76.

[3] Theodore H. White and Annalee Jacoby, *Thunder Out of China* (New York, 1946), p. 201.

cally iron-clad army in China." The Red commandants, and presumably the servicemen under their command, were revolutionary veterans, or as Snow phrased it, "conscious fighters for Socialism." [4]

Subsequent foreign contacts with the Eighth Route Army served to underline and reinforce the favorable image projected by Edgar Snow in *Red Star over China*. Helen Foster Snow's characterization of the Communist military apparatus coincided closely with that of her husband. She was moved by the energy, idealism, "organic precision," and political awareness which permeated the ranks of the Eighth Route Army. Above all, she was impressed "with two special qualities which gave this army a unique personality—Youth and the Spirit of Sacrifice." To her these were truly "fighting Chinese on crusade, taking history in their stride." Finally, Mrs. Snow subscribed to her spouse's notion that the Red Army was a consciously revolutionary force, "under the absolute control of the [Chinese] Communist Party." [5] Agnes Smedley heaped praise on the "indestructible" warriors of the Red Army and agreed with Edgar Snow that they were "sexual ascetics." [6] Haldore Hanson's overriding conviction about the Communists was that the spirited legions of the Eighth Route Army were unsurpassed in their dedication to the struggle against the Japanese invader.[7] Harrison Forman observed that the principled Communist regulars were the best-fed, best-disciplined, and best-trained troops in China.[8]

---

[4] Edgar Snow, *Red Star over China* (New York, 1961), pp. 43, 63, 67, 278–279, 281–283, 306, 313.

[5] Nym Wales [Helen Foster Snow], *Inside Red China* (Garden City, New York, 1939), pp. 38–39, 62.

[6] Agnes Smedley, *China Fights Back: An American Woman with the Eighth Route Army* (London, 1939), pp. 19, 34.

[7] Haldore Hanson, *"Humane Endeavour": The Story of the China War* (New York and Toronto, 1939), p. 313.

[8] Harrison Forman, *Report from Red China* (New York, 1945), pp. 42, 225–226.

Victor Keen was struck by the youthfulness, "fanatic zeal," and spartan character of the Red Army.[9]

Even those writers who harbored a fundamental distrust of anything associated with Bolshevism felt compelled to say a good word about the Eighth Route Army. Theodore H. White and Annalee Jacoby belittled the Communist military establishment for its lack of technological and logistical sophistication and suggested that Communist battle statistics were "stained with overvivid propaganda." Somewhat reluctantly, they granted that there was one quality of the Eighth Route Army which "made it great—its fighting spirit." [10] In a similar vein, Joy Homer endeavored to minimize the Communist contribution to the overall war effort. She concluded, nonetheless, that the Communists were the "best-trained veterans" in China.[11] Although Cormac Shanahan scoffed at the notion that the Reds were playing a major role in the Sino-Japanese conflict, even he conceded that they had "fighting spirit." [12]

The glowing appraisals of American journalists can be discounted on the grounds that these people were only amateur military analysts. Evans F. Carlson's assessment of the Red Army is, therefore, of particular interest. Carlson thought that the mobile guerrilla bands of the Eighth Route Army were "the answer to the challenge of Japan's modern military machine." As a Marine, he was profoundly impressed by this unorthodox armed force and believed that the clue to its dynamism lay in what he ambiguously called "ethical indoctrination." This was a phrase loosely employed by Carlson to designate a lethal combination of observed

[9] Victor Keen, "Chinese Soviet's Youthful Army a Merger of Private Battalions," *New York Herald Tribune,* June 6, 1937, II, 6.

[10] White and Jacoby, *Thunder Out of China,* pp. 207, 210.

[11] Joy Homer, *Dawn Watch in China* (Boston, 1941), p. 226.

[12] Cormac Shanahan, "China's Communist Puzzle," *China Monthly,* VI (June 1945), 10.

traits: political consciousness, high moral standards, democratic camaraderie between officers and men, and individual motivation dynamically coordinated with group cooperation.[13]

Carlson detailed what he meant by his elusive terminology in a letter of December 24, 1937, to the White House. Emphasizing that the Red Army's military style was novel, he contended that the Communists had been able to inculcate "the spirit of willing service" in their troops by establishing the simple principle that an individual behaves in an upright manner "because it is the right thing to do." Secondly, Carlson reasoned that, since Communist officers confided in their men and freely discussed strategy with them, "a strong bond of understanding" had been built up between the leaders and the led. This combination of voluntary motivation and mutual understanding, a kind of dialogue between the collective mass and the individual soul, produced what Carlson judged to be a superior fighting machine endowed with a magnificent spirit.[14]

Carlson's enthusiasm for the Eighth Route Army, then, tended to confirm the images projected by American correspondents. Evans F. Carlson was so convinced of the viability of the Communist approach to the art of warfare that after being recommissioned in 1941 he patterned the famous Marine Raider battalions after the Chinese Red Army. The rallying cry of the Raiders was *"Gung Ho!"* an adaptation of the Chinese slogan for "working together." Like "ethical in-

[13] Evans Fordyce Carlson, *Twin Stars of China: A Behind-the-Scenes Story of China's Valiant Struggle for Existence by a U.S. Marine Who Lived and Moved with the People* (New York, 1940), pp. 110–111, 121. See also Carlson, *The Chinese Army: Its Organization and Military Efficiency* (New York, 1940), pp. 35–43, and Michael Blankfort, *The Big Yankee: The Life of Carlson of the Raiders* (Boston, 1947), pp. 23–25, 200–202.

[14] Carlson to Miss Marguerite Le Hand, December 24, 1937, Franklin D. Roosevelt papers.

doctrination," "*Gung Ho!*" implied cooperative comradeship and selfless personal dedication.[15] The Raider actions at Makin Island and Guadalcanal in 1942 would seem to indicate that Colonel Carlson was successful in applying the knowledge he had accumulated from his observations of the Eighth Route Army.[16]

While Western observers adduced many factors to explain the vitality of the Red Army, nearly all of them emphasized the phenomenon of its popularity with the peasant masses. Perhaps Harrison Forman best described this underlying source of Communist power when he observed that the Eighth Route Army had "achieved a miracle in China—the respect and cooperation of the people." [17] In the main, foreign correspondents attributed the Red Army's widespread popularity to its policy of treating civilians with respect and courtesy. Communist officers were not chary in articulating the rationale behind the exemplary behavior of their troops. As General P'eng Teh-huai told Edgar Snow: "But nothing, absolutely nothing is more important than this—that the Red Army is a people's army, and has grown because the

[15] Blankfort, *The Big Yankee*, pp. 23–25. One can get a pretty good idea of what Carlson meant by "ethical indoctrination" by viewing the 1943 film "Gung Ho!" Carlson acted as technical adviser to Walter Wanger for this Hollywood version of the Makin raid. "Gung" and "Ho" are Chinese words for "to work" and "harmony." As suggested in the movie, the Raiders were to think for themselves but to help each other. They were to live in a democratic fashion with one another, as well as to be ready to die for democracy.

[16] For information on Carlson's 2nd Raider Battalion and its activities during the Second World War, see Frank O. Hough, Verle E. Ludwig, and Henry I. Shaw, Jr., *Pearl Harbor to Guadalcanal: History of U.S. Marine Corps Operations in World War II* (Vol. I, Washington, D.C., 1958), pp. 285–286, 350; Benis M. Frank and Henry I. Shaw, Jr., *Victory and Occupation: History of U.S. Marine Corps in World War II* (Vol. V, Washington, D.C., 1968), pp. 707–710, 744–745; and Robert Debs Heinl, Jr., *Soldiers of the Sea: The United States Marine Corps, 1775–1962* (Annapolis, Maryland, 1962), pp. 357–358, 372.

[17] Forman, *Report from Red China*, p. 203.

people helped us."[18] Another oft-quoted statement which journalists usually attributed to P'eng was that "the Eighth Route Army is like the fish, and the people like the water"; the one could not live and grow without the medium of the other.[19] Accordingly, as almost every reporter observed, the Red Army implemented strict rules of polite conduct in its dealings with the peasantry.[20] The result was, as Carlson recognized, that the Eighth Route Army was an object of enthusiastic acclaim in the villages of northern China.[21]

A well-known Chinese proverb says that "one does not make good iron into nails, or good men into soldiers." The typical Red warrior, as depicted in the Western literature on the Chinese Communist movement, was just about as far removed from this assessment as one could possibly imagine. He was made not of iron but of steel. The soldier-hero of the Red Army was young, valiant, disciplined, perservering, and popular. He was upright in his moral behavior and willing to die for his values. This awesome fighter was superbly officered by men like Lin Piao, he had mastered the arts of guerrilla warfare, and he was unexcelled in his capacity for endurance and mobility. Above all, this Red knight in straw sandals was distinguished by his revolutionary *élan*. Finally, while the abundance of the complimentary adjectives listed above can readily be translated into factors explaining the resilience of the Eighth Route Army, contemporaries judged that it was this army's "organic connection with the people," as Agnes Smedley phrased it, which primarily accounted for its strength and success.[22] Mao

[18] Snow, *Red Star over China*, p. 304.

[19] For example, see Smedley, *China Fights Back*, p. 175.

[20] For a listing of the Red Army's disciplinary rules and a commentary on the importance of this code in gaining peasant support see Snow, *Red Star over China*, p. 176; Smedley, *China Fights Back*, pp. 122–123; Wales, *Inside Red China*, p. 291.

[21] Carlson, *Twin Stars of China*, p. 89.

[22] Smedley, *China Fights Back*, p. 31. For an interesting evaluation of the successor to the Eighth Route Army, the People's Liberation

Tse-tung best summarized the reality behind the image
when he reported to the Seventh CCP Congress in 1945 that
the Red Army was powerful "because all who have joined
it are conscientiously disciplined." [23] There was, as Samuel
B. Griffith wrote, "an iron hand in the velvet glove." [24]

Army, by a retired marine general with firsthand experience in China
see Samuel B. Griffith, II, "Communist China's Capacity to Make
War," *Foreign Affairs*, XLIII (January 1965), 217–236. In a number of
important particulars, Griffith's assessment of the P.L.A. parallels the
earlier appraisals of the Red Army by Carlson, Snow, and others.

[23] Conrad Brandt, Benjamin Schwartz, and John K. Fairbank, eds., *A
Documentary History of Chinese Communism* (Cambridge, Mass.,
1952), p. 298.

[24] Griffith, *The Chinese People's Liberation Army*, p. 255. For an
analysis of the elaborate system of Communist Party political control
over military units, see John Gittings, *The Role of the Chinese Army*
(London, New York, and Toronto, 1967), pp. 99–118.

[13]

"The Land of
Five Withouts"

If reporters identified the behavior of the Red Army toward civilians as a cardinal reason for the popularity of the CCP, another factor they singled out in explaining peasant approbation was the nature of the domestic program sponsored by the Chinese Communists. This many-faceted prospectus for internal modernization encompassed a broad range of political, economic, and social reforms. The primary agencies employed by the Communists to implement their blueprint for a new China were the mass associations. These were the organizations through which the CCP labored to create an environment favorable to the prosecution of guerrilla warfare. Westerners recognized that the driving energy of Communist administrators had succeeded in rousing the apathetic populace of North China and had invigorated the fabric of an impoverished society. As Lieutenant George Uhlmann put it, "a new China is developing in these guerrilla regions." [1]

Firsthand observers commonly described the contours of this new China with adjectives like democratic, dynamic, liberal, nationalistic, and reformist. They generally agreed that whatever label should be attached to the policies being fostered by the CCP, developments in the Border Regions

[1] Lieutenant George Uhlmann, "Land of Five Withouts," *Far Eastern Survey*, XII (May 3, 1943), 86.

moved in an enlightened and progressive direction. Many of them summed up the process of change in Red China with the phrase "mass mobilization." But whatever conceptual device foreign visitors to the Communist strongholds employed, most of them were certain that momentous stirrings with potentially far-reaching consequences were taking place behind the Japanese lines.

One aspect of the Communist program to reconstruct the fabric of Chinese society was to stamp out certain traditional evils. Edgar Snow contended that opium growing, unemployment, beggary, infanticide, footbinding, prostitution, child slavery, and official corruption had been all but eliminated in the Soviet areas.[2] Other writers emphasized the liquidation of one or another of these social diseases, but it was the Communist offensive against human avarice that struck most of them as being particularly noteworthy. Thus, Gunther Stein suggested that the greatest administrative achievement registered by the Yenan regime was the "virtual disappearance of corruption."[3] G. Martel Hall made a special point of trying to unearth scandal and misconduct in the administration of the Chin-Ch'a-Chi. This professional banker was frankly astonished when he could not find a single example of "squeeze."[4] A Communist political director explained to Evans F. Carlson how the problem of cupidity was dealt with. If an official was found guilty of embezzling less than $500, he was imprisoned. However, if the amount exceeded $500, the grafter became a victim of guerrilla justice: he was shot.[5] Therefore, it is not surprising that firsthand observers

[2] Edgar Snow, *Red Star over China* (New York, 1961), p. 241.

[3] Gunther Stein, *The Challenge of Red China* (New York and London, 1945), p. 138.

[4] John Carter Vincent, Chungking, March 15, 1943, dispatch to the Secretary of State, 893.00/14981, Department of State files.

[5] Evans Fordyce Carlson, *Twin Stars of China: A Behind-the-Scenes Story of China's Valiant Struggle for Existence by a U.S. Marine Who Lived and Moved with the People* (New York, 1940), p. 222.

found the Communist areas singularly free of corruption and mismanagement. Cormac Shanahan and Gustav Soderbom were the only visitors to the guerrilla areas whose testimony damaged the Communist reputation for upright behavior. Shanahan pictured the Shen-Kan-Ning as an oppressive police state where subdued peasants were terrorized by an army of spies.[6] Soderbom contended that the opium poppy was under cultivation in Shansi and suggested that the Communists were bolstering their uncertain finances by marketing the finished product in Japanese-occupied territory.[7] George Uhlmann, however, more accurately reflected the Western consensus about the expurgatory activity which was an important part of the Communist program to reconstruct Chinese society. He labeled the Border Regions " 'The Land of Five Withouts'—without beggars, without opium, without prostitution, without corruption, and without unjust taxes." [8]

As Uhlmann's final "without" suggests, the Communist internal program incorporated economic policies which were designed to improve the lives of the inhabitants of the Border Areas. Edgar Snow felt that the introduction of progressive taxation, the redistribution and reclamation of land, the abolition of usury, and the encouragement of producers' cooperatives helped to explain the CCP's rapport with the peasant masses.[9] In the interest of the united front, the Communists ceased the practice of land redistribution after 1937, except for the property of "traitors." Nonetheless, they promoted moderate enactments such as graduated taxation and

[6] Cormac Shanahan, "China's Communist Puzzle," *China Monthly,* VI (June 1945), 11–12.

[7] Everett F. Drumright, Sian, August 16, 1943, memorandum of conversation with Mr. Gustav Soderbom, 893.00/15134, Department of State files.

[8] Uhlmann, "Land of Five Withouts," 86.

[9] Snow, *Red Star over China,* pp. 238–241.

the lowering of rents and interest rates. Anna Louise Strong believed that even these temperate measures had succeeded in arousing "intense loyalty from the greater part of the population," while Haldore Hanson went so far as to credit the viability of the guerrilla governments to the " 'rice bowl' appeal" of their agrarian reforms.[10]

By the mid-1940's the economic policies of the CCP were bearing tangible fruit. Late visitors to the Border Regions were impressed by the comparative affluence of these areas. Not long after Gunther Stein passed from KMT to CCP territory, he began to notice unmistakable indications that the standard of living of the common man in the Communist zone was higher than that of his Nationalist counterpart. The Border Area farmers were better supplied with the necessities of life than any he had seen elsewhere in the country.[11] Brooks Atkinson arrived in Yenan at harvest time. The rich abundance of the good earth was much in evidence. The people, furthermore, looked "better fed, huskier and more energetic than in other parts of China." [12] Harrison Forman also was struck by the visible prosperity of the guerrilla strongholds. He suggested that Border Region economic progress was, in large part, a by-product of the self-production movement. In order to ease the tax burdens of the peasantry, the Eighth Route Army was officially encouraged to provide its own material requirements. Consequently, the Communist soldier expended a substantial portion of his energy wielding a hoe rather than a rifle. According to Forman, by 1944 the Communist army and bureaucracy were producing sixty-four per cent of their own clothing and food and were rapidly approaching "complete

[10] Anna Louise Strong, *One-Fifth of Mankind* (New York, 1938), p. 193; Haldore Hanson, "The People behind the Chinese Guerrillas," *Pacific Affairs*, XI (September 1938), 295.

[11] Stein, *The Challenge of Red China*, pp. 61–62, 201.

[12] Brooks Atkinson, "Yenan Is Well Fed with Big Harvest," *New York Times*, September 25, 1944, 9.

self-sufficiency." [13] Even Mao Tse-tung cultivated, appropriately enough, a tobacco patch. Chu Teh tended cabbages. Theodore H. White judged that the self-sufficiency drive of the CCP "had been superlatively successful, and the party and its functionaries lived not on taxes but on the sweat of their own brow." [14] The Western literature on Chinese communism was punctuated with such enthusiastic compliments for the manifest accomplishments of an economic program which seemed to be the quintessence of moderate progressivism. [15]

The CCP supplemented its economic policies with a broad range of social action programs. Men, women, and children were encouraged to participate in at least one of a large number of possible activities. An individual might join a sewing club, become part of a drama group, or simply attend that staple of guerrilla society—the mass meeting. Westerners could not help but notice this aspect of the Chinese Communist movement. Indeed, they applauded the CCP's effort to enrich the lives of the Border Area peoples. For-

[13] Harrison Forman, *Report from Red China* (New York, 1945), pp. 83–85. See also Stein, *The Challenge of Red China*, pp. 66–74, 133–142.

[14] Theodore H. White and Annalee Jacoby, *Thunder Out of China* (New York, 1946), p. 228. Apparently, the Red Army is still active in areas of agricultural and industrial production. According to Samuel B. Griffith, the People's Liberation Army "grows a high percentage of the cereals it consumes, raises its own hogs, chickens and ducks, and where conditions permit, augments its rations by hunting and fishing. It also manufactures its own uniforms, shoes, blankets and bedding, builds its barracks, and other facilities, and maintains all its installations." See Samuel B. Griffith, II, "Communist China's Capacity to Make War," *Foreign Affairs*, XLIII (January 1965), 226–227.

[15] For an evaluation of the self-production movement see John Gittings, *The Role of the Chinese Army* (London, New York, and Toronto, 1967), pp. 55–57. Gittings suggests that except for a few model army units, it was not possible for military and governmental personnel to approach self-sufficiency and that the level of taxation continued to be high throughout the Border Regions.

eigners were struck also by the educational focus of the Communist drive to activate the Chinese masses. The CCP's pedagogical network was a vast enterprise, including both formal and informal institutions and devices. Peasants were sent into the classroom on the primary, secondary, and adult levels. In community associations the common man casually discussed politics and learned to decipher a few Chinese characters. Gunther Stein was articulating a widely shared image when he observed that the Shen-Kan-Ning "seems like a big elementary school." [16]

Many Western reporters commented on the didactic focus of the CCP's domestic program, but Edgar Snow was more incisive than most when it came to analyzing this phenomenon. After observing the grateful response of culture-starved peasants to a performance of the Red theater, he suggested that there was "no more powerful weapon of propaganda . . . than the Reds' dramatic troupes, and none more subtly manipulated." Snow remarked that the Chinese Communist movement could be understood as a "grand propaganda tour." He acknowledged that the emphasis was crudely propagandistic and frankly political. When a farmer's child learned to read for the first time, Snow noted, he knew who had taught him. Such a person had been carefully indoctrinated with the "basic fighting ideas of Chinese Communism." [17] Helen Snow's evaluation of the CCP's accent on mass education, however, was more characteristic of

[16] Stein, *The Challenge of Red China,* p. 260.

[17] Snow, *Red Star over China,* pp. 114–116, 255–256. For interesting examples of the kind of dramas performed by the Border Region theatrical groups, see J. Clayton Miller, "The Drama in China's Anti-Japanese Propaganda," *Pacific Affairs,* XI (December 1938), 465–477. This article consists of translations from the Chinese of two propaganda plays: "Weapons" and "The Little Hero." In "Weapons" one of the characters, an informed peasant, says to his dispirited companions: "Look at the People's Army! They don't take the harvest from us, and they even want to reduce the land tax and give us a better chance to live, so that we farmers will see better days."

the typical Western assessment. The Communist instructional agencies were, she concluded, establishing the foundations of a "new cultural and political democracy." [18]

The axial mechanism of the Communist program to revolutionize Chinese society was the mass association. Edgar Snow called the Border Regions the "scene of the greatest effort at mass mobilization in the history of China." [19] Nothing struck Harrison Forman more than the CCP's "will to organize." [20] Skilled Communist agitators feverishly labored to mobilize a rural populace into a grand army of regimented partisans. Brigading apathetic farmers was, as Theodore H. White realized, "work for fanatics." White judged that the Communists filled the bill. These were, he wrote, "men who worked with history as if it were a tool and with peasants as if they were raw material." [21] Chinese Communists waged a relentless campaign to enlist every villager in any number of a bewildering variety of community groups. Michael Lindsay distinguished seven different categories of mass associations, two of a military and five of a civil nature: the self-defense corps and the militia, the worker's, the peasant's, the young people's, the women's and the children's groups.[22] The Communists' obsession for administrative comprehensiveness was total; their Leninist organizational talents were extraordinary.

In village after village Western travelers observed the monumental efforts of Communist organizers and marveled at their superlative achievements. With the exception of Cormac Shanahan, Agnes Smedley's comment about the Shansi countryside could have been written by any of the

[18] Nym Wales [Helen Foster Snow], *Inside Red China* (Garden City, N.Y., 1939), p. 141.

[19] Snow, *The Battle For Asia* (New York, 1941), p. 252.

[20] Forman, *Report from Red China*, p. 160.

[21] White and Jacoby, *Thunder Out of China*, pp. 201–202.

[22] Michael Lindsay, "The North China Front: Part II," *Amerasia*, VIII (April 14, 1944), 119–120.

foreign visitors to Red China. The common people, she said, had been "aroused, organized, trained, and armed . . . so that often the whole population of a town, including women and children and the aged, fight the enemy with every weapon at their command." [23] Haldore Hanson used Hopei to illustrate the general mobilization pattern employed by the CCP. Individuals broadly representative of the social classes in a particular locality were enlisted in a front mobilization committee which assumed comprehensive wartime powers. Under the auspices of this governing body, men's, women's, and young people's associations were established. At colorful mass meetings, the people were inundated with propagandistic speeches, inspirational dramas, and patriotic songs. They were encouraged to join the Village Self-Defense Corps, the Young Vanguards, the Children's Brigade, or some other partisan assemblage. They usually joined.[24] Moreover, the various community gatherings were, as Edgar Snow perceived, "all skillfully interwoven, and each directly under the guidance of some Communist, though decisions of organization, membership, and work seemed to be carried out in a democratic way by the peasants themselves." [25] Under the overall direction of the Border Area regimes, these mass associations became the functional agencies which institutionalized and promoted the CCP's political, social, and economic reform programs. As they proliferated across the Chinese landscape, Communist power grew by leaps and bounds.

The CCP had a powerful ally in its frantic drive to mobilize the Chinese peasant—the Japanese Army. About all Chinese Communists had demonstrated to 1937 was their stubborn capacity to survive. Chiang Kai-shek's bandit-suppression campaigns had failed to suppress them. But the

[23] Agnes Smedley, *China Fights Back: An American Woman with the Eighth Route Army* (London, 1939), p. 238.

[24] Hanson, "The People behind the Chinese Guerrillas," 286–289.

[25] Snow, *Red Star over China*, p. 236.

CCP had not been able to maintain the Kiangsi Soviet Republic, much less to extend its territorial base. Reliance on peasant radicalism and agrarian reform had not been enough to gain significant and lasting influence for the CCP. Chinese Communists were simply unable to establish a secure foothold prior to the Sino-Japanese War.[26]

Japan's occupation of North China, as one scholar wrote, was the "decisive ingredient" in preparing the ground for the success of the Chinese Communist movement. Landlords and KMT officials fled before the advance of the Japanese Army, thereby reducing the potential opposition to the CCP. More important, the vicious military tactics of the Japanese welded the peasantry into a solidary mass of oppressed nationalists. It is suggestive that the Communists made little headway in areas where the peasants were treated well by, or had no direct contact with, the Japanese Army.[27]

"What the Japanese have done to occupied China," an outraged journalist wrote, "is one of the most monstrous historic crimes ever perpetrated against one people by another." [28] After observing the Japanese armed forces in action, the Commander-in-Chief of the American Asiatic Fleet concluded that they had discarded all of the rules of warfare and had become savages armed with bombs and machine guns.[29] In 1941, the Japanese supplemented haphazard sadism with a blueprint for systematic savagery. General Yasuji Okamura's "three-all" policy, patterned after German techniques, was a bankrupt response to the challenge of guerrilla activity. The slogans were self-explanatory: "kill all, burn

[26] Barrington Moore, Jr., *Social Origins of Dictatorship and Democracy: Lord and Peasant in the Making of the Modern World* (Boston, 1967), pp. 221–222.

[27] *Ibid.*, pp. 223–224.

[28] White, "Inside Red China," *Life*, XVII (December 18, 1944), 40. White goes on to detail atrocities committed against the Chinese people which are almost unbelievable in their bestiality.

[29] Harry E. Yarnell to Stanley K. Hornbeck, March 10, 1939, Hornbeck papers, Stanford University.

all, destroy all!" A given area was encircled, all of its inhabitants were butchered, and the countryside was leveled. Instances of this program of total atrocity were not hard to come by.[30] The importance of the invader's behavior to the appeal and effectiveness of the CCP's domestic program of mass mobilization can scarcely be overestimated. As James Bertram phrased it, war was the "great educator." [31] It transformed politically backward peasants into nationalistic patriots ready to cooperate with those who offered them an alternative to enslavement and poverty. Japanese terrorist reprisals may have done more to arouse the people of North China, as Bertram suggested, than the considerable propaganda efforts of the CCP.[32] In this psychological sense, then, Japan's legions were the allies of the Chinese Red Army.

Like Bertram, other firsthand observers emphasized the Japanese factor in explaining the viability of the Communist governments. Helen Snow felt that invasion was rapidly accomplishing what both Sun Yat-sen and the Communists had been unable to do—"awakening the greatest mass of people on earth." [33] Haldore Hanson characterized a Japanese annihilation campaign in south Shansi as "totalitarian warfare at its maximum efficiency" and concluded from extensive conversations with peasants that the invader's cruelty had served only to harden their "spirit of resistance." [34] T. A. Bisson suggested that instead of "saving China from bolshevism," the Japanese onslaught had made it easier for

[30] Chalmers A. Johnson, *Peasant Nationalism and Communist Power: The Emergence of Revolutionary China, 1937–1945* (Stanford, 1962), pp. 55–56. See also White and Jacoby, *Thunder Out of China,* p. 205.

[31] James M. Bertram, *Unconquered: Journal of a Year's Adventures among the Fighting Peasants of North China* (New York, 1939), p. 271.

[32] *Ibid.,* p. 228.

[33] Wales, *Inside Red China,* p. 301.

[34] Hanson, *"Humane Endeavour": The Story of the China War* (New York and Toronto, 1939), pp. 272–275.

the CCP to organize partisan bands.[35] Theodore H. White judged that reforms made up half of the Communist appeal. He credited the military primacy of the Red Army with the other fifty per cent and implied that the Communists had achieved their "real popularity" by countering a barbarous foe.[36] G. Martel Hall contended that popular support for the Eighth Route Army in an occupied region varied with the length of time a particular locality had been subjected to Japanese mistreatment.[37] Michael Lindsay maintained that the Communist leaders themselves recognized that the behavior of the Japanese troops had been "the most important factor" in unifying the masses.[38] A comment made to Anna Louise Strong by a leading political commissar indicated that Lindsay knew what he was talking about. Jen Pi-shih told her that "the savagery of the Japanese is our best argument" in mobilizing the people.[39] The Chinese Communists' internal program should be viewed in this wartime context. While the CCP gained peasant support through reform programs, it was the Japanese Army which provided the prod that roused the Chinese peasant from his apathy. The unquestionable popularity of the CCP had many roots, but none went deeper than its nationalistic appeal to a beleaguered people.

Political developments also drew attention and acclaim. After observing that voting and officeholding rights had been extended to all classes in the Shen-Kan-Ning, James Bertram surmised that the Yenan regime "could fairly claim to be the nearest thing to a complete democracy in

[35] T. A. Bisson, *Japan in China* (New York, 1938), pp. 300–301.

[36] White and Jacoby, *Thunder Out of China*, p. 205. See also White, "Inside Red China," 40.

[37] Vincent, Chungking, March 15, 1943, dispatch to the Secretary of State, 893.00/14981, Department of State files.

[38] Lindsay, "The North China Front: A Study of Chinese Guerrillas in Action," *Amerasia*, VIII (March 31, 1944), 105.

[39] Strong, *One-Fifth of Mankind*, p. 241.

China." [40] On similar grounds, Haldore Hanson characterized the Chin-Ch'a-Chi as a political utopia, "a replica of
Plato's Republic." This guerrilla stronghold had been organized, he wrote, by a "strange congregation" of Buddhists,
Christians, Communists, lamas, unlettered farmers, and college students. Hanson was informed that the governor of the
Chin-Ch'a-Chi and two-thirds of its executive committee
were not even Communists. He concluded that a "democratic experiment" had been instituted in the Shansi-Hopei-
Chahar Border Region. [41] To Evans F. Carlson, Yenan incar-
nated the "spirit of liberalism" and representative government was the "backbone" of the Chin-Ch'a-Chi. The
basis for Carlson's assessment was his conviction that the
peoples of North China were actively participating in the
selection of local officials and that they were content. [42] The
Bands, who personally attended such important convocations
as the Hopei Border Region Congress, were persuaded that
the Reds had successfully established a "modern scientific democracy . . . that really worked." China's Communists had
accomplished this, they mused, behind Japanese lines and
"in less time than it takes to train one class of students in the
red tape of the British civil service." [43]

Especially after 1941, the CCP promoted a technique of
government which convinced several foreign visitors that
Communist democracy was the genuine article. This was the
widely publicized "three-thirds" system. Communists voluntarily restricted themselves to one-third of the total membership of any elective body. The remaining two-thirds were
drawn from such nonparty elements as "left progressives"
and "middle elements." Lin Piao said that the non-CCP
group was made up of national and petty bourgeoisie, en-

[40] Bertram, *Unconquered*, pp. 125–126.

[41] Hanson, *"Humane Endeavour,"* pp. 241, 245.

[42] Carlson, *Twin Stars of China*, pp. 176, 216–217.

[43] Claire and William Band, *Dragon Fangs: Two Years with Chinese
Guerrillas* (London, 1947), p. 133.

lightened gentry, "and those members of the Kuomintang who stood for resistance to Japan and did not oppose the Communist Party." [44] Although the composition of two-thirds of the "three-thirds" system was never defined precisely, Gunther Stein and Harrison Forman were enthusiastic about this remarkable tripartite arrangement. Accordingly, both of them concluded that a salient feature of Border Area rule was its representative character. [45] The "three-thirds" strategy, the extension of civil rights, the implementation of familiar electoral procedures, and the widespread participation of the masses in the political process persuaded most firsthand observers that the governmental apparatus of Red China could be understood as a species of democracy.

There were, however, skeptics and dissenters. Joy Homer depicted the Communist leaders as benevolent "overlords." She believed that the CCP, like other Leninist parties, was governed by a "small clique of men." Unfortunately, she did not bother to develop either of these notions; her comments were delivered as obiter dicta. [46] Although the Bands claimed that the CCP had instituted a democratic system, they also observed that there was no organized political opposition in the Communist strongholds. The contradiction apparently did not disturb them. [47] Brooks Atkinson classed Yenan's political structure as a species of "agrarian or peasant democracy." Yet, he suggested that this democracy had a "strong authoritarian direction." [48] Atkinson's suspicions had been aroused by Mao Tse-tung's dogmatic personality and by the

[44] Lin Piao, "Long Live the Victory of People's War!" in *China after Mao,* by A. Doak Barnett (Princeton, 1967), p. 209.

[45] Stein, *The Challenge of Red China,* pp. 86, 102, 128–132; Forman, *Report from Red China,* p. 56.

[46] Joy Homer, *Dawn Watch in China* (Boston, 1941), pp. 229, 235.

[47] Claire and William Band, *Dragon Fangs,* p. 336.

[48] Atkinson, "Chinese Still Try to Unify Factions," *New York Times,* November 26, 1944, 43.

psychological dynamics of a "struggle meeting" in which peasants were encouraged to "confess" and become "corrected." [49] Like Homer and the Bands, however, Atkinson did not provide a detailed analysis of the totalitarian aspects of the Chinese Communist movement. Although Cormac Shanahan also dealt in generalities, he made a special effort to refute the notion that the CCP practiced true democracy. He called the "three-thirds" system "a farce," voting a "mere formality," and insisted that all political power lay in the hands of a Communist elite. The Reds were nothing more than outsiders and usurpers who had imposed themselves on the Chinese masses.[50]

The most searching critique of the political style of Chinese communism was advanced by Theodore H. White, who granted that Yenan encouraged freedom of discussion and criticism but felt that this eventuated in a mere "administrative" debate, a parody of democracy. High policy, White contended, was framed by a politburo whose directives were not considered proper matters for argumentation. White also pointed out that the proportional arrangements of the "three-thirds" system were of no great import as the Communists were the only group "with a cohesive program." Finally, this skeptical American reporter asked some pointed questions. He associated minority rights and civil liberties with the American concept of representative government and wondered how the Communists would behave if they had to cope with authentic political adversaries. Would they, White wrote, "permit an opposition press and opposition party to challenge them by a combination of patronage and ideology?" [51] It was a good question, but it was not one which White and his peers could answer on the basis of experience.

Since Edgar Snow's views fall somewhere between the as-

[49] Atkinson to the author, May 28, 1965.
[50] Shanahan, "China's Communist Puzzle," 11.
[51] White and Jacoby, *Thunder Out of China*, pp. 231–237.

surance of a Haldore Hanson and the anxiety of a Theodore H. White, they provide a suggestive epilogue to the question of Communist democracy. The uncertainties inherent in an ambiguous situation are reflected in Snow's analysis of CCP politics. Snow was circumspect in that he never definitely labeled Chinese Communists "democrats." One can discern, nonetheless, an interesting progression in his thought. In *Red Star over China* he intimated that the Communists had temporarily abandoned the doctrine of proletarian hegemony for a program which envisioned a "union of all classes" in bourgeois-democratic-style institutions, but he recognized that this "great shift in strategy" did not mean that ultimate socialist aspirations had been deserted. He implied, on the one hand, that the CCP's democratic slogans were genuine. On the other, he acknowledged their tactical nature. He did not, however, attempt to reconcile means with ends.[52]

The contrast between a semidictatorial KMT and a democratic CCP forms a central theme in *The Battle for Asia*. Snow praised the Communists for their democratic political and economic reforms, called the Border Area regimes the most democratic administrations ever known to the Chinese peasantry, and posited a "democratic republic" as the immediate goal of Chinese communism. He even suggested that the CCP was the great democratic alternative to a feudal China. Snow made it clear, however, that the CCP did not advocate bourgeois democracy as an end in itself. He recognized that bourgeois democracy represented only an historical stage in the CCP's larger vision of transforming China into a socialist state.[53]

By 1944, Snow had sharpened the Chinese dialectic. In *People on Our Side* he wrote with passion and thought in stereotypes. He played down the importance of the CCP's commitment to Marxism, characterized the Shen-Kan-Ning

[52] Snow, *Red Star over China*, pp. 487–490.
[53] Snow, *The Battle for Asia*, pp. 113–114, 258, 293–295, 365–366.

as a functioning popular democracy, and pictured the KMT as a repressive dictatorship completely divorced from the Chinese people.[54] In 1945, Snow became even more explicit with regard to the question of Communist democracy. Early in the year he wrote a harsh review of Lin Yutang's anti-Communist *The Vigil of a Nation.* Among other things, Snow praised the CCP for having an administration "more democratic than any China has yet known." [55] In a withering reply Lin insisted that the Chinese Communists were "not true democrats but totalitarians of the Russian type in theory and practice." [56] In a feeble rejoinder which shed more heat than light on the problem of Border Region politics, Snow did not defend the notion that Chinese Communists were democrats, but rather reiterated his conviction that they were Marxist revolutionaries.[57] In a subsequent article Snow refined his position. He rejected the idea that the CCP would establish "a liberal democracy in China in the American sense." He believed, however, that the Communists probably would institute "a kind of democratic equalitarianism such as is now practiced in the areas they control." [58]

Although Snow's vague pronouncements on the matter of Communist democracy defy a confident explication, practiced means and not projected ends seem to have become uppermost in his thinking. He never called the Chinese Communists democrats, and yet he described the Border Area regimes as popular democracies. Snow's Communists, then,

[54] Snow, *People on Our Side* (New York, 1944), pp. 278–279, 282, 289–290, 302. See also Snow, "Sixty Million Lost Allies," *Saturday Evening Post,* CCXVI (June 10, 1944), 44, 46.

[55] Snow, "China to Lin Yutang," *Nation,* CLX (February 17, 1945), 180.

[56] Lin Yutang, "China and Its Critics," *Nation,* CLX (March 24, 1945), 324.

[57] Snow, "China to Lin Yutang—II," *Nation,* CLX (March 31, 1945), 359.

[58] Snow, "Must China Go Red?" *Saturday Evening Post,* CCXVII (May 12, 1945), 67.

were not democrats but they practiced democracy. This paradoxical analysis can be reconciled in a Leninist framework. In *Red Star over China* Snow distinguished between democratic means and Communist ends. His subsequent writings, however, indicate that, like most firsthand observers, Snow also interpreted Border Region developments in existential terms. Mass participation and enthusiasm, the extension of civil rights, and a governmental sensitiveness to the aspirations of the people—the outward trimmings—were understood as genuinely democratic manifestations and not as expedient vehicles on a highway which led from democracy to communism.

Nearly every Western traveler to the Border Areas judged that, in one sense or another, Communist political developments could be viewed as a species of democracy. They tended to equate mass participation and elective bodies with democracy and to overlook the monolithic hold of the CCP on the effective levers of power. On the other side, several firsthand observers qualified their statements or raised questions about the nature of the CCP's commitment to democracy. Those who were most discriminating faced a difficult problem of analysis. While Edgar Snow, for example, knew enough to refrain from calling a member of the CCP a democrat, he could not deny that Western-style political institutions and patterns of behavior had been instituted in the Border Regions. It was reasonable in 1940 for a perceptive scholar like George E. Taylor to recognize both the superficialities and the potentialities of the political apparatus in the Chin-Ch'a-Chi. This was not, Taylor wrote, a "real democratic" government; the initiative came from the top. Nonetheless, he could also justifiably suggest that the Chin-Ch'a-Chi's mass associations constituted a lasting and spectacular step "toward an institutional basis for democracy." [59] Only hindsight has enabled us to answer the important question

[59] George E. Taylor, *The Struggle for North China* (New York, 1940), pp. 107–109.

which Theodore H. White posed about how Chinese Communists would react to authentic political opposition.

Democracy, nationalism, progress and reform—these were the component parts of the Western image of the Border Area governments. It was, on the whole, a bright image replete with complimentary adjectives and some wishful thinking. A person like Evans Carlson was certain that the Communist system approximated a "pure democracy" and inferred that the CCP was advocating social and economic ideals which could be associated with the ethics of Christianity.[60] Of course, not everyone spoke in ecstatic terms of a utopia in the Chinese hinterlands. Many did, however, and most were deeply impressed by what they had seen.

In retrospect, firsthand reports can be criticized for being unsystematic and imprecise in describing the domestic policies of the CCP. More impressed by the absence of corruption than by specific reform programs, travelers to the Border Regions seldom provided detailed analyses of how Communists were restructuring Chinese society. The most obvious defect of firsthand reports is optimism about the democratic proclivities of the CCP. Many observers were unable to recognize that Communist "democracy" was primarily a means for obtaining popular support and not an end in itself. The main objectives of the "three-thirds" system, for example, had little to do with the promotion of self-government. Rather, the system was designed to complement and to make more effective the authority of the CCP. A directive of March 6, 1940, enjoined cadres to take care that "Communists play the leading role in the organs of political power." The governmental bodies to which the tripartite arrangement was applied were forums for discussion and implementation, not policy-making institutions. Outsiders were not admitted to such ruling circles of power as the Red Army or the CCP itself.[61] The democratic stereotype which character-

[60] Carlson, *Twin Stars of China,* p. 231.

[61] Lyman P. Van Slyke, *Enemies and Friends: The United Front in Chinese Communist History* (Stanford, 1967), pp. 143–151. See also Je-

izes much of the Western literature on Chinese communism rests on a failure to make a distinction between a totalitarian regime's manipulation of democratic symbols and a republican government's sufferance of competing power centers.[62] Much more striking than the defects of the Western literature on Chinese communism is the tendency of recent scholarship to uphold the findings of firsthand observers. Few question the sincerity of the CCP's attempt to eradicate baneful social legacies or the moderate nature of the CCP's land policy from 1937 to 1945. Jerome Ch'en describes the agrarian program in the Border Areas as one of reducing rent and interest rates while eschewing the confiscation of property.[63] Chalmers Johnson points to the significance of partisan organizations in the "social mobilization" of the peasant masses. Like virtually every American and European traveler to the Border Regions, he also underscores the critical role of the Japanese Army in generating the merger of peasant nationalism and agrarian radicalism which underlay the phenomenal success of the CCP's domestic program.[64] If present-day scholarship is taken as the measure of what actually happened, firsthand observers projected a generally realistic image of "the Land of Five Withouts." To put the matter another way, the accounts written by those who visited the Communist areas help to validate subsequent insights into the Chinese Communist movement.

---

rome Ch'en, *Mao and the Chinese Revolution* (New York, 1967), pp. 247–248.

[62] Tang Tsou, "The American Political Tradition and the American Image of Chinese Communism," *Political Science Quarterly*, LXXVII (December 1962), 583–587.

[63] Ch'en, *Mao and the Chinese Revolution*, p. 248. See also Lin Piao, "Long Live the Victory of People's War!" p. 209.

[64] Johnson, *Peasant Nationalism and Communist Power*, pp. 19–22. See also Moore, *Social Origins of Dictatorship and Democracy*, pp. 221–223.

[14]

Loyal Partners in
an Uneasy Enterprise

A fourth topic of general concern to Western observers was the relationship of the CCP to the KMT. What was, they wondered, the nature of the CCP's commitment to the united front? Since external events impinged heavily on evaluations of this problem, the subject must be understood in its chronological setting.

Edgar Snow's *Red Star over China* was written during the formative stages of the united front. By relying on Mao Tse-tung's unequivocal statements and his own affinity for the dialectical method, Snow was able to comprehend the issue in hardheaded terms. As refracted through Snow's dialectical lens, the united front became an unstable and impermanent synthesis which "might break up again whenever the internal denials outweighed the present external ones." Although Mao had pledged that the Communists would "not utilize any wartime situation in an opportunist way," he also viewed war as a mighty accelerator of, and vehicle for, revolutionary social change. Snow recognized the tactical aspect of the CCP's alliance with the KMT. He emphasized that while the Communists were disposed to make the necessary alterations "in form and nomenclature," they were bent on retaining their politico-military autonomy and Marxist doctrines. As Snow expressed it: "Marxism, and the basic tenets of social revolution, it was quite clear, they would never give up. Every new step taken, every change made, was examined, debated, decided, and integrated in terms of Marxism—and the proletarian Revolution, which the Communists did not abandon as their ultimate purpose." While there had been an exchange of concessions between the KMT and the CCP, there were, as Mao said, "definite limits" beyond which the Communists would not go.[1]

During the uncertain months between Chiang Kai-shek's return from Sian and the outbreak of the Sino-Japanese War, the Communists muffled talk of the conditional nature of their commitment to a united front and emphasized the importance of Chinese national unity. Agnes Smedley was enjoying an evening of comradeship and conversation with General P'eng Teh-huai and his staff in early 1937. As the radio was turned on, everyone stopped to listen when the Nanking broadcaster began to expound on the sadistic activities of Red bandits. Miss Smedley indignantly asked whether anything could be done about such lies. In an unguarded moment, P'eng harshly declared that "the only answer is our final victory!" Someone switched off the radio; silence filled the room. "The stillness was," Miss Smedley recalled, "heavy, burdensome." [2] Apparently, P'eng's indiscretion was not duplicated, for the Communists presented a different face to Miss Smedley's immediate successors.

In their discussions with Helen Snow, Communist leaders like Chou En-lai stressed the CCP's willingness to abandon revolutionary practices in order to attain a *rapprochement* with the KMT. She was impressed by what she heard and saw. She observed that the crimson stars had disappeared from Red Army uniforms and that even Chu Teh wore a Nationalist cap. Mrs. Snow concluded that the CCP had

[1] Edgar Snow, *Red Star over China* (New York, 1961), pp. 97, 476–478, 487–488, 492–494.
[2] Agnes Smedley, *Battle Hymn of China* (New York, 1943), pp. 163–164.

given up its attempt to erect a Soviet system and felt that the Communists were sincere in their advocacy of a united front.[3] Philip Jaffe recalled that in the summer of 1937 the Chinese Communists were preoccupied with the question of national unity. He remembered that they talked incessantly about the united front and tried to impress him with its overriding importance.[4] T. A. Bisson also found Yenan determined to close the breach separating it from Nanking, "irrespective of the difficulties to be surmounted."[5] Owen Lattimore's assessment of the situation confirmed the statements of his traveling companions. Lattimore acknowledged that the Communists were eager to make whatever concessions were necessary in order to achieve a united front. Lattimore's analysis, however, was less superficial than either Jaffe's or Bisson's. He posed the question of whether the patriotic fervor of the CCP meant that the Communists were deserting their revolutionary goals. "It seems to me," Lattimore answered, "as foolish to think so as to suppose that the Soviet Union is on its way back to capitalism."[6] Lattimore's unpublished comment was atypical. Indeed, Agnes Smedley did not choose to tell her revealing story about General P'eng's slip of the tongue until 1943. In August 1937 she was writing that the spirit of national unity was a "firm reality" in Yenan and glorifying the Communists for their ardent patriotism.[7] She was a bit premature, but with the publication of the CCP's statement on cooperation and concord on September 22, the united front did become a formal "reality."

From late 1937 to 1939, visitors to the Border Regions

[3] Nym Wales [Helen Foster Snow], *Inside Red China* (Garden City, N.Y., 1939), pp. 209–212.

[4] Philip J. Jaffe, interview with the author, June 14, 1965.

[5] T. A. Bisson, *Japan in China* (New York, 1938), p. 195.

[6] Owen Lattimore, "The Present and Future of Chinese Communism: The Theory of the United Front," 893.00/14179, Department of State files, 2.

[7] Smedley, *China Fights Back: An American Woman with the Eighth Route Army* (London, 1939), p. 18.

tended to promote an image of patriotic Communists whose
fidelity to the principles of national solidarity and the person of Chiang Kai-shek were beyond reproach. After a number of fascinating conversations with Mao Tse-tung, Chu
Teh, and Chou En-lai, James Bertram was persuaded that
"there could be no question of the loyalty of the Chinese
Communists to the leadership of Chiang Kai-shek." By 1938
the Communists were disclaiming any intention of seizing
control of the National government and were talking about
a united front that would continue into the postwar era.
Such professions help to account for Bertram's conviction
that any threat to Chinese unity would not come from the
CCP.[8] Anna Louise Strong similarly pictured the Communists as resolute supporters of the Central regime.[9] Although
Evans F. Carlson knew otherwise, he claimed that a bond of
mutual confidence existed between the Generalissimo and
the leaders of the CCP.[10] Even "Asiaticus" characterized the
cadres of the New Fourth Army as steadfast and exemplary
upholders of the united front.[11] On the whole, then, the
portrait drawn by Westerners in 1937–1938 was appropriate
to the spirit of the time. They looked at the brighter side of
the landscape and refrained from smudging their canvases
with shaded pastels. The exceptions were George E. Taylor
and Haldore Hanson.

While Taylor recognized that in practice and pronounce-
ment the Communists were paragons of propriety, he implied that the united front was a Comintern tactic. He sug-

[8] James M. Bertram, *Unconquered: Journal of a Year's Adventures
among the Fighting Peasants of North China* (New York, 1939), pp.
118, 297.

[9] Anna Louise Strong, *One-Fifth of Mankind* (New York, 1938), pp.
191–192.

[10] Evans Fordyce Carlson, *Twin Stars of China: A Behind-the-Scenes
Story of China's Valiant Struggle for Existence by a U.S. Marine Who
Lived and Moved with the People* (New York, 1940), p. 276.

[11] "Asiaticus," "The Yangtze Triangle Guerrilla War," *Amerasia*, III
(August 1939), 275–281.

gested, moreover, that national unity was built less on loyalty to Chungking than on a determination to defeat Japan. Taylor wrote that the united front was "based on a postponement of fundamental social change by the Communists" and speculated that it would not outlive either the wartime threat or any serious attempt to upset China's social structure.[12] Although Hanson thought that the Communist desire to cooperate with the KMT was genuine and did not believe that the CCP's prospectus encompassed a subversive effort, he discerned a future of revolution and class struggle "below the surface."[13] Hanson did not, furthermore, hesitate to record the manifestations of KMT-CCP hostility which could be found by any acute observer of the Chinese scene. It is important to realize, however, that Hanson, Taylor, and their fellow reporters consistently attributed whatever friction they chose to document to "right-wing" elements in the Kuomintang.[14] In Occidental eyes, the Communists were, if not entirely blameless, the more accommodating advocates of national solidarity.

By 1939, Western images of the united front were being formulated against the backdrop of a renewed KMT blockade of the Shen-Kan-Ning. The general deterioration in Chinese solidarity—which had its beginnings with the fall of Hankow and reached a climax with the New Fourth Army Incident of early 1941—was obvious to anyone interested in the problem. On the other side, both Nationalists and Communists loudly proclaimed their dedication to the spirit and principles of the united front. For some firsthand observers,

[12] George E. Taylor, *The Struggle for North China* (New York, 1940), pp. 96–97, 175–176.

[13] Haldore Hanson, "The People behind the Chinese Guerrillas," *Pacific Affairs*, XI (September 1938), 297–298.

[14] Hanson, *"Humane Endeavour": The Story of the China War* (New York and Toronto, 1939), pp. 349–350; Taylor, *The Struggle for North China*, pp. 175–176.

actions spoke louder than words. To most, it was the ver-
biage which counted.

Most of those who traveled to the Border Areas in 1939
did not question the solidarity of the united front. Ralph
Lapwood recorded that the Chin-Ch'a-Chi was plentifully
stocked with standards bearing the inscription "Long Live
Chiang Kai-shek, Leader of National Resistance." [15] Joy Homer's encounter with Chinese Communists led her to minimize rumored clashes between the Red Army and Nationalist troops. She concluded that the KMT and CCP were
"cemented in uncomfortable but dependable partnership by
the cold knowledge that they must battle together or be
defeated." [16] In his review of *Dawn Watch in China*, T. A.
Bisson rebuked Miss Homer for her naïveté in glossing over
the seriousness of KMT-CCP tensions.[17] Yet, as late as November 1940, the Communists were playing down their differences with Chungking. When Stanton Lautenschlager was
in Yenan, Chinese Communists told him of their enormous
admiration for the Generalissimo. "From the lowest to the
highest," he wrote, "the communist leaders . . . all declared
that they were for the United Front." [18] Joy Homer, Lapwood, and Lautenschlager had optimistically evaluated the
united front on the superficial level of patriotic propaganda
and had ignored such unpleasant realities as the KMT
blockade.

Edgar Snow refused to minimize the impending crisis.
The course of events convinced him that the "fundamental
dialectic" of China remained: "the rivalry for leadership be-

[15] Ralph and Nancy Lapwood, *Through the Chinese Revolution*
(London, 1954), p. 26.

[16] Joy Homer, *Dawn Watch in China* (Boston, 1941), p. 238.

[17] Bisson, "New Dimensions in China," *Saturday Review of Literature*, XXIII (April 26, 1941), 16.

[18] Stanton Lautenschlager, *Far West in China* (New York, 1941), p.
21. See also George A. Fitch, "China's Northwest Life-Line," *Amerasia*,
IV (September 1940), 305.

tween the Kuomintang and the Communist Party." Snow's villain, to be sure, was a dictatorial KMT, and most of his peace doves were roosting in Yenan. Nonetheless, after his visit in 1939 to the blockaded Shen-Kan-Ning, he pessimistically informed the public that "the cleavage between the two parties was still very wide." Snow even suggested that the KMT might be preparing to abandon the struggle against Japan in order to concentrate "on what appeared to be its main interest: a renewed civil war against 'the Reds.'" [19]

After the New Fourth Army Incident, it required a flight of the imagination to maintain that all was well with the united front. In 1941, Anna Louise Strong excitedly wrote of the possibility of civil war, pleaded that international pressure be applied to the KMT and insinuated that there was an Axis plot afoot to bring Chungking into the Fascist camp.[20] "Asiaticus" also spoke darkly about Fascist intrigues, pro-Japanese Nationalist leaders, and the likelihood of renewed internal strife.[21] After a few days in Chungking and a conversation with Chou En-lai, Vincent Sheean proclaimed that the united front was defunct.[22] Michael Lindsay described KMT-CCP relations as "unfortunately bad" and gently chided the Nationalists for their "unreasonable" attitude.[23] Indeed, from the Western point of view it was the

---

[19] Snow, *The Battle for Asia* (New York, 1941), pp. 109–114, 354. With the passage of time, Snow's prognosis became progressively more pessimistic. For example, see *People on Our Side* (New York, 1944), p. 284.

[20] Strong, "The Kuomintang-Communist Crisis in China," *Amerasia,* V (March 1941), 11, 21–23.

[21] "Asiaticus," "The Fascist Axis vs. the United Front in China," *Amerasia,* IV (February 1941), 543–546; "Autobiography of General Yeh Ting," *ibid.,* V (March 1941), 29; "China's Internal Friction Aids Japan," *ibid.,* 118–122.

[22] Vincent Sheean, *Between the Thunder and the Sun* (New York, 1943), pp. 343–345.

[23] Michael Lindsay, "The North China Front: Part II," *Amerasia,* VIII (April 14, 1944), 124–125.

KMT that had been recalcitrant. When George Uhlmann walked through the guerrilla areas in the spring of 1942, he did not see a single anti-KMT placard. Instead, the French lieutenant listened to the Generalissimo being extolled and noticed that Nationalist banners were prominently displayed. The Communist leaders, Uhlmann wrote, "deplored the Kuomintang's apparent unwillingness to help them, but they never went beyond that." [24]

During their first two years in the Border Regions, Claire and William Band had not heard a single word uttered against Chiang Kai-shek. At a mass meeting in Paoteh on September 10, 1943, the Bands were startled by the conspicuous absence of the Generalissimo's portrait "in the gallery of honor." This was a new experience for these British academicians, but the worst was yet to come. The Bands were appalled when the local guerrilla commander opened the session with a violent speech denouncing the national leader and his party. After the treacherous sins of the KMT had been eloquently catalogued, an agitated crowd thundered the slogans: "Down with the Kuomintang traitors! Down with Chiang Kai-shek! Long live Mao Tse-tung!" "It seemed to us," the Bands sagaciously observed, that the Communists "were getting a lot of things off their chests that had been bursting to come out for a long time; the United Front seemed to have involved quite a strain on their self-restraint, and they were thoroughly enjoying themselves for a change." [25] Hereafter, it is not probable that any subordinate had the audacity or the inclination to switch off the radio on P'eng Teh-huai.

The reporters who reached Yenan in 1944 concluded that the shambles euphemistically styled the united front was beyond repair. Nobody would have disputed Brooks Atkinson's

[24] Lieutenant George Uhlmann, "Land of Five Withouts," *Far Eastern Survey*, XII (May 3, 1943), 89.

[25] Claire and William Band, *Dragon Fangs: Two Years With Chinese Guerrillas* (London, 1947), pp. 210–211.

statement that there was a "complete lack of trust on both sides." [26] In their talks with Harrison Forman and Gunther Stein, the Communists seldom failed to include a parting shot at the KMT. Not surprisingly, Forman visualized the united front as an "armed truce." [27] Indeed, the Communist stance had drastically altered. Instead of minimizing differences and praising the Generalissimo as the national hero, Chinese Communists were openly and even belligerently hostile toward the Central government. When Stein quizzed Mao on what the CCP would do if the Nationalists invaded their territory, he got a direct answer. "We shall," Mao replied, "fight back." [28]

The Western image of the united front was largely a product of external events. It was modified and altered by the uncertain vicissitudes of KMT-CCP relations and reflected the situation at any given moment. However, there was one highly important constant in Western appraisals. Either implicitly or explicitly, nearly all firsthand observers placed the blame for opprobrious conduct on the Kuomintang. Theodore H. White, certainly no friend of China's Communists, suggested that Chiang Kai-shek's determination to maintain dictatorial control of China was the rock on which unity had foundered.[29] Chinese Communists were always careful, even in 1944, to preface their remarks about KMT-CCP strife with righteous protestations of a desire to avoid civil war and to compromise. The only thing they insisted on was that the KMT grant them modest representation in a truly

[26] Brooks Atkinson, "Chinese Still Try to Unify Factions," *New York Times,* November 26, 1944, 43.

[27] Harrison Forman, *Report from Red China* (New York, 1945), p. 172.

[28] Gunther Stein, *The Challenge of Red China* (New York and London, 1945), p. 459.

[29] Theodore H. White and Annalee Jacoby, *Thunder Out of China* (New York, 1946), p. 255.

democratic government.[30] By and large, Westerners took the Communists at their word and judged that their commitment to a united front policy was genuine.

If understood within a certain framework, the CCP's adherence to the united front can be seen as something more than a Bolshevik deception. Derived from the imperatives of the Chinese situation in 1937, the united front advanced the self-interest of the CCP. It allowed the Communists to appeal to both Chinese and foreigners in unfeigned nationalistic terms. At the same time, Chinese Communists never let the rhetoric of wartime unity take precedence over party objectives. Limited cooperation with the KMT was seen as a means to ultimate power, not as an end in itself. The united front represented the deferral of, not the forsaking of, revolutionary goals.[31] In the phraseology of Lin Piao: "The line of our Party during the War of Resistance aimed not only at winning victory in the war, but also at laying the foundations for the nation-wide victory of the new-democratic revolution." Selected cadres were assigned underground work in KMT and Japanese-controlled areas. Under the slogan "alliance and struggle," CCP policy, as Lin wrote, was "to accumulate strength and to bide our time." [32]

Image seldom coincided with reality. Western visitors were not, of course, aware of the intrigues of undercover agents or privy to Maoist statements of long-range strategy. On the other side, they were too inclined to be more cynical about Chinese Nationalists than about Chinese Communists and to accept the propaganda of the CCP while rejecting

[30] For example, see Mao's remarks to Gunther Stein prior to the "We shall fight" statement in Stein, *The Challenge of Red China*, pp. 455–459.

[31] Lyman P. Van Slyke, *Enemies and Friends: The United Front in Chinese Communist History* (Stanford, 1967), pp. 2–3, 48, 105–121.

[32] Lin Piao, "Long Live the Victory of People's War!" in *China after Mao*, by A. Doak Barnett (Princeton, 1967), pp. 205, 208–209, 213.

that of the KMT. Lacking a firm grasp of ideological subtleties, most firsthand observers evaluated the Chinese Communist movement in terms of its immediate anti-Japanese rather than its ultimate anti-Nationalist goals.

[15]

Are They Moscow's Minions?

Foreign visitors to Red China made a special effort to detect any ties which the Chinese Communists might have with the Communist International or the Soviet Union. They generally assumed, with substantial justification, that the Comintern and the U.S.S.R. were Siamese twins. They did not distinguish, therefore, between the Comintern and the Russian state, nor has this writer. Working on the premise that Russian agents and material assistance were the likely concomitants of Soviet influence, travelers to the Border Areas always looked for either of these commodities. Their futile search for tangible evidence that the Chinese Communists were tools of Moscow provides an absorbing chapter in the Western literature on the Chinese Communist movement.

As in so many other matters, Edgar Snow made the first determined effort to ferret out Comintern agents and gold. He found little of either. Snow suggested that after the CCP's physical isolation from the Soviet Union in 1927–1928, the Chinese Communists had been compelled to "limp along as a kind of poor stepchild." The amount of financial assistance which they received from the Russians prior to 1936, Snow wrote, had been "amazingly small." He concluded that it was "rubbish to assert that Russia had been propping up the Chinese Reds." As for Soviet advisers, Snow ascertained that the German Communist Otto Braun had been the only Comintern expert with the Red Army since 1933. Braun, moreover, does not seem to have possessed much influence in the inner counsels of the CCP. His Chinese comrades held him chiefly responsible for the Red Army's defeat during Chiang Kai-shek's fifth bandit-suppression campaign.[1] For his part, Braun complained that pro-Maoist Chinese officers had sabotaged his carefully devised German battle plans.[2] In the first edition of *Red Star over China,* Snow described Braun as a "saddened and chastened ex-Prussian officer" who had been demoted to "a very subordinate position." [3] Braun left Yenan in 1939 on what may have been the only Russian airplane to have landed there during the Second World War.[4]

Snow's declaration in *Red Star over China* that Chinese Communists were not puppets of Stalin did not discourage his journalistic successors from behaving like private detectives.[5] The persistent quest for proof of an international conspiracy continued through 1937 and 1938. When James Bertram was introduced to Skvontsov in Shansi, the New Zealander thought that he had at last uncovered one of those fabled Russian advisers whose escapades had been vividly

[1] Edgar Snow, *Red Star over China* (New York, 1961), pp. 415–417, 420; *Red Star over China* (rev. and expanded ed., New York, 1968), p. 437. See also Snow, "The Man Alongside Mao: Deputy Lin Piao's Thoughts and Career," *New Republic,* CLV (December 3, 1966), 15.

[2] Snow, *Red Star over China* (rev. and expanded ed., 1968), p. 429.

[3] Snow, *Red Star over China* (New York, 1938), pp. 383–384. In this first edition, Snow was critical of Braun and scored the German Communist for his military blunders. In subsequent editions, Snow eliminated his harsher statements and wrote in a more friendly manner. The journalists who followed Snow into the Border Regions discovered that Braun was not enthusiastic about talking to correspondents. Evidently, Snow's initially uncomplimentary remarks had made him wary of reporters.

[4] Snow, *Red Star over China* (rev. and expanded ed., 1968), pp. 479–480.

[5] Snow, *Red Star over China* (1961), p. 421.

portrayed in the capitalist press. Skvontsov, however, disappointed Bertram by turning out to be nothing more than a *Tass* correspondent.[6] Helen Snow, who failed to find a single Russian during her lengthy stay in Yenan, later speculated that Skvontsov must have been the first Soviet citizen to set foot in the Communist areas since 1927. She had been informed that prior to her visit in 1937 no Russian had entered the Communist strongholds.[7] Haldore Hanson tried to "track down the old bogy that Soviet Russia is directing the activities of the Chinese Communists." He returned from the Border Regions persuaded that Moscow's arms and men were unknown quantities to the Eighth Route Army and somewhat startled by the independent attitude adopted by certain CCP officials toward the U.S.S.R.[8] Evans F. Carlson and Agnes Smedley also were curious about the Red Army's ties with the Comintern. Both of them concluded that the Chinese fighting machine had not been the recipient of direct material aid from the Russians.[9] When Earl Leaf made inquiries about the relationship of Chinese communism to the Soviet Union, he received an unequivocal response from Chu Teh. "Our movement," Chu demanded, has "sprung from the soil of China and not from any foreign source."[10]

Despite the abundance of debunking evidence presented by the early scrutinizers of the Communist regions, the myth

[6] James M. Bertram, *Unconquered: Journal of a Year's Adventures among the Fighting Peasants of North China* (New York, 1939), p. 284.

[7] Nym Wales [Helen Foster Snow], *My Yenan Notebooks* (Madison, Conn., 1961), p. 11; *Inside Red China* (Garden City, N.Y., 1939), p. 70.

[8] Haldore Hanson, *"Humane Endeavour": The Story of the China War* (New York and Toronto, 1939), p. 312.

[9] Evans Fordyce Carlson, *Twin Stars of China: A Behind-the-Scenes Story of China's Valiant Struggle for Existence by a U.S. Marine Who Lived and Moved with the People* (New York, 1940), p. 281; Agnes Smedley, *Battle Hymn of China* (New York, 1943), pp. 369–370.

[10] Earl H. Leaf, "Soviet Russia Has Given Chinese Reds No Aid, Declares Commander-in-Chief Chu Teh of Chinese Communist Forces," *North China Star*, July 9, 1937, 1, 24.

of Soviet support to the CCP never really died out. Westerners persevered in their quest for Comintern plotters and mu-
nition crates bearing the imprint "Made in the U.S.S.R."
Joy Homer was terribly excited at the prospect of observing
inflexible Russian conspirators in action. Much to her cha-
grin, she could locate in Yenan only one "homesick Russian
photographer." She learned disconcertingly that Americans
were more popular than Russians among the younger generation of Communist officials and students. Miss Homer noticed that the lower cadres of the CCP were "lukewarm" in
their attitude toward the Soviet Union and contended that
"the average young party member is scarcely aware of Russian affiliations." Although she tried to salvage her crum-
bling assumptions by suggesting that the leaders of the CCP
spent part of their time taking airplane trips to Moscow, her
encounter with China's Communists adds up to a cataloguing of abused suppositions.[11] George A. Fitch similarly concluded that rumors that the Russians were trying to establish
a Communist enclave in northwest China were groundless.
There was not, he wrote, "a single Russian adviser" or bun-
dle of Soviet supplies in either Shensi or Shansi.[12] The year
1939, then, was not a good year for anyone interested in documenting Sino-Soviet complicity.

The journalists who were permitted to enter Yenan in the
summer of 1944 continued the hunt for Russian influence.
Harrison Forman, Gunther Stein, and Theodore H. White
did come across three Soviet citizens. Two of them were *Tass*
correspondents and the other was a surgeon. All three had
entered Communist territory with Chungking's knowledge,
permission, and passports. As for Russian material aid, it was
conspicuously absent. Forman even tried counting the available photographs of Karl Marx and Vladimir I. Lenin. But

[11] Joy Homer, *Dawn Watch in China* (Boston, 1941), pp. 214,
226–228.
[12] George A. Fitch, "China's Northwest Life-Line," *Amerasia*, IV
(September 1940), 305.

for every occasional picture of these heroes of world communism, Forman found a hundred of Roosevelt, Churchill, Chiang Kai-shek, and Stalin.[13] For several years, Brooks Atkinson had made a point of studying the relationship of the CCP to Moscow. On the basis of what he learned in Chungking and Yenan, Atkinson concluded that there was no discernible liaison between Chinese and Russian Reds.[14] This was not only Atkinson's opinion. No foreign investigator of the guerrilla redoubts could discover any concrete evidence of a strong bond between Moscow and Yenan. As far as anyone was able to determine, the *Tass* reporters and the Russian surgeon were just what they claimed to be. Some CCP officials may have flown to Moscow, the possibility of radio communications exists, and the *Tass* men could have done more than simply report the news. The notion that the Russians were supplying their Chinese comrades with advisory personnel and war materiel, however, seems to have had no basis in reality. If there was any intimate contact between Moscow and Yenan, it was extraordinarily well concealed.[15]

The absence of Soviet advisory personnel and Russian ru-

[13] Harrison Forman, *Report from Red China* (New York, 1945), p. 176; Gunther Stein, *The Challenge of Red China* (New York and London, 1945), p. 437; Theodore H. White and Annalee Jacoby, *Thunder Out of China* (New York, 1946), p. 240. The Russian doctor in question was probably I. Orlov. He is mentioned in the China Defence League's pamphlet *In Guerrilla China: Report of China Defence League* (Chungking, 1943), p. 21. During the Bands's three months' stay in Yenan in late 1943 and early 1944, they met one *Tass* correspondent. According to the Bands, this *Tass* reporter was on Communist soil with the knowledge and consent of Chungking. See Claire and William Band, *Dragon Fangs: Two Years With Chinese Guerrillas* (London, 1947), pp. 262–263.

[14] Brooks Atkinson, "Chinese Still Try to Unify Factions," *New York Times,* November 26, 1944, 43.

[15] For a detailed report on the three Russians in Yenan and the possibility of radio contact see *Foreign Relations of the United States: Diplomatic Papers, 1945. The Far East and China* (Washington, D.C., 1969), pp. 301–304.

bles was enough to convince some that the CCP had no substantial links with international communism. Other reporters, however, were uneasy with this mode of analysis and approached the problem of CCP-Comintern relations differently. While Gunther Stein recognized that there were no Russians in Yenan, he was troubled by Yenan's proclivity for endorsing Moscow's "line" or theoretical position in world affairs. Stein discussed the matter with Po Ku (Ch'in Pang-hsien), a leading Chinese theoretician. Po maintained that the CCP had developed its pronouncements without instructions from the Comintern and insisted that any given CCP statement was the Chinese estimate of a situation. Stein accepted Po Ku's reasoning and concluded that the "common political philosophy of the Chinese and Russian Communist parties is sufficient explanation for similar reactions to general world events." He was convinced that China's Communists were "nationalists," not tools of Moscow.[16]

While Stein stressed the philosophical or ideological ties between the Chinese and the Russian Communists, James Bertram emphasized their psychological or emotional solidarity. Bertram had not seen a single Russian weapon during months of travel with the Eighth Route Army, but he believed that the Chinese had received an important legacy from the Soviet Union. Chinese Communists felt, in Bertram's estimation, a sense of oneness with the Russians "in a world struggle." Bertram noticed that to Red Army commanders like Ho Lung the U.S.S.R. was the "socialist fatherland." The unavailability of Russian material support did not, the New Zealander suggested, destroy the CCP's unwavering confidence and faith in their Russian comrades.[17]

In *Red Star over China*, Edgar Snow went further than either Bertram or Stein. While Snow knew that the Russians had no direct physical contact with the Chinese Commu-

16 Stein, *The Challenge of Red China*, pp. 443–446.
17 Bertram, *Unconquered*, p. 282.

nists, he drew attention to their "spiritual and ideological" ties. He stressed the exemplary role of the Soviet Union. The CCP, he argued, viewed Russia with an almost religious fervor as the "mighty fatherland," the guiding light in their "dream of a Socialist world brotherhood." Snow believed, moreover, that "the political ideology, tactical line, and theoretical leadership of the Chinese Communists had been under the close guidance, if not positive direction, of the Communist International." [18] But Snow considerably qualified his appraisal of CCP-Comintern kinship by suggesting that Chinese communism was largely an indigenous species of Marxism "and no mere orphan adopted from abroad, as some writers naïvely suppose." He contended further that the role of the Comintern in Chinese affairs after 1927 had been "colossally magnified in the anti-Communist press." [19] Whether Snow was aware of his ambiguous and contradic-

[18] Snow, *Red Star over China* (New York, 1961), pp. 405–406, 410. In the first edition, Snow wrote: "And finally, of course, the political ideology, tactical line, and theoretical leadership of the Chinese Communists have been under the close guidance, if not positive detailed direction, of the Communist International, which during the past decade has become virtually a bureau of the Russian Communist Party. In the final analysis this means that, for better or worse, the policies of the Chinese Communists, like Communists in every other country, have had to fall in line with, and usually subordinate themselves to, the broad strategic requirements of Soviet Russia, under the dictatorship of Stalin" (p. 374). In subsequent revisions, Snow modified his first sentence and dropped the second one entirely. The complete passage from the 1944 edition reads as follows: "And finally, of course, the political ideology, tactical line, and theoretical leadership of the Chinese Communists had been under the close guidance, if not positive direction, of the Communist International." While these alterations do not detract substantially from Snow's analysis of the CCP-Comintern connection, they do erase the harsher aspects of his appraisal of Stalin and the Communist International. Snow included, moreover, a rather invidious paragraph about Russian domination of the Comintern on page 378 of the first edition which does not appear in the subsequent editions.

[19] *Ibid.*, pp. 119, 414.

tory thinking is not certain, but the reader of *Red Star over China* could find incompatible views of the CCP-Russian connection in the same volume.

In his later writings, Snow took a firmer stand. By 1941 he had determined that the CCP occupied a unique position of independence vis-à-vis the Communist International.[20] In *People on Our Side,* Snow defined the Chinese Communist Party as a "distinctly Chinese offspring of Marxism firmly rooted in the national problems of China's 'semi-colonial' revolution." Although Snow thought that the Comintern occasionally exerted a "directive influence" on the CCP, he concluded that the Chinese party enjoyed a relationship of "relative independence" toward its Soviet brethren.[21]

It was Snow's final image of an independent CCP which dominated the Western literature on the Chinese Communist movement. Anna Louise Strong's characterization of Chinese Communists as "members in good standing" of the Communist International and Cormac Shanahan's oblique suggestion that perhaps Mao Tse-tung had to "wait for the 'green light' from Stalin" before making a move were exceptional.[22] Theodore H. White voiced the consensus when he described the CCP as an autonomous organization whose ties with Moscow were "nominal" and when he pictured the Chinese Communist Party as a "Sinified" and "nationalistic" entity "rooted in its own soil." [23]

Edgar Snow once asked Mao Tse-tung whether a Soviet China would be dominated by the U.S.S.R. Mao replied that if this notion had any validity then it was "also possible to build a railway to Mars and buy a ticket from Mr. H. G.

---

[20] Snow, *The Battle for Asia* (New York, 1941), p. 289.

[21] Snow, *People on Our Side* (New York, 1944), pp. 290–291.

[22] Anna Louise Strong, *One-Fifth of Mankind* (New York, 1938), pp. 189–190. Coming from Miss Strong, this was a compliment; Cormac Shanahan, "China's Communist Puzzle," *China Monthly,* VI (June 1945), 12.

[23] White and Jacoby, *Thunder Out of China,* pp. 45, 240.

Wells." [24] The sense of absurdity conveyed by Mao's remark parallels the emotional tone of every observer's attempt to deal with the problem of Moscow's relationship to Yenan. Where were the Russian agents and supplies? During the early stages of the Sino-Japanese War, the Russians did in fact provide the Chinese with advisers, armaments, and money. As Evans F. Carlson, Haldore Hanson, and others realized, however, this assistance went solely to the Kuomintang. [25] The most likely place to interview a Russian military expert was somewhere in Nationalist China; there were none in Red China. This was the situation which confronted foreign reporters. Not surprisingly, they associated the image of the Chinese Communists as tools of Moscow with fertile bourgeois imaginations and relegated it to the status of a myth. None of them believed that one could build a railroad to Mars.

Image and reality coincided. Under the leadership of Mao Tse-tung and Chu Teh the CCP had graduated from an urban-based dealer agency of the Comintern to a rural-based independent Marxist vehicle for revolutionary change. As early as 1936, Mao told Edgar Snow that the Chinese Communist Party was "not fighting for an emancipated China in order to turn the country over to Moscow!" [26] The Chinese

---

[24] Snow, "Chinese Communists and World Affairs: An Interview With Mao Tse-tung," *Amerasia*, I (August 1937), 267.

[25] For example, see Carlson, *Twin Stars of China*, p. 56; Hanson, "*Humane Endeavour*," p. 354; Fitch, "China's Northwest Life-Line," 301–306. For a detailed scholarly analysis of Russian aid to Nationalist China by a former adviser to the Chinese government see Arthur N. Young, *China and the Helping Hand, 1937–1945* (Cambridge, Mass., 1963), pp. 16, 22, 26, 28, 51, 54–57, 72, 125–130, 206–209, 252–253, 347–350, 423. Young's findings confirm the impression of Western visitors to Red China that Soviet assistance, in men and materiel, found its way to the KMT, not the CCP.

[26] Cited in Stuart R. Schram, *The Political Thought of Mao Tse-tung* (rev. and enlarged ed., New York, Washington, and London, 1969), p. 419.

Red Army, Marshal Lin Piao proudly proclaimed in com-
memoration of the twentieth anniversary of the defeat of
Japan, had fought and won "great victories" from 1937 to
1945 "without any material aid from the outside." [27] Twenty
years earlier, in April 1945, Mao Tse-tung told the delegates
to the Seventh CCP Congress that even as the Russian system had been created by Russian history, so the Chinese system would be created by Chinese history.[28] Chinese Communists may have derived inspiration from Leninist doctrine
and have been impressed by the Soviet model, but they
made their own way. "It was no secret," as Gabriel Kolko
has written, that Chiang Kai-shek used part of the $250 mil-
lion the Russians loaned him for arms purchases "as much to
contain the Communists as the Japanese." [29] Lin Piao was
speaking from experience when he warned the revolutionaries of the future that no war of national liberation could rely
on external support and advised them to adhere to a policy
of "self-reliant struggle." [30] Present-day scholars will find un-
tapped and illuminating information on the relationship between Russian and Chinese Communists in the works of firsthand observers.

[27] Lin Piao, "Long Live the Victory of People's War!" in *China after
Mao,* by A. Doak Barnett (Princeton, 1967), p. 235.

[28] Conrad Brandt, Benjamin Schwartz, and John K. Fairbanks, eds.,
A Documentary History of Chinese Communism (Cambridge, Mass.,
1952), p. 305.

[29] Gabriel Kolko, *The Politics of War: The World and United
States Foreign Policy, 1943–1945* (New York, 1968), p. 233. See also
Richard J. Barnet, *Intervention and Revolution: The United States in
the Third World* (New York and Cleveland, 1968), especially pp.
47–76, and Charles B. McLane, *Soviet Policy and the Chinese Communists, 1931–1946* (New York, 1958).

[30] Lin Piao, "Long Live the Victory of People's War!" pp. 231–236,
256–257.

[16]

Are They Really Communists?

Much nonsense has been written about the "agrarian reformer" myth. In 1944 Chiang Kai-shek denounced the "agrarian democrats" idea as "clever Communist propaganda" to mask the CCP's ties with the Third International.[1] Subsequent evaluations have expanded on Chiang's statement. A retired American diplomat maintains that the agrarian reformer slogan was a cunning artifice devised by the CCP to conceal its intentions and affiliations.[2] Another former Foreign Service officer diagnoses the agrarian-democrats illusion as a "disinformation" conspiracy: a Russian-inspired contrivance circulated by seemingly reliable non-Communist sources and calculated to demoralize the West, to secure American economic assistance, and to obscure the emergence of a Sino-Soviet monolith.[3] Allen Dulles, former director of the Central Intelligence Agency, contends that

one of the most successful long-range political deceptions of the Communists convinced gullible people in the West before and during World War II that the Chinese people's movement was

[1] *United States Relations with China: With Special Reference to the Period 1944–1949* (Washington, D.C., 1949), p. 553.

[2] Charles W. Thayer, *Guerrilla* (New York, Evanston, and London, 1963), pp. 42, 97.

[3] Natalie Grant [Mrs. Richard Wraga], "Disinformation," *National Review*, IX (November 5, 1960), 41–46.

not Communistic, but a social and "agrarian" reform movement. This fiction was planted through Communist-influenced journalists in the Far East and penetrated organizations in the West.[4] Finally, writers like John T. Flynn have argued that the American people were seduced and led astray by the fantastic hoax that the Chinese Reds were not true Communists but "agrarian reformers" and "old-fashioned democrats."[5] Flynn and others sharing his convictions have identified nearly every Westerner who had a firsthand encounter with China's Communists as an insidious propagandist linked with an international conspiracy.[6] They have conveyed the impression that most, if not all, foreign reporters denied that the Chinese Communists were bona fide Leninists. If anyone has misled the reading public, however, it is not these much maligned American and European journalists. Rather, Flynn

[4] Allen Dulles, *The Craft of Intelligence* (New York, Evanston, and London, 1963), pp. 149–150.

[5] John T. Flynn, *While You Slept: Our Tragedy in Asia and Who Made It* (New York, 1951), p. 22.

[6] *Ibid.*, pp. 59–70. See also Anthony Kubek, *How the Far East was Lost: American Policy and the Creation of Communist China, 1941–1949* (Chicago, 1963), pp. 363–384, and Freda Utley, *The China Story* (Chicago, 1951), pp. 139–163. The specific chapters in these volumes which deal with the Western literature on the Chinese Communist movement are suggestively titled: "The Pool of Poison," "Subversion Along the Linotype Front: Reviewers at Work," and "How the Communists Captured the Public."

For a recent study which comes very close to arguing that the Chinese Communists were in fact merely agrarian reformers, see Gabriel Kolko, *The Politics of War: The World and United States Foreign Policy, 1943–1945* (New York, 1968), pp. 236–241. Working from the existential premise that the historian understands the true nature of a system only "from its practice, as opposed to its rhetoric," Kolko calls the Chinese Communists pragmatic and self-guiding "ideological opportunists." In what can only be described as a massive overstatement, Kolko says that after 1940, Mao Tse-tung's "only constant inspiration" was the Chinese classics and Chinese folklore "rather than Marxism."

and a number of other publicists have done the American people—and the Chinese Communists—a disservice by propagating simplistic evaluations of the Western literature on communism in China. Their stereotyped appraisals have given birth to the legend that the Chinese Communists, aided by a cabal of foreign reporters, tried to disguise their true nature by promoting the beguiling slogan "agrarian reformers." In this chapter the "agrarian reformer" myth is reappraised through an examination of the writings of those who had direct contacts with Chinese Communists before and during the Second World War.

There were, of course, firsthand observers who described Chinese Communists as either agrarian reformers or some comparably innocuous species of political moderates. T. A. Bisson, for example, defined Chinese communism as "the essence of *bourgeois* democracy" applied to agricultural conditions.[7] This position typifies one kind of response to the question of whether the Chinese Communists were actually Communist revolutionaries committed to a Marxist-Leninist reorganization of society. At the other extreme, some Western reporters were persuaded that the Chinese Reds were truly Red. A third school of thought, comprising the majority of informed Far Eastern observers, straddled the issue. The writers in this category expressed views that fluctuated uncertainly between the two polar appraisals.

An articulate, and perhaps the first, exponent of the view that the Chinese Communists were not communists was a British journalist, Freda Utley. From 1927 to 1931, she had been a member of the British Communist Party. In 1928, she made a brief trip to China as a courier for the Comintern and held discussions with the underground leaders of the CCP in Shanghai. Six years of residence in the Soviet Union (1930–1936) and the victimization of her Russian husband in a purge were, for her, profoundly disillusioning

[7] T. A. Bisson, "China's Part in a Coalition War," *Far Eastern Survey*, XII (July 14, 1943), p. 139. The emphasis is Bisson's.

experiences.[8] By 1938, when she returned to China as special correspondent for the London *News-Chronicle,* Freda Utley considered herself "a fugitive from Stalin's tyranny," [9]

Miss Utley's background of hostility to Soviet communism makes her meeting with Chinese Communists in Hankow in 1938 a particularly fascinating episode. Edgar Snow discreetly inquired of Po Ku and Chou En-lai whether they would see an "exiled comrade." He was astonished when Po and Chou remarked that "they were immediately engaged in fighting the Japanese, not the battles of the Comintern," and did not object to talking with Miss Utley.[10] Instead of being shunned as an apostate, Freda Utley was warmly welcomed by the Chinese Communists. Chou En-lai paid her a personal visit and the Eighth Route Army held a reception in her honor. Reasoning that the leaders of the CCP must have known of her husband's arrest and that she was out of favor with the Soviet authorities, Freda Utley concluded that the Chinese Communists "really were a different breed." [11] In

[8] Utley, *Odyssey of a Liberal: Memoirs* (Washington, D.C., 1970), pp. 84–85, 90–93, 270–271, 306. Freda Utley emigrated to the United States in 1939 and became an American citizen in 1950. She did not learn until 1963 that her husband, Arcadia J. Berdichevsky, had died in a Russian prison camp in 1938.

[9] Utley, *The China Story,* p. 108. See also Miss Utley's statement of May 1, 1950, in U.S. Senate, Subcommittee of the Committee on Foreign Relations, 81st Cong., 2nd Sess., *State Department Employee Loyalty Investigation, Hearings* (Part I, Washington, D.C., 1950), pp. 737–797.

[10] Edgar Snow, *The Battle for Asia* (New York, 1941), pp. 289–290. See also Snow's vindictive remarks in *Journey to the Beginning* (New York, 1958), pp. 227–228. Snow's comments in *Journey to the Beginning* are colored by his hostility toward Freda Utley for her role in the McCarthy era, but those in *The Battle for Asia* seem to have been written before her anticommunism had been publicly directed at the Chinese Reds.

[11] Utley, *Odyssey of a Liberal,* pp. 211–212; *China at War* (New York, 1939), pp. 73–74; *The China Story,* p. 108; Snow, *The Battle for Asia,* pp. 289–290.

1939, she wrote *China at War*. This volume reflects the nature of her persuading encounter with the CCP.

In *China at War*, Freda Utley asserted that the CCP had ceased to be a revolutionary Leninist organization and had become a party of "social reformers and patriots." After losing their proletarian base in 1927, she explained, the Chinese Communists had been compelled to adapt themselves to an agrarian environment. She believed that by 1935, Chinese communism had been "transmuted by the logic of history into a movement of peasant emancipation." She maintained too that the CCP had abandoned the idea of establishing a one-party dictatorship. The aim of Chinese communism was political and social reform along democratic and capitalistic lines.[12] Chinese charm and the peasant base of the CCP had led Miss Utley to conclusions that she was later to regret and repudiate.

Freda Utley was not the only person who thought that the Chinese Communists were not Bolsheviks. Evans F. Carlson was of a similar persuasion. His observations convinced him that the doctrines of the CCP were "in their political aspects, representative government (democracy), in their economic aspect, the co-operative theory, and that only in their social application could they be called communistic, for emphasis is placed on social equality." Carlson's Communists were an ill-defined species of utopian democrats whose teachings were closer to Christianity than to Leninism.[13] Unlike Freda Utley, Carlson specifically discounted the importance of ideologies and had little conception of the philosophical tenets of Marxist-Leninism.[14] Although Agnes Smedley was herself no paragon of theoretical expertise, it would be difficult to find fault with her evaluation of Carlson. The marine

12 Utley, *China at War*, pp. 251–254.
13 Evans Fordyce Carlson, *Twin Stars of China: A Behind-the-Scenes Story of China's Valiant Struggle for Existence by a U.S. Marine Who Lived and Moved with the People* (New York, 1940), pp. 176, 299.
14 *Ibid.*, p. 210.

knew nothing, she sneered, of the principles which inspired Communist behavior.[15]

Claire and William Band were in the same class as Evans F. Carlson. These British educators were equally ignorant of the theoretical underpinnings of communism. Their explanation of Bolshevism was that it constituted a kind of communal sharing of material goods, "each for all." Like Carlson, the Bands viewed the Chinese Communists as progressive democrats and suggested that their prospectus for building a new China was identical with that of the KMT. The Bands felt that it was a pity that the Chinese Communists had not changed the name of their party. After all, the program of the CCP did not resemble communism "as it is understood anywhere else in the world." [16]

Harrison Forman holds the dubious honor of being the American journalist who most emphatically rejected the notion that the CCP might be Bolsheviks. Chinese Communists were not, he wrote, "Communists—not according to the Russian definition of the term." Forman believed that years of earthy contact with property-conscious peasants had forced the CCP to compromise its earlier Marxist-Leninism. The Chinese Communists of 1944, he suggested, were no more communistic than Americans.[17] Although Forman refrained from explicitly stating what he did think Chinese Communists were, it is not likely that he would have dissented from the view of the *New York Times* China reporter that they were agrarian democrats.[18]

A second school of thought either avoided the question of

[15] Agnes Smedley, *China Fights Back: An American Woman with the Eighth Route Army* (London, 1939), p. 253.

[16] Claire and William Band, *Dragon Fangs: Two Years with Chinese Guerrillas* (London, 1947), pp. 62, 244, 332, 335.

[17] Harrison Forman, *Report from Red China* (New York, 1945), p. 177.

[18] Brooks Atkinson, "Chinese Still Try to Unify Factions," *New York Times*, November 26, 1944, 43.

the CCP's revolutionary commitment or leaned only tentatively toward one side or the other of the issue. Owen Lattimore consciously tried to avoid using what he considered to be the misleading clichés of the day and to describe social phenomena in concrete terms. The only time he came close to using the phrase "agrarian reformers" was to satirize it. In an article in which he warned that there was a definite possibility that China would "go Bolshevik," Lattimore ridiculed the assumption that "the heavily agrarian structure of society in China makes it necessary for even the Chinese Communists to be 'agrarian radicals' rather than 'true Communists,' and that the Chinese family system is notably resistant to Marxist ideas." [19] Stanton Lautenschlager simply observed that "Yenan is not very radical" and left it at that.[20] On an equally superficial level, the press correspondent for the Interdenominational Church Committee for China Relief wrote that ideologically Russian and Chinese Bolshevism were "many miles apart." [21]

In discussing Mao Tse-tung's important exposition of Chinese communism, *On the New Democracy,* Michael Lindsay was inattentive to statements proclaiming the CCP's solidarity with the Soviet Union, the vanguard role of the proletariat, and the revolutionary commitment to a socialist society. Although Lindsay spent more time in the Communist-controlled regions of China than any of the other transient foreigners who visited these areas during the Second World War, he stressed the immediate and tactical aspects of the Chinese Communist movement. He noted that the CCP's peasant constituency would oppose such Stalinist innovations as collectivism and remarked that the CCP looked

[19] Owen Lattimore, "American Responsibilities in the Far East," *Virginia Quarterly Review,* XVI (Spring 1940), 164–165; Lattimore, conversation with the author, April 16, 1969.

[20] Stanton Lautenschlager, *Far West in China* (New York, 1941), p. 19.

[21] Joy Homer, *Dawn Watch in China* (Boston, 1941), p. 228.

forward "to a long period of development under capitalist democratic institutions." [22] In Lindsay's appraisal of the situation, communism in China was not a pressing matter. As he wrote on October 7, 1944, the real issue between the KMT and the CCP was democratic government.[23]

Although Gunther Stein approached the problem differently, his response to the question of how far the CCP were genuine Communists was similar to that of Lindsay. Stein began his analysis by taking exception to the agrarian reformer thesis. Nevertheless, he could not bring himself to accept statements by CCP leaders that they were and intended to remain true Communists. Instead of supporting either of these positions, Stein groped to find a middle ground. He pictured the CCP as a tightly disciplined elite, recognized the party's control over mass organizations, and pointed to the absence of a free press in Red China. On the other side, Stein was impressed by the undogmatic character of Chinese Communists, by their willingness to adopt an independent stance vis-à-vis the Comintern, and by their attempt to sinify their theory. He thought that nationalism was the dominant characteristic of the CCP's ideology, not Marxism.[24] As Tang Tsou has pointed out, Stein minimized the revolutionary components of Chinese communism and reduced the CCP's political philosophy "to an innocuous tool of intellectual analysis." [25] Stein pushed his tortured logic to the conclusion that the Chinese Communists were democratic nationalists only slightly tinted with an evolutionary brand of

[22] Michael Lindsay, "The North China Front: Part II," *Amerasia,* VIII (April 14, 1944), 124–125.

[23] U.S. Senate, Committee on the Judiciary, Subcommittee on Internal Security, 89th Cong., 1st Sess., *Morgenthau Diary: China,* II (Washington, D.C., 1965), p. 1333.

[24] Gunther Stein, *The Challenge of Red China* (New York and London, 1945), pp. 143–147, 179, 230.

[25] Tang Tsou, *America's Failure in China, 1941–50* (Chicago, 1963), pp. 233–234.

"Marxism." Although Stein did not use the analogy, his Communists bore a remarkable resemblance to the British Labour Party. Theodore H. White's interpretation of the nature of Chinese communism coincided with Stein's in that both men decided that the Chinese Communists were essentially nationalists. White described the Communist leaders as "grim, hard-headed pragmatists who cast away tenet after tenet" of Marxist theory. The CCP had become a party of empiricists deriving theory from experience and of "out-and-out" nationalists.[26] White realized that the Communists flatly denied the assumption that they were mere agrarian reformers and insisted that they were Communists "in the full sense of the word." He minimized, however, the philosophical aspects of what they said and emphasized that they were "among the world's greatest empiricists, trial-and-error artists par excellence." [27]

White was uneasy with his own appraisal. Like Michael Lindsay, he was familiar with Mao Tse-tung's *On the New Democracy*. Unlike Lindsay, White distinguished between CCP means and ends and confessed his uncertainty about the future. Mao's *On the New Democracy*, White wrote, left certain questions unanswered. How long would the new democracy period last? Was the Communist alliance with other Chinese groups to be permanent or temporary? If they had the power, would the CCP permit opposition parties or pursue an authoritarian reorganization of society along socialist lines? Would a triumphant CCP bind China to the Soviet Union in a revolutionary front against other nations? In a real sense, then, White's analysis of the Chinese Communist movement was open-ended. He called the Chinese Commu-

[26] Theodore H. White, "Inside Red China," *Life,* XVII (December 18, 1944), 44, 46.
[27] White and Annalee Jacoby, *Thunder Out of China* (New York, 1946), p. 234.

nists pragmatic nationalists but took the precaution of telling the reader of his own uncertainty.[28]

At the session of the State Department Employee Loyalty Investigation Hearings on March 13, 1950, Senator Joseph R. McCarthy accused Haldore Hanson of being "a man with a mission—a mission to communize the world." [29] The Senator from Wisconsin rested his case on copious citations from Hanson's *"Humane Endeavour."* In a vigorous rebuttal on March 28, Hanson denied any subversive affiliations and demanded that a fair reading of his book would reveal a realistic appraisal of the nature of Chinese communism. Hanson disassociated himself from the agrarian-reformer interpretation. He stated that he had pointed out in *"Humane Endeavour"* that Mao Tse-tung collected translations of the principal Marxist works, that certain members of the CCP had been trained in the Soviet Union, and that the Chinese Communists flew a hammer and sickle standard.[30]

A close reading of *"Humane Endeavour"* and Hanson's other writings partially sustains his effort to vindicate his reputation. He did mention, in a factual manner, such items as the public display of the hammer and sickle emblem along with the KMT flag. But Hanson stressed the presence of the Nationalist symbol, not the conspicuousness of the Soviet standard.[31] When discussing the education of Chinese Communists, he emphasized that only a few of them had received their training in Moscow.[32] Hanson did, however, ask the right questions. He quizzed Mao Tse-tung on whether the CCP had abandoned communism and got a forthright

---

[28] *Ibid.,* pp. 234–237.

[29] U.S. Senate, *State Department Employee Loyalty Investigation* (Part 1), p. 82.

[30] *Ibid.,* pp. 342–343, 364.

[31] Haldore Hanson, "The People behind the Chinese Guerrillas," *Pacific Affairs,* XI (September 1938), 290.

[32] Hanson, *"Humane Endeavour": The Story of the China War* (New York and Toronto, 1939), p. 312.

reply. "The Chinese Communist party," Mao responded, "has not ceased to be communist. Our final goal is unchanged." When Mao went on to suggest that the ultimate transition from a democratic to a socialist republic might be through evolutionary rather than revolutionary means, a startled Hanson protested that there was "no historical precedent" for the peaceful introduction of Marxian socialism. Mao smiled as he observed that: "We are trying to make history, not to imitate it." [33]

Hanson was struck more by the professed desire of the CCP to "make history" and to cooperate with the KMT in building a democratic China than he was by references to a distant socialist utopia. The Chinese Communist Party, he wrote, had demonstrated the sincerity of its desire to create a genuine democracy.[34] In short, Hanson recognized the long-range aims of the CCP but chose to emphasize their remoteness and to focus on the moderate character of the immediate program sponsored by Yenan. Communism in China simply was not a vital issue to Haldore Hanson in 1938–1939.

Anna Louise Strong provides the final example of an American journalist who failed to take an unequivocal stand on the question of whether the Chinese Reds were Communists. The implication of the analyses by Hanson, Homer, Lautenschlager, Lindsay, Stein, and White was that the CCP could not be understood as an orthodox Stalinist party. While none of these writers can be associated meaningfully with the agrarian-reformer school, their firsthand observations did incline them to discount the revolutionary commitment of the CCP. Anna Louise Strong's controlling supposition, however, was that the Chinese Reds were revolutionary comrades in arms with the Russians and legitimate members of the Communist International.

[33] *Ibid.*, pp. 308–310.
[34] Hanson, "Firebrands and Chinese Politics," *Amerasia*, III (April 1939), 82.

This assumption did not inhibit her from concluding that there was no reason to fear a Communist takeover in China. She belittled the possibility of a Bolshevized China on the grounds that the immediate CCP goal was a democratic republic and that it would require a relatively long period of time to achieve even this limited aim. Without any qualms, she praised the Chinese Communists as firm supporters of the united front and Generalissimo Chiang Kai-shek.[35] Anna Louise Strong chose to accentuate the wartime strategy of the CCP and to relegate the problem of a Communist China to a dimly outlined future. In this "presentism," she was at one with nearly all of her contemporaries.

In 1939 the *New Statesman and Nation* published a letter from Freda Utley in which she announced that "there are no 'Bolsheviks' to-day in China; they have all become 'Mensheviks.' "[36] A few issues later, the *New Statesman* carried a forthright critique of this position. James Bertram attacked Miss Utley's ideas as being "dangerously misleading," saying that if the Reds had "ceased to be revolutionary, then the hammer-and-sickle flag now furled in Yenan should properly be hoisted over Transport House." Bertram suggested that the CCP had emulated Stalin in discarding Trotsky's thesis of a revolution by the proletariat in a semicolonial state, adding that the Chinese Communists were advocates of the "three stages" theory of the Chinese Revolution. According to this strategy, the anti-imperialist phase would be followed by the bourgeois-democratic period and the whole process would be terminated in a socialist upheaval. If this made the Chinese Communists and Stalin "Mensheviks," Bertram concluded, "then that is a matter for Miss Utley to fight out with those who attach more importance to these labels than I do." Bertram rested his interpre-

[35] Anna Louise Strong, *One-Fifth of Mankind* (New York, 1938), pp. 188–200.

[36] Utley, "Correspondence: China," *New Statesman and Nation,* XVII (January 28, 1939), 131.

tation on the claim that his views reflected those of the many Chinese Communists with whom he had talked.[37]

Bertram was not the only Western journalist who had the perspicacity to recognize the Leninist commitment of the Chinese Communist Party. Although Agnes Smedley never dealt with the problem in a comprehensive fashion, she occasionally made random comments which must have given her readers a start. For example, she noted in *Battle Hymn of China* that most Chinese Communists thought "in terms of Marx, Engels, Lenin, and Stalin," and that some took pride "in their ability to quote chapter and verse of these or lecture on them for three or four hours."[38] In an interview on March 1, 1937, she asked Mao directly whether the Chinese Communists had become simple nationalists and had forsaken the class struggle. Mao replied that the Chinese Communists were internationalists who favored the world Communist movement.[39] A Lutheran missionary who had frequently heard Agnes Smedley extol the CCP as a party of dedicated Marxist revolutionaries at Bishop Roots's dinner table in the 1930's was surprised to learn in the 1950's that she had supposedly fooled correspondents and diplomats into thinking that the Chinese Communists were agrarian reformers.[40] One can minimize her written and oral statements on the valid grounds that they were disconnected snippets written in an overall context of adoration for China's Communists. Nevertheless, the implication of much that she wrote and said was that the Chinese comrades were revolutionary Marxists.

Although Cormac Shanahan had a low opinion of Gunther Stein's *The Challenge of Red China*, he empha-

---

[37] James Bertram, "Correspondence: The Chinese Revolution," *New Statesman and Nation*, XVII (February 11, 1939), 208–209.

[38] Smedley, *Battle Hymn of China* (New York, 1943), p. 169.

[39] Cited in Stuart Schram, *Mao Tse-tung* (New York, 1966), p. 184.

[40] Paul Frillmann and Graham Peck, *China: The Remembered Life* (Boston, 1968), p. 24.

sized that parts of the book disproved propaganda claiming that the CCP were not real Communists. Shanahan, who had been told by Mao Tse-tung in Yenan that the principles of the CCP were those of international communism, deplored Stein's failure to include more statements by Mao on the Marxist commitment of the Chinese Communists. Nevertheless, he felt there was sufficient information in the volume to jar gullible people from their intellectual stupor. Since eighty-five per cent of the Chinese population was rural, it was only natural that the Communist apparatus would "show something of an agrarian character." This, however, was nothing more than a façade. Shanahan concluded that the organizational and thought patterns apparent in Yenan were definitely products of communism and bore no relation to the precepts taught by Sun Yat-sen.[41]

By 1941, Freda Utley had changed her mind about the Chinese Communists. She later recalled that it was the response of the CCP to the Nazi-Soviet Pact of 1939 which convinced her of the error of her ways.[42] An article she wrote in the spring of 1941 substantiates her memory.[43] It is apparent that Freda Utley was particularly disturbed by Mao Tse-tung's observations on international affairs in an interview with Edgar Snow in Yenan on September 26, 1939. Mao defended Russian neutrality in the European conflagration on the grounds that all of the protagonists were imperialists in a "robber war with justice on neither side." He called Neville Chamberlain "the world's Public Enemy No. 1," vindicated the Soviet invasion of eastern Poland as an ef-

[41] Cormac Shanahan, "The Challenge of Gunther Stein," *China Monthly*, VII (February 1946), 66; *Foreign Relations of the United States: Diplomatic Papers, 1944. China* (Washington, D.C., 1967), pp. 482–483.

[42] U.S. Senate, *State Department Employee Loyalty Investigation* (Part 1), pp. 785, 787. See also Utley, *Odyssey of a Liberal*, p. 225.

[43] Utley, "Will Russia Betray China?" *Asia*, XLI (April 1941), 170–173.

fort to liberate minority peoples, and exonerated the Nazi-Soviet agreement as having put Hitler "in Stalin's pocket" and provided the U.S.S.R. with national security.[44] Considering Freda Utley's deep loathing of both Nazism and Stalinism and her British lineage, it is not unreasonable to assume that Mao's comments did indeed give her second thoughts about the nature of Chinese communism.

In that article in 1941, Freda Utley discarded the idea that the Chinese Communists were agrarian reformers. She now pictured the CCP as a pliant tool of Comintern totalitarianism. Although she chided Chiang Kai-shek for his shortsightedness and undemocratic assumptions, she sympathized with his misgivings about trusting the CCP, a party more responsive to Russian than to Chinese interests. Freda Utley's moody essay reflects her personal disappointment and disillusionment. "It is the tragedy of the progressive movement in China," she wrote, "and the tragedy of the Chinese masses, that the Communist Party is under the orders of a foreign power which is not in the least interested in them, but only in the survival of the Stalinist bureaucracy."[45] From 1941 on, and into the McCarthy period of American history, Freda Utley became a vocal critic of China's Communists. Her abandonment of the agrarian-reformer thesis, however, was overshadowed by the writings of the two most perceptive exponents of the notion that the CCP was genuinely Communist: Helen and Edgar Snow.

In approaching the problem of the nature of Chinese communism, Helen Foster Snow began by opposing the view that the Red Army was a purely peasant force. She denied that it had an agrarian ideology and accepted the proposi-

[44] Snow, "The Chinese Communists and Wars on Two Continents: Interviews with Mao Tse-tung," *China Weekly Review,* XCI (January 20, 1940), 277–280. Miss Utley refers to this interview and Snow's *The Battle for Asia* as sources for her new appraisal of Chinese communism.

[45] Utley, "Will Russia Betray China?" 170–173.

tion that the CCP represented "proletarian leadership." Mrs. Snow pointed out that the ultimate goal of the CCP was the triumph of "Socialism" and contended that the Red Army considered itself an integral part of the international revolutionary movement. She even had the temerity to suggest that the Chinese Reds should place more emphasis on their "*Leninist* character" in order that "outsiders would not confuse their theories with the pre-Leninist era of Marxism." Mrs. Snow possessed a working knowledge of the doctrine of proletarian hegemony and understood the important thesis of telescoping the revolution and thereby passing the "orthodox bourgeois stage." Mrs. Snow's Communists certainly were not "Mensheviks," but rather faithful disciples of Bolshevism.[46]

Despite Mrs. Snow's recognition of the Leninist character of Chinese communism, she did not think that the CCP's moderate professions were simply a ploy to enable them to seize power. After talking with Chinese Communists, she was convinced that they earnestly desired "some form of democracy" as the most effective vehicle for organizing mass resistance to the Japanese. Indeed, Mrs. Snow was not disturbed at the possibility of a "liberal-Leftist" take-over in China. There was, she explained in one of the most common expressions in the Western literature on the Chinese Communist movement, "no danger of 'Bolshevism' in China for many years to come." [47]

Edgar Snow was the most articulate and staunch advocate of the thesis that the Chinese Communists were Marxist rev-

[46] Nym Wales [Helen Foster Snow], *Inside Red China* (Garden City, N.Y., 1939), pp. 51–52, 62. The italics are Mrs. Snow's. In Mao's interviews with Mrs. Snow, he referred to the possibility of avoiding the capitalist stage of the Chinese Revolution and of transforming it into a "Socialist" revolution. Mao also equated the CCP with the proletariat and enunciated the doctrine of proletarian hegemony. Moreover, Mao emphasized that his opinions were in harmony with the resolutions of the Comintern. See pp. 223–226.

[47] *Ibid.*, pp. 320–322.

olutionaries aspiring to the attainment of absolute political power. Perhaps the most striking statement in *Red Star over China* was an affirmation of faith by Mao Tse-tung. The CCP, Mao proclaimed, "was, is, and will ever be, faithful to Marxist-Leninism, and it will continue its struggles against every opportunist tendency. In this determination lies one explanation of its invincibility and the certainty of its final victory." [48] The CCP, Mao asserted in the clearest of possible terms, "will never abandon its aims of Socialism and Communism, it will still pass through the stage of democratic revolution of the bourgeoisie to attain the stages of Socialism and Communism." [49] Since Snow understood the nature of Chinese communism through the eyes of the party leader, it is not surprising that he believed that the CCP was genuinely Communist.

By taking Snow's thoughts out of context, Harold R. Isaacs has been able to maintain that *Red Star over China* is the birthplace of the agrarian-reformer myth. [50] This conclusion is hardly justified. In the section referred to by Isaacs, Snow did write that whatever Chinese communism may have been in the South, the Soviet society of the Northwest could more accurately be described as one of "rural equalitarianism" than a Marxist prototype. Snow went on to emphasize, however, that the moderate agrarian-reform program being sponsored by the CCP was only a means to an end. The Chinese Communists, he explained, had never regarded their current activities as more than a tactical phase in their struggle for power. Snow understood the reformist orientation of the CCP as "only a very provisional affair." The ultimate aim re-

[48] Edgar Snow, *Red Star over China* (New York, 1961), p. 188.

[49] *Ibid.*, p. 488. See also Mao's statement of ultimate intentions in a report of April 1945 titled "On Coalition Government" in Conrad Brandt, Benjamin Schwartz, and John K. Fairbank, eds., *A Documentary History of Chinese Communism* (Cambridge, Mass., 1952), p. 304.

[50] Harold R. Isaacs, *Images of Asia: American Views of China and India* (New York, 1962), p. 163. See also Utley, *Odyssey of a Liberal*, p. 210.

mained "a true and complete Socialist State of the Marx-Leninist conception."[51] If the Chinese Communists advocated a united front with the KMT and democracy for China, it was *"simply because"* these were necessary initial steps toward the realization of their revolutionary goals.[52]

There were but two significant qualifications to Snow's realistic analysis of the revolutionary commitment of the CCP in *Red Star over China*. In the first instance, Snow implied that the socialist phase of the Communist vision was many years away. Second, he envisaged the Chinese brand of communism as an indigenous Bolshevik hybrid. Snow recognized that the Chinese Communists had copied many of their notions, organizations, and methods from the Russians. He maintained, however, that in all of the borrowing from the U.S.S.R. there had been considerable adaptation of ideas and institutions to the Chinese milieu.[53] Nevertheless, to assert that *Red Star over China* was the incubator for the agrarian-reformer myth is to overlook a major thesis of the book. When Snow prophesied that one day the Red Star would gain ascendancy in China, he meant exactly what he said.

By the time Snow returned to the Northwest in the fall of 1939, the agrarian-reformer cliché had gained sufficient currency to prompt him to ask Mao Tse-tung a pointed question. Mao replied quite clearly to Snow's observation that a number of people were asserting that Chinese Communists had become bourgeois in their objectives and methods by insisting that the Chinese Communists "are always social revolutionaries; we are never reformists." Mao explained that, at that time, the Chinese revolution had a democratic and national character. But, he added: "after a certain stage it will be transformed into social revolution."[54] Fortified with

---

[51] Snow, *Red Star over China*, pp. 232–233.

[52] *Ibid.*, p. 455. The italics are Snow's.

[53] *Ibid.*, pp. 409, 479–480.

[54] Snow, "The Chinese Communists and Wars on Two Continents: Interviews with Mao Tse-tung," *China Weekly Review*, XCI (January 13, 1940), 246.

the information that Mao Tse-tung still considered himself to be a Marxist, Snow launched a full-scale assault on the agrarian reformer school in *The Battle for Asia.*

Snow began his critique by noting that an assorted collection of well-wishers had done their best to convince others that Chinese Communists were not true Communists. After commenting further along this line, Snow confessed that he could not understand how such people reconciled their views with the CCP's consistent support of the Comintern. He then suggested that liberals who build up hopes that the Chinese Reds were merely reformers who had discarded revolutionary techniques were "doomed to ultimate disillusionment." The "religion" of China's Communists remained "international socialism." If conditions changed, the CCP might embrace whatever methods it believed necessary "in order 'to stay on the locomotive of history.'" Snow went on to parry possible objections from the agrarian reformer partisans by drawing an analogy between Christianity and communism. It was just as logical, he argued, for a Chinese devotee of Marx to label himself a Communist as it was for a follower of Christ to call himself a Christian. Although admitting that those in Yenan had never practiced communism, were not then living in a Red utopia, and had not advocated the immediate establishment of Bolshevism in China, he said that this did not lessen their firm conviction that they were "fighting in the vanguard of a world revolution." [55]

In 1944–1945, a shift occurred in Snow's analysis of Chinese communism.[56] Perhaps from a desire to present his

[55] Snow, *The Battle for Asia,* pp. 290–292.

[56] For an interpretation of Snow's writings different from that which follows see Tang Tsou, *America's Failure in China,* pp. 231–233. Professor Tsou draws a sharp distinction between Snow's reporting before and after 1944. He identifies the former as realistic but feels that after 1944, Snow altered his characterization of China's Communists to the extent that he succumbed to the agrarian-reformer illusion. This interpretation fails to take into account Snow's particular mode of analysis and rests on evidence that is inconclusive.

Chinese friends in the best possible light, Snow played down the revolutionary commitment of the CCP. He stressed that even to the CCP the attainment of socialism in China was a very remote goal.[57] The Chinese Communist Party, he asserted, had become a "purely Chinese offspring of Marxism" with communism as a "quite distant" objective.[58] In consistently appraising Chinese communism in terms of means and ends, Snow had come to emphasize the means and minimize the ends.

There were, however, definite limits to Snow's change in emphasis, evidence of which appears in his squabble with the popular Chinese author Lin Yutang. In a biting review of Lin's *The Vigil of a Nation,* Snow defended China's Communists on the grounds that they had long ago renounced "any intention of establishing communism" in the foreseeable future.[59] Lin employed his sarcastic wit to full advantage in replying. He supported his thesis that the Chinese Communists were genuine Communists by citing Snow's *The Battle for Asia.* As for the notion that the CCP had no intention of erecting a Stalinist system soon, Lin declared that "that harmless 'near future' happens to be defined by Mao Tse-tung as 'several years,' no longer than the Nazi incubation period after the Munich *putsch.*" [60] Possibly sobered by Lin's barbed critique, Snow could only reply that there was nothing startling in the idea that the CCP had not abandoned its aspiration to implant socialism in China. The Communists, Snow continued, had never concealed their objectives. He even reiterated his original position that the

[57] For illustrations of this shift in analysis see Snow, *People on Our Side* (New York, 1944); "Sixty Million Lost Allies," *Saturday Evening Post,* CCXVI (June 10, 1944), 12–13, 44, 46; "Must China Go Red?" *ibid.,* CCXVII (May 12, 1945), 9–10, 67–68, 70.

[58] Snow, "Sixty Million Lost Allies," 44.

[59] Snow, "China to Lin Yutang," *Nation,* CLX (February 17, 1945), 180.

[60] Lin Yutang, "China and Its Critics," *Nation,* CLX (March 24, 1945), 326.

Chinese Communists were "very close in their sympathies" to the Russians and had "sought to defend Soviet policies." [61]

In an article published after the altercation with Lin Yutang, Snow elaborated his position. He began by equating Chinese communism with an "agrarian-reform movement." Viewed historically, the Chinese Communists were the successors to a century of peasant uprisings. At the moment, moreover, the CCP espoused a moderate program "with a Marxist coloration." If by Chinese communism one meant the policies being enforced in the Border Areas, Snow explained, it was a "watered-down thing today." The leaders of the CCP, he continued, admitted that many years might elapse before China could pass beyond the "bourgeois-democratic" stage of development. Even under the most favorable conditions, Snow wrote, it would require a decade for the CCP to realize its moderate platform of agrarian reform. Theoretically, he suggested, there was "no reason why the Kuomintang and Kungchantang [Communist Party] couldn't work together in a coalition government during that decade." [62]

Snow had scarcely completed this ostensibly agrarian-reformer interpretation, when he appended a "word of warning." It was wrong, he wrote, to think that the Chinese Reds did not aspire to complete power. He rejected the notion that the Communists would originate a liberal democratic system "in the American sense," but he did think they would institute a "kind of democratic equalitarianism." He fortified his disclaimers by adding that it was misleading to suggest that Chinese Communists were not Marxists, were not sympathetic to the Soviet Union, and were not intent on building a classless socialist society. Those who tried to ingratiate the Chinese Reds with the American public "on the ground

[61] Snow, "China to Lin Yutang—II," *Nation*, CLX (March 31, 1945), 359.

[62] Snow, "Must China Go Red?" 67.

that they are not real Communists, in the foregoing sense," Snow concluded, were either dishonest or misinformed.[63]

The notion that the agrarian-reformer myth was a stratagem devised by Chinese Communists and disseminated by a captive group of Far Eastern journalists is rooted in a lack of familiarity with the Western literature on communism in China. In assessing the nature of the CCP, firsthand observers did not present a united front. The conceptual variety and interpretive subtlety incorporated in Western reporting cannot be understood in terms of the simplistic "agrarian reformer" formula. Evaluations ranged from the naïveté of Harrison Forman through the uncertainty of Theodore White to the authenticity of Edgar Snow.

Despite this discordancy, foreign reporters did concur in the judgment that, however one looked at the CCP, communism was not immediately relevant to the Chinese situation. Westerners generally approached the subject of Chinese communism from an empirical, present-minded frame of reference. That is, they viewed Red China in existential terms. It was the existing, immediate environmental facts of life in the Border Areas that structured their analyses. Even those who understood Marxist theory were more impressed by what they could or could not see than by what they were told. There was less concern for what Chinese Communists said they were striving for ultimately than for what they were doing in the present. This led most reporters to underestimate the CCP's attachment to Marxism as an ideal and to Leninism as an organizational technique for the attainment of complete power.

It can, then, justly be charged that firsthand observers minimized the imminence of a Communist threat to China. This underestimation was the natural product of a wartime atmosphere of friendliness for the opponents of Japan and Nazi Germany, of the fact that the Soviet Union offered the

[63] *Ibid.*

only authoritative model for communism, of the personal attractiveness and moderate reform policies of Chinese Communists and, above all, of the mode of analysis favored by Western reporters. After 1945, the Russian Red Army proved that Bolshevism could be spread in the wake of a Stalin tank, and their Chinese comrades demonstrated that Communist totalitarianism could be established in a predominantly agricultural society. Western reporters of the Chinese scene failed to rise above the assumptions and perspectives of their own time; few of them would have qualified as prophets.

In retrospect, however, it seems that firsthand observers of the 1930's and 1940's were closer to the truth than those who condemned them in the 1950's. During the McCarthy era, it was easy to conclude that the CCP was just another subservient satellite of the Soviet Union. But the Sino-Soviet split and the emergence of Communist polycentrism have necessitated a reappraisal of basic assumptions. Anyone who talks about a monolithic Communist conspiracy today is thought to be discussing a phenomenon that no longer exists, perhaps one that never existed. Historians like Stuart Schram argue persuasively that the movement led by Mao Tse-tung always exhibited a measure of independence from Moscow not normally associated with the affiliates of Stalin's Comintern.[64] At the very least, it now is clear that Maoism was never a flawless reproduction of Stalinism. Although Mao Tse-tung is a revolutionary whose basic world view is colored by the precepts of Marxism-Leninism, he also is "a very 'Chinese' Marxist," more concerned with his nation's destiny than with the proletarian world revolution.[65] If the firsthand reporters of the 1930's and 1940's often seemed uncertain

[64] Schram, *Mao Tse-tung*, pp. 72, 175 *et seq.*
[65] Schram, *The Political Thought of Mao Tse-tung* (rev. and enlarged ed., New York, Washington and London, 1969), p. 114. See also Schram, "What Makes Mao a Maoist," *New York Times Magazine,* March 8, 1970, 36–37, 58, 60, 62, 75–76, 80, 82.

and sometimes bewildered analysts of the nature of Chinese communism, they can take comfort in the fact that their contention that the CCP could not be understood as a replica of Stalinism commands more respect today than it once did.[66] Even within the framework of the now dubious assumption that the CCP was an orthodox Stalinist party, people in the 1930's and 1940's did have a means of obtaining a balanced view. Edgar and Helen Snow, James Bertram, the reformed Freda Utley, Cormac Shanahan and, to a lesser degree, Agnes Smedley all argued that the Chinese Communists were truly Communist revolutionaries. One could rely on the statements, as reported by Western journalists, of the CCP itself. Mao Tse-tung's frank declarations alone should have been enough, Snow reminisced, to have destroyed any illusion that the CCP "sought to establish anything less than all-out proletarian" power.[67] Chinese Communists, as a Foreign Service officer recalled, "always strongly rejected the label of 'agrarian reformers' " and insisted that they were "a lot more than that." [68] Perhaps most important, the student of Chinese affairs had at his disposal Edgar Snow's forthright censure of the purely existential interpretation of the Chinese Communist movement. The historian does not have to avail himself of hindsight in order to criticize the agrarian-reformer myth; contemporaries did the job for him.

[66] With the advantage of twenty years of perspective and scholarship, historians are still debating the nature of Chinese communism in terms of how far the CCP deviated in theory and practice from the Soviet model. For example, see the spirited discussion by Stuart Schram, Arthur A. Cohen, Benjamin Schwartz, Mostafa Rojai, Joseph R. Levenson, and Leonard Schapiro of "What Is Maoism?: A Symposium" in *Problems of Communism,* XV (September–October, 1966), 1–30. Even those who assume an intimate relationship between Soviet and Chinese communism, such as Cohen, find important instances where the Chinese departed from the Russian model.

[67] Snow, *Red Star over China* (rev. and expanded ed., New York, 1968), p. 438.

[68] John F. Melby, *The Mandate of Heaven: Record of a Civil War, China, 1945–49* (London, 1968), p. 16.

[17]

The Image

John Gunther's brief characterization of the Chinese Communists in *Inside Asia* is the most concise summation of the image of the CCP projected by firsthand observers.[1] Although he spoke to Chou En-lai in Hankow, Gunther did not visit Yenan. He based his sketch on a conversation with Evans F. Carlson and the publications of Helen and Edgar Snow and Agnes Smedley. While Gunther's depiction primarily reflects the influence of *Red Star over China*, it can be taken as a reasonably accurate précis of the Western literature on Chinese communism.

Gunther conveyed an engaging image. Mao Tse-tung is a philosopher, a dreamer, a creator, a builder—an intellectual who can match wits with the best China has to offer. Colorful personalities like Ho Lung, "a terrific fellow . . . the most Robin Hood-like of all," give a warm and even comic touch to the Communist hierarchy. The Eighth Route Army is a people's army. This patriotic force possesses a morale and morality unmatched in China. The Communists fight for ideals and country, not profit. Informality and social equalitarianism characterize the relations between officers and men.[2]

[1] John Gunther, *Inside Asia* (New York and London, 1939), especially pp. 219–222.
[2] *Ibid.*, pp. 216, 219–221.

While the CCP styles itself "Communist," subscribes to
Marxist theory, and organizes itself along Soviet lines, the
prospect for communism in China is "for the remote future."
The Chinese Communist Party is a member of the Comin-
tern and hails the U.S.S.R. as its loyal ally. Yet, there are no
Russian advisers with the Eighth Route Army. The Chinese
Communists are autonomous. They "run their own show." [3]

In spite of the pressure of incessant warfare and with limited material resources, the Communists have registered
achievements in social and educational reform "to make you
blink." The moderate nature of the CCP's program bears no
resemblance to developments in Russia. Rents have been reduced and corruption assaulted, but little property has been
confiscated or nationalized. Child marriages and opium are
forbidden and Confucianism scorned. Literacy, cooperatives,
technology, and athletics are promoted. The emphasis is on
"education above all—more and better education." Truly,
the Border Area is "a new Chinese world. . . . China alight
and alive." [4]

Although John Gunther wrote his assessment of the
Chinese Communists in 1939, an essay composed by Owen
Lattimore in 1945 demonstrates that the passage of six years
had not diminished or changed in essentials the romantic
image of the CCP. In a review of Harrison Forman's *Report
from Red China,* Lattimore described China's Communists
as "strange newcomers" in an "ancient land." The Chinese
Communist movement incorporated, he continued, "bespec-
tacled intellectuals, girls with bobbed hair, earnest, bustling
doctors, puritanical troops who fight the way Cromwell's
Ironsides would have fought if they had all managed to be
simultaneously Ironsides and Daniel Boones." In their spare
hours, he concluded, "they clear the land like CCC boys,

---

[3] *Ibid.,* pp. 219–220.
[4] *Ibid.,* pp. 214, 219–220.

farm like 4-H boys and girls in Iowa, and do good deeds like politically star-struck Boy Scouts." [5]

As the comments by Lattimore and Gunther suggest, there was a tendency to picture Mao's followers as a Chinese version of Robin Hood. Like those fabled bandits of Sherwood Forest, the Red guerrillas were on the right side. They warred against tyranny and for the common man. These ably officered Communists were enormously popular, loyal to their comrades, independent of any outside agency, and revolutionary in an acceptable way. The only great difference was that the Communists wore caps emblazoned with a red star. They might even constitute a threat to the established regime. This, however, was judged to be a hopeful, not a dreadful omen. After all, even if Robin Hood had sported a red constellation on his cap, he would not have frightened the people who counted—the downtrodden masses.

The analogy and the characterization are, of course, overdrawn. But the connotation is a valid approximation of the Western view of the Chinese Communists. Visitors to the Border Regions came back enthusiastically impressed by what they had seen. Their books and articles projected an image of China's Communists which was favorable in nearly every respect. This can be seen in their response to the six questions which were posed at the beginning of this section.

Westerners judged that the leaders of the CCP were brilliant, dedicated, and decisive. Above all, they were likeable and modern men. The Red Army was a dynamic military machine which waged incessant warfare against a depraved invader. Peasants living in the Border Areas were relatively fortunate people. They were the beneficiaries of a reform program which was democratically oriented and which was structured to provide for their needs. The united front left

[5] Owen Lattimore, "Report from Red China," *Atlantic Monthly,* CLXXV (April 1945), 133.

something to be desired, but the Communists were not basically at fault. They were the loyal partners who asked only for an equitable role in promoting republican institutions. Perhaps most important, the CCP was not a tool of Moscow. Indeed, there was some question as to whether the Chinese Communists were Communists. But even if the Chinese Reds were really Red, they were Red with a difference. These Marxist or peasant reformers were a long way from Stalinism. Weighed in the balance, the Chinese Communists were the best China had to offer. In a land of limited alternatives, they were surmounting formidable obstacles and laying the foundations for a new, a better, a modern China. The adjectives employed to describe the Chinese Communist movement constitute the component parts of an engaging image: youthful, dynamic, spartan, popular, progressive, democratic, reformist, and patriotic. One could scarcely ask for more.

After 1945, the idealized image of China's Communists categorically exploded. Our present-day conceptualizations of China, as Harold R. Isaacs has suggested, are "almost all images of anathema." [6] Analogies between the CCP and the Boy Scouts are no longer in good taste. The Korean war took all of the lightheartedness and attractiveness out of the Western image of the Chinese Communists. Genghis Khan came back. The People's Liberation Army came to be viewed as a nerveless and inscrutable human sea of vicious barbarians. Naturally, people living in the 1950's and 1960's asked how it was possible for the writers of the 1930's and 1940's to be so mistaken and wrongheaded. Perhaps this is not the best way of posing the problem. It is important, however, to understand why our predecessors thought they had found a glowing Red Star rather than a hostile planet in northwest China.

[6] Harold R. Isaacs, *Images of Asia: American Views of China and India* (New York, 1962), pp. 215ff.

★ PART IV

PERSUADING ENCOUNTER

[18]

The Conspiracy Thesis

Firsthand encounters with the Chinese Communists present the historian with an unusual problem. It is axiomatic that two people looking at the same phenomenon never render their perceptions in precisely the same way. There is, however, practically no record of any Western visitor to Red China from 1936 to 1945 who came away disenchanted or hostile. The sole exception was Cormac Shanahan. While foreign observers did not agree on every specific, similarities in their reports are far more striking than differences. Impressions of the Chinese Communists ranged from favorable to highly enthusiastic. The spectrum of value judgments was narrow, the conceptual congruity remarkable.

Contemporaries recognized this startling uniformity, and a few scholars like Nathaniel Peffer seriously tried to explain it.[1] But most writers were content to catalogue favorable reports of China's Communists by Western correspondents and to cite them as documentary proof of the validity of their well-disposed appraisals.[2] Publicists of a different persuasion

[1] Nathaniel Peffer, "Contrasting Yenan and Chungking," *New York Times Book Review*, October 28, 1945, 4.

[2] For example, see John Gunther, *Inside Asia* (New York and London, 1939), pp. 214–222; Lawrence K. Rosinger, *China's Crisis* (New York, 1945), pp. 81–89; Maxwell S. Stewart, "The Chinese Communists," *Nation*, CLX (March 24, 1945), 338–339; "Impasse in China," *New Republic*, CXIII (March 26, 1945), 407–408; Richard Watts, Jr., "The Chinese Giant Stirs," *ibid.* (May 28, 1945), 733–736.

were not noticeably vocal prior to the end of the Second World War, and militantly anti-Communist organizations like Alfred Kohlberg's America China Policy Association were not established until 1946 or later.[3] Nevertheless, there were a few people writing before 1945 who laid the groundwork for what eventually blossomed into the conspiracy thesis.

Both Chiang Kai-shek and Ambassador Patrick J. Hurley privately suggested that many American correspondents had Communist leanings.[4] In March 1941, Freda Utley publicly labeled Edgar Snow a Communist sympathizer. She did not accuse Snow of deliberately manipulating facts, but simply contended that he was politically naïve and did not understand the nature of Communist totalitarianism.[5] In a speech delivered before the House of Representatives on March 15, 1945, Congressman Walter H. Judd, formerly a medical missionary in China, suggested that the American public was being sold a "gold brick." While Judd admitted that he had been "taken in for a time" by the notion that the Chinese Communists were just agrarian reformers, he attributed anti-KMT and pro-CCP attitudes to a "concerted propaganda campaign" spearheaded by Communists and their "fellow-travelers."[6] The most outspoken advocates of the conspiracy hypothesis before the end of the Second World War, however, were Rodney Gilbert and the Right Reverend Monsignor George Barry O'Toole.

[3] Ross Y. Koen, *The China Lobby in American Politics* (New York, 1960), p. 57.

[4] *United States Relations with China: With Special Reference to the Period 1944–1949* (Washington, D.C., 1949), p. 553; Walter Millis, ed., *The Forrestal Diaries* (New York, 1951), pp. 98–99.

[5] Freda Utley, "A Terse, Authentic Report of the Terror in China: Edgar Snow Writes that the 'Deliberate Degradation of Man Has Been Thoroughly Systematized by the Japanese Army,'" *New York Times Book Review*, March 9, 1941, 9. See also Utley, *Odyssey of a Liberal: Memoirs* (Washington, D.C., 1970), pp. 210, 285.

[6] U. S., *Congressional Record*, 79th Cong., 1st Sess., 1945, XCI, Part 2, pp. 2297–2299.

In two articles in the *New York Herald Tribune,* Gilbert denounced the rising tide of criticism directed at the Kuomintang. He believed that anti-Nationalist remarks stemmed from two sources—disillusioned American military personnel and Communist propagandists. Gilbert called the first group misguided and aimless, the second "decidedly purposeful." [7] Writers like Agnes Smedley and T. A. Bisson, according to Gilbert, were laboring to discredit the Chungking regime in order to "pave the way for a Communist takeover in postwar China." Such people, he concluded, were aiding and abetting the subversion of a loyal ally and promoting the expansion of "Red 'democracy.' " [8]

Monsignor O'Toole's statements constitute the most explicit articulation of the conspiratorial viewpoint prior to 1945. Born in Ohio in 1886 and ordained in 1911, he had earned two doctorates at Urban University of the Propaganda in Rome before going to China in 1920. In 1925, he became the co-founder and first rector of Catholic University (Fu Jen) in Peking, a position which he held until 1933. From 1934 to 1937, he was head of the department of philosophy at Duquesne University. Subsequently, he accepted a professorship at the Catholic University of America. More important, when the *China Monthly* was established in 1939, he became its editor. Before his death on March 26, 1944, he had molded the *China Monthly* into a staunchly pro-Nationalist organ.[9]

As early as January 1942, O'Toole identified international communism as the source of comments disparaging the

[7] Rodney Gilbert, "Belittling China's War Effort," *New York Herald Tribune,* August 16, 1943, 14.

[8] Gilbert, "Belittling China's War Effort: Part II," *New York Herald Tribune,* August 17, 1943, 18.

[9] On O'Toole see Matthew Hoehn, ed., *Catholic Authors: Contemporary Biographical Sketches, 1930–1947* (Newark, New Jersey, 1948), pp. 603–605, and John J. Delaney and James Edward Tobin, *Dictionary of Catholic Biography* (Garden City, N.Y., 1961), p. 884. O'Toole was posthumously awarded the Order of the Brilliant Star by the Chinese government for his work as cofounder of Fu Jen.

KMT. His primary target was Vincent Sheean. Sheean was, according to O'Toole, a godless visionary and a "parlor pink." The Monsignor attributed Sheean's views to an "inordinate attachment" to the memory of Rayna Prohme, a "red-haired Red inamorata." He also called Edgar Snow and Ernest Hemingway "paid partisans of Stalin." By 1944, he had compiled a list of "Red Snipers" which included T. A. Bisson, Nathaniel Peffer, Agnes Smedley, and Ilona Ralf Sues.[10]

Despite the efforts of Gilbert and O'Toole, it was only after the Communists had defeated Chiang Kai-shek's forces that the conspiracy theory received wide attention and support.[11] The publication of two books in 1951 heralded its arrival as a force to be reckoned with. John T. Flynn's *While You Slept* and Freda Utley's *The China Story*, which was a best-seller for three months, were parallel attempts to interpret dramatic developments in East Asia in conspiratorial terms.[12] Chiang Kai-shek had been driven from the main-

[10] G. Barry O'Toole, "U.S. Reds Reopen Attack on Kuomintang," *China Monthly*, III (January 1942), 17, 21; "Debunking an 'Imperial' Debunker," V (February 1944), 12–13. O'Toole's successor as editor of the *China Monthly*, Father Mark Tsai, fully embraced the conspiracy thesis. Tsai's editorials and selection of articles and news reports leave little to the imagination. See "Institute of Pacific Relations Called Nest of Reds," *China Monthly*, VI (May 1945), 15; " 'The Six' Arrested" (July–August 1945), 7–10; Geraldine T. Fitch, "My Country and China's People," 17–19, 31; Mark Tsai, "Half Truth and False Friend" (October 1945), 24–26; Alfred Kohlberg, "Owen Lattimore: 'Expert's Expert'—The Monocle, the Commissar, the Old Homestead, and Snafu," 10–13, 26. The book reviews in the *China Monthly* also provide a rich depository for anyone interested in the conspiratorial mentality. See especially Father Roland Norris, "Report From Red China," VI (May 1945), 30, and Father Cormac Shanahan, "The Challenge of Gunther Stein," VIII (February 1946), 65–66.

[11] Koen, *The China Lobby in American Politics*, p. 133.

[12] John T. Flynn, *While You Slept: Our Tragedy in Asia and Who Made It* (New York, 1951); Freda Utley, *The China Story* (Chicago, 1951).

land to Formosa, the United States faced the Chinese Red Army in Korea, and Senator Joseph R. McCarthy was crusading against treason in high places.[13] These developments helped to create an atmosphere that provided Flynn and Miss Utley with a rationale and an audience.

John T. Flynn placed the blame for the "fantastic snarl" of American Far Eastern policy on a "little junta" of correspondents and State Department officials. Newspaper and magazine reporters assumed a prominent role in Flynn's analysis. Enjoying ready access to the mass media, they were able to poison the mind of the American public. Flynn's list of subversive propagandists included a large number of those who had encountered the Chinese Communists at first hand: Claire and William Band, Israel Epstein, Harrison Forman, Philip J. Jaffe, Owen Lattimore, Edgar Snow, Agnes Smedley, Gunther Stein, Anna Louise Strong, George E. Taylor, Nym Wales, and Theodore H. White. He suggested that some of these writers and journalists were members of a Communist party or agents of a Communist apparatus, and that many of them were "mere dupes." Flynn concluded that "almost all" of them were "passionately committed" to international communism.[14]

Freda Utley expanded Flynn's list and refined his argument. *The China Story* is a more artful attempt to demonstrate how Communists influenced the course of American foreign policy. Like Flynn, Freda Utley assumed that the central deception practiced on the American public was the notion that Chinese Communists were not true Communists but agrarian reformers. Unlike Flynn, she recognized the dif-

---

[13] Relying primarily on Freda Utley's *The China Story*, Senator McCarthy called into question the loyalty and activities of Evans F. Carlson, Harrison Forman, Haldore Hanson, Owen Lattimore, Agnes Smedley, and Gunther Stein. See Joseph R. McCarthy, *America's Retreat from Victory: The Story of George Catlett Marshall* (New York, 1951), pp. 68, 118, 158.

[14] Flynn, *While You Slept*, pp. 66–70, 142–143, 154.

ficulty of distinguishing between the "real" and the "crypto-Communists" who popularized misleading images of the CCP.[15]

Freda Utley faced a dilemma when it came to writing about individuals like Agnes Smedley, Evans F. Carlson, and Edgar Snow. She had known them in Hankow in 1938 and had substantially agreed with their appraisals of the Chinese Communists. While she was quick to apologize for her earlier assessment of the CCP in *China at War,* she avoided any suggestion that her acquaintances were members of a Communist organization. Instead she established motivational categories of guilt and complicity. Agnes Smedley, who had been her close friend, "resembled the best of the old Bolsheviks liquidated by Stalin." Although completely devoted to the Chinese Communists, Miss Smedley was not a Stalinist. She was a warmhearted, basically honest, Leninist-style radical. Evans F. Carlson was a "simple soldier" beguiled into thinking that Chinese Communists "were 'true Christians.'" He exemplified romantic idealism, naïveté, and eccentricity. Edgar Snow, an extraordinarily effective promoter of the Communist cause, was a "careerist"—a dissimulator lacking both integrity and principles. In sum, Freda Utley believed that it was sheer ignorance, romanticism, misguided humanitarianism, and careerism that impelled Western reporters to write favorable accounts of the CCP.[16]

Despite Miss Utley's apparent efforts to avoid guilt-by-association arguments in interpreting the China story, her conclusions were the same as John T. Flynn's. Through their control of the mass media, a small clique of Communist sympathizers had exerted a detrimental influence on the American government and public. Although some fools had been mistaken for villains and although some American journalists were "dupes" rather than conscious agents, the effect was

[15] Utley, *The China Story,* pp. 238–239.
[16] *Ibid.,* pp. 106–108, 157–158, 239–240.

the same. In fact, Freda Utley concluded, Red sympathizers constituted "a greater danger to the Republic than all the Communists in America." Motivation, then, really did not matter. A Communist conspiracy had been fostered "in our midst" and American correspondents had contributed mightily to its success.[17]

The propounders of the conspiracy theory have failed to define clearly the nature of the China conspiracy. They have nebulously interpreted it to include espionage, the promotion of a naïve view of Chinese communism, the spreading of calculated lies, the undermining of government policy, and the praising of Chinese Communists at the expense of Chinese Nationalists. The accusers have also devoted more effort to formulating accusations than to gathering evidence. Their hypothesis is based on the plausible assumption that an opinion-forming elite of China experts had the capacity strongly to influence public opinion, but they have not presented the evidence necessary to demonstrate the validity of the hypothesis.

Although the propounders of the conspiracy theory have been unable to show either that collusion took place or that the inspiration behind firsthand assessments of the CCP was a commitment to Communist dogma, their point of view is not necessarily bankrupt. Were Western reporters guilty of fostering a calculated and covert plot to further the interests of the Chinese Communist Party? No documentation exists which might answer this question authoritatively, but there is some evidence indicating that a handful of those who had face-to-face encounters with the CCP were highly sympathetic to Communist goals, and the possibility exists that a few of them were acting as operatives for Communist organizations. Among those most frequently accused of being conspirators are Anna Louise Strong, Agnes Smedley, Gunther

17 *Ibid.,* pp. ix, 124, 139, 165, 171–175, 238, 240–241.

Stein, and Philip J. Jaffe. The limits and strengths of the conspiracy thesis can be suggested through case studies of these individuals.

Anna Louise Strong was a vigorous proponent of both the Russian and the Chinese Communists. Her autobiography, *I Change Worlds,* is a panegyric to the virtues of Russian socialism and an ardent personal profession of faith in its principles. In an introspective vein, she narrates her abandonment of capitalism and conversion to Stalinism. America had become the chief of sinners, an imperialist warmonger. The Soviet Union was the world's best hope, offering salvation through socialism. She repeatedly requested permission to be granted membership in the Russian Communist Party. Her petitions were denied. Instead, she was encouraged to continue her friendly reporting on the U.S.S.R. in the bourgeois press. Although she wanted to be a "comrade-creator," Anna Louise Strong reluctantly accepted the argument that she could be more useful to the cause by operating outside the official fold. She rationalized her ambiguous position by reasoning that it was better to slave for communism and thereby contribute to the building of a brave new society than to be a lackey for capitalism.[18]

Philip J. Jaffe has suggested that Anna Louise Strong "never really understood either socialism or Marxism." [19] This seems to be a valid observation. None of her books or articles reflects knowledge of the subtleties of dialetical materialism. Indeed, she confessed in her autobiography that she found abstractions dull and perplexing.[20] She once told Helen Snow that after completing her requirements for a doctor of philosophy degree she hated philosophy so much

[18] Anna Louise Strong, *I Change Worlds: The Remaking of an American* (New York, 1935), pp. 126, 153, 301–302.

[19] Philip J. Jaffe, "The Strange Case of Anna Louise Strong," *Survey,* No. 53 (October 1964), 129.

[20] Strong, *I Change Worlds,* pp. 153–155.

that she "never wanted to read a book of it again." [21] Hers was a radicalism of the heart, not of the intellect. She claimed to have discovered a "partial antidote" to her emotional approach by a conscientious reading of *Pravda*. This may be, but theoretical naïveté is evident in her failure to grasp the differences between Trotsky and Stalin. Despite her relative ignorance of theory, she was persuaded that Communists were "really new people, getting newer all the time!" [22]

In addition to her inability to fathom Marxist doctrine, Anna Louise Strong also probably never became a member of any Communist organization. By all accounts, she was a disagreeable and self-willed woman. As one who admired her put it, she left the impression that as far as she was concerned "you could go to hell with her compliments." [23] She was given to quarreling with her superiors and found it difficult to suppress her own feelings in order to follow the party "line" without question.[24] She balked at the idea of taking orders from a petty bureaucrat or of suspending her own judgment. Philip Jaffe and Helen Snow, both of whom knew her for thirty years, do not believe that she ever joined a Communist party.[25]

Anna Louise Strong seems to have been what Mrs. Snow called a "classic fellow-traveler": a radical journalist who honestly saw only one side of the picture. Convinced that socialism was right, she was "as uncritical as a camera." [26] Her

[21] Nym Wales [Helen Foster Snow], "Anna Louise Strong: The Classic Fellow-Traveler," *New Republic,* CLXII (April 25, 1970), 19.

[22] Strong, *I Change Worlds,* pp. 289–290, 392, 415.

[23] Ilona Ralf Sues, *Shark's Fins and Millet* (Boston, 1944), p. 188. See also Jaffe, "The Strange Case of Anna Louise Strong," 129, and Wales, "Anna Louise Strong," 18.

[24] Strong, *I Change Worlds,* pp. 313–315.

[25] Jaffe, interview with the author, June 14, 1965; Wales, "Anna Louise Strong," 17.

[26] Wales, "Anna Louise Strong," 17–19.

faith in communism weathered the Nazi-Soviet nonaggression pact of 1939 and even her expulsion from Russia a decade later, and she was scornful of those who became ex-Communist anti-Communists.[27] One of the few foreigners to survive the Cultural Revolution unmolested, from 1958 until her death on March 29, 1970, she lived in Peking and wrote articles extolling the Chinese Communist movement. The wreaths presented by Mao Tse-tung and Lin Piao at the ceremony paying last respects to her bore an appropriate inscription: "To the progressive American writer Miss Anna Louise Strong, a friend of the Chinese people." [28] To the end, she was an unswerving advocate of the Chinese Communists.

As early as 1937, Agnes Smedley had gained public notoriety as an abettor of Red insurrection.[29] This prompted the New York *Daily Worker* to issue an unusual front-page statement on January 29, 1937. Earl Browder, secretary-general of the American Communist Party, warned that Miss Smedley in no way represented either the Chinese or American party. He described her as merely a free-lance journalist.[30]

On February 10, 1949, the United States Army released a 32,000-word report on the espionage activities of the Sorge spy ring. This account, which had been prepared by General Douglas MacArthur's intelligence staff, identified Agnes

[27] Daniel Aaron, *Writers on the Left: Episodes in American Literary Communism* (New York, 1961), p. 376. See also Frank A. Warren, *Liberals and Communism: The 'Red Decade' Revisited* (Bloomington and London, 1966), p. 71.

[28] "Ceremony in Peking to Pay Last Respects to Anna Louise Strong Before Her Portrait and Ashes," *Peking Review* (April 10, 1970), 37–38. See also Strong, "Why I Came to China at the Age of 72," *Peking Review* (September 20, 1963), 19–22, and her *Letters from China* (3 vols.; Peking, 1963–1965).

[29] For example, see "American Woman Recruits Reds for Revolt in Northwest China," *New York Herald Tribune,* January 8, 1937, 1, 4.

[30] "A Warning Regarding News from China," New York *Daily Worker,* January 29, 1937, 1.

Smedley as a secret agent for the Soviet government.[31] Calling the accusation a "despicable lie," Agnes Smedley threatened to institute legal action against the Army.[32] The Army publicly admitted that it had no proof that she was a participant in the Sorge cabal and labeled the report a blunder.[33] Miss Smedley expressed gratitude to the War Department for clearing her reputation but was thrown back on the defensive when Major General Charles A. Willoughby, MacArthur's chief of intelligence, assumed responsibility for the document of February 10. He defiantly invited libel suits by any persons named as subversives. Agnes Smedley sidestepped Willoughby's challenge by demanding that General MacArthur, as the "responsible officer," waive his immunity so that she could sue him.[34] Willoughby reiterated his position in a volume published in 1952, *Shanghai Conspiracy*. According to Willoughby, Agnes Smedley was a leading perpetrator of the agrarian-reform myth and a member of the Sorge group. Nevertheless, as Willoughby recognized, there was no evidence proving her involvement in a Communist organization and she repeatedly denied any such connection.[35]

Chalmers A. Johnson's careful examination of available materials indicates that Miss Smedley was associated with Richard Sorge's activities. From 1930 to 1933 Sorge was engaged in gathering information in Shanghai for the Russian army. While Johnson doubts that Miss Smedley was a mem-

[31] Walter H. Waggoner, "Tokyo War Secrets Stolen by Soviet Spy Ring in 1941," *New York Times*, February 11, 1949, 1, 4.

[32] "Army Withholds Spy Data Backing," *New York Times*, February 12, 1949, 4; "Army Admits Spy Faux Pas; No Proof on Agnes Smedley," *ibid.*, February 19, 1949, 1.

[33] "Army Admits Spy Faux Pas," 1, 6.

[34] " 'Faux Pas' Inquiry on Spies Demanded," *New York Times*, February 20, 1949, 22; "Officer Welcomes Suit on Spy Report," *ibid.*, February 22, 1949, 11.

[35] Charles A. Willoughby, *Shanghai Conspiracy: The Sorge Spy Ring* (New York, 1952), pp. 31–33, 252.

ber of Sorge's spy ring, it is clear that she collaborated with him. She introduced Sorge to Chinese with pro-Communist leanings, permitted him to use her residence for meetings, and helped establish a "listening post" in Peiping. Apparently, she thought that Sorge was a Comintern agent and did not know that he was working for Soviet military intelligence. Johnson also concludes that Agnes Smedley never became a member of a Communist party. Her role in Sorge's operation was minor, was confined to his Shanghai phase, and did not extend to his more important intrigues in Japan after 1933. [36]

While Johnson does an effective job of discrediting most of Willoughby's accusations against Agnes Smedley, the problem of her relationship to the Chinese Communist movement remains. Willoughby was not far from the truth when he observed that she supported the CCP "without reservation." [37] The only qualification to her commitment to the CCP is that she rejected membership in the party. She deplored capitalism, considered it an honor actively to support the CCP, and admitted her sympathy with the Chinese Communists.[38] Yet, she never wanted to join the party. She was an irreverent woman, outspoken and blunt in her appraisals. As Hollington K. Tong wrote, she "had a way of saying what she thought when she thought it, which some-

[36] Chalmers A. Johnson, *An Instance of Treason: Ozaki Hotsumi and the Sorge Spy Ring* (Stanford, 1964), pp. 62–67, 80–90.

[37] Willoughby, *Shanghai Conspiracy*, p. 266.

[38] Agnes Smedley, *Battle Hymn of China* (New York, 1943), pp. 10, 81, 209. In this respect, the biographical sketch of Miss Smedley in *Twentieth Century Authors* is quite interesting. She is described as having changed her ideology from socialism to communism. Many of the articles in this volume are based on autobiographical materials submitted by those being characterized. The format of the essay on Miss Smedley suggests that it is, at least in part, a self-appraisal. See Stanley J. Kunitz and Howard Haycraft, eds., *Twentieth Century Authors: A Biographical Dictionary of Modern Literature* (New York, 1942), pp. 1301–1302.

times proved troublesome." [39] She disliked the "intellectual arrogance" of certain Chinese Communists, would quarrel with leading figures like Chu Teh on the spur of the moment, and refused to become "a mere instrument in the hands of men who believed that they held the one and only key to truth." [40]

Agnes Smedley was too individualistic and independent in judgment to place her life and mind unquestioningly at the disposal of others. She consistently denied that she was a Communist, telling her friends that she could not bring herself to accept party discipline. In June 1939 she wrote Freda Utley that she would retain the right to determine how her life would be spent. Only "backward, stupid people," she explained, blindly obeyed orders and considered that all except Communist party members were, as she put it, either idiots or feebleminded.[41] While American, European, and Chinese Communists supported the Russo-German pact of August 1939, Agnes Smedley was openly critical of the agreement.[42] Instinctively recognizing that she might one day be disappointed with those for whom she fought, she was neither doctrinaire nor particularly interested in Marxist theory. She gave boundlessly of her time, money, and energy to the CCP, but she remained, as Anna Wang observed, a passionate individualist her entire life.[43]

Freda Utley has written what is perhaps the most incisive appraisal of Agnes Smedley. Unable to accept oppression

[39] Hollington K. Tong, *Dateline—China: The Beginning of China's Press Relations with the World* (New York, 1950), p. 57.

[40] Smedley, *Battle Hymn of China,* pp. 10, 251. For an example of Miss Smedley's brashness even when dealing with top Chinese Communist officials, see Michael Blankfort, *The Big Yankee: The Life of Carlson of the Raiders* (Boston, 1947), pp. 209–210.

[41] Utley, *Odyssey of a Liberal,* p. 207.

[42] Paul Frillmann and Graham Peck, *China: The Remembered Life* (Boston, 1968), p. 23.

[43] Anna Wang, *Ich kämpfte für Mao: Eine deutsche Frau erlebt die chinesische Revolution* (Hamburg, Germany, 1964), pp. 86–89.

under the name of any ideal, "at heart she was more of an anarchist than anything else." [44] She was more radical and idealistic than the members of the CCP, a fact which they recognized. [45] According to Philip Jaffe, the Chinese Communists considered her a nuisance. [46] When Helen Foster Snow was in Yenan in 1937, she was startled to learn that the Communists had taken "such a dislike" to Miss Smedley. For one thing, they resented her unorthodox ideas on marriage, an institution which she equated with slavery. [47] And James M. Bertram recalled that they were critical of the romantic and unsystematic nature of Miss Smedley's writings. From their point of view, "Agnes was a near-Trotskyist or anarchist or something: not really reliable anyway." [48] This rebel against all kinds of authority could never accept the discipline of a Communist party. Owen Lattimore has suggested that had she lived long enough she would have been one of the first to be shot when the CCP took power. [49]

The second Western correspondent who had been associated with the Sorge spy ring was not an American. Gunther Stein was a German Jew who became a naturalized British citizen in 1941. He earned a reputation as an authoritative reporter on financial matters and was known for his pronounced antipathy to fascism. [50] Like Agnes Smedley,

---

[44] Utley, *China at War* (New York, 1939), pp. 215–216.

[45] Owen Lattimore, conversation with the author, April 16, 1969.

[46] Jaffe, interview with the author, June 14, 1965.

[47] Helen Foster Snow to the author, April 19, 1965. Miss Smedley once characterized marriage as "a relic of human slavery." See *Battle Hymn of China*, p. 8.

[48] James M. Bertram to the author, April, 1965. See also Utley, *Odyssey of a Liberal*, p. 201.

[49] Lattimore, conversation with the author, April 16, 1969.

[50] Johnson, *An Instance of Treason*, p. 107. Ambassador Nelson T. Johnson assessed Stein as a very interesting and well-informed journalist. See Johnson to Stanley K. Hornbeck, November 11, 1936, Hornbeck papers, Stanford University.

Stein was named in the United States Army report of 1949.[51] Charles A. Willoughby believed that Stein was a "top level" operative in Richard Sorge's organization.[52] Stein dismissed the charge as ridiculous.[53]

Before Richard Sorge was hanged in 1944, he described Gunther Stein as a "sympathizer but never an actual member of our group," a person who "did give us positive cooperation."[54] General Willoughby thought that the distinction was insignificant.[55] Chalmers A. Johnson has disagreed and contended that Willoughby was wrong to identify Stein as a Soviet agent. Johnson recognizes, however, that Stein was very close to Sorge's activities. In the late 1930's, Stein helped Sorge gather information in Japan. Sorge even operated his transmitter from Stein's home in Tokyo. Johnson suggests that Stein was motivated by his antifascism and that although he must have known he was "assisting the Comintern by aiding Sorge," he probably did not realize that Sorge was working for Russian military intelligence. Johnson concludes that Willoughby's charge that Stein was a henchman of Moscow "cannot be sustained by the evidence."[56]

While it is not possible to sustain the charge that Stein was a leading member of the spy ring, it is clear that he was more deeply involved with Richard Sorge than was Agnes Smedley. Stein participated in the ring's operations by acting

[51] Waggoner, "Tokyo War Secrets Stolen by Soviet Spy Ring in 1941," 4.

[52] Willoughby, *Shanghai Conspiracy*, p. 77.

[53] "Army Admits Spy Faux Pas," 6. When Willoughby repeated his accusation against Stein in 1951, Stein reiterated his denial. See "Stein Denies Spy Charge: British Writer Refers to Word by Gen. Willoughby," *New York Times*, August 11, 1951, 5.

[54] John D. Morris, "Soviet Knew Ahead of Tokyo War Plan," *New York Times*, August 10, 1951, 3.

[55] *Ibid.*

[56] Johnson, *An Instance of Treason*, pp. 107–109.

as a courier of microfilms from Tokyo to Hong Kong. Although Sorge was guarded in his statements to the Japanese police about Stein, he did say that Stein was aware of the activities of his organization. Max Clausen, one of Sorge's partners, stated under interrogation that Stein was a member of the ring. There also is a possibility that Stein knew about Sorge's connection with Soviet military intelligence. And yet, the charges against Gunther Stein, like those against Agnes Smedley, remain unproven.[57]

Philip J. Jaffe was born of poor Jewish parents in Russia. When Jaffe was about eleven years old, his family immigrated to the United States. After earning bachelor's and master's degrees at Columbia University, Jaffe built up a successful greeting card business. Before becoming the managing editor of *Amerasia* in 1937, he had been associated with the left-wing New York periodical *China Today*.[58]

David J. Dallin singled out Jaffe in his study of Soviet espionage. Jaffe was, Dallin concluded, a Communist expert on the Far East, a devoted adherent to the Stalinist line, and the probable supplier of confidential information on the United States to Russian agents.[59] In a statement of June 1955, which Dallin appended to his text, Jaffe denied ever having been implicated in a Soviet intrigue. He protested that the securing and divulging of government data in the columns of *Amerasia* were legitimate journalistic activities.[60]

The magazine *Amerasia* deserves a separate study. By all odds, it was the best-informed American periodical on the Chinese Communist movement. Although its total circulation was under 2,000, *Amerasia* was widely read in Washington, by people like Joseph C. Grew, Stanley K. Hornbeck,

[57] F. W. Deakin and G. R. Storry, *The Case of Richard Sorge* (New York, 1966), pp. 165, 208, 342–343.

[58] Jaffe, interview with the author, January 11, 1966.

[59] David J. Dallin, *Soviet Espionage* (New Haven, 1955), pp. 445–448.

[60] *Ibid.*, pp. 448–450n.

and Nelson T. Johnson.[61] Its declared purpose was to promote the development of an informed public opinion regarding United States relations with the Pacific countries. Ostensibly, its editors eschewed a dogmatic editorial line and did not intend the journal to be a "propaganda organ" for any particular doctrine, policy, institution, or nation.[62] Yet, from the appearance of its first issue in March 1937 to its final installment in July 1947, *Amerasia* championed the cause of Chinese communism. It also provided its readers with much factual material on the Far East.

Many of the contributors to *Amerasia* could claim that their enthusiastic assessments of the Chinese Communists were based on firsthand observations: for example, Edgar Snow, T. A. Bisson, Anna Louise Strong, J. Clayton Miller, Evans F. Carlson, Haldore Hanson, "Asiaticus," James M.. Bertram, and Michael Lindsay.[63] Views critical of the Chi-

[61] Jaffe, interview with the author, June 14, 1965; Joseph C. Grew to Hornbeck, April 13, 1937, and Johnson to Hornbeck, April 19, 1937, Hornbeck papers, Stanford University.

[62] "Topics in Brief: On Amerasia," *Amerasia,* I (March 1937), 2–3; "Topics in Brief: On Amerasia Again" (April 1937), 51.

[63] Edgar Snow, "Chinese Communists and World Affairs: An Interview with Mao Tse-tung," *Amerasia,* I (August 1937), 263–269; T. A. Bisson, "Mao Tse-tung Analyzes Nanking in Interview" (October 1937), 360–365; Anna Louise Strong, "Political Work of a Chinese Army," II (August 1938), 304–308; J. Clayton Miller, "The Chinese Still Rule North China: Political and Military Strategy of the Hopei-Shansi-Chahar Border Government" (September 1938), 336–345; Evans F. Carlson, "The Unorthodox War Continues," III (March 1939), 12–15; Haldore Hanson, "Firebrands and Chinese Politics" (April 1939), 78–82; "Asiaticus," "Chou En-lai on the New Stage of the Anti-Japanese War" (June 1939), 184–190; "Asiaticus," "The Yangtze Triangle Guerrilla War" (August 1939), 275–281; Carlson, "European Pacts and Chinese Prospects" (October 1939), 345–349; Carlson, "Whither China?" (December 1939), 458–463; Carlson, "America Faces Crisis in the Orient" (February 1940), 555–560; "Asiaticus," "The Fascist Axis vs. the United Front in China," IV (February 1941), 543–546; Strong, "The Kuomintang-Communist Crisis in China," V (March 1941), 11–23; "Asiaticus," "Autobiography of General Yeh Ting," 24–29; "Asiaticus," "China's In-

nese Communists did not appear in *Amerasia,* but the journal
published a substantial number of unfriendly evaluations of
the Kuomintang.[64]

Amerasia's editorials on China were characterized by an
intense interest in KMT-CCP relations and sympathy for the
Chinese Communists. In 1937–1938, *Amerasia*'s columns reflected the optimism of a united front that was really working.[65] From 1939 to 1941, *Amerasia*'s writers praised the
CCP as the most progressive element in the Far East and
fretted over ominous rumors that all was not well between
Chungking and Yenan.[66] When the New Fourth Army Incident of 1942 demonstrated the reality of Nationalist-Communist hostility, *Amerasia* openly adopted a partisan stance.

---

ternal Friction Aids Japan" (May 1941), 118–122; James M. Bertram,
"Japanese Offensive in North China" (July 1941), 215–216; "Asiaticus,"
"New Fourth Army Area Revisited" (September 1941), 287–294; "Asi-
aticus," "Behind the Japanese Lines in Central Asia" (October 1941),
355–360; Michael Lindsay, "The North China Front: A Study of
Chinese Guerrillas in Action," VIII (March 31 and April 14, 1944),
100–110, 117–125; Strong, "A World's Eye View from a Yenan Cave:
An Interview with Mao Tse-tung," XI (April 1947), 122–126; Strong,
"Communist Regime in Manchuria" (May 1947), 137–143; Strong,
"The Thought of Mao Tse-tung" (June 1947), 161–174.

[64] Most of the articles listed in note 63 contain either direct or implied criticisms of the Kuomintang. Other examples of unfriendly commentary on the Nationalists can be found in Frederick V. Field, "Are
Chinese Again Fighting Chinese?" *Amerasia,* III (September 1939),
315–319; Kate L. Mitchell, "Political Crisis in China," IV (February
1941), 538–542; Hugh Deane, "Political Reaction in Kuomintang
China," V (July 1941), 209–214; John Taylor [pseud.], "Nazi Front in
China" (December 1941), 433–438; Mitchell and Philip J. Jaffe, "The
China Controversy," VII (September 1943), 274–285. Meribeth E. Cam-
eron's "China: Three Half Centuries," VI (October 25, 1942), 347–354,
is an exception to the rule of negative appraisals of the Kuomintang.

[65] For example, see "Topics in Brief: Kuomintang and Communists,"
Amerasia, I (June 1937), 147–148.

[66] For example, see Frederick V. Field, "Are Chinese Again Fighting
Chinese?"; Kate L. Mitchell, "Political Crisis in China," IV (February
1941), 538–542; Philip J. Jaffe, "Communist Aims in China," 547–577.

The KMT was criticized for its reactionary behavior, and the CCP was lauded as China's best hope. Lengthy statements from official CCP sources were printed and Communist policies supported.[67] After 1941, *Amerasia's* editorials became more and more one-sided. In 1942, Chiang Kai-shek was depicted as a great Asian leader, but strong reactionary remnants in the KMT were credited with instituting a blockade of the guerrilla areas. On the other side, the Eighth Route Army was eulogized for its military, political, economic, and social achievements.[68] By 1943, *Amerasia* was calling for an end to Chungking's "repressive policies against all popular movements" and for a relaxation of the blockade of the Shen-Kan-Ning.[69] *Amerasia's* editors had formulated distinctive conceptions of the "two Chinas" by 1944. Nationalist China was a dictatorial, stagnant police state trying to preserve a monopoly of power by suppressing the emergence of a modern, progressive, pro-democratic Communist China.[70] As the Second World War drew to a close, *Amerasia* deplored the political impasse in China, published statements by Communist leaders, and sharply criticized the American policy of unconditional support of the Chungking regime.[71]

[67] For example, see Jaffe, "The Soviet-Japanese Neutrality Pact," *Amerasia*, V (May 1941), 109–114; "Developments on China's United Front" (June 1941), 167–172.

[68] For example, see Jaffe, "Is China the Number One Front?" *Amerasia*, VI (August 1942), 255–263; "Economic Trends in Asia" (December 1942), 441–443.

[69] "The China Front and the Future of Asia," *Amerasia*, VI (January 1943), 463. See also Jaffe, "China Can Win and Yet Lose: A Challenge to America and China," VII (July 25, 1943), 195–205; Jaffe and Kate L. Mitchell, "The China Controversy" (September 1943), 274–285.

[70] For example, see "The 'Communist Problem' in China," *Amerasia*, VIII (April 28, 1944), 134–141.

[71] "Political Impasse in China: Parts I, II, and III," *Amerasia*, IX (March 23, April 6, April 20, 1945), 83–94, 99–109, 115–126; "Two Roads for China: China's Leaders Speak" (May 18, 1945), 147–158; "The Outlook for Democracy in China" (September 1945), 253–258.

Three characteristics make *Amerasia* an unusual journal: its abundance of detailed information on Chinese developments, its sustained interest in KMT-CCP relations, and its pro-Communist editorial line. From 1937 to 1945, the journal was controlled and operated by Philip J. Jaffe. Much of its material was sent from China by people like Anna Louise Strong and by Chinese Communists. Conversations were held with reporters who had returned from the Far East, and newspapers from all over the world were watched for information on the CCP.[72] This helps to explain the quality of the articles and editorials in *Amerasia*.

The reasons for *Amerasia*'s overriding concern with, and partisan appraisal of, China's Communists are to be found in part in the composition of its staff. Jaffe, Frederick V. Field, T. A. Bisson, Chi Ch'ao-ting, Kenneth W. Colegrove, Owen Lattimore, Cyrus H. Peake, Robert K. Reischauer, and William T. Stone comprised the original board of editors. There is no doubt that Chi was a Communist, and it is generally thought that Field was a strong sympathizer. Chi joined the American Communist Party in 1926 while a student at the University of Chicago on a Boxer indemnity scholarship. In 1927, he married Harriet Levine, a third cousin of Philip Jaffe's. The newlyweds spent their first year of marriage in Moscow, where Chi attended the Sixth Congress of the Comintern. In the 1930's Chi worked for the China bureau of the Central Committee of the American Communist Party, contributed articles under various pseudonyms to the *Daily Worker* and other journals, served on the editorial board of *China Today,* and earned a Ph.D. degree from Columbia University. His dissertation won the Seligman Economics Prize and was published under the title *Key Economic Areas in Chinese History.* From 1937 to 1940 he was a member of the research staff of the Institute of Pacific Relations and an editor of *Amerasia.* Returning to China in 1941, he worked as an underground agent for the

[72] Jaffe, interview with the author, June 14, 1965.

CCP in H. H. Kung's Ministry of Finance. In 1944, he became Kung's confidential secretary and attended the Bretton Woods Conference as secretary-general of the Chinese delegation. After 1949, he held a series of important posts in the Communist regime. When Edgar Snow met him in Peking in 1960, he was director of foreign trade for the Chinese People's Republic. It was not until after his death in 1963 that Chi's remarkable career was revealed by the CCP.[73]

According to Philip Jaffe, Chi was a spy for the CCP and Field was closely associated with the American Communist Party.[74] Frederick Vanderbilt Field was a radical millionaire whose strong sympathy for communism has been accepted as a fact by both friends and enemies alike and has not been denied by Field himself.[75] Jaffe has denied any affiliation with a Communist party, and there is no evidence to prove otherwise. He was on close personal terms with Earl Browder. He conveyed Browder's greetings to the leaders of the CCP during his trip to Yenan in the summer of 1937 and returned to the United States with letters from the Chinese Communists to the secretary-general of the American CP.[76] Until 1945,

[73] Howard L. Boorman, ed., *Biographical Dictionary of Republican China* (Vol. 1; New York and London, 1967), pp. 293–297; Snow, *The Other Side of the River: Red China Today* (New York, 1962), pp. 20, 73, 75, 108, 678.

[74] Jaffe, interview with the author, June 14, 1965.

[75] See the testimony of the following individuals in U.S. Senate, Committee on the Judiciary, Subcommittee on Internal Security, 82nd Cong., 1st and 2nd Sess., *Institute of Pacific Relations, Hearings* (15 parts; Washington, D.C., 1951–1952): Elizabeth Bentley (Part 13, pp. 4787–4788), John K. Fairbank (Part 11, pp. 3775–3776), Frederick V. Field (Part 1, pp. 75–127, and Part 12, pp. 4033–4152), William L. Holland (Part 11, pp. 3898–3899), Owen Lattimore (Part 9, p. 2953), William W. Lockwood (Part 11, p. 3874), Harvey M. Matusow (Part 11, pp. 3843–3844), John Carter Vincent (Part 6, p. 1933), and Nathaniel Weyl (Part 8, pp. 2804–2805).

[76] Earl Browder, "The American Communist Party in the Thirties," in *As We Saw the Thirties: Essays on Social and Political Movements of a Decade,* ed. Rita James Simon (Urbana, Chicago, and London, 1967), p. 247.

Jaffe was, as he styled himself, a left-wing "utopian"—an idealist who sincerely believed that Russian-American cooperation was possible and that the united front strategy was desirable.[77] Earl Latham has charged that *Amerasia* was "a magazine under the control of Communist supporters." [78] Although Latham's assessment minimizes the presence of non-Communist scholars like Kenneth Colegrove, Owen Lattimore, and Robert Reischauer, there is little question that Jaffe and the journal he edited were favorably inclined toward the Chinese Communists.

With few exceptions, it has become fashionable in academic circles to discount or ridicule the conspiratorial mentality.[79] In a recent study, Richard Hofstadter has censured what he calls the "paranoid style" in American politics and its central image of a "vast, insidious, preternaturally effective international conspiratorial network designed to perpetrate acts of the most fiendish character." Nonetheless, Hofstadter grants that there are subversive acts in history and that there is "just enough reality at most points along the line to give a touch of credibility to the melodramatics" of the conspiratorial imagination.[80] After all, Communists do employ espionage to further their aims. The writings of John T. Flynn, Freda Utley, and others of their persuasion

[77] Jaffe, interview with the author, June 14, 1965.

[78] Earl Latham, *The Communist Controversy in Washington: From the New Deal to McCarthy* (Cambridge, Mass. 1966), p. 203.

[79] For example, see Charles A. Beard, *The Devil Theory of War: An Inquiry into the Nature of History and the Possibility of Keeping Out of War* (New York, 1936), pp. 17–29; Richard H. Rovere, *Senator Joe McCarthy* (New York, 1960), p. 40; Tang Tsou, *America's Failure in China, 1941–50* (Chicago, 1963), pp. 219–221, 538–546; Arthur M. Schlesinger, "Extremism in American Politics," *Saturday Review*, XLVIII (November 27, 1965), 21–25; Harry Eckstein, "On the Etiology of Internal Wars," *History and Theory*, IV, No. 2 (1965), 133–163.

[80] Richard Hofstadter, *The Paranoid Style in American Politics and Other Essays* (New York, 1965), pp. 14, 29, 62–63.

cannot be dismissed as sheer fantasy. The conspiracy thesis deserves to be examined on its own merits.

There is no reason to doubt the sincerity or sanity of those who have characterized favorable reporting on the Chinese Communist movement as a purposeful distortion of the truth. From the militantly anti-Communist perspective, the Chinese Communists, like all other Communists, were part of an international plot against the "free world." Individuals who wrote friendly assessments of the CCP thereby became objects of suspicion—probable perpetrators of an enormous artifice. The conspiracy thesis serves a purpose. It is a convenient way of discrediting enthusiastic appraisals of the Chinese Communists written from 1936 to 1945. Yet, any attempt to prove the validity of the conspiracy hypothesis encounters serious obstacles.

"Conspiracy" may not even be an operational concept that can be tested. In the ethereal realm of espionage and intrigue concrete evidence is rare. Accusation and denial constitute the normal pattern of response to the question of any particular individual's affiliations or intentions. The historian must try to understand what happened in the absence of a meaningful dialogue between the accusers and the accused. The basic dilemma is that one must try to document the nearly undocumentable. Even if it could be shown that an individual held membership in a Communist organization, it would not necessarily follow that he was implicated in a conspiracy to undermine established governments or that he accepted orthodox Marxist-Leninist concepts. People joined or supported Communist parties for a great variety of reasons. In the context of the 1930's and early 1940's, communism meant jobs to some, peace to others. This was a period of tremendous domestic and international ferment. The international scene was dominated by the rise of fascism in Europe and militarism in Asia. In the United States, it was the era of the Great Depression and the New Deal.

Thousands of citizens joined or supported Communist-dominated organizations like the American League Against War and Fascism for reasons unrelated to the doctrines of the class struggle or the dictatorship of the proletariat. The American Communist Party, Earl Browder recalled, rose to a position of national influence in the 1930's precisely because its activities were "essentially *reformist*" and not revolutionary. Championing such causes as unemployment relief, equal rights for Negroes, trade unionism, and the struggle against Hitler's Germany, the American CP "relegated its revolutionary socialist goals to the ritual of chapel on Sundays on the pattern long followed by the Christian Church." [81] By emphasizing limited and immediate practical reform aims, the Communists seemed to individuals like Granville Hicks, the literary editor of the *New Masses* and a member of the American Communist Party, different "from other critics of the status quo only insofar as they were more realistic and more determined." [82]

The broadly conceived tactics of the anti-Fascist, pro-New Deal Popular Front help to account for the "Communist vogue" among intellectuals from 1935 to 1939.[83] A considerable number of artists, journalists, and literary figures were attracted to Communist organizations out of a liberal-humanitarian impulse.[84] When Stalin and Hitler signed a nonaggression pact on August 23, 1939, however, many became disillusioned and broke with the party. The "turn towards communism," Hicks explained, was a "hasty impulse, soon regretted." [85]

In 1939, the American League Against War and Fascism

[81] Browder, "The American Communist Party in the Thirties," pp. 219–246. The italics are Browder's.

[82] Granville Hicks, "Writers in the Thirties," in *As We Saw the Thirties,* ed. Rita James Simon, p. 85.

[83] Arthur M. Schlesinger, Jr., *The Crisis of the Old Order: 1919–1933* (Boston, 1957), pp. 222–223.

[84] See Aaron, *Writers on the Left,* p. 391, and Warren, *Liberals and Communism,* pp. 87–88, 220–225.

[85] Hicks, "Writers in the Thirties," p. 89.

was replaced by the American Peace Mobilization. The Nazi-Soviet agreement had destroyed the Popular Front and caused a massive defection of liberal intellectuals from Communist organizations. With the invasion of the Soviet Union on June 22, 1941, the American CP reversed itself and adopted an ultra-patriotic stance. During the Second World War, the party was able to regain much of its lost popularity. From 1941 to 1945 there was an idealization of the U.S.S.R. in the United States. This was the season when prominent members of the Daughters of the American Revolution spoke in glowing terms of Stalin and the Soviet Union.[86] The vast majority of Americans were friendly toward Russians and were prepared, as one scholar put it, "to sup with the devil" in order to defeat Nazi Germany.[87] For most of the period 1929–1945, then, it was possible to support or join Communist movements out of a genuine concern for social betterment or from revulsion against fascism.

Particularly in light of the historical context of the 1930's and early 1940's, unless there is strong reason to suspect dissimulation, the scholar is obliged to accept the testimony of the accused. With respect to Gunther Stein and Philip Jaffe, there is cause to question the credibility of their statements. Stein emphasized that he sought "objective information" and presented his work as an exercise in nonpartisan, eyewitness journalism.[88] His association with Richard Sorge in Japan, however, casts doubt on Stein's claim to be a disinterested observer. *Amerasia* described itself as a nonaligned organ of

[86] See Irving Howe and Lewis Coser, *The American Communist Party: A Critical History* (New York, 1962), pp. 315–436, and David A. Shannon, *The Decline of American Communism: A History of the Communist Party of the United States since 1945* (New York, 1959), pp. 3–33.

[87] Richard W. Leopold, "The United States in World Affairs: 1941–1968," in *Interpreting American History: Conversations with Historians,* ed. John A. Garraty (Vol. 2; London, 1970), pp. 225–226.

[88] Gunther Stein, *The Challenge of Red China* (New York and London, 1945), pp. 13, 83–84, 470.

public discussion. Under Jaffe's editorship, however, the magazine consistently presented only one side of the China story. The presence of Chi Ch'ao-ting and Frederick V. Field on the editorial staff enhances the possibility that *Amerasia* was offering to its readers something less than an objective view of the CCP. On the other side, the behavior of both Stein and Jaffe can be explained by their attraction to the anti-Fascist leadership of Communist organizations.

Anna Louise Strong and Agnes Smedley were true believers, individuals committed to the Chinese Communist movement. Both were avowed advocates, and they made no attempt to conceal their partisanship. Secrecy, as Lenin emphasizes in his handbook on how to make a revolution, is "such a necessary condition" that "all other conditions" must be "subordinated to it." [89] Since secrecy is at the very heart of the concept of conspiracy, it is difficult to understand how these self-styled spokesmen for radicalism can be charged with conspiring to deceive.

Contemporaries recognized that Agnes Smedley was biased, and they had Anna Louise Strong's frank autobiography at their disposal.[90] In 1949, Mrs. Snow asked Anna Louise Strong whether she was a Communist. She replied that she did not know whether she was or not. "I never had a card and I never paid dues," she elaborated, "if that's what you mean. But of course, I have always thought of myself as a Communist. Surely everybody knows where I stand." [91] In 1934, Richard Sorge forbade one of his agents to contact Agnes Smedley because she was known to be a Communist sympathizer.[92] When Evans F. Carlson cautioned her that

[89] V. I. Lenin, *What Is To Be Done?* (New York, 1929), p. 127.

[90] For example, see Chen Yih, "Agnes Smedley's Stories of China," *New York Times Book Review,* September 5, 1943, 3; Clifton Fadiman, "Books: Everyman's Guide to Tokyo," *New Yorker,* XIX (September 11, 1943), 84; Mark Gayn, "Thirteen Years in China," *Saturday Review of Literature,* XXVI (September 18, 1943), 22.

[91] Wales, "Anna Louise Strong," 17.

[92] Johnson, *An Instance of Treason,* p. 64.

her intense commitment to the Eighth Route Army militated against objectivity, her rejoinder was in character. "Of course I am not impartial and make no such pretense. . . . With all my heart, with all that gives me consciousness, I am convinced of the high purpose . . . of this army." [93] An open conspiracy is a contradiction in terms.

If conspiracy is defined as an organized and secret plan employing deception in order to advance subversive goals, do any of those under consideration qualify as conspirators in a plot to undermine the government of Chiang Kai-shek and to prepare the American people for Mao Tse-tung's triumph? Philip Jaffe, Agnes Smedley, Gunther Stein, and Anna Louise Strong were acquainted with one another, they shared a dislike for the Kuomintang, and they possessed a strong bias in favor of the Chinese Communists. Both Jaffe and Anna Louise Strong worked with Communists, Stein was intimately associated with the Sorge spy ring, and the possibility exists that Agnes Smedley could have been recruited into the Soviet intelligence network during her stay in Russia in 1933.[94] None of them would have been disappointed to see Chiang defeated and Mao triumphant. But even the most compromising evidence now available does not prove that any of these individuals were conspirators.

If one works from the premise that the burden of proof rests with the accusers, there is little to substantiate the conspiracy theory. There is no evidence that Jaffe, Agnes Smedley, Stein, or Anna Louise Strong ever held membership in a Communist party. It has not been shown that their behavior was coordinated or directed through a centrally controlled agency. That all four wrote glowing reports about the CCP is indisputable. They presented China's Communists to their readers in the best possible light. But there is no convincing evidence that their books and articles were part

[93] Smedley, *China Fights Back: An American Woman With the Eighth Route Army* (London, 1939), p. 255.
[94] Deakin and Storry, *The Case of Richard Sorge*, pp. 72, 340–341.

of a covert plan to deceive the American public or a deliberate misrepresentation of the Chinese situation as they saw it. The accusers have not even shown that their criticisms of Chinese Nationalists and praise of Chinese Communists was objectively wrong or, for that matter, exaggerated. Until it can be demonstrated that firsthand observers characteristically used deception in a secretive and organized fashion to promote subversive goals, their writings cannot be dismissed as "disinformation." Hypothetically provable, the conspiracy thesis has not been proved.

If what Charles A. Beard called the "devil theory" of history cannot convincingly be applied to the activities of individuals like Agnes Smedley or Anna Louise Strong, it is totally inadequate for dealing with the writings of most of those who had firsthand encounters with Chinese Communists. To accuse a man like Evans F. Carlson of being a Communist is presumptuous. He was anything but a Marxist. As the wife of an important Chinese Communist official remarked, Carlson could not even be called a revolutionary.[95] To suggest that conscientious journalists like Edgar Snow and Theodore H. White were Communist propagandists is to engage in unsubstantiated obloquy. In the search for viable explanations of the phenomenon of favorable reporting on the Chinese Communist movement, one must look elsewhere. Although the possibility remains that one or two of those accused were in fact conspiring with Communist organizations to subvert the government of Chiang Kai-shek or to indoctrinate the American public, the "devil theory" is just too simple.

[95] Wang, *Ich kämpfte für Mao*, p. 202.

[19]

The American Perspective

Tang Tsou has offered an interesting alternative to the conspiracy thesis. His critique of the American image of Chinese communism focuses on the notion that the Chinese Communists were democrats or agrarian reformers. Tsou argues that this widely accepted misunderstanding "could not have been the product of a group of conspirators and agents, however clever they may have been." [1] Instead, he views such misconceptions of the CCP as a logical extension of the American political tradition.

Following the lead of scholars like Louis Hartz and Daniel J. Boorstin, Tsou reasons that a tacit agreement among Americans on basic principles blunted their capacity to understand the political dynamics of other societies. This consensus of values is held responsible for a "profound ignorance" of alien ideologies such as communism, a tendency to discount the importance of theory, and a deplorable lack of insight into American institutions and ideals. The moral unanimity of American life, the argument continues, accentuates the natural inclination to view foreign things "in terms of an image of one's self and to judge foreign life in

[1] Tang Tsou, *America's Failure in China, 1941–50* (Chicago, 1963), p. 235. See also Tang Tsou, "The American Political Tradition and the American Image of Chinese Communism," *Political Science Quarterly*, LXXVII (December 1962), 570–600.

terms of one's own assumptions." Thus, American reporters, scholars, and diplomats, being ill-informed of the essence of both communism and democracy and lacking adequate conceptual tools, were unable to recognize the speciousness of Chinese Communist "democracy." Presumably, if Americans had not been so naïve, they would have diagnosed the CCP as a highly disciplined and tightly organized elite group of "professional revolutionaries, aiming at the seizure of power whenever possible, exploiting mass discontent from whatever sources are at hand, and employing a multiplicity of means and a variety of institutional forms to achieve its purpose." [2]

Although Tang Tsou's thesis provides a valuable corrective of the American image of Chinese communism, it rests on an oversimplification or homogenization of the writings of American and European reporters. Another objection is that he has the advantage of a hindsight denied to contemporaries and possesses analytical devices they lacked. The danger inherent in Tsou's perspective is illustrated when he comes close to identifying favorable views of communism with plain stupidity. [3]

Despite the shortcomings of Tsou's analysis, his general approach to the problem of unanimity in American reporting on the Chinese Communist movement is enlightening. If the question of ignorance is left in abeyance, the notion that Americans "tended to view Chinese things in terms of an American image and to judge Chinese affairs by American

[2] *Ibid.*, pp. 219–230. Although Haldore Hanson was deficient in knowledge of Communist theory, his characterization of the qualities exhibited by CCP leaders is close to Tang Tsou's understanding of what constitutes an intelligent definition of communism. For this interesting parallel see Haldore Hanson, "The People behind the Chinese Guerrillas," *Pacific Affairs*, XI (September 1938), 298.

[3] See especially Tsou's remarks about Owen Lattimore's lack of intellectual sophistication: "Lattimore's naïveté about the Soviet Union led him sometimes to hold unduly favorable views of Soviet life and to tolerate pro-Communist views. In this sense, he was ignorant of communism." Tang Tsou, *America's Failure in China*, p. 222n.

standards" provides a fertile starting point for an assessment of the Western experience in Red China.[4] The writings of those who had firsthand encounters with Chinese Communists suggests that they implicitly accepted certain values as being inherently superior to other values. Most important, their usually inarticulate assumptions of what constituted progress and propriety in the human condition were compatible with what they found in the Border Regions.

A set of values is implicit in the favorable image of the Chinese Communists projected by firsthand observers. To begin with, Americans and some Europeans had a bias toward social egalitarianism. They attached importance to informality, directness, simplicity, and spontaneity in human relations. In the context of this affinity for naturalness and forthrightness, traditional Chinese behavior patterns could be a source of friction. Chinese humanism, with its emphasis on man-in-society, was preoccupied with the problem of social conduct. This engrossment with proper deportment can be understood best under the Confucian concept of *li*. *Li,* which has been translated "the rule of propriety" or "ritual," comprehends both morality and courtesy. By placing a premium on correct form, Chinese etiquette for social intercourse became intricate and elaborate. Polite conventions included the custom of speaking depreciatingly of oneself, of clasping one's own hands instead of shaking hands, of bowing, of reserving seats of honor, of exchanging name cards, of sustaining surface affability, of serving tea in a ritualistic manner, of making stylized inquiries of one's guest, of avoiding bluntness and relying on indirectness in conversation.[5] In sum, the canons of *li* dictated that an individual comport himself

---

[4] *Ibid.,* p. 223.

[5] John King Fairbank, *The United States and China* (rev. ed., New York, 1958), pp. 102–105; H. G. Creel, *Chinese Thought: From Confucius to Mao Tse-tung* (New York, 1963), pp. 32–35; Kenneth Scott Latourette, *The Chinese: Their History and Culture* (4th rev. ed., 2 vols. in 1; New York and London, 1962), pp. 582–587.

in a disciplined fashion according to the rules of society. This stress on propriety and ritual could be frustrating and even alienating to an Occidental. As an authority on Chinese civilization wrote, "most of us in the modern West have little use for ceremony." [6]

Americans, and especially American reporters, were impatient with Chinese formalism. In this respect, whatever annoyance they felt was directed toward Nationalist, not Communist Chinese. While many Kuomintang officials were equipped with both Western educations and manners, a foreigner was more likely to encounter devoted practitioners of *li* in Chungking than in Yenan. Indeed, as H. G. Creel has pointed out, Mao Tse-tung specifically repudiated *li* as an aspect of China's "semi-feudal" culture.[7] In *On the New Democracy,* Mao inveighed against "the worship of Confucius, the study of the Confucian canon, the old ethical code, and the old ideologies." This was a reactionary inheritance which had to be "swept away." [8] Chinese Communists were determined to live like contemporary men. As Helen Snow recognized, they wanted to be "as modern as possible" in ideas, dress, and customs.[9]

The personal attractiveness of Chinese Communists helps to account for the enthusiasm of Western reporters. Journalists returned from the Border Regions with the conviction they had been among modern men, men in their own image. Agnes Smedley claimed that all of the journalists who visited Yenan "felt remarkably at ease." She remembered Mao Tse-tung casually dropping by to chat with his guests, He brought along a bag of peanuts! None of the dissimulation

[6] Creel, *Chinese Thought,* p. 209.

[7] *Ibid.,* p. 205.

[8] Dan N. Jacobs and Hans H. Baerwald, eds., *Chinese Communism: Selected Documents* (New York, Evanston, and London, 1963), p. 73.

[9] Nym Wales [Helen Foster Snow], *Inside Red China* (Garden City, N.Y., 1939), p. 92.

and ceremony of official Chinese life, she continued, existed among the Communists.[10] On James Bertram's first day at Eighth Route Army headquarters in Shansi, Chu Teh entered his room. The commander-in-chief of the Red Army sat on the edge of Bertram's bed and modestly asked whether the foreign correspondent wanted to talk with him. Chu's invitation was so disarming that Bertram "abandoned any pretense at formalities."[11] Philip J. Jaffe was increasingly impressed by Mao's utter sincerity and lack of ostentation. He called these "typical" traits of the CCP leaders and remembered Chinese Communists as definitely more informal and "Western" than other Chinese.[12]

Edgar Snow enjoyed compote with Mao and taught his hosts to play poker. Snow recognized that one reason for his affinity to the Reds was their practice of fraternity and equality.[13] The "un-Chinese" character of Chinese Communists is a recurrent theme of *Red Star over China*. They had discarded "much of the insincere ceremony of traditional Chinese etiquette" and were more open and undevious than other Chinese. He was "as completely at ease in their company as if I were with some of my own countrymen."[14]

Further examples of the remarkable sense of familiarity Westerners felt in the company of Chinese Communists are not hard to unearth. Helen Snow found the plain life of the Eighth Route Army a refreshing departure from the conventions of the official and merchant classes of China. She was

[10] Agnes Smedley, *Battle Hymn of China* (New York, 1943), p. 179.

[11] James M. Bertram, *Unconquered: Journal of a Year's Adventures among the Fighting Peasants of North China* (New York, 1939), p. 150.

[12] Philip J. Jaffe, "China's Communists Told Me: A Specialist in Far Eastern Affairs Interviews the Leading Men of Red China in Their Home Territories," *New Masses*, XXV (October 12, 1937), 5; Jaffe, interview with the author, January 11, 1966.

[13] Edgar Snow, *Journey to the Beginning* (New York, 1958), pp. 160, 178.

[14] Snow, *Red Star over China* (New York, 1961), p. 409.

particularly delighted to discover that the Communists had adopted the "democratic foreign custom" of handshaking.[15] After being elaborately feted by KMT officials in Sian, Gunther Stein was struck by the unpretentiousness of his welcome to the Shen-Kan-Ning. "There was none of the usual scraping and bowing, no exchange of name cards and of solemnly mumbled phrases of courtesy." The Communists met Stein and his party with awkward handshakes, friendly smiles, and a few simple words of salutation. "Nobody made a fuss about us." Stein was both relieved and perplexed at the contrast to the round of receptions and parades in Nationalist territory.[16] When James Bertram first encountered the soldiers of the Red Army, he immediately discerned "an openness of manner that is curiously Western." [17] He later remarked that the way to distinguish a KMT from a CCP officer was by the "frank and unceremonious" greeting of the Communist.[18]

While the personality factor was of importance to every assessment of the CCP, it was the central element in Evans F. Carlson's persuading encounter. Carlson had an aversion for social distinctions, circumspection, and luxurious living. He prized democratic comradeship, candor, and equalitarian simplicity. This spartan marine's experiences in Red China were a confirmation of his predilections.

Prior to his departure for the Border Areas, Carlson had been led to expect something novel. Edgar Snow informed him that the Communists were different. They had, Snow said, renounced the Chinese principle of saving "face" and were unalterably opposed to evasiveness and procrastination.

[15] Wales, *Inside Red China*, pp. 64, 69.

[16] Gunther Stein, *The Challenge of Red China* (New York and London, 1945), pp. 59–60.

[17] Bertram, *First Act in China: The Story of the Sian Mutiny* (New York, 1938), p. 241.

[18] Bertram, *Unconquered*, p. 150.

These were honest, self-critical, and straightforward men.[19] It did not take Carlson long to find himself in total agreement with Snow. Carlson felt thoroughly at home with Chinese Communists. By the end of his first evening at Red Army headquarters, he was calling his hosts "comrades." Carlson self-consciously explained: "Well, it was a comradely atmosphere and no one could have resisted its infectious appeal." [20]

Evans F. Carlson was impressed by Communist informality at meals, uninhibited friendliness, and alertness. He did not evaluate the Chinese Communists in ideological terms. Carlson had no interest in philosophical abstractions. He cared about people and judged them on the basis of an American soldier's standards. General P'eng Teh-huai was lauded because he ate millet, "the peasant food," at each meal. Li Tsung-jen was Carlson's favorite KMT officer. This was because Li's "simple manner of living" more nearly approached that of the Eighth Route Army than any other Nationalist leader. Carlson was comfortable with Madame Sun Yat-sen, since she had the "don't stand on ceremony" attitude of the Chinese Communists.[21]

What Carlson disliked is equally clear. Traditional Chinese middle-class cultural mores left the marine weary. Nationalist officials often subjected Carlson to the ordeal of *li*—sipping tea and exchanging platitudes. The Chinese Communists offered, from his point of view, a happy contrast. He thought the Communists were more like Americans than any other group in Chinese society—they "looked you

---

[19] Evans Fordyce Carlson, *Twin Stars of China: A Behind-the-Scenes Story of China's Valiant Struggle for Existence by a U.S. Marine Who Lived and Moved with the People* (New York, 1940), p. 35.

[20] *Ibid.*, p. 72.

[21] *Ibid.*, pp. 74, 137, 316. Like Carlson, Freda Utley was impressed by the frankness of General Li Tsung-jen. See Freda Utley, *China at War* (New York, 1939), p. 263.

squarely in the eye." [22] In a revealing statement, Carlson suggested why the CCP had captured his sympathies. Among the Communists he found

a desire for directness in speech and action, a desire to avoid the superficial politeness which has been so much a part of Chinese official etiquette since the days of Confucius. No orthodox Chinese official, for example, would have come out to greet me in the spontaneous manner of Chu Teh. Instead I would have been received by ceremonious secretaries and ushered into the presence of the Great One with pompous unctuousness. There would have followed twenty minutes of tea sipping, as we sat stiffly on the edges of our chairs and exchanged meaningless platitudes. But here was an ease of manner and an absence of reserve which was refreshingly genuine.[23]

Chinese Communists seemed more familiar to Carlson than Chinese Nationalists. He could act and talk with the Communists the way he would with an American. Like Americans, they were straightforward and truthful.[24] All men may be brothers, but Evans F. Carlson and other Americans enjoyed a sense of brotherhood in only one part of China.[25]

---

[22] Carlson, *Twin Stars of China*, pp. 92, 96–97, 164.

[23] *Ibid.*, p. 68.

[24] Carlson to Marguerite Le Hand, December 24, 1937, Franklin D. Roosevelt papers; Carlson to Miss Le Hand, March 4, 1938, Roosevelt papers.

[25] For further examples of the preference of Westerners for equalitarianism see Claire and William Band, *Dragon Fangs: Two Years with Chinese Guerrillas* (London, 1947), pp. 56, 122; Israel Epstein, *The People's War* (London, 1939), p. 92; Harrison Forman, *Report from Red China* (New York, 1945), p. 97; Hanson, *"Humane Endeavour": The Story of the China War* (New York and Toronto, 1939), pp. 244, 304; Anna Louise Strong, *One-Fifth of Mankind* (New York, 1938), p. 130; Utley, *China at War*, pp. 73–74; Theodore H. White and Annalee Jacoby, *Thunder Out of China* (New York, 1946), pp. 227–228. For a delightful account of one Westerner's reaction to the *"opera bouffe"* style of a tradition-minded Chinese official see Bertram, *Unconquered*, pp. 223–235.

If it was the engaging mien of the Chinese Communists that captivated Evans F. Carlson, it was the CCP's reform program to alleviate the miseries of the peasantry that primarily accounts for the enthusiasm of Agnes Smedley. She falls into no easily recognizable category. While her approach to social problems was collectivistic, she was a staunch individualist. She was deficient as a theorist but did not hesitate to criticize others for their lack of philosophical expertise. She had a rebellious spirit. Her rhetoric was anarchical, her behavior bizarre. Yet, she accepted Marxist clichés with remarkable composure. What she opposed— marriage, the family, capitalism, exploitation, constituted authority—is more readily apparent than what she supported. She told Carlson that she liked the Chinese Communists because they were seeking a formula which would "effectively serve the interests of all the people." [26]

As James Bertram has pointed out, Agnes Smedley had an "incurable fondness for the word 'masses.' " [27] She possessed, Freda Utley wrote, a "burning sympathy" for mankind.[28] In China, Miss Smedley found much on which to lavish her compassion. The grinding poverty of her own youth was paralleled by the destitution of the Chinese people. One of the most important realities of the China Westerners knew was the incessant suffering of the vast majority of its inhabitants. Theodore H. White recalled the cruelty of life in the Chinese village—starving people, bloated children, constant indignities to human beings, and deadening boredom. He observed that after a few weeks foreigners accepted the normality of this perpetual grief.[29] The war years were a time when, as Bertram put it, "only the dogs fed well in

[26] Carlson, *Twin Stars of China,* p. 74.

[27] Bertram, *First Act in China,* p. 175.

[28] Utley, *China at War,* p. 214.

[29] White made these remarks in the introduction to the paperback edition of *Thunder Out of China.* See White and Jacoby, *Thunder Out of China* (New York, 1961), p. vii.

China." [30] Agnes Smedley called Chinese history an "intermittent record of mass death." [31] She graphically summarized a dominant image of China shared by her generation when she wrote: "In China death moved about as bold as a lord." [32] But Miss Smedley could not accept such conditions as normal, and she made the struggle of the oppressed Chinese peasant for change her own.

Carlson perceptively evaluated Miss Smedley as a person dominated by strong emotional feelings. Human distress touched her deeply, and she constantly labored to relieve it. When suffering was the result of exploitation, Carlson noted, "her wrath knew no bounds, and the offenders felt the lash of her vitriolic tongue and pen." [33] Her standard for judging any particular individual was consistent. Those who tried to improve the livelihood of the Chinese masses were heroic figures.

Although she found religion shallow, despised missionaries as a matter of principle, and styled herself a "heathen," she warmly praised an American Lutheran medical missionary and a group of Catholic nuns. The fundamentalist Lutheran pastor was, as she described him, a "grim, dour Christian" who talked about unbelievers the way Southerners talked about Negroes. But he kept his hospital open to everyone and was committed to helping the sick and wounded, and Miss Smedley "saw only a man dedicated to the service of mankind." [34] Since the Canossian Sisters of Nanyang, Honan, "served mankind and did not try to pre-

---

[30] Bertram, *Unconquered,* p. 321.

[31] Smedley, *China Fights Back: An American Woman with the Eighth Route Army* (London, 1939), p. 22.

[32] Smedley, *Battle Hymn of China,* p. 54.

[33] Carlson, *Twin Stars of China,* p. 69.

[34] Smedley, *Battle Hymn of China,* pp. 383–388. Miss Smedley was so interested in this Lutheran missionary that she attended one of his prayer meetings.

vent the emancipation of the poor," they also passed her test for being decent human beings.[35] Agnes Smedley was disgusted with the KMT because she considered it to be a tool of privileged classes who were indifferent to the well-being of the masses.[36] She was a partisan of the CCP because she believed that it was striving for the "liberation of the poor." [37] Her identification with the CCP was complete. She frequently used the word "we" when referring to the Eighth Route Army.[38] This was not simply a literary device. The Chinese Communists and Miss Smedley shared what she called *"Weltschmerz"* or "world pain." [39] Angered by the misery and injustice of the world, she felt a sense of brotherhood with the poor Chinese peasant. Most Westerners who travel to foreign lands are from upper- or middle-class backgrounds. Agnes Smedley, a washer-woman's daughter, came honestly by her class hatreds and revolutionary instincts.[40] Her vision of the future China was a society "free from exploitation." [41] She was confident that this was also the goal of the CCP.

Although Miss Smedley certainly cannot be described as typical in nearly any respect, the rationale behind her advocacy of Chinese communism illustrates a second value widely held by Western reporters. They were humanitarians. Americans and Europeans shared a humanitarian bias; concern for

[35] *Ibid.*, p. 396. Although Agnes Smedley preferred to rely on the Chinese armies, she was "not too much repelled" when the Sisters gave her a religious charm to wear during air raids.

[36] For example, see Smedley, *Battle Hymn of China*, pp. 36, 50.

[37] *Ibid.*, p. 81.

[38] For example, see *ibid.*, p. 195.

[39] *Ibid.*, p. 216. While Miss Smedley's translation of *Weltschmerz* is not the usual one, "world pain" can be accepted on the grounds that it suggestively conveys her system of values.

[40] Anna Wang, *Ich kämpfte für Mao: Eine deutsche Frau erlebt die chinesische Revolution* (Hamburg, Germany, 1964), pp. 86–89.

[41] Smedley, *China Fights Back*, p. 243.

promoting the welfare of the common man, especially through the elimination of hardship and poverty. While few experienced *Weltschmerz* with the intensity of Agnes Smedley, all favored the Communist reform program, had an affinity for the underdog, and were people-minded.

James Bertram's upbringing was markedly different from that of Agnes Smedley. But they shared, as Bertram wrote, "an unbounded admiration for the common Chinese people" and a feeling of disappointment toward a Nationalist regime which had failed to provide a better living for the masses.[42] Bertram was enthusiastic about the progressive reformism he saw in the Border Regions.[43] He denied any commitment to communism. The only creed he professed was "liberal humanism." [44]

In his autobiography, Edgar Snow commented that anyone who had been in the Far East long enough could become so accustomed to the commonplace suffering of others that it no longer bothered him.[45] Yet, like Agnes Smedley, Snow was unable to rid his mind of scenes of horror and devastation. He remembered his tour of the famine stricken areas of the Northwest in 1929 as "hours of nightmare." [46] "Corpses frequently disappeared before they could be interred and human flesh was openly sold in some villages." This experience remained the "most shocking" of Snow's career, until he got a look at Hitler's gas chambers.[47]

Edgar Snow loved China and the Chinese people. Whatever the shortcomings of Chinese Communists, he reasoned, they had "returned to the people" and were laboring to arouse China's millions to a more abundant life.[48] Snow ac-

[42] Bertram, *First Act in China,* pp. 216–217.
[43] Bertram, *Unconquered,* pp. 126–127.
[44] Bertram, *Return to China* (London, Melbourne, and Toronto, 1957), pp. 242–243.
[45] Snow, *Journey to the Beginning,* p. 34.
[46] Snow, *Red Star over China,* p. 226.
[47] Snow, *Journey to the Beginning,* pp. 3, 9.
[48] Snow, *Red Star over China,* p. 117.

cepted the philosophy of the greater good. He pictured Red firing squads not as totalitarian monstrosities but as surgical instruments shedding blood in behalf of human freedom.[49] The CCP was liberating the oppressed and building a government "of, by and for the people." [50] Snow's strongest bias was a commitment to suffering humanity. He espoused the principle of human brotherhood and opposed backwardness, poverty, exploitation, despotism, and profiteering. He was a humanitarian.[51]

Theodore H. White offers a final illustration of the humanitarian ethic as a determinant in American reporting. Despite his comment about the familiarity of human degradation in China, White's sharpest condemnations are the response of an outraged humanitarian. He returned from a trip with Harrison Forman to famine-ridden Honan sickened and embittered. Chungking officials phlegmatically responded that "the dead bodies were lies; the dogs digging cadavers from the loess were figments of our imagination." [52] White saw China as a part of the world where people literally lived in such "terrible bondage" that they had "nothing to lose but their chains." [53]

Thunder Out of China is an intensely personal indictment of a system of government which blandly looked on while squalor engulfed millions of its citizens. It is not that Theodore White liked communism or even Chinese Communists. Indeed, he distrusted both the party leaders and their dogmas. Yet, these "cold-blooded" and intolerant Reds had bound their interests to those of the "masses of poverty-stricken, suffering peasants, from whom they have always

[49] *Ibid.*, pp. 390–391.
[50] *Ibid.*, p. 514.
[51] For some of Snow's more explicit statements of his personal values see *Journey to the Beginning*, pp. 25, 138, 168; *The Battle for Asia* (New York, 1941), pp. 88–90.
[52] White and Jacoby, *Thunder Out of China* (New York, 1946), p. 77.
[53] *Ibid.*, p. xiii.

drawn their greatest support." [54] The CCP was given qualified praise in *Thunder Out of China* because its policies represented a hopeful response to the desperate needs of the
Chinese people.

A strong preference for democracy constitutes the third
and most commonly articulated bias of firsthand observers.
They assumed that democracy was the best form of government and way of life designed by man. Nearly every foreign
visitor to the Border Regions judged that, in one sense or
another, the Chinese Communist movement was democratic.
While democracy is unquestionably a central criterion in
American and European assessments, its content defies generalization. Democracy meant something different to each individual but was cherished by all as an important ideal. It
was, as Tang Tsou suggests, a "given" or automatically accepted value.[55] In an unreflective and imprecise fashion, firsthand observers projected a democratic image of Chinese
communism that encompassed a bewildering variety of situations and standards.

To Evans F. Carlson, democracy was the absence of hierarchical distinctions in social intercourse. It was more a spirit
than a theory.[56] For Agnes Smedley, democracy was a humanitarian concern for the economic needs of the oppressed,
not an institutional arrangement. Its essence was an
equitable distribution of wealth.[57] To Claire and William
Band, democracy was a system of elections held by secret bal-

---

[54] *Ibid.,* p. 314. For further illustrations of the humanitarian ethic as
a factor in Western appraisals of Chinese communism see Carlson,
Twin Stars of China, pp. 216–217, 224–225; Ralph and Nancy Lapwood, *Through the Chinese Revolution* (London, 1954), pp. 7–21;
Vincent Sheean, *Between the Thunder and the Sun* (New York, 1943),
p. 347; Ilona Ralf Sues, *Sharks' Fins and Millet* (Boston, 1944),
pp. 220–222; Wales, *My Yenan Notebooks* (Madison, Conn., 1961), p. 6.

[55] Tang Tsou, *America's Failure in China,* pp. 219–220.

[56] Carlson, *Twin Stars of China,* pp. 72–74.

[57] Smedley, *China Fights Back,* pp. 34, 115–116, 243.

lot in which all classes could vote.[58] For Edgar Snow, democracy was both a decision-making process involving widespread participation and an administrative responsiveness to the aspirations of the people. It was a government designed to promote the greater good.[59] To Harrison Forman, G. Martel Hall, and Haldore Hanson, the "three-thirds" device was democracy in action. It provided for the political representation of the different factions in Chinese society.[60] Thus, the content of democracy could be psychological, financial, procedural, or structural. According to the predisposition of the particular individual involved, it was defined in social, economic, or political terms.

Since Helen Snow's analysis incorporates the multiplicity of observations which led reporters to use the adjective "democratic" when describing Chinese Communists, it can be used to summarize the value under consideration. The democratic image is at the heart of *Inside Red China*. Chinese Communists were praised for their adoption of "democratic" social mannerisms. Since Border Region reform programs such as that in education were geared to reaching the masses, they were enthusiastically described as fostering "democracy." Mrs. Snow was also happy to report that the Chinese Communists held "democratic" elections in which officials were chosen by the people. Although she un-

[58] Claire and William Band, *Dragon Fangs*, pp. 133, 145–149, 336. The monolithic political power of the CCP was also recognized by writers like Gunther Stein, George E. Taylor, and Theodore H. White. It did not prevent them from employing the term "democratic" in their analyses of the CCP.

[59] Snow, *Red Star over China*, pp. 235–236; *The Battle for Asia*, pp. 113–114, 252, 258, 365–366; *People on Our Side* (New York, 1944), p. 293.

[60] Forman, *Report from Red China*, pp. 56, 179; John Carter Vincent, Chungking, April 2, 1943, dispatch to the Secretary of State, 893.00/14996, Department of State files; Hanson, *"Humane Endeavour,"* pp. 241, 244.

derstood the Leninist commitment of the CCP, Helen Snow
was convinced that the Communists earnestly desired "some
form of democracy." She believed that the immediate goal of
China's Communists was the promotion of a "Democratic
Republic." [61] Prejudices in favor of informality, humanitarianism, and representative instructions are intermingled in
her democratic image of Chinese communism.[62]

The democratic value, then, is a broad and all-encompass-
ing predisposition. It includes both attitudes, activities, and
institutions in its purview. Despite the indistinct focus of the
Western propensity for democracy, its importance cannot be
overestimated. In one respect or another, firsthand observers
thought that the Chinese Communists were "democratic."
Whether it was the CCP's social equalitarianism, employment of familiar electoral procedures, or concern for the
Chinese people which attracted attention, foreign visitors to
Red China did believe they had found men in their own
image.

Tang Tsou has argued that the image of the Chinese
Communists as democrats is a product of theoretical ignorance about both communism and democracy.[63] To some extent, this is true. Individuals like Evans F. Carlson, Harrison
Forman, and Haldore Hanson did not possess the analytical
tools to enable them to grasp the distinctions between a popular totalitarian administration and a functional democracy.
Hanson frankly admitted his incompetence as an interpreter
of Marxist philosophy.[64] There is, however, another side to
the picture.

[61] Wales, *Inside Red China*, pp. 69, 92, 110, 123, 141, 211–215, 262, 320.

[62] For another interesting illustration of the tendency to define democracy in social, economic, and political terms see Sues, *Shark's Fins
and Millet,* pp. 287–288.

[63] Tang Tsou, "The American Political Tradition and the American
Image of Chinese Communism," 577–587.

[64] Hanson, *"Humane Endeavour,"* p. 303.

Helen Snow, James Bertram, and especially Edgar Snow comprehended the CCP's dedication to Leninism and the theoretical subtleties of Communist doctrine. Snow's mode of analysis was dialectical, and he had considerably more than a novice's acquaintance with Marxism. *Red Star over China,* for example, contains numerous references to the works of Lenin, Trotsky, and Stalin.[65] Snow recalled that his reading in the 1930's included "some basic Marxist-Leninist texts" and histories of European and Asian communism.[66] When "Asiaticus" reprehended Snow for distorting Marxist theory in *Red Star over China,* Snow responded in kind. While he called himself "only an amateur at theory," Snow's explanation of the principle of proletarian hegemony proved that he was even better at splitting theoretical hairs than "Asiaticus." [67] To varying degrees, Philip J. Jaffe, Gunther Stein, Agnes Smedley, Anna Louise Strong, George E. Taylor, Freda Utley, and Theodore H. White had at least some knowledge of Communist ideology.

Whether or not Snow and his contemporaries had an adequate conceptual understanding of democracy is almost an academic question. They were writing books about Chinese communism, not learned treatises on the American political tradition. With a few individuals such as Evans F. Carlson and Harrison Forman, one suspects that Tang Tsou's critique is applicable. They employed the term "democracy" so loosely that even the textual context of their writings does not inform the reader precisely of what they had in mind. In most cases, however, there is no convincing evidence either

---

[65] See especially pp. 380, 410–414, and 478–495 of *Red Star over China.*

[66] Snow, *Journey to the Beginning,* p. 138.

[67] "Comment and Correspondence: 'Asiaticus' Criticizes 'Red Star over China,'" *Pacific Affairs,* XI (June 1938), 237–244; "Edgar Snow Replies: To the Editor of Pacific Affairs," *ibid.,* 244–248. See also "Asiaticus'" abstruse rejoinder: "'Asiaticus' Holds His Ground: To the Editor of Pacific Affairs," *ibid.,* 248–252.

for or against ignorance. It is worth noting, moreover, that most observers refrained from explicitly labeling the Chinese Communists democrats or agrarian reformers.

In light of the inclusive nature of the democratic bias, a distinction should be made between "democracy" and "democratic." Reporters used the adjective "democratic" to describe those particular aspects of the Chinese Communist movement which seemed familiar. They often characterized the Communist system as the "more democratic" or the "most democratic" in China. What Western observers meant is not always clear, but very few of them indiscriminately equated American democracy with Chinese communism. Finally, there were correspondents like Theodore H. White whose conception of democracy was not very far removed from Tang Tsou's rigid definition of it as a system of government where "more than one center of power" competes for the support and consent of the governed through a constitutional process.[68] Ignorance is, at best, only a partial explanation for the American image of Chinese communism. A factor of more importance was the distorting effect of a culturally conditioned political vocabulary.

Words like "democracy" bear Western connotations which can distort Asian reality. In order to explain the CCP to themselves and to their readers, firsthand observers used terminology that was Western in origin and implication. Whether they believed that Chinese Communists were true Communists or agrarian democrats, foreigners instinctively grasped at what seemed familiar. When Evans F. Carlson wrote that the so-called Chinese Communists were really a party of "Liberal Democrats" seeking only honest government and equality of opportunity, he was projecting onto an Asian society an American liberal's conception of what is

[68] White and Jacoby, *Thunder Out of China*, pp. 236–237; Tang Tsou, "The American Political Tradition and the American Image of Chinese Communism," 584.

good and right.[69] Edgar Snow called Chinese Communists Marxists, but he also employed words like "democratic" to characterize the CCP. Since "democratic" had anti-Communist overtones in the West, the consequence was a blurred image. In order to place Chinese Communists into their own scale of values, firsthand observers characteristically used words and phrases which made the unfamiliar seem familiar. As Akira Iriye has suggested, Americans and Europeans took their language from the limited vocabulary of Western institutions, compared "things Chinese with things more familiar," and thereby read into an Asian society with "different historical roots" what may have been inappropriate concepts.[70]

Firsthand observers attached importance to equalitarianism in social relations, humanitarianism, and democracy. While these values were not often explicitly articulated, they constitute the central components of the self-image through which Americans and some Europeans looked at China. Westerners discovered much that was compatible with their standards in the Border Areas. Chinese Communists were engagingly informal, they ardently promoted moderate but progressive reforms, and they selectively adopted Western electoral and governmental procedures. Foreign visitors thought they had met men in their own image. This conviction of commonality in ideals, attitudes, and behavior goes far toward explaining the warm and enthusiastic response of firsthand observers to Chinese Communists.

People-minded, democratic, egalitarian Chinese Communists galvanizing peasants to fight Japanese and to overcome misery were hard to be against before 1945, even for bourgeois Americans. While the romanticism that clustered about the image of the Chinese Communist as revolutionary

[69] Carlson to Le Hand, March 4, 1938, Roosevelt papers.

[70] Akira Iriye, *Across the Pacific: An Inner History of American–East Asian Relations* (New York, 1967), pp. 248–249.

may seem unreal today, it was believable to firsthand observers in the 1930's and 1940's.[71] How closely the image corresponded to reality is perhaps an unanswerable question. What has happened since 1945 imposes a perspective on both communism and Chinese Communists radically different from that of the 1930's and early 1940's. Individuals like Helen Foster Snow were neither forewarned nor entrapped by the psychology and clichés of the Cold War. During the 1930's, as she emphasized, nobody had "the least idea of what the Chinese Communists represented." It did not occur to anyone of her generation that the CCP would ever intrude on the Western hemisphere and try to stir up anti-Americanism in places like Cuba.[72] Indeed, before the end of the Second World War, the values of Chinese communism seemed to have operated more as a bridge to the West than as a barrier to mutual understanding.

Maurice Meisner has suggested that it may be more fruitful to understand Chinese Communists as radical, modernizing, antitraditionalist carriers of "many of the values which we associate with modern Western rationalism" than as simply Marxist totalitarians.[73] Mao's new China is, as John K. Fairbank wrote, "science-minded, people-minded, dynamic and convinced of its own creativity." [74] Products of the May Fourth Movement, Mao and the Chinese Communists were essentially modern men in that they repudiated Confucian

[71] For general comments on the romantic mystique sometimes associated with revolutionaries, see Ronald Hingley, "The Revolutionary: On the Persistence of Myths and Mystiques," *Problems of Communism,* XIII (May–June 1964), 63–70, and Richard J. Barnet, *Intervention and Revolution: The United States in the Third World* (New York and Cleveland, 1968), pp. 47–59.

[72] Mrs. Helen Foster Snow to the author, May 1, 1965.

[73] Maurice Meisner, "A Review Article: Sinological Determinism," *China Quarterly,* No. 30 (April–June 1967), 182.

[74] John K. Fairbank, *China: The People's Middle Kingdom and the U.S.A.* (Cambridge, Mass., 1967), p. 42.

ethics and called for a complete transformation of Chinese society.[75] As an iconoclastic Chinese of the May Fourth generation, Mao admired the institutions, ideas, and machines that had enabled the West to mobilize the energies of its people. Passionately nationalist and impatiently utilitarian, Mao and the CCP emphasized that the human will could overcome all obstacles, wrench the Middle Kingdom from its tradition-bound inertia, and thrust China forward into the modern age of science and industry. Many facets of the Chinese Communist movement seem distinctly Western in spirit and character: the stress on human resolution, on organization, on popular education, and on the direct participation of citizens in public affairs.[76]

Marxism itself is a product of the West. It has a morality and an appeal. Marxism favors the underdog, disdains class distinctions, and claims to represent the interests of the common man. These were the aspects of the Chinese Communist movement underscored in the writings of firsthand observers. "The Chinese chose the channel of 'Marxism-Leninism' to reach Western civilization," Helen Snow wrote in a retrospective commentary, "and we can be glad they still like to feel this much identification with the West, however Sinicized." [77] In an even more suggestive recollection, Edgar Snow remembered that perhaps the strongest attraction of the Chinese Communists "to me as a Westerner was their decisive rejection of mysticism and the gods that had failed the

[75] See Chow Tse-tsung, *The May Fourth Movement: Intellectual Revolution in Modern China* (Cambridge, Mass., 1960). The CCP still exalts the May Fourth Movement as the beginning of modern China. For example, see "The Jubilee of the May 4th Movement," *Peking Review*, No. 19 (May 5, 1969), 20–22.

[76] See Stuart Schram, *Mao Tse-tung* (New York, 1966), and Howard L. Boorman, "Mao Tse-tung as Historian," *China Quarterly*, No. 28 (October–December, 1966), 82–105.

[77] Wales, "Old China Hands," *New Republic*, CLVI (April 1, 1967), 14.

poor, in favor of the rationalist's faith in man's ability to solve the problems of mankind." [78]

If firsthand observers emphasized those features of the Chinese Communist movement which coincided with their values, they minimized, perhaps unconsciously, the incompatible. In *On the New Democracy,* Mao Tse-tung made no secret of the fact that he would use democracy to end democracy, at least as that elusive concept was generally understood in the United States. But Mao's rejection of liberal Western political and economic institutions, his intolerance of certain social classes, and his repudiation of personal individuality went largely unnoticed by firsthand observers.[79] This minimization is explained in part by the climate of opinion at the time. As Arthur M. Schlesinger, Jr., has pointed out, one of the common attitudes of educated Americans in the decade after 1935 was complacency toward communism.[80] Agnes Smedley idealized the Soviet Union as a brave new world struggling to ennoble the life of its citizens, Evans Carlson characterized the U.S.S.R. as the friend of oppressed peoples, and James Bertram was more alarmed by the fascism of Germany, Italy, and Japan than by the ideological solidarity of Russian and Chinese Communists.[81] Edgar Snow had some qualms about communism, but he knew what he was against. By 1935 he had decided that

whatever the ultimate truth about Russia might turn out to be, *"as between Nazi-Fascism and Communism* my sympathies were with Communism," not of love for its friends but of dislike of its enemies. One enemy at a time was enough for me; and it was

[78] Snow, *Journey to the Beginning,* p. 178.

[79] See Arthur A. Cohen, *The Communism of Mao Tse-tung* (Chicago and London, 1964), pp. 188–206.

[80] Arthur M. Schlesinger, Jr., *The Politics of Upheaval* (Boston, 1960), pp. 94–95.

[81] Smedley, *Battle Hymn of China,* p. 127; Carlson, "European Pacts and Chinese Prospects," *Amerasia,* III (October 1939), 345–346; Bertram, *First Act in China,* pp. vii–xviii; *Unconquered,* pp. 281–282.

Hitler, not Russia, who denied even the principle of human brotherhood and glorified barbarism and racial engorgement.[82]

The specter of German fascism and Japanese militarism facilitated a misjudgment that was commonplace in the era of the New Deal—a confusion of Chinese Communist and American liberal values.[83]

If firsthand observers overlooked or minimized the totalitarian propensities inherent in the Chinese Communist movement, it was more a malady of their age than a flaw in their moral values. For if those who wrote glowing accounts of the CCP opposed anything, it was tyranny. What repulsed Westerners is implicit in the ideals they espoused. They disliked ostentation and evasiveness, they deplored exploitation and indifference to human suffering, and they despised dictatorship. They found all of these unlovely traits in Kuomintang China.

[82] Snow, *Journey to the Beginning*, p. 138. The italics are Snow's.

[83] See Earl Latham, *The Communist Controversy in Washington: From the New Deal to McCarthy* (Cambridge, Mass., 1966), pp. 359–360.

[20]

The Chinese Perspective

Words scarcely convey the intensity of the revulsion that a surprisingly large number of Americans felt toward the Kuomintang. Hostility toward Chiang Kai-shek's government is a hard and irreducible fact of the American experience in China. The crucial shortcoming of the conspiracy thesis and the American self-image rationale lies in the tendency of both to underestimate the American response to the Kuomintang. American values operated in a Chinese environment. Any meaningful approach to the problem of unanimity in reporting on China's Communists must take into account the reaction to China's Nationalists.

"Living in China is always a searing experience," Mrs. Helen Foster Snow wrote, "the letter 'C' remains branded on every China Hand." [1] Americans were charmed by China and the attractive Chinese people. An entry Agnes Smedley made in her diary on August 31, 1939, is representative of the emotions of other firsthand reporters. She wrote: "As China conquers most people, so has it conquered me." [2] One important consequence of this sympathetic identification with China was a feeling of outrage against a government whose behavior seemed to constitute a perpetual travesty of

[1] Nym Wales [Helen Foster Snow], "Old China Hands," *New Republic*, CLVI (April 1, 1967), 15.

[2] Agnes Smedley, *Battle Hymn of China* (New York, 1943), p. 299.

justice on its citizens. From the viewpoint of Western corre-spondents, the KMT was rotten at the core. As it appeared to them, the KMT was an old-fashioned dictatorship, feudal, decadent, and probably beyond repair. If Americans had a persuading encounter with Chinese Communists, they had a repelling encounter with Chinese Nationalists. Their biases were turned against the KMT.

Personal contacts with Chiang Kai-shek and other Nation-alist officials left Westerners uncomfortable and dissatisfied. Evans F. Carlson refrained from publicizing his innermost doubts about the Generalissimo and the KMT, because he did not want to say anything which might disrupt the united front.[3] But his sensitive conscience compelled him to make a few revealing statements. Two interviews with the Generalis-simo in 1938 left Carlson with one firm impression. Chiang Kai-shek, he wrote, had a face which "could be called inscru-table without exaggeration." After a rather feeble attempt to explain why Chiang had not been more active in eliminat-ing corruption and inefficiency in the KMT, Carlson went out of his way to comment on the Generalissimo's Christian-ity. Chiang had been baptized a Methodist in 1931. While Carlson did not contest the sincerity of Chiang's conversion, he pointedly remarked that he would not try to reconcile the Generalissimo's faith with his un-Christian and un-humani-tarian policies.[4]

Considerations similar to those which inhibited Carlson from giving a frank appraisal caused Edgar Snow to moder-ate his own statements. But Snow also was not able to dis-guise his true feelings. He described Chiang Kai-shek's face as an "austere mask" and suggested that the Generalissimo was a somewhat hypocritical Confucian moralizer. Snow also

[3] Michael Blankfort, *The Big Yankee: The Life of Carlson of the Raiders* (Boston, 1947), pp. 276–277.

[4] Evans Fordyce Carlson, *Twin Stars of China: A Behind-the-Scenes Story of China's Valiant Struggle for Existence by a U.S. Marine Who Lived and Moved with the People* (New York, 1940), pp. 131, 272–278.

credited the Nationalist leader with a "messiah complex or egotism" and characterized his ethics as "semi-feudal and Confucianist." [5] Ilona Ralf Sues, who worked for a short time as Madame Chiang Kai-shek's adviser on publicity, compared the Generalissimo unfavorably with Chu Teh. She remembered that Chu was always available, friendly, and easy to talk to, while Chiang was cold and remote. Miss Sues had to muster a lot of courage even to attempt to secure an interview with the Generalissimo.[6] Theodore H. White contrasted the composed but smiling face of Mao Tse-tung to the "disciplined countenance" of Chiang Kai-shek.[7] Gunther Stein depicted Chiang as a rigid and stern figure "poles apart" from the nonchalant and "mellow" Mao.[8] Even though Freda Utley was impressed by the Generalissimo, she thought that he was totally "inscrutable." "I felt that I knew no more about him after I had met him than before." [9]

Graham Peck, a thoughtful American who spent the Second World War working for the United States Office of War Information in China, best summarized the American brief against the Generalissimo. "Perhaps the worst that should be said of him," Peck wrote, was that Chiang Kai-shek "was not a modern man." [10] Of course, Chiang Kai-shek was not the only figure of prominence in the Kuomintang. But he was the head of the party and dwarfed all others as a symbol of

[5] Edgar Snow, *The Battle for Asia* (New York, 1941), pp. 116–120.

[6] Ilona Ralf Sues, *Shark's Fins and Millet* (Boston, 1944), pp. 231–232.

[7] Theodore H. White and Annalee Jacoby, *Thunder Out of China* (New York, 1946), p. 229.

[8] Gunther Stein, *The Challenge of Red China* (New York and London, 1945), p. 84.

[9] Freda Utley, *China at War* (New York, 1939), pp. 244–245. For the sake of the record, it should be noted that Agnes Smedley described Mao Tse-tung's face as "inscrutable." As far as the author can tell, however, no other American reporter who had a face-to-face encounter with Mao agreed with her. See *Battle Hymn of China*, p. 168.

[10] Graham Peck, *Two Kinds of Time* (Boston, 1950), p. 99.

the KMT. It is therefore a fact of some importance that when Chiang was compared with the leaders of the CCP he came out second best.

Not all Nationalists struck Americans as being chilly and distant. Many KMT luminaries, including Madame Chiang Kai-shek, possessed American educations and mannerisms. Snow had a high regard for Hollington K. Tong, Chungking's efficient Vice-Minister of Publicity. They shared the distinction of being alumni of the University of Missouri.[11] Agnes Smedley had about as much use for the Kuomintang as Freda Utley had for the Russian Communist Party. Yet, Miss Smedley considered T. V. Soong, the Generalissimo's brother-in-law, to be a decent and progressive person.[12] Modern men, then, could be found in the Kuomintang. Graham Peck has suggested that a chief reason for the KMT's ability to get along with the United States was that "un-typical Americanized Chinese" like Madame Chiang and T. V. Soong handled their foreign relations.[13]

The higher echelons of the KMT also included individuals like Ch'en Li-fu, the tradition-minded minister of education who actively promoted an atavistic revival of Confucianism.[14] Freda Utley pictured Ch'en as an obscurantist and a remnant of feudalism.[15] Whether Ch'en Li-fu or Hollington Tong was a more typical representative of the KMT is debatable. But there can be little question that the personalities of many Chinese Nationalists and the philosophy they espoused were alien and repulsive to Americans.

Lin Yutang, who among other things was a spokesman for the KMT, observed that the concept of *li* covered both gov-

---

[11] Snow, *The Battle for Asia*, p. 115; *Journey to the Beginning* (New York, 1958), p. 206.

[12] Smedley, *Battle Hymn of China*, pp. 60, 220.

[13] Peck, *Two Kinds of Time*, p. 181.

[14] John King Fairbank, *The United States and China* (rev. ed., New York, 1958), pp. 193–194.

[15] Utley, *China at War*, p. 58.

ernment by good manners and government by rituals. He went on to identify *li* as the "central concept of Confucian teachings" and said that it extended to include the idea of "establishing political order by a prevailing sense of moral order." In this respect, *li* emphasized "the psychological attitude of orderliness." Lin concluded his defense of government by courtesy by paraphrasing Mencius' aphorism that "only good manners . . . distinguish men from the beasts." [16]

While Americans had nothing against good manners and orderliness per se, they had little use for either Confucian ceremony or philosophic moralizing. To Chinese, rites and propriety were lubricants for human relationships. To most Westerners, they were obstacles. Western dislike of Chinese formality was discussed in the preceding chapter. The discomfort Americans experienced when confronted by Confucian ritual, however, is a small matter when compared to their hostility toward the Confucian ethic. This aversion to *li* as a moral principle is best exemplified in the reaction of Western reporters to Chiang Kai-shek's *China's Destiny*.

China's Destiny, which was first published in 1943, has been called the "political bible of the Kuomintang." [17] It was required reading for the youth of Nationalist China. In *China's Destiny*, as John King Fairbank wrote, Chiang "sought by exhortation to revive the ancient Confucian virtues." [18] The Generalissimo's leading assumption was the superiority of Confucianism to "any other philosophy." [19] Chiang's prospectus for the future direction of China in-

[16] Lin Yutang, *Between Tears and Laughter* (New York, 1943), pp. 81–82, 86. Chapter ten of this volume, "Defense of Courtesy," is an interesting exemplification of the neo-Confucian attitude which Americans found strange and "feudal."

[17] Chiang Kai-shek, *China's Destiny and Chinese Economic Theory*, ed. Philip Jaffe (New York, 1947), p. 20.

[18] Fairbank, *The United States and China*, pp. 191–192.

[19] Chiang Kai-shek, *China's Destiny*, p. 95.

cluded, in their order of importance, psychological, ethical, political, and economic reconstruction.[20] He called for a revival, expansion, and glorification of the ancient Chinese ethical system. "The most important task," he proclaimed,

is to increase the emphasis on propriety and righteousness, and on the virtues of integrity, understanding, and sense of honor. These virtues are the source of the four basic principles and the eight virtues, which in turn are based on "loyalty" and "filial piety." To fulfill the principle of complete loyalty to the state and of filial piety toward the nation; to be altruistic and not seek personal advantage; to place the interests of the state ahead of those of the family; such is the highest standard of loyalty and filial piety.[21]

China's Destiny was, in the words of Chiang Kai-shek, a survey of the present "in the light of the past" and a "planning for the future on the basis of the lessons of history." He proposed to meet the demands of the twentieth century by perpetuating "the spirit that has upheld this country during the last five thousand years" and by reviving "our ancient virtues." [22]

Gunther Stein recalled that while *China's Destiny* was available in Yenan, foreign correspondents had a difficult time trying to obtain the volume in Chungking.[23] According to Theodore H. White, the book was withdrawn from circulation after having sold 500,000 copies. The censorship, he added, would not permit Western journalists to quote from *China's Destiny*.[24] Despite the fact that *China's Destiny* be-

---

[20] *Ibid.*, pp. 157–182.

[21] *Ibid.*, p. 165. The four basic principles referred to by Chiang Kaishek are: propriety (*li*), justice or righteousness (*i* or *yi*), integrity or modesty (*lien*), and conscience or honor (*ch'ih*). The eight virtues or ethical tenets can be translated as: benevolence, faithfulness, filial piety, harmony, love, loyalty, peace, and righteousness.

[22] *Ibid.*, pp. 43, 237.

[23] Stein, *The Challenge of Red China*, p. 235.

[24] White and Jacoby, *Thunder Out of China*, p. 126.

came almost a collector's item, its contents were known to the Bands, Edgar Snow, and Michael Lindsay.

Claire and William Band referred to Chiang Kai-shek's work as an "Oriental version of *Mein Kampf.*" They refused to believe that Chiang had written a single word of *China's Destiny* and speculated that his signature had been secured by forgery or blackmail.[25] Snow did not contest the Generalissimo's authorship. *China's Destiny,* in Snow's appraisal, seemed feudal and almost fascist. He felt that it represented a plea for dictatorship, not democracy.[26] Writing from Yenan in 1944, Lindsay told his father he was in the process of reading *China's Destiny*—"which they have not dared to translate into English." He acidly remarked that part of Chiang's masterpiece "is simply Chinese style fascism with praise of the old hierarchical imperial structure of society." It seemed that the Generalissimo had definitely come out against democracy and was starting to behave like a typical dictator. Lindsay concluded that the KMT's *pao-chia* system of collective responsibility was paralleled by the "Nazi hostage system."[27]

China's Destiny did not appear until 1943, and no English translation was published before 1947. But Western reporters had decided that the KMT was a relic of Confucianism long before they read *China's Destiny*. Public veneration of Confucius had been resumed in 1928, and by 1931 the sage's birthday was celebrated as a national holiday. In 1934, the Standing Committee of the KMT resolved to observe and re-

[25] Claire and William Band, *Dragon Fangs: Two Years with Chinese Guerrillas* (London, 1947), p. 228. In a similar vein, Philip Jaffe maintained that *China's Destiny* was "widely known as the *Mein Kampf* of China." See Chiang Kai-shek, *China's Destiny and Chinese Economic Theory,* p. 19.

[26] Snow, *People on Our Side* (New York, 1944), pp. 280–282.

[27] U.S. Senate, Committee on the Judiciary, Subcommittee on Internal Security, 89th Cong., 1st Sess., *Morgenthau Diary: China,* II (Washington, D.C., 1965), p. 1328. For a brief description of the *pao-chia* system see: Fairbank, *The United States and China,* pp. 189–190.

spect the teachings of Confucius as an antidote to such alien doctrines as Marxism.[28] A few months later, the government of Chiang Kai-shek launched the New Life Movement. This movement sought to rouse the spirit of China's millions through a revival of the Confucian ethic.[29] It was, as James C. Thomson, Jr., has written, "a hybrid composite of Confucian, fascist, Japanese, and Christian elements." [30] Emphasizing YMCA-like character building, the New Life Movement prescribed moralistic remedies for China's economic distresses. There were national campaigns against smoking, spitting, and littering public buildings with watermelon seeds.[31]

James Bertram had been in China little more than a year when he viewed a New Life film. He felt that it was "as remote from modern China as the morality it strove to inculcate." [32] Freda Utley thought it a shame for Madame Chiang Kai-shek to waste so much of her time on the New Life Movement. Miss Utley visualized the New Life Movement as a "semi-Y.M.C.A., semi-neo-Confucian" attempt to solve China's problems by moralistic preachments from above. She believed that the Chinese people needed social and economic reforms, not sermons on how to live virtuous lives.[33] This conviction was shared by other Western correspondents. Agnes Smedley's favorite Chinese historical figure was Ch'in-shih Huang-ti, the founder of the Ch'in dynasty. She particularly admired his effort to eradicate the "feudal" philosophy of Confucianism. Miss Smedley was prone to

[28] James C. Thomson, Jr., *While China Faced West: American Reformers in Nationalist China, 1928–1937* (Cambridge, Mass., 1969), pp. 152–153; Jerome Ch'en, *Mao and the Chinese Revolution* (New York, 1967), pp. 179–180.

[29] Fairbank, *The United States and China*, p. 191.

[30] Thomson, *While China Faced West*, p. 152.

[31] *Ibid.*, pp. 158–159.

[32] James M. Bertram, *First Act in China: The Story of the Sian Mutiny* (New York, 1938), p. 254.

[33] Utley, *China at War*, pp. 198–202.

equating Nationalist China with the Middle Ages.[34] Even
individuals favorably disposed toward the KMT were soon
calling the New Life Movement the "Return-to-the-Old-Life
Movement." Chiang's Confucian version of the YMCA
seemed too clearly to be an attempt to substitute for social
reform an archaic behavioral code.[35]

If the KMT represented an outmoded Confucianism to
Western reporters, the CCP represented modernity. Freda
Utley called the Reds the "greatest realists" and the "most
modern-minded element" in China.[36] Gunther Stein, who
had no affinity for the ancient virtues, observed that the "ideological enemies" of Chinese communism were "Confucius
and the other sages of China's distant past."[37] Edgar Snow
believed that the Confucianism of the KMT was a key to the
weakness of its wartime leadership. He was also aware that
the CCP was "specifically anti-Confucianist."[38] Firsthand
observers did not explicitly compare Chiang Kai-shek's
China's Destiny to Mao Tse-tung's *On the New Democracy.*
It is reasonably safe to assume that had they done so they
would have found Mao's orientation more to their liking.[39]
At the very least, they would have agreed with the conclusion of a United States Foreign Service officer that *China's
Destiny* was "a real Confucian feudal document."[40]

People-minded Americans tended to identify with the de-
sires of the lowly Chinese peasant. They had an interest in

[34] Smedley, *China Fights Back: An American Woman With the
Eighth Route Army* (London, 1939), pp. 185–186; *Battle Hymn of
China*, p. 135. Miss Smedley titled the chapter describing her initial re-
action to Nationalist China "Into the Middle Ages."

[35] Thomson, *While China Faced West*, pp. 226, 234.

[36] Utley, *China at War*, p. 256.

[37] Stein, *The Challenge of Red China*, p. 245.

[38] Snow, *The Battle for Asia*, p. 248

[39] For a comparison of *China's Destiny* and *On the New Democracy*
see Jerome Ch'en, *Mao and the Chinese Revolution*, pp. 256–259.

[40] John F. Melby, *The Mandate of Heaven: Record of a Civil War,
China, 1945–49* (London, 1968), p. 186.

his welfare and were troubled by the problem of man's inhumanity to man. The KMT did not seem to share their concerns. Theodore H. White and Annalee Jacoby observed that despite the "humane paper legislation" of the Nationalist government, some scholars thought that China was probably the only nation in the world where the people ate less, lived more bitterly, and were clothed worse "than they were five hundred years ago." [41] Only the Communists had provided effective leadership "to the peasant's irresistible longing for justice in his daily life." [42] Vincent Sheean could not imagine how the lot of the Chinese masses could have been more desperate than it was under the KMT—"they were dying of starvation." [43] The plight of the Chinese people moved Agnes Smedley to chastize "a ruling class made up of venal landlords, merchants, and politicians." [44]

It was not the fact that hundreds of thousands of Chinese were living and dying in misery that turned foreign reporters against the KMT. All of them realized that China was not the United States and that a war was being fought. What really upset Westerners was their belief that Chiang Kai-shek's government was, as Brooks Atkinson put it, "cold-hearted" or indifferent to the well-being of its citizens.[45] Edgar Snow thought that the KMT was committed to a "semi-feudal economy" of usury, peasant bondage, and land-lordism. He felt that Chungking was completely divorced from the aspirations of the Chinese people.[46] Many others agreed with Snow. A Christian missionary who spent all of his years in China in the Nationalist areas assailed the KMT

[41] White and Jacoby, *Thunder Out of China*, p. 32.

[42] *Ibid.*, p. 314.

[43] Vincent Sheean, *Between the Thunder and the Sun* (New York, 1943), p. 347.

[44] Smedley, *Battle Hymn of China*, p. 217.

[45] Brooks Atkinson, "Long Schism Seen," *New York Times*, October 31, 1944, 4.

[46] Snow, *People on Our Side*, pp. 279–282.

for regarding peasants "as nothing but an endlessly exploitable source of money, food, and conscripts." [47] But the most poignant testimony to the importance of the humanitarian ethic as an engine for disillusionment with the KMT is to be found in the writings of one of its defenders.

In China, Freda Utley wrote, "wherever you go, you can find people poor enough to carry your things for you." [48] Miss Utley admired the common Chinese peasant and was "horrified" at his neglect. She believed that if China was to survive, ancient social, economic, ideological, and administrative injustices had to give way to reforms.[49] Her criticisms of the Kuomintang in *China at War* focus on its failure to respond to the needs of the people. She spoke of "official callousness or negligence" toward the masses.[50] Although Freda Utley admired the Generalissimo, she was disturbed by his insensitivity to the suffering of China's millions.[51]

Even after Freda Utley had decided that the Chinese Reds were Stalinists, she recognized that the KMT left much to be desired. She continued to take Chiang Kai-shek to task for his "lack of vision" and his lack of confidence in his own people. In a revealing statement, she labeled the Russian domination of the CCP a "tragedy"—a tragedy for the Chinese masses and the progressive movement in China.[52] *The China Story* was Freda Utley's most fervent anti-Communist manifesto. Despite her bitter assault against the CCP, she could not bring herself to excuse the shortcomings of the KMT. While she garnered an abundance of extenuating factors to help explain the illiberal behavior of Chiang Kai-

[47] Paul Frillmann and Graham Peck, *China: The Remembered Life* (Boston, 1968), p. 261.
[48] Utley, *China at War*, p. 167.
[49] *Ibid.*, p. ix.
[50] *Ibid.*, p. 22; see also pp. 70–82.
[51] *Ibid.*, p. 243.
[52] Utley, "Will Russia Betray China?" *Asia*, XLI (April 1941), 172–173.

shek, she felt that it had taken a "great disaster"—the flight to Formosa in 1949—to awaken the Generalissimo to the drastic necessity for improving the livelihood of the Chinese peasant. Her main argument for supporting Chiang was that he had proved himself a "valiant enemy of totalitarianism." [53] Freda Utley's hatred for communism had triumphed over her humanitarian sympathies. It was a Pyrrhic victory.

Americans may have been ignorant of democratic theory, but they knew that the Kuomintang was not a democratic party. "Decadent, unprincipled, corrupt governing party" was Theodore H. White's brief formula for understanding the KMT.[54] He felt that it was dominated by a dissolute political faction which combined some of the "worst features" of the Spanish Inquisition and Tammany Hall.[55] White believed that a China entirely ruled by the KMT would be a "historical monstrosity." [56] Agnes Smedley thought that the party harbored "notoriously proto-Fascist" elements.[57] She wrote that the provincial branch of the KMT in Anhwei represented "all that was dark and treacherous." [58] Gunther Stein concluded that the party was rigidly controlled by a reactionary and "Fascist" clique.[59]

The Kuomintang was both a political party and the government of China. As a government, it seemed equally undemocratic. To Mrs. Snow, the ten years of KMT rule from

[53] Utley, *The China Story* (Chicago, 1951), pp. 64–65, 74–75. See also Utley, *Odyssey of a Liberal: Memoirs* (Washington, D.C., 1970), pp. 196–199, 214.

[54] White and Jacoby, *Thunder Out of China*, p. 293.

[55] White, " 'Life' Looks at China: Through the Blockade One of Its Correspondents Brings this Firsthand Report," *Life*, XVI (May 1, 1944), 103. This article was written before White visited the Border Areas.

[56] White and Jacoby, *Thunder Out of China*, p. 322.

[57] Smedley, "Crisis in China: Defeat and Disunity," *PM*, October 22, 1944, 3.

[58] Smedley, *Battle Hymn of China*, p. 349.

[59] Stein, *The Challenge of Red China*, p. 475.

1927 to 1937 had been a "Fascist aberration." [60] Brooks Atkinson described Chiang Kai-shek's political ideas as those of
a warlord and his government as "anti-democratic." [61] Edgar
Snow was amazed at the bland assumption of Chinese officials that the peasant was unfit for self-rule and asserted that
the KMT had a genuine fear of its own people. He did not
anticipate that an "autocratic dictatorship" like the KMT
would ever voluntarily relinquish its monopoly of power.[62]
The Nationalists, Agnes Smedley observed, always found one
pretext or another for postponing the introduction of democracy.[63]

There were individuals like Joy Homer who could see no
wrong in the Chungking regime. Most Americans, however,
disliked Confucian morality and ceremony, doubted that Nationalist reform projects were worth more than the paper
they were written on, and disbelieved the Kuomintang's
pledges of eventual democracy. Theodore H. White eloquently summarized the thinking of the vast majority of firsthand observers: "The manners of the Kuomintang in public
were perfect; its only faults were that its leadership was corrupt, its secret police merciless, its promises lies, and its
daily diet the blood and tears of the people of China." [64]
The Kuomintang violated the values Americans held dear.

Few scholars have doubted the substance of the firsthand
critique of Chiang Kai-shek and the Kuomintang. Chow
Tse-tsung's study of the May Fourth Movement indicates that
to the present day a conservative faction of the KMT has
glorified traditional Chinese ethics and has strongly
opposed the iconoclasm of reform-minded Chinese. In the
1930's, anyone who even mentioned the May Fourth Movement in public risked the displeasure of the Nationalist

[60] Wales, *Inside Red China* (Garden City, N.Y., 1939), p. 303.
[61] Atkinson, "Long Schism Seen," 4.
[62] Snow, *The Battle for Asia*, pp. 209–213.
[63] Smedley, *Battle Hymn of China*, p. 338.
[64] White and Jacoby, *Thunder Out of China*, p. 256.

government. Chiang himself has long been a fervent admirer of Tseng Kuo-fan, the Confucian soldier-statesman who crushed the Taiping rebellion.[65] Jerome Ch'en suggests that the Generalissimo was "essentially a Confucian" who emphasized psychology and moral principles as the means to reconstruct Chinese society.[66] Gabriel Kolko advances "gangsterism" as a serious analytical tool for understanding the KMT.[67] Bot Kolko and Barrington Moore, Jr., interpret the Nationalist regime as fundamentally antidemocratic, criticize Chinese Nationalists for insensitivity to the needs of their own people, and regard KMT reform decrees as little more than window dressing to disguise the victimization of the peasantry.[68] Moore finds "striking resemblances" between KMT doctrine as expressed in *China's Destiny* and Western fascism.[69]

More striking than alleged similarities between Chinese Nationalists and European fascists is the resemblance between the analyses of contemporary scholars and the writings of firsthand observers. Kolko flails the Nationalist Army as "more an institution for taxing the peasantry than a military body."[70] Theodore H. White and Annalee Jacoby described

[65] Chow Tse-tsung, *The May Fourth Movement: Intellectual Revolution in Modern China* (Cambridge, Mass., 1960), pp. 343–346. For an able analysis of the "neo-Restoration" of Confucianism by the Kuomintang see Mary Clabaugh Wright, *The Last Stand of Chinese Conservatism: The T'ung-Chih Restoration, 1862–1874* (Stanford, 1957), pp. 300–312. Mrs. Wright points out that the "issue of Confucianism" was "squarely joined in the Kuomintang-Communist struggle for control of China's destiny" (p. 301).

[66] Jerome Ch'en, *Mao and the Chinese Revolution*, pp. 257–259.

[67] Gabriel Kolko, *The Politics of War: The World and United States Foreign Policy, 1943–1945* (New York, 1968), pp. 229–230.

[68] Kolko, *The Politics of War*, pp. 227–230; Barrington Moore, Jr., *Social Origins of Dictatorship and Democracy: Lord and Peasant in the Making of the Modern World* (Boston, 1967), pp. 193–197.

[69] Moore, *Social Origins of Dictatorship and Democracy*, pp. 197–201.

[70] Kolko, *The Politics of War*, p. 200.

the same institution as "a pulp, a tired, dispirited, unorganized mass, despised by the enemy, alien to its own people, neglected by its government, ridiculed by its allies." [71] Barrington Moore pictures the KMT as an unpopular, totalitarian, fascist-like party with "gangster attributes." [72] Twenty-five years earlier, General Joseph W. Stilwell made the following entry in his celebrated diary: "Sympathy here for the Nazis. Same type of government, same outlook, same gangsterism." [73] Although it can be argued that the findings of Kolko and Moore are the product of a quarter of a century of historical scholarship, Akira Iriye's warning that to say Chiang Kai-shek was a fascist is to compare "things Chinese with things" not Chinese bears repeating.[74] But it is not altogether remarkable that historians operating under assumptions similar to those of firsthand observers have been equally affronted by Chinese Nationalists and have arrived at conclusions which seem familiar.

[71] White and Jacoby, *Thunder Out of China*, p. 132.
[72] Moore, *Social Origins of Dictatorship and Democracy*, p. 214.
[73] White, ed., *The Stilwell Papers* (New York, 1948), p. 124.
[74] Akira Iriye, *Across the Pacific: An Inner History of American-East Asian Relations* (New York, 1967), p. 248.

[21]

Two Kinds of Time

In a thoughtful review article in October 1945, Nathaniel Peffer made an attempt to resolve the problem of unanimity in Western reporting on the Chinese Communists. He began by pointing out that there was something in Red China which captured the imagination of "all sorts and conditions of men." Regardless of occupation, class, previous attitudes or social convictions, a series of individuals, including objective intellectuals, emotional radicals, military officers and neutral correspondents, had returned from Yenan "ardent defenders if not enthusiasts" of the CCP. Peffer could find no record of an Occidental visitor to the Border Areas who came away antagonistic.[1]

Peffer thought it unreasonable to believe that all foreign travelers to the Border Regions had been gulled by propaganda. The personalities, programs, and patriotism of Chinese Reds appealed to Westerners. These straightforward Communists seemed dedicated to improving the livelihood of the Chinese people and defeating the Japanese aggressors. Yenan had all the qualities of a social settlement. Its atmosphere was charged with optimism and anticipation. But there was something more.[2]

[1] Nathaniel Peffer, "Contrasting Yenan and Chungking," *New York Times Book Review,* October 28, 1945, 4.
[2] *Ibid.*

If Americans and Europeans gave the Communists the benefit of every doubt, Peffer wrote, it was because they were "predisposed to do so." They were inclined to favor Yenan because they came from Chungking. "A current of fresh air appears to blow through Communist China, and those who come there from Chungking seem to find themselves suddenly breathing deeply again." Yenan was nearly all that Chungking was not—activity, hope, public honesty, official concern for the masses. This "irrepressible contrast" explains American enthusiasm for the Chinese Communists. Firsthand observers left Yenan "aglow and moved to testify" because they had been to Chungking first.[3]

Nathaniel Peffer's perceptive interpretation of American reporting on the Chinese Communists is atypical. There has been nothing quite like it before or since 1945. Evidently Peffer was not acquainted with the writings of Cormac Shanahan. He also erred in assuming the universality of a prior disenchantment with Nationalist China. Joy Homer certainly was not predisposed toward finding a mecca in Yenan, and the Bands decided that the Kuomintang was less attractive than the Chinese Communist Party only after their sojourn in the Border Areas. Despite these oversights, Peffer's analysis goes to the very heart of the American experience in Red China.

Favorable images of the CCP were more a product of experiential than of ideological influences. The Americans and Europeans who had firsthand contacts with the Chinese Communists did not share a common political orientation. While many of them had a certain degree of tolerance toward communism, few were Communists. The spectrum of their political convictions ranged from the anti-Stalinism of Freda Utley to the nihilistic radicalism of Agnes Smedley. Western reporters did exhibit preferences for social equalitarianism, humanitarianism, and democracy. With the ex-

[3] *Ibid.*

ception of a person like Freda Utley, however, these predilections were defined in and were in part a reflection of
their response to the Chinese environment. Norman Bethune was as struck by the contrasts between the KMT and
CCP areas as any of the non-Communist firsthand observers.[4]

The experiential pattern took different directions. Joy
Homer, Stanton Lautenschlager, and Cormac Shanahan entered the Border Regions with no apparent misgivings about
the KMT. Shanahan's rabid anticommunism colored everything he wrote, Lautenschlager did not compare Nationalist
and Communist China, and Joy Homer adored both sides. It
is of some significance, however, that both Miss Homer and
Lautenschlager had persuading encounters with the Chinese
Communists. Shanahan—who liked neither communism nor
Chinese Communists—inconveniently disrupts all generalizations. Perhaps what the Catholic priest saw can only be explained in terms of his preconceived notions about all Communist societies. But on the basis of existing information,
Father Shanahan remains inexplicable.

Claire and William Band are unique but explicable. They
seem to have lived in an ivory tower at Yenching University
before escaping to the guerrilla redoubt. Their political conservatism made them suspicious of communism, and they
discounted Communist accusations against the Nationalists
as transparent propaganda. Then they went to Chungking.
To their dismay, the Bands discovered that the charges
"seemed more than true." Claire and William Band were
hopeful that the KMT would reform itself, but they unfavorably contrasted Chungking with Yenan.[5]

The Bands went through the experiential process in reverse. Although no firsthand observer's persuading encoun-

[4] See Jonathan Spence, *To Change China: Western Advisers in
China, 1620–1960* (Boston and Toronto, 1969), p. 219.

[5] Claire and William Band, *Dragon Fangs: Two Years With Chinese
Guerrillas* (London, 1947), pp. 307–325.

ter was precisely the same as another's, Helen Snow typifies the normal pattern. By the winter of 1935, Mrs. Snow had given up hope in the Kuomintang. She and her husband were always on the verge of leaving Peiping in despair.[6] Mrs. Snow visualized China as "one big, pathological, soggy mess, sick to death and about to be taken over by the Japanese." She did not think that much of the "ancient regime" was worth saving and had decided that China desperately needed a thoroughgoing revolution from top to bottom.[7] Mrs. Snow was disillusioned with the KMT before she went to Yenan in 1937. She had a compulsion to learn whether the Communists "were the same old degenerate Chinese or if they were something new and different." [8]

Mrs. Snow called her trip to Red China "a journey of discovery . . . of a new mind and a new people, creating a new world in the heart of the oldest and most changeless civilization on earth." The Communists were a "new species" of Chinese.[9] Against the background of Kuomintang China, they "showed up very well indeed." They shook hands with visitors, behaved in a more forthright, open and friendly manner, seemed less secretive and deceptive, and opposed physical torture. In comparison with other Chinese, the Communists were "extremely humanitarian"—a character trait which appealed to Mrs. Snow "very much." Chinese Communists "seemed more 'like us.' " [10]

While the Nationalists had repudiated "the values we represent," the Communists wanted to find a "common ground." The Chinese Communists were "reaching out for a bridge to the Western world through their Marxian concept and were trying to become men of their own century." [11]

[6] Mrs. Helen Foster Snow to the author, May 1, 1965.

[7] Mrs. Snow to the author, April 17, 1965.

[8] Mrs. Snow to the author, May 1, 1965.

[9] Nym Wales [Helen Foster Snow], *Inside Red China* (Garden City, N.Y., 1939), pp. xi, 38.

[10] Mrs. Snow to the author, May 1, 1965.

[11] Mrs. Snow to the author, April 17, 1965.

Chinese Communists always called Chiang Kai-shek and his followers "barbarians." Mrs. Snow was of the same opinion. She was enthusiastic about the CCP primarily because it strove to "DESTROY FEUDALISM AND ESTABLISH A MODERN SOCIETY." Sickened by her experiences in Nationalist China, she had gone to Yenan with a "kind of categorical imperative" to learn what sort of people the Communists were—to see "if they belonged to the same human race as myself." [12] They did.

The experiential pattern of revulsion to the KMT and attraction to the CCP epitomized by Mrs. Snow is not singular. It is duplicated in the careers of the preponderant majority of firsthand reporters. Those whose experiences fall within the schema of a repelling encounter with Chinese Nationalists followed by a persuading encounter with Chinese Communists include Brooks Atkinson, James M. Bertram, T. A. Bisson, Evans F. Carlson, Israel Epstein, Harrison Forman, Haldore Hanson, Philip J. Jaffe, Ralph Lapwood, Michael Lindsay, Vincent Sheean, Agnes Smedley, Edgar Snow, Gunther Stein, Anna Louise Strong, Ilona Ralf Sues, and Theodore H. White. Not everyone entered the guerrilla strongholds with attitudes and emotions identical to those of Mrs. Snow. Agnes Smedley had written eulogies of the Communists and diatribes against the Nationalists years before she actually set foot on Red territory. Her trips to the Border Regions simply reinforced longstanding convictions. Despite some alienating personal contacts with Chiang Kai-shek's government, Haldore Hanson maintained a remarkable sense of balance toward the KMT. These deviations from Mrs. Snow's point of view were, however, largely a matter of emphasis. Both Agnes Smedley and Hanson were predisposed to give the CCP the benefit of the doubt.

The importance of coming from Nationalist to Communist China is underscored in the writings of Western observ-

[12] Mrs. Snow to the author, May 1, 1965.

ers. In a widely discussed article, T. A. Bisson divided China into two parts—Nationalist or *"feudal* China" and Communist or *"democratic* China." [13] Israel Epstein chose three suggestive subtitles for his essay on Chinese affairs: "The Military Contrast," "The Political Contrast," and "The Economic Contrast." The KMT "dictatorship" pursued "defeat-breeding feudal fascist" policies, while the CCP was liberating China from exploitation and the Japanese.[14] Evans F. Carlson "could not resist contrasting" the spartan self-discipline of the Eighth Route Army with the physical comforts enjoyed by Kuomintang leaders.[15] *Red Star over China* is an exercise in comparative analysis. Always implicitly and often explicitly, Edgar Snow evaluated Chinese Communists on the basis of their difference from other Chinese. Snow digressed from his description of factory conditions in the Shen-Kan-Ning to emphasize that one had to compare the life of Communist workers with the miserable lot of those elsewhere in China to understand the improvement. The average American laborer would have found either situation unbearable, but that was not the point.[16]

Gunther Stein also stressed that Red China had to be judged "on its own merits." There was no imaginable parallel with the events taking place in China to the United States. But Stein continually paired Yenan with Chungking. The memory of Chiang Kai-shek's "pathetic city" kept coming back to him "like a nightmare." When Stein flew from Yenan to Chungking, he was traveling "from one Chinese world to another." [17]

[13] T. A. Bisson, "China's Part in a Coalition War," *Far Eastern Survey,* XII (July 14, 1943), 138. The italics are Bisson's.

[14] I. Epstein, "Light on the Chinese Puzzle," *Labour Monthly,* XXVII (June 1945), 173–178.

[15] Evans Fordyce Carlson, *Twin Stars of China: A Behind-the-Scenes Story of China's Valiant Struggle for Existence by a U.S. Marine Who Lived and Moved with the People* (New York, 1940), p. 133.

[16] Edgar Snow, *Red Star over China* (New York, 1961), p. 274.

[17] Gunther Stein, *The Challenge of Red China* (New York, and London, 1945), pp. 5, 88, 460.

After having lived in Nationalist China, foreign visitors were enchanted by the Border Areas. In Red China there was a sense of history in the making so strong that it almost had substance. The atmosphere was pungent with energetic activity, fellowship, and good will. Joy Homer found her Communist hosts young, carefree, efficient, and "all on fire." They seemed "exasperating and ridiculous and lovable." [18] The excitement Ilona Ralf Sues had felt while in Yenan sagged when she got back to Hankow, where there was selfishness, suffering, and indifference to the common people.[19] Ralph Lapwood had one experience during his fifteen years in China which "contrasted sharply with the rest"—his trek through the guerrilla regions. Lapwood left Peiping outraged at the poverty, lack of humanitarian justice, and nepotism which was rampant in Kuomintang China. After the inertia and decadence which characterized most of the country, the partisan bases were like a fresh breeze of hope and confidence. He discerned a "marked degeneration" in morale once out of Red China.[20] Owen Lattimore speculated that firsthand reports were heavily weighted in favor of the CCP because many thought the Chinese Communists were too nationalistic to emerge from the war firmly tied to the Soviet Union, were too economically backward to pose a serious threat to other nations, and because the KMT was so rotten and corrupt.[21]

James Bertram compared the bleak conditions of Mao Tse-tung's unheated cave to the grand style of life formerly indulged in by Nanking officials. The New Zealander did not rue the Japanese bombings of Nanking. Perhaps the explosions would shake the "old face-saving" bureaucrats from their lethargy. Stimulating Yenan seemed to Bertram a good

[18] Joy Homer, *Dawn Watch in China* (Boston, 1941), p. 228.
[19] Ilona Ralf Sues, *Shark's Fins and Millet* (Boston, 1944), pp. 257, 293–294.
[20] Ralph and Nancy Lapwood, *Through the Chinese Revolution* (London, 1954), pp. 19–22, 32.
[21] Owen Lattimore, conversation with the author, April 16, 1969.

place to be as opposed to "Old China." [22] Bertram thought that a number of factors accounted for the favorable views of foreign reporters toward Chinese Communists. Westerners had a "natural sympathy for the underdog," and they admired the ability of the CCP to accomplish so much with so little. The Communists were frank and ready to talk with correspondents, and the Eighth Route Army was spirited, skilled, and popular with the peasants. Bertram felt that it was

impossible to convey the contrast between Nanking, with its shabby-pretentious buildings, its white cotton gloves and shabby roguery; and Yenan—this Spartan capital, bare loess and millet, but everyone young, brown, bubbling over with enthusiasm—and so damned efficient, so unlike "Old China" in so many ways.[23]

Brooks Atkinson had never been to Nanking, but he had reported the news from Chungking. He remembered the KMT as a "medieval organization." The Nationalists treated the peasants as if they were "rubbish." Atkinson stressed that "after the stagnation of Kuomintang China, the vitality of Communist China was tonic." [24] The Chinese Communists seemed more able, effective, and interested in the masses than the Chinese Nationalists.[25]

Atkinson's encounter with the Chinese Communists was of brief duration, and he certainly was more anti-KMT than pro-CCP. His assessment of the CCP as a "farm labor party" suggests that his reports are more notable for literary felicity than for political insight.[26] Nevertheless, posterity would

[22] James M. Bertram, *Unconquered: Journal of a Year's Adventures among the Fighting Peasants of North China* (New York, 1939), pp. 115, 131.

[23] Bertram to the author, April 1965.

[24] Brooks Atkinson to the author, May 28, 1965.

[25] Atkinson to the author, May 4, 1965.

[26] Atkinson, "Chinese Still Try to Unify Factions," *New York Times,* November 26, 1944, 43.

have been the loser if Brooks Atkinson had not wielded his formidable pen from two perspectives, Chungking and Yenan.

Like Atkinson, Theodore H. White spent most of the Second World War in Nationalist territory. The best-selling volume which he wrote jointly with Annalee Jacoby, *Thunder Out of China,* is only secondarily concerned with the topic of Chinese communism. The major theme of this journalistic masterpiece is not the attractiveness of the Communist alternative, but rather the progressive bankruptcy of the Chungking government. While a writer like Edgar Snow spoke of a Red star rising over China, White thought more in terms of a Nationalist regime which was in the process of surrendering the Mandate of Heaven by default—rotting away through moral deterioration and political misrule.

White's characterization of the Chinese Communists in generally favorable terms did not stem from any affinity on his part for communism as a political doctrine. Indeed, his sentiments lay in the opposite direction. He distrusted Communist intentions and had no desire to see China engulfed in a Red tide. White did not care much for the CCP, but he cared even less for the KMT. If the Nationalists were "decadent," the Communists were "dynamic." White described Chungking as a city of "unbridled cynicism, corrupt to the core." Yenan was a place of excitement and bustle. The people were healthier and ruddier. Those who visited Yenan escaped from the oppressiveness of Chungking into what appeared to be "an area of light." The key to White's assessment of the Chinese Communist movement lies in his conviction that the CCP had "shone by comparison" with the KMT.[27]

Harrison Forman wrote that most foreign newsmen were neither Communists nor Communist sympathizers.[28] This

[27] Theodore H. White and Annalee Jacoby, *Thunder Out of China* (New York, 1946), pp. 18, 226, 293, 313–314, 317.

[28] Harrison Forman, *Report from Red China* (New York, 1945), p. 1.

seems true. Michael Lindsay could not muster much hope for the Kuomintang.[29] Neither could many other firsthand reporters. Agnes Smedley remembered that journalists never returned from the Border Areas "without feeling they had been among modern men, men much like themselves." [30] She had a reasonably accurate memory. Philip J. Jaffe emphasized that the contrast between the KMT and the CCP was "the important thing." Life in the United States was so far removed from conditions in China that it would have been absurd to compare the two nations. A person came from Nationalist to Communist China—"that was the difference." [31] Jaffe was accurately summarizing the preconditioning of his generation.

As Edgar Snow remarked, China was not Missouri. One part of the country was poverty, filth, brutality, ignorance, indifference, chaos, helplessness. The other was youth, enthusiasm, dedication, and hope. Snow speculated that if he had just arrived in China from America in 1936, he might have been less responsive to the Chinese Communists. He might have recognized that Chinese communism constituted a future menace to the United States. But Snow had been in East Asia since 1928. His thought was "largely environed" by the Chinese setting.[32] Some of those who went to Yenan had been in China longer than Snow, others for a shorter period. All of them came from some point in Chiang Kai-shek's China.

The "irrepressible contrast" between Nationalist and Communist China permeates the Western literature on Chinese communism. Few writers formulated their assessments of the CCP against the backdrop of American na-

[29] U.S. Senate, Committee on the Judiciary, Subcommittee on Internal Security, 89th Cong., 1st Sess., *Morgenthau Diary: China,* II (Washington, D.C., 1965), p. 1327.

[30] Agnes Smedley, *Battle Hymn of China* (New York, 1943), p. 181.

[31] Philip J. Jaffe, interview with the author, January 11, 1966.

[32] Snow, *Journey to the Beginning* (New York, 1958), pp. 177–178.

tional interests. None compared the Border Areas to the United States. Western observers had an absorbing concern with the Chinese milieu. Yenan was matched against Chungking. This Chinese contrast is the central feature of the American and European experience. In a land of narrow alternatives, the Communists were, as Snow put it, "the lesser evil." [33] The "plain fact," he recalled, "was that the Reds *were* 'better' people than their enemies. They said they were pro-poor and anti-rich and they practiced it." [34] Snow did not apologize for his reporting, and it is of some significance that neither did most of his contemporaries. In 1965, Brooks Atkinson scrawled in a letter: "I very much liked, and still like, Chou En-lai, who is a modern man." [35] The only thing he could have done to improve the symbolic value of his comment would have been to underline the word "modern."

Transplanted into a different cultural environment, Americans were subjected to many subtle influences. They loved China and the Chinese, but they disliked and exaggerated such traditional aspects of Chinese society as *li*, "face," and Confucianism. What they seemed to like most were the least "Chinese" aspects of China. Tending to view China in terms of their own cultural values, they admired Chinese Communists most especially for being familiar and "un-Chinese."

In 1950, Graham Peck published a volume with the usual title *Two Kinds of Time*.[36] Peck began this fascinating account of his experiences in China by comparing the ancient Chinese conception of abstract time with that of the modern West. According to the Chinese view, man's position in time is that of an individual sitting near a river. He always faces downstream watching the water flow by. The future is above

[33] *Ibid.*, p. 231.
[34] Snow to the author, September 26, 1969. The emphasis is Snow's.
[35] Atkinson to the author, May 28, 1965.
[36] Graham Peck, *Two Kinds of Time* (Boston, 1950).

and behind him where it cannot be seen, while the past is below and before him where it can be examined. In the American view, the perspective is different. Man looks upstream with his gaze fixed on the dim horizon. He is more like a person in an airplane than a river sitter.[37]

Like airplane passengers arriving from a distant land, Americans evaluated China through the eyes of the modern West. When they arrived in the Far East, Americans brought along their cultural baggage. Coming from an optimistic society accustomed to the ideals of aggregate betterment, social movement, and democratic progress, they speculated about the future with expectations of a rising level of improvement in the well-being and intelligence of the masses. They made the common man their hero, trusted change, and treasured social mobility.[38] The fatalism implicit in the philosophy of the river sitter was alien to Americans of the generation which came to maturity before 1945.

On a hypothetical index, the values of the CCP were more compatible with American values than were those of the KMT. The dominant historic optimism of Marxism and its utopian materialism struck a responsive chord in the Western mind.[39] The behavior and attitudes of Chinese Communists were somehow familiar and acceptable to Americans, while those of Chinese Nationalists were strange and repulsive. Chungking represented one kind of time, Yenan another.

[37] *Ibid.,* pp. 3–4.
[38] Robert L. Heilbroner, *The Future as History* (New York, 1961), pp. 21, 27, 38, 52.
[39] *Ibid.,* pp. 48, 113–114.

★

BIBLIOGRAPHY
AND INDEX

Bibliography

Certain characteristics of the sources on which this study is based have presented difficulties. The published materials which have been examined include books, pamphlets, and articles, book reviews, the appropriate volumes of the *Foreign Relations* series, congressional documents, selected magazine and newspaper files, and relevant secondary works. These are commonplace funds of historical information. When related to the subject of Chinese communism, however, some of these materials have specific shortcomings.

Although most of those who wrote accounts of their encounters with Chinese Communists were given to autobiographical reminiscing, few of them paid much attention to chronology. When one of their number later attempted to compile a list of the foreigners who had visited Red China after 1927, she ended up with little but frustration as a reward for her effort. She concluded that it was "impossible to discover any dates" in the writings of her contemporaries and even peevishly suggested that this phenomenon was a plot contrived to confuse the reader.[1]

While the tendency of firsthand observers to be lax in the matter of chronology clearly is more a reflection of indifference than of purposeful evasiveness, it has presented genuine

[1] Nym Wales [Helen Foster Snow], *My Yenan Notebooks* (Madison, Conn., 1961), p. 11.

problems. In far too many instances, the author has been compelled to make educated guesses as to exactly when certain firsthand observers traveled in the Chinese Communist regions. Fortunately, it has been possible in a few cases to submit these calculations for verification to the individuals involved. The fact remains, nonetheless, that some of the dates cited in this study are only approximate.

A large number of book reviews have been sampled with the object of providing the reader with contemporary appraisals of the volumes in question. These essays, however, are severely limited as sources of information and insight. Many critics reveal more about themselves than they do about the work they are reviewing. They often find what they had hoped to discover and not necessarily what was really there. T. A. Bisson, for example, rated nearly every study he examined as being the best on the market, indispensable, or required reading. At times, one is confronted with the ironic spectacle of a romanticizer criticizing another author for being too much of a romantic.[2] Add to this the marked variation in quality of any random selection of review essays and the shortcomings of such writings is readily apparent. These critiques are useful, however, to the extent that they reflect the contemporary response to American reporting on the Chinese Communist movement.

On the other side, the writer has been impressed by the quality of the *Foreign Relations* series on China. A comparison of these printed materials with the manuscript files from which they have been drawn has led him to the conclusion that in terms of frankness, representativeness, and comprehensiveness, these volumes are an embodiment of the high editorial standards of the Historical Office of the Department of State. The same cannot be said, however, for the manifold volumes produced by sundry congressional investi-

---

[2] For example, see Nym Wales' review of Joy Homer's *Dawn Watch in China*: "China Station," *New Republic*, CV (September 8, 1941), 316.

gating committees. Neither the taxpayer nor the historian can obtain much benefit from this wasteland of incoherence. For example, the writer finds himself in essential agreement with Edgar Snow's evaluation of the hearings on the Institute of Pacific Relations. They constitute, Snow observed, a "fifteen-volume monument to the art of irrelevance." [3]

As for the relevant secondary works, their number is not legion. This study has been slowed and limited by the absence of detailed scholarly monographs on certain phases of the history of both the Kuomintang and the Chinese Communist Party. Despite a recent upsurge in the publication of scholarly works on China, just discovering the facts about revolutionary China remains, as John King Fairbank has written, "no easy task." [4]

In addition to published materials, several manuscript collections have been examined in the effort to reconstruct the American experience in Red China. Foremost among the primary sources are the files of the Department of State. While the writer was unable to look at the small percentage of documents which are still restricted, he was allowed to examine most of the materials relevant to this study.

The other manuscript collections which have been scrutinized are the Patrick J. Hurley, Franklin D. Roosevelt, Nelson T. Johnson, Stanley K. Hornbeck, and Cordell Hull papers. Containing approximately a thousand boxes, the Hurley collection is rich and fascinating. In addition to the Ambassador's official and private correspondence, it includes a considerable amount of revealing supplementary materials. This latter category includes Chinese Nationalist and Chinese Communist documents, American and Chinese press releases, speeches of all description and origin, and clipping books. The Roosevelt materials reveal almost nothing about the President's thinking on the subject of Chinese

[3] Edgar Snow, *Journey to the Beginning* (New York, 1958), p. 332.

[4] John King Fairbank, *The United States and China* (rev. ed., New York, 1958), p. 2.

communism. They do contain, however, an interesting file of correspondence from Evans F. Carlson, the first American military observer to travel with the Chinese Red Army. Considerably more can be learned of Ambassador Johnson's views from his dispatches to the Department of State than from the unexceptional allusions he makes to the Chinese Communists in his private letters. Nevertheless, the Johnson manuscripts do contain a few pertinent communications from Edgar Snow and Evans F. Carlson. Although the Hornbeck collection is not yet adequately organized, it promises to be a valuable source for those interested in American–East Asian relations. The Cordell Hull papers, which are not fully open to investigators, were an unqualified disappointment.

While many of the customary materials have not been entirely satisfactory, the writer has found personal correspondence and interviews to be useful sources of information. He owes a particular debt of gratitude to Brooks Atkinson, James M. Bertram, Philip J. Jaffe, Owen Lattimore, J. Clayton Miller, Edgar Snow, and Mrs. Helen Foster Snow. All of these individuals went out of their way to probe their memories and to answer many questions.

Because of the proximity of the period under consideration, the bibliographical groupings are somewhat arbitrary. The line between primary sources and secondary works is drawn functionally to fit the nature of the study. Under "Primary Sources," the author includes the writings of all those who were eyewitness observers of the Chinese Communist movement, regardless of the date of their reports. This category also incorporates the publications of interpreters of the CCP who were contemporaries of those who penned firsthand accounts. "Secondary Works" refers primarily to scholarly monographs of a more recent date which are derived from primary materials.

The bibliography does not list a number of publications which have been used in the preparation of this study. With the exception of specific review articles which are important in themselves as commentaries on Chinese communism, book reviews are excluded. They are, however, cited in the footnotes. While the standard biographical and reference guides have been consulted, only those which have been particularly helpful are entered in the bibliography. Finally, the list of articles under "Primary Sources" is incomplete. Although *Amerasia* and *Pacific Affairs* have been examined issue-by-issue, it seems unreasonable to record all of the relevant essays in these journals. Only those articles which have been especially revealing sources of information are listed. Using the same principle of selectivity, some of the newspaper articles which are cited in the footnotes have not been included in the bibliography.

PRIMARY SOURCES

Manuscripts

Department of State files. National Archives, Washington, D.C.
"Dixie Mission" papers. Office of the Chief of Military History, Washington, D.C.
Hornbeck, Stanley K., papers. Hoover Institution on War, Revolution and Peace, Stanford University, Stanford, California.
Hull, Cordell, papers. Division of Manuscripts, Library of Congress.
Hurley, Patrick J., papers. The University of Oklahoma Library, Norman, Oklahoma.
Johnson, Nelson T., papers. Division of Manuscripts, Library of Congress.
Roosevelt, Franklin D., papers. Franklin D. Roosevelt Library, Hyde Park, New York.

Newspapers and Periodicals

Amerasia: A Review of America and the Far East, 1937–1947.
Baltimore *Sun,* 1944–1945.
The China Monthly: The Truth about China, 1940–1946.
Daily Worker (New York), 1936–1945.
The New Republic, 1944–1945.

New York Herald Tribune, 1936–1937.
The New York Times, 1944–1945.
Pacific Affairs, 1928–1945.

Government Documents

Foreign Relations of the United States: Diplomatic Papers, 1936.
5 vols. Washington, D.C., 1953–1954.
Foreign Relations of the United States: Diplomatic Papers, 1937.
5 vols. Washington, D.C., 1954.
Foreign Relations of the United States: Diplomatic Papers, 1938.
5 vols. Washington, D.C., 1954–1956.
Foreign Relations of the United States: Diplomatic Papers, 1939.
5 vols. Washington, D.C., 1955–1957.
Foreign Relations of the United States: Diplomatic Papers, 1940.
5 vols. Washington, D.C., 1955–1961.
Foreign Relations of the United States: Diplomatic Papers, 1941.
7 vols. Washington, D.C., 1956–1963.
Foreign Relations of the United States: Diplomatic Papers, 1942.
China. Washington, D.C., 1956.
Foreign Relations of the United States: Diplomatic Papers, 1943.
China. Washington, D.C., 1957.
Foreign Relations of the United States: Diplomatic Papers, 1944.
China. Washington, D.C., 1967.
Foreign Relations of the United States: Diplomatic Papers, 1945.
The Far East and China. Washington, D.C., 1969.
U.S. Congress. *Congressional Record.* 79th Cong., 1st Sess. Vol.
XCI, parts 1 and 2, Washington, D.C., 1945.
*United States Relations with China: With Special Reference to
the Period 1944–1949.* Washington, D.C., 1949.
U.S. Senate, Committee on Armed Services and the Committee
on Foreign Relations. *Military Situation in the Far East, Hear-
ings.* 82nd Cong., 1st Sess. 5 parts, Washington, D.C., 1951.
——, Committee on the Judiciary, Subcommittee to Investigate
the Administration of the Internal Security Act and Other Internal Security Laws. *The Amerasia Papers: A Clue to the Catastrophe of China.* 91st Cong., 1st Sess. 2 vols., Washington,
D.C., 1970.
——, Committee on the Judiciary, Subcommittee to Investigate
the Administration of the Internal Security Act and Other In-

ternal Security Laws. *Institute of Pacific Relations, Hearings.* 82nd Cong., 1st and 2nd Sess. 15 parts, Washington, D.C., 1951–1952.

——, Committee on the Judiciary, Subcommittee to Investigate the Administration of the Internal Security Act and Other Internal Security Laws. *Morgenthau Diary: China.* 89th Cong., 1st Sess. 2 vols., Washington, D.C., 1965.

——, Subcommittee of the Committee on Foreign Relations. *State Department Employee Loyalty Investigation, Hearings.* 81st Cong., 2nd Sess. 3 parts, Washington, D.C., 1950.

Printed Documents

Brandt, Conrad, Benjamin Schwartz, and John K. Fairbank, eds. *A Documentary History of Chinese Communism.* Cambridge, Massachusetts, 1952.

Jacobs, Dan N., and Hans H. Baerwald, eds. *Chinese Communism: Selected Documents.* New York, Evanston, and London, 1963.

Schram, Stuart R. *The Political Thought of Mao Tse-tung.* Rev. and enlarged ed. New York, Washington, and London, 1969.

Books

Abend, Hallett. *My Life in China, 1926–1941.* New York, 1943.

——. *Tortured China.* New York, 1930.

——, and Anthony J. Billingham. *Can China Survive?* New York, 1936.

"Asiaticus." *Von Kanton Bis Schanghai: 1926–1927.* Wien-Berlin, 1928.

Auden, W. H., and Christopher Isherwood. *Journey to a War.* New York, 1939.

Band, Claire and William. *Dragon Fangs: Two Years with Chinese Guerrillas.* London, 1947.

Belden, Jack. *China Shakes the World.* New York, 1949.

Bertram, James M. *Beneath the Shadow: A New Zealander in the Far East, 1939–46.* New York, 1947.

——. *First Act in China: The Story of the Sian Mutiny.* New York, 1938.

——. *Return to China.* London, Melbourne, and Toronto, 1957.

——. *Unconquered: Journal of a Year's Adventures among the Fighting Peasants of North China.* New York, 1939.

Bisson, T. A. *Japan in China.* New York, 1938.

Bland, J. O. P. *China: The Pity of It.* London, 1932.

Bosshardt, Rudolf Alfred. *The Restraining Hand: Captivity for Christ in China.* London, 1932.

Byrnes, James F. *All in One Lifetime.* New York, 1958.

——. *Speaking Frankly.* New York and London, 1947.

Carlson, Evans Fordyce. *The Chinese Army: Its Organization and Military Efficiency.* New York, 1940.

——. *Twin Stars of China: A Behind-the-Scenes Story of China's Valiant Struggle for Existence by a U.S. Marine Who Lived and Moved with the People.* New York, 1940.

Chiang Kai-shek. *China's Destiny and Chinese Economic Theory.* Ed. Philip J. Jaffe. New York, 1947.

Clark, Grover. *The Great Wall Crumbles.* New York, 1935.

——. *A Place in the Sun.* New York, 1937.

Clubb, O. Edmund. *Communism in China: As Reported From Hankow in 1932.* New York and London, 1968.

Dolsen, James H. *The Awakening of China.* Chicago, 1926.

Epstein, Israel. *From Opium War to Liberation.* Rev. ed. Peking, 1964.

——. *The People's War.* London, 1939.

——. *The Unfinished Revolution in China.* Boston, 1947.

Fitch, George A. *My Eighty Years in China.* Taiwan, Republic of China, 1967.

Flynn, John T. *While You Slept: Our Tragedy in Asia and Who Made It.* New York, 1951.

Forman, Harrison. *Report from Red China.* New York, 1945.

Frillmann, Paul, and Graham Peck. *China: The Remembered Life.* Boston, 1968.

Gannes, Harry. *When China Unites: An Interpretive History of the Chinese Revolution.* New York, 1937.

Gayn, Mark J. *Journey from the East: An Autobiography.* New York, 1944.

Gilbert, Rodney. *What's Wrong with China.* New York, 1926.

Gunther, John. *Inside Asia.* New York and London, 1939.

Hanson, Haldore. *"Humane Endeavour": The Story of the China War.* New York and Toronto, 1939.

Hedin, Sven. *The Silk Road.* Trans. F. H. Lyon. London, 1938.

Hogg, George. *I See a New China.* Boston, 1944.

Holcombe, Arthur N. *The Chinese Revolution: A Phase in the Regeneration of a World Power.* Cambridge, Massachusetts, 1930.

———. *The Spirit of the Chinese Revolution.* New York, 1930.

Homer, Joy. *Dawn Watch in China.* Boston, 1941.

Hull, Cordell. *The Memoirs of Cordell Hull.* 2 vols. New York, 1948.

Hutchinson, Paul. *What and Why in China.* Chicago, 1927.

Ickes, Harold L. *The Secret Diary of Harold L. Ickes.* 3 vols. New York, 1953–1954.

Isaacs, Harold R. *No Peace for Asia.* New York, 1947.

———. *The Tragedy of the Chinese Revolution.* London, 1938; 2nd rev. ed., Stanford, 1961.

Jaffe, Philip J. *New Frontiers in Asia: A Challenge to the West.* New York, 1945.

Lapwood, Ralph and Nancy. *Through the Chinese Revolution.* London, 1954.

Lattimore, Owen. *Ordeal by Slander.* Boston, 1950.

———. *Solution in Asia.* Boston, 1945.

———. and Eleanor. *The Making of Modern China: A Short History.* New York, 1944.

Lindsay, Michael. *Notes on Educational Problems in Communist China, 1941–47.* New York, 1950.

McCarthy, Senator Joseph R. *America's Retreat From Victory: The Story of George Catlett Marshall.* New York, 1951.

MacNair, Harley Farnsworth. *China in Revolution: An Analysis of Politics and Militarism Under the Republic.* Chicago, 1931.

———. *China's International Relations and Other Essays.* Shanghai, 1926.

Melby, John F. *The Mandate of Heaven: Record of a Civil War, China, 1945–49.* London, 1968.

Millard, Thomas F. *China: Where It Is Today and Why.* New York, 1928.

Millis, Walter, ed. *The Forrestal Diaries.* New York, 1951.

Monroe, Paul. *China: A Nation in Evolution.* New York, 1928.

Morley, Felix. *Our Far Eastern Assignment.* Garden City, New York, 1926.

Nearing, Scott. *Whither China?: An Economic Interpretation of Recent Events in the Far East.* New York, 1927.

Norton, Henry Kittredge. *China and the Powers.* New York, 1927.

Peck, Graham. *Through China's Wall.* Boston, 1940.

———. *Two Kinds of Time.* Boston, 1950.

Peffer, Nathaniel. *China: The Collapse of a Civilization.* New York, 1930.

Powell, John B. *My Twenty-Five Years in China.* New York, 1945.

Ransome, Arthur. *The Chinese Puzzle.* Boston and New York, 1927.

Rasmussen, O. D. *What's Right with China: An Answer to Foreign Criticisms.* Shanghai, 1927.

Rea, George Bronson. *The Case for Manchoukuo.* New York and London, 1935.

Roosevelt, Elliott. *As He Saw It.* New York, 1946.

Rosinger, Lawrence K. *China's Crisis.* New York, 1945.

———. *China's Wartime Politics, 1937–1944.* Princeton, 1944.

Russell, Bertrand. *The Problem of China.* London, 1922.

Sheean, Vincent. *Between the Thunder and the Sun.* New York, 1943.

———. *Personal History.* Garden City, New York, 1935.

———. *This House against This House.* New York, 1945.

Smedley, Agnes. *Battle Hymn of China.* New York, 1943.

———. *China Fights Back: An American Woman with the Eighth Route Army.* London, 1939.

———. *China's Red Army Marches.* New York, 1934.

———. *Chinese Destinies: Sketches of Present-Day China.* New York, 1933.

———. *Daughter of Earth.* Rev. ed. New York, 1935.

———. *The Great Road: The Life and Times of Chu Teh.*

Snow, Edgar. *The Battle for Asia.* New York, 1941.

———. *Far Eastern Front.* New York, 1933.

———. *Journey to the Beginning.* New York, 1958.

———. *The Other Side of the River: Red China Today.* New York, 1962.

———. *People on Our Side.* New York, 1944.

——. *Random Notes on Red China, 1936–1945.* Cambridge, Massachusetts, 1957.

——. *Red Star over China.* New York, 1938; rev. eds. 1938, 1944, 1961; rev. and enlarged ed., 1968.

——, ed. *Living China: Modern Chinese Short Stories.* New York, 1937.

Snow, Helen Foster. *See* Nym Wales.

Sokolsky, George E. *The Tinder Box of Asia.* Garden City, New York, 1932.

Stein, Gunther. *The Challenge of Red China.* New York and London, 1945.

Stimson, Henry L. *The Far Eastern Crisis: Recollections and Observations.* New York and London, 1936.

Strong, Anna Louise. *China's Millions.* New York, 1928.

——. *China's Millions: The Revolutionary Struggles from 1927 to 1935.* New York, 1935.

——. *The Chinese Conquer China.* Garden City, New York, 1949.

——. *A Consideration of Prayer From the Standpoint of Social Psychology.* Chicago, 1908.

——. *I Change Worlds: The Remaking of an American.* New York, 1935.

——. *One-Fifth of Mankind.* New York, 1938.

Sues, Ilona Ralf. *Shark's Fins and Millet.* Boston, 1944.

Taylor, George E. *America in the New Pacific.* New York, 1942.

——. *The Struggle for North China.* New York, 1940.

Tong, Hollington K. *China and the World Press.* Nanking [?], 1948 [?].

——. *Dateline—China: The Beginning of China's Press Relations with the World.* New York, 1950.

Townsend, Ralph. *Ways That Are Dark: The Truth about China.* New York, 1933.

Trotsky, Leon. *Problems of the Chinese Revolution.* Trans. Max Shachtman. New York, 1932.

Utley, Freda. *China at War.* New York, 1939.

——. *The China Story.* Chicago, 1951.

——. *The Dream We Lost: Soviet Russia Then and Now.* New York, 1940.

——. *Japan's Feet of Clay*. London, 1936.

——. *Last Chance in China*. Indianapolis and New York, 1947.

——. *Odyssey of a Liberal: Memoirs*. Washington, D.C., 1970.

Van Dorn, Harold Archer. *Twenty Years of the Chinese Republic: Two Decades of Progress*. New York, 1932.

Vandenberg, Arthur H., Jr., ed. *The Private Papers of Senator Vandenberg*. Boston, 1952.

Wales, Nym [Helen Foster Snow]. *China Builds for Democracy: A Story of Cooperative Industry*. New York, 1941.

——. *The Chinese Labor Movement*. New York, 1945.

——. *Inside Red China*. Garden City, New York, 1939.

——. *My Yenan Notebooks*. Madison, Connecticut, 1961.

——. *New China*. Calcutta, India, 1944.

——. *Red Dust: Autobiographies of Chinese Communists*. Stanford, 1952.

Wang, Anna. *Ich kämpfte für Mao: Eine deutsche Frau erlebt die chinesische Revolution*. Hamburg, Germany, 1964.

Weale, Putnam [Bertram Lenox Simpson]. *Why China Sees Red*. New York, 1925.

White, Theodore H., ed. *The Stilwell Papers*. New York, 1948.

——, and Annalee Jacoby. *Thunder Out of China*. New York, 1946, 1961. AMS Press

Williams, Edward Thomas. *China: Yesterday and Today*. Rev. ed. New York, 1927.

——. *A Short History of China*. New York and London, 1928.

Woodhead, H. G. W., Julean Arnold, and Henry Kittredge Norton. *Occidental Interpretations of the Far Eastern Problem*. Chicago, 1926.

Yakhontoff, Victor A. *The Chinese Soviets*. New York, 1934.

Yorke, Gerald. *China Changes*. New York, 1936.

Yutang, Lin. *Between Tears and Laughter*. New York, 1943.

——. *The Vigil of a Nation*. New York, 1945.

Pamphlets

Browder, Earl. *Civil War in Nationalist China*. Chicago, 1927.

Clark, Grover. *In Perspective: A Review of the Politico-Military Situation in China*. Peking, 1927.

Gannett, Lewis S. *Young China*. Rev. ed. New York, 1927.

Hornbeck, Stanley K. *China To-Day: Political*. Boston, 1927.

Hu Shih, Grover Clark and Stanley K. Hornbeck. *Forward or Backward in China?* New York, 1927.

Hung, William, Arthur N. Holcombe and David Z. T. Yui. *Nationalist China.* New York, 1929.

In Guerrilla China: Report of China Defence League. Chungking, 1943.

James, M., and R. Doonping [Chi Ch'ao-ting]. *Soviet China.* New York, 1932.

Lautenschlager, Stanton. *Far West in China.* New York, 1941.

———. *With Chinese Communists.* London, 1941.

Lindsay, Michael. *North China Front* [1944?].

Mif, P. *Heroic China: Fifteen Years of the Communist Party of China.* New York, 1937.

Snow, Edgar, *et al. China: The March toward Unity.* New York, 1937.

Stewart, Maxwell S. *War-Time China.* New York, San Francisco, and Honolulu, 1944.

Stewart, Ray. *War in China.* New York, 1932.

Strong, Anna Louise. *Letters from China.* 3 vols. Peking, 1963–1965.

Wittfogel, Karl August. *New Light on Chinese Society: An Investigation of China's Socio-Economic Structure.* New York, 1938.

Yang Chien. *The Communist Situation in China.* Nanking, 1931.

Articles

"Asiaticus." "Autobiography of General Yeh Ting," *Amerasia,* V (March 1941), 24–29.

———. "Behind the Japanese Lines in Central Asia," *Amerasia,* V (October 1941), 355–360.

———. "China's Internal Friction Aids Japan," *Amerasia,* V (May 1941), 118–122.

———. "Chou En-lai on the New Stage of the Anti-Japanese War," *Amerasia,* III (June 1939), 184–190.

———. "The Fascist Axis vs. the United Front in China," *Amerasia,* IV (February 1941), 543–546.

———. "New Fourth Army Area Revisited," *Amerasia,* V (September 1941), 287–294.

———. "The Yangtze Triangle Guerrilla War," *Amerasia,* III (August 1939), 275–281.

Atkinson, Brooks. "Chinese Still Try to Unify Factions," *New York Times,* November 26, 1944, 43.

——. "Critic at Large: Publication of State Department Papers on China of 1943 Evokes Reflections," *New York Times,* April 10, 1962, 40.

——. "Long Schism Seen," *New York Times,* October 31, 1944, 1, 4.

——. "Yenan, a Chinese Wonderland City on 3 Kinds of Time, Has One Clock," *New York Times,* October 6, 1944, 12.

——. "Yenan Is Well Fed with Big Harvest," *New York Times,* September 25, 1944, 9.

Baldwin, Hanson W. "Review of the Chinese Situation," *New York Times,* July 20, 1943, 7.

——. "Too Much Wishful Thinking about China," *Reader's Digest,* XLIII (August 1943), 63–67.

Barnett, Robert W. "An Interview With Chou En-lai," *Amerasia,* V (May 1941), 123–127.

Bertram, James M. "Correspondence: The Chinese Revolution," *New Statesman and Nation,* XVII (February 11, 1939), 208–209.

——. "Japanese Offensive in North China," *Amerasia,* V (July 1941), 215–216.

Bisson, T. A. "China's Part in a Coalition War," *Far Eastern Survey,* XII (July 14, 1943), 135–141.

——. "Mao Tse-tung Analyzes Nanking in Interview," *Amerasia,* I (October 1937), 360–365.

Braun, Otto. "In wessen Namen spricht Mao Tse-tung?" *Neues Deutschland,* May 27, 1964.

Browder, Earl. "The American Communist Party in the Thirties," in *As We Saw the Thirties: Essays on Social and Political Movements of a Decade,* ed. Rita James Simon. Urbana, Chicago, and London, 1967.

Buck, Pearl S. " 'The Darkest Hour' in China's History," *New York Times Magazine,* December 17, 1944, 9, 45–46.

——. "A Warning About China: A Great Friend of the Chinese People Points to Dangers That May Lose Us a Valuable Ally," *Life,* XIV (May 10, 1943), 53–54, 56.

Carlson, Evans Fordyce. "America Faces Crisis in the Orient," *Amerasia,* III (February 1940), 555–560.

——. "European Pacts and Chinese Prospects," *Amerasia*, III (October 1939), 345–349.

——. "The Unorthodox War Continues," *Amerasia*, III (March 1939), 12–15.

——. "Wither China?" *Amerasia*, III (December 1939), 458–463.

"China's International Peace Hospitals," *Far Eastern Survey*, XII (April 19, 1943), 79–80.

"The Chinese Communists," *New York Times*, August 17, 1945, 16.

"The Chinese Crisis," *New York Times*, November 1, 1944, 22.

"Comment and Correspondence: 'Asiaticus' Criticizes 'Red Star over China,' " *Pacific Affairs*, XI (June 1938), 237–244; "Edgar Snow Replies: To the Editor of *Pacific Affairs*," *ibid.*, 244–248; " 'Asiaticus' Holds His Ground: To the Editor of *Pacific Affairs*," *ibid.*, 248–252.

"Correspondents Complain to Chinese on Censorship," *New York Times*, October 12, 1944, 16.

"Divided China," *New York Times*, June 10, 1944, 14.

Durdin, Tillman. "Second U.S. Writer Barred by Chinese," *New York Times*, July 23, 1945, 3.

Eastman, Max, and J. B. Powell. "The Fate of the World Is at Stake in China," *Reader's Digest*, XLVI (June 1945), 13–22.

Epstein, Israel. "Light on the Chinese Puzzle," *Labour Monthly*, XXVII (June 1945), 173–178.

[——]. "China Communists Confer with Rich," *New York Times*, August 6, 1944, 19.

[——]. "China Communists from All Classes," *New York Times*, August 20, 1944, 23.

[——]. "Communist Army in China Is Strong," *New York Times*, July 1, 1944, 6.

[——]. "No Opium Poppies on Way to Yenan," *New York Times*, August 14, 1944, 5.

"The Far Eastern Muddle," *New Republic*, CX (March 13, 1944), 334–335.

Fitch, George A. "China's Northwest Life-Line," *Amerasia*, IV (September 1940), 301–306.

Fitch, Geraldine T. "Letters to the Times: China Ends Eighth War Year," *New York Times*, July 7, 1945, 12.

[Forman, Harrison.] "The Camera's Story of History-in-the-Making: China's Communists," *Current History,* XLVIII (February 1938), 66–69.

Gayn, Mark. "Crisis in China," *Collier's,* CXIV (October 28, 1944), 17–18, 44.

Gilbert, Rodney. "Belittling China's War Effort," *New York Herald Tribune,* August 16 and 17, 1943, 14, 18.

Gould, Randall. "Communism Wanes in China," *Christian Science Monitor,* April 7, 1937, 1–2, 12.

Hanson, Haldore. "Firebrands and Chinese Politics," *Amerasia,* III (April 1939), 78–82.

———. "The People behind the Chinese Guerrillas," *Pacific Affairs,* XI (September 1938), 285–298.

Hanwell, Norman D. "The Chinese Red Army," *Asia,* XXXVI (May 1936), 317–322.

———. "When Chinese Reds Move In," *Asia,* XXXVI (October 1936), 631–634.

———. "Within Chinese Red Areas," *Asia,* XXXVII (January 1937), 58–61.

Hicks, Granville. "Writers in the Thirties," in *As We Saw the Thirties: Essays on Social and Political Movements of a Decade,* ed. Rita James Simon. Urbana, Chicago, and London, 1967.

"Impasse in China," *New Republic,* CXII (March 26, 1945), 407–408.

"In Guerrilla China," *New York Times,* April 16, 1944, IV, 8.

Isaacs, Harold R. "China: Today's Bitter Fiasco, Tomorrow's Sure Battleground and a Problem That Must Be Solved before World Peace Is Won," *Newsweek,* XXV (April 23, 1945), 60–61.

———. "Perspectives of the Chinese Revolution: A Marxist View," *Pacific Affairs,* VIII (September 1935), 269–283.

Jaffe, Philip J. "China's Communists Told Me: A Specialist in Far Eastern Affairs Interviews the Leading Men of Red China in Their Home Territories," *New Masses,* XXV (October 12, 1937), 3–10.

Keen, Victor. "China's Reds Offer Olive Branch in Belief That Anti-Japan Front Is More Vital Than Class Fight," *New York Herald Tribune,* May 23, 1937, II, 7, 14.

———. "Chinese Soviet Goes to School: 60% Politics and 40% Education Is Recipe in the Mental Diet," *New York Herald Tribune,* June 13, 1937, II, 4.

——. "Chinese Soviet's Youthful Army a Merger of Private Battalions," *New York Herald Tribune,* June 6, 1937, II, 5–6.

Kohlberg, Alfred. "Owen Lattimore: 'Expert's Expert'—The Monocle, the Commissar, the Old Homestead, and Snafu," *China Monthly,* VI (October 1945), 10–13, 26.

Lattimore, Owen. "American Responsibilities in the Far East," *Virginia Quarterly Review,* XVI (Spring 1940), 161–174.

——. "Reply to Mr. Kohlberg," *China Monthly,* VI (December 1945), 15–17.

——. "Report from Red China," *Atlantic Monthly,* CLXXV (April 1945), 133.

Leaf, Earl H. "Chinese Reds in Shensi Work and Play Hard; Soviet Capital Scene of Much Laughter, Fun and Sports," *North China Star,* April 26, 1937, 1, 6.

——. "Mao Tse-tung's Life Is Thrilling, Hectic Story; Has Become Almost Legend to Chinese During 10 Years," *North China Star,* May 6, 1937, 1, 8.

——. "Persons and Personages: Six Women of China," *Living Age,* CCCLIV (March 1938), 40–42.

——. "Soviet Russia Has Given Chinese Reds No Aid; Declares Commander-in-Chief Chu Teh of Chinese Communist Forces," *North China Star,* July 9, 1937, 1, 24.

Lin Piao. "Long Live the Victory of People's War!" in *China after Mao,* by A. Doak Barnett. Princeton, 1967.

Lindsay, Michael. "The North China Front: A Study of Chinese Guerrillas in Action," *Amerasia,* VIII (March 31 and April 14, 1944), 100–110, 117–125.

Miller, J. Clayton. "The Chinese Still Rule North China: Political and Military Strategy of the Hopei-Shansi-Chahar Border Government," *Amerasia,* II (September 1938), 336–345.

——. "The Drama in China's Anti-Japanese Propaganda," *Pacific Affairs,* XI (December 1938), 465–477.

——. "Japan Turns Back the Clock," *Amerasia,* II (October 1938), 397–404.

——. "Japan's China versus China's China," *World Youth,* III (October 22, 1938), 21.

——. "Japs Battle a Reborn China: Former Clevelander Tells of

New Government That Is Functioning Smoothly within Nipponese Lines," *Cleveland Plain Dealer,* January 8, 1939, 1, 6.

O'Toole, G. Barry. "Debunking an 'Imperial Debunker,' " *China Monthly,* V (February 1944), 12–13.

——. "U.S. Reds Reopen Attack on Kuomintang," *China Monthly,* III (January 1942), 17, 21.

"Pacific Affairs Bibliographies: No. III—Literature on the Chinese Soviet Movement," *Pacific Affairs,* IX (September 1936), 421–435.

Peffer, Nathaniel. "The Chinese Idea of Communism," *Current History,* XXXVI (July 1932), 400–404.

——. "Contrasting Yenan and Chungking," *New York Times Book Review,* October 28, 1945, 4.

——. "Our Distorted View of China," *New York Times Magazine,* November 7, 1943, 7, 40–41.

Prohme, William. "Internal Conflict in China," *Nation,* CXXVII (December 26, 1928), 724–725.

——. "Soviet China," *New Republic,* LXVII (August 12, 1931), 334–335.

Reizo Otsuka. "Recent Developments in the Chinese Communist Movement," in *Problems of the Pacific, 1936: Aims and Results of Social and Economic Policies in Pacific Counties, Proceedings of the Sixth Conference of the Institute of Pacific Relations, Yosemite National Park, California, 15–29 August 1936,* ed. W. L. Holland and Kate L. Mitchell. Chicago, 1937.

Roth, Andrew. "China's Civil Conflict," *New Republic,* CXIII (August 27, 1945), 248–250.

Russell, Maud. "Letters to the Editors: Dr. Lin and Mr. Snow," *Nation,* CLX (April 21, 1945), 471.

Sevareid, Eric. "Censors in the Saddle," *Nation,* CLX (April 14, 1945), 415–417.

Shanahan, Cormac. "America's Place in the World," *China Monthly,* VI (November 1945), 30–32.

——. "The Challenge of Gunther Stein," *China Monthly,* VII (February 1946), 65–66.

——. "China's Communist Puzzle," *China Monthly,* VI (June 1945), 9–12.

——. "False Solution in Asia," *China Monthly,* VI (December 1945), 22–24, 26.

Smedley, Agnes. "Crisis in China: Defeat and Disunity," *PM,* October 22, 1944, 3–5.

Snow, Edgar. "Boyhood of a Chinese Red: The Autobiography of Mao Tse-tung," *Asia,* XXXVII (July 1937), 480–484; "Schooling of a Chinese Red: The Autobiography of Mao Tse-tung," *ibid.* (August 1937), 570–576; "How the Red Army Began: The Autobiography of Mao Tse-tung," *ibid.* (September 1937), 619–623; "The Red Army in Action: The Autobiography of Mao Tse-tung," *ibid.* (October 1937), 682–688.

———. "China to Lin Yutang," *Nation,* CLX (February 17, 1945), 180–183; "China to Lin Yutang: II," *ibid.* (March 31, 1945), 359.

———. "The Chinese Communists and Wars on Two Continents: Interviews With Mao Tse-tung," *China Weekly Review,* XCI (January 13 and 20, 1940), 244–246, 277–280.

———. "Chinese Communists and World Affairs: An Interview with Mao Tse-tung," *Amerasia,* I (August 1937), 263–269.

———. "Direct From the Chinese Red Area," *Asia,* XXXVII (February 1937), 74–75.

[———]. "First Pictures of China's Roving Communists," *Life,* II (January 25, 1937), 9–15; "An Army of Fighting Chinese Communists Takes Possession of China's Northwest," *ibid.* (February 1, 1937), 42–45.

———. "I Went to Red China: The Inside Story of China's United Front against Japan," *Saturday Evening Post,* CCX (November 6, 1937), 100–103.

———. "Interview with Mao," *New Republic,* CLII (February 27, 1965), 17–23.

———. "Interview with Mao Tse-tung: Communist Leader," *China Weekly Review,* LXXVIII (November 14 and 21, 1936), 377–379, 420–421.

———. "The Long March," *Asia,* XXXVII (October 1937), 689–692; "The Long March: Part II," *ibid.* (November 1937), 741–747.

———. "The Man Alongside Mao: Deputy Lin Piao's Thoughts and Career," *New Republic,* CLV (December 3, 1966), 15–18.

———. "Must China Go Red?" *Saturday Evening Post,* CCXVII (May 12, 1945), 9–10, 67–68, 70.

———. "Reds and Northwest: A Visitor to Communist Areas Tells

His First-Hand Observations," *Shanghai Evening Post and Mercury,* February 3, 4, 5, 1937, 10–11.

——. "Sixty Million Lost Allies," *Saturday Evening Post,* CCXVI (June 10, 1944), 12–13, 44, 46.

——. "Soviet China I: What the Chinese Communists Want," *New Republic,* LXXXI (August 4, 1937), 351–354; "Soviet China II: The Long March," *ibid.,* LXXXII (August 11, 1937), 9–11; "Soviet China III: Chinese Communist Industry," *ibid.* (August 18, 1937), 42–44; "Soviet China IV: Moscow and the Chinese Communists," *ibid.* (September 8, 1937), 124–125.

——. "Soviet Society in Northwest China," *Pacific Affairs,* X (September 1937), 266–275.

——. "The Strength of Communism in China: The Bolshevik Influence," *Current History,* XXXIII (January 1931), 521–526.

——. "Will Stalin Sell Out China?" *Foreign Affairs,* XVIII (April 1940), 450–463.

Snow, Helen Foster. *See* Nym Wales.

Steele, A. T. "Chinese Reds Plan to Keep Army: American Learns at Stronghold," *New York Times,* March 1, 1937, 8.

Strong, Anna Louise. "The Kuomintang-Communist Crisis in China," *Amerasia,* V (March 1941), 11–23.

——. "Political Work of a Chinese Army," *Amerasia,* II (August 1938), 304–308.

——. "Why I Came to China at the Age of 72," *Peking Review* (September 20, 1963), 19–22.

Sweetland, Reginald E. "The Strength of Communism in China —II: Banditry in a New Guise," *Current History,* XXXIII (January 1931), 526–529.

Taylor, George E. "Reconstruction After Revolution: Kiangsi Province and the Chinese Nation," *Pacific Affairs,* VIII (September 1935), 302–311.

Uhlmann, Lieutenant George. "Land of Five Withouts," *Far Eastern Survey,* XII (May 3, 1943), 86–89.

Utley, Freda. "Correspondence: China," *New Statesman and Nation,* XVII (January 28, 1939), 130–131.

——. "Will Russia Betray China?" *Asia,* XLI (April 1941), 170–173.

Wales, Nym [Helen Foster Snow]. "Anna Louise Strong: The

Classic Fellow-Traveler," *New Republic,* CLXII (April 25, 1970), 17–19.

——. "Old China Hands," *New Republic,* CLVI (April 1, 1967), 13–15.

——. "Why the Chinese Communists Support the United Front: An Interview with Lo Fu," *Pacific Affairs,* XI (September 1938), 311–322.

"A Warning Regarding News from China." New York *Daily Worker,* January 29, 1937, 1.

Watts, Richard, Jr. "The Chinese Giant Stirs," *New Republic,* CXII (May 28, 1945), 733–736.

Wedemeyer, Lt. General Albert C., as told to George Creel. "Don't Count China Out," *Collier's,* CXVI (July 7, 1945), 24–25, 46.

White, Theodore H. "Inside Red China," *Life,* XVII (December 18, 1944), 39–40, 42, 44, 46.

——. " 'Life' Looks at China: Through the Blockade One of Its Correspondents Brings This Firsthand Report," *Life,* XVI (May 1, 1944), 98–101, 103–104, 106, 109–110.

Yakhontoff, Victor A. "The U.S.A. and the U.S.S.R.," *Asia and the Americas,* XLIII (September 1943), 513–516.

Yutang, Lin. "China and Its Critics," *Nation,* CLX (March 24, 1945), 324–327.

Interviews and Personal Correspondence

Atkinson, Brooks. Three letters to the author, May 4, 18, and 28, 1965.

Bertram, James M. Two letters to the author, April 12 and April, 1965.

Bisson, T. A. Letter to the author, October 16, 1964.

Blankfort, Michael. Two letters to the author, October 1964 and March 5, 1965.

Jaffe, Philip J. Two interviews with the author, June 14, 1965 and January 11, 1966.

Lattimore, Owen. Conversation with the author, April 16, 1969.

Mandel, Benjamin J. Two letters to the author, August 5 and August 26, 1965.

Miller, J. Clayton. Three letters to the author, August 31, December 7, 1965, and January 30, 1966.

Snow, Edgar. Three letters to the author, August 23, 1964, November 16, 1968, and September 26, 1969.

Snow, Helen Foster. Two letters to the author, April 17 and May 1, 1965.

White, Theodore H. Letter to the author, May 27, 1965.

SECONDARY WORKS

References and Guides

Boorman, Howard L., ed. *Biographical Dictionary of Republican China,* vol. 1. New York and London, 1967.

Ethridge, James M., and Barbara Kopala, eds. *Contemporary Authors: The International Bio-Biographical Guide to Current Authors and Their Works.* 14 vols. Detroit, 1962–1965.

Kunitz, Stanley J., and Howard Haycraft, eds. *Twentieth Century Authors: A Biographical Dictionary of Modern Literature.* New York, 1942.

——, and Vineta Colby, eds. *Twentieth Century Authors: A Biographical Dictionary of Modern Literature.* 1st Supplement. New York, 1955.

Kwang-ching, Liu. *Americans and Chinese: A Historical Essay and Bibliography.* Cambridge, Massachusetts, 1963.

Langer, William L., *et al.,* eds. *Foreign Affairs Bibliography: A Selected and Annotated List of Books on International Relations.* 4 vols. New York and London, 1933–1964.

Lust, John. *Index Sinicus: A Catalogue of Articles in Periodicals and Other Collective Publications, 1920–1955.* Cambridge, England, 1964.

Books

Aaron, Daniel. *Writers on the Left: Episodes in American Literary Communism.* New York, 1961.

Barnet, Richard J. *Intervention and Revolution: The United States in the Third World.* New York and Cleveland, 1968.

Beard, Charles A. *The Devil Theory of War: An Inquiry into the Nature of History and the Possibility of Keeping Out of War.* New York, 1936.

Blankfort, Michael. *The Big Yankee: The Life of Carlson of the Raiders.* Boston, 1947.

Blum, John Morton. *From the Morgenthau Diaries.* 3 vols. Boston, 1959–1967.

Borg, Dorothy. *American Policy and the Chinese Revolution, 1925–1928.* New York, 1947.

———. *The United States and the Far Eastern Crisis of 1933–1938: From the Manchurian Incident through the Initial Stage of the Undeclared Sino-Japanese War.* Cambridge, Massachusetts, 1964.

Brandt, Conrad. *Stalin's Failure in China, 1924–1927.* Cambridge, Massachusetts, 1958.

Buhite, Russell D. *Nelson T. Johnson and American Policy toward China, 1925–1941.* East Lansing, Michigan, 1969.

Ch'en, Jerome. *Mao and the Chinese Revolution.* New York, 1967.

Chow, Tse-tsung. *The May Fourth Movement: Intellectual Revolution in Modern China.* Cambridge, Massachusetts, 1960.

Clubb, O. Edmund. *20th Century China.* New York and London, 1964.

Cohen, Arthur A. *The Communism of Mao Tse-tung.* Chicago and London, 1964.

Compton, Boyd. *Mao's China: Party Reform Documents, 1942–44.* Seattle, 1952.

Creel, H. G. *Chinese Thought: From Confucius to Mao Tse-tung.* New York, 1963.

Deakin, F. W. and G. R. Storry. *The Case of Richard Sorge.* New York, 1966.

Dulles, Allen. *The Craft of Intelligence.* New York, Evanston, and London, 1963.

Fairbank, John K. *China: The People's Middle Kingdom and the U.S.A.* Cambridge, Massachusetts, 1967.

———. *The United States and China.* Rev. ed. New York, 1958.

Feis, Herbert. *The China Tangle: The American Effort in China from Pearl Harbor to the Marshall Mission.* Princeton, 1953.

Frank, Benis M., and Henry I. Shaw, Jr. *Victory and Occupa-*

tion: History of U.S. Marine Corps in World War II, vol. V. Washington, D.C., 1968.

Gillin, Donald G. *Warlord: Yen Hsi-shan in Shansi Province, 1911–1949.* Princeton, 1967.

Gittings, John. *The Role of the Chinese Army.* London, New York, and Toronto, 1967.

Gordon, Sydney, and Ted Allan. *The Scalpel, the Sword: The Story of Dr. Norman Bethune.* London, 1954.

Greene, Felix. *A Curtain of Ignorance: How the American Public Has Been Misinformed About China.* Garden City, New York, 1964.

Griffith, Samuel B., II. *The Chinese People's Liberation Army.* New York, Toronto, London, Sydney, 1967.

Heilbroner, Robert L. *The Future as History.* New York, 1961.

Heinl, Robert Debs, Jr. *Soldiers of the Sea: The United States Marine Corps, 1775–1962.* Annapolis, Maryland, 1962.

Hoffer, Eric. *The True Believer: Thoughts on the Nature of Mass Movements.* New York, 1951.

Hofstadter, Richard. *The Paranoid Style in American Politics and Other Essays.* New York, 1965.

Hohenberg, John. *Between Two Worlds: Policy, Press and Public Opinion in Asian-American Relations.* New York, Washington, and London, 1967.

——. *Foreign Correspondence: The Great Reporters and Their Times.* New York and London, 1964.

Hough, Frank O., Verle E. Ludwig, and Henry I. Shaw, Jr. *Pearl Harbor to Guadalcanal: History of U.S. Marine Corps Operations in World War II,* vol. I. Washington, D.C., 1958.

Howe, Irving, and Lewis Coser. *The American Communist Party: A Critical History.* New York, 1962.

Hucker, Charles O. *The Censorial System of Ming China.* Stanford, 1966.

Iriye, Akira. *Across the Pacific: An Inner History of American-East Asian Relations.* New York, 1967.

Isaacs, Harold R. *Images of Asia: American Views of China and India.* New York, 1962.

Johnson, Chalmers A. *An Instance of Treason: Ozaki Hotsumi and the Sorge Spy Ring.* Stanford, 1964.

——. *Peasant Nationalism and Communist Power: The Emer-*

gence of Revolutionary China, 1937–1945. Stanford, 1962.

Koen, Ross Y. *The China Lobby in American Politics*. New York, 1960.

Kolko, Gabriel. *The Politics of War: The World and United States Foreign Policy, 1943–1945*. New York, 1968.

Kubek, Anthony. *How the Far East Was Lost: American Policy and the Creation of Communist China, 1941–1949*. Chicago, 1963.

Latham, Earl. *The Communist Controversy in Washington: From the New Deal to McCarthy*. Cambridge, Massachusetts, 1966.

Latourette, Kenneth Scott. *The Chinese: Their History and Culture*. 4th rev. ed., 2 vols. in 1. New York and London, 1962.

Leng, Shao-chuan, and Norman D. Palmer. *Sun Yat-sen and Communism*. New York, 1960.

Liu, F. F. *A Military History of Modern China, 1924–1949*. Princeton, 1956.

Lohbeck, Don. *Patrick J. Hurley*. Chicago, 1956.

McLane, Charles B. *Soviet Policy and the Chinese Communists, 1931–1946*. New York, 1958.

Moore, Barrington, Jr. *Social Origins of Dictatorship and Democracy: Lord and Peasant in the Making of the Modern World*. Boston, 1967.

North, Robert C. *Moscow and Chinese Communists*. 2nd ed. Stanford, 1963.

Pratt, Julius W. *Cordell Hull, 1933–44*. 2 vols. New York, 1964.

Reston, James. *The Artillery of the Press: Its Influence on American Foreign Policy*. New York and Evanston, 1967.

Romanus, Charles F. and Riley Sunderland. *United States Army in World War II: China-Burma-India Theater*. 3 vols. Washington, D.C., 1953–1959.

Rovere, Richard H. *Senator Joe McCarthy*. New York, 1960.

Schlesinger, Arthur M., Jr. *The Crisis of the Old Order: 1919–1933*. Boston, 1957.

——. *The Politics of Upheaval*. Boston, 1960.

Schram, Stuart. *Mao Tse-tung*. New York, 1966.

Schwartz, Benjamin I. *Chinese Communism and the Rise of Mao*. Cambridge, Massachusetts, 1952.

Shannon, David A. *The Decline of American Communism: A*

History of the Communist Party of the United States Since 1945. New York, 1959.

Sheridan, James E. *Chinese Warlord: The Career of Feng Yü-hsiang.* Stanford, 1966.

Spence, Jonathan. *To Change China: Western Advisers in China, 1620–1960.* Boston and Toronto, 1969.

Steele, A. T. *The American People and China.* New York, Toronto, and London, 1966.

Thayer, Charles W. *Guerrilla.* New York, 1965.

Thomson, James C., Jr. *While China Faced West: American Reformers in Nationalist China, 1928–1937.* Cambridge, Massachusetts, 1969.

Tong, Hollington K. *Chiang Kai-shek: Soldier and Statesman.* 2 vols. London, 1938.

Tsou, Tang. *America's Failure in China, 1941–50.* Chicago, 1963.

Van Slyke, Lyman P. *Enemies and Friends: The United Front in Chinese Communist History.* Stanford, 1967.

Varg, Paul A. *Missionaries, Chinese, and Diplomats: The American Protestant Missionary Movement in China, 1890–1952.* Princeton, 1958.

Warren, Frank A. *Liberals and Communism: The 'Red Decade' Revisited.* Bloomington and London, 1966.

Willoughby, Charles A. *Shanghai Conspiracy: The Sorge Spy Ring.* New York, 1952.

Wright, Mary Clabaugh. *The Last Stand of Chinese Conservatism: The T'ung-Chih Restoration, 1862–1874.* Stanford, 1957.

Young, Arthur N. *China and the Helping Hand, 1937–1945.* Cambridge, Massachusetts, 1963.

Articles

Boorman, Howard L. "Mao Tse-tung: The Lacquered Image," *China Quarterly,* No. 16 (October–December 1963), 1–55.

———. "Mao Tse-tung as Historian," *China Quarterly,* No. 28 (October–December 1966), 82–105.

Butterfield, Fox. "A Missionary View of the Chinese Communists, 1936–1939," in *Papers on China,* vol. XV. Cambridge, Massachusetts, 1961.

Cohen, Warren I. "The Development of Chinese Communist Policy Toward the United States, 1922–1945," *Orbis,* XI (Spring and Summer, 1967), 219–237, 551–569.

Eckstein, Harry. "On the Etiology of Internal Wars," *History and Theory,* IV, No. 2 (1965), 133–163.

Fairbank, John K. "Assignment for the '70's," *American Historical Review,* LXXIV (February 1969), 861–879.

Garavente, Anthony. "The Long March," *China Quarterly,* No. 22 (April–June 1965), 89–124.

Gittings, John. "The Chinese Army," in *Modern China's Search for a Political Form,* ed. Jack Gray. London, New York, and Toronto, 1969.

Grant, Natalie [Mrs. Richard Wraga]. "Disinformation," *National Review,* IX (November 5, 1960), 41–46.

Griffith, Samuel B., II. "Communist China's Capacity to Make War," *Foreign Affairs,* XLIII (January 1965), 217–236.

Hingley, Ronald. "The Revolutionary: On the Persistence of Myths and Mystiques," *Problems of Communism,* XIII (May–June 1964), 63–70.

Hudson, G. F. "From Marx to Mao," *Problems of Communism,* XVII (May–June 1968), 59–63.

Jaffe, Philip J. "The Strange Case of Anna Louise Strong," *Survey: A Journal of Soviet and East European Studies,* LIII (October 1964), 129–139.

Leopold, Richard W. "American Policy and China, 1937–1950: A Review," *Journal of Conflict Resolution,* VIII (December 1964), 505–510.

Meisner, Maurice. "A Review Article: Sinological Determinism," *China Quarterly,* No. 30 (April–June 1967), 175–183.

Mirsky, Jonathan. "Report From the China Sea," *New York Review of Books,* XIII (August 21, 1969), 35–37.

Nolan, John M. "The Long March: Fact and Fancy," *Military Affairs,* XXX (Summer 1966), 77–90.

Peck, James. "The Roots of Rhetoric: The Professional Ideology of America's China Watchers," *Bulletin of Concerned Asian Scholars,* II (October 1969), 59–69.

Schlesinger, Arthur M. "Extremism in American Politics," *Saturday Review,* XLVIII (November 27, 1965), 21–25.

Schlesinger, Arthur, Jr. "Franklin D. Roosevelt and Foreign Affairs, *New York Times Book Review,* July 6, 1969, 1–2, 20–21.

Schram, Stuart R. "What Makes Mao a Maoist," *New York Times Magazine,* March 8, 1970, 36–37, 58, 60, 62, 75–76, 80, 82.

——, Arthur A. Cohen, Benjamin Schwartz, Mostafa Rejai, Joseph R. Levenson, and Leonard Schapiro. "What Is Maoism?: A Symposium," *Problems of Communism,* XV (September–October 1966), 1–30.

Selden, Mark. "The Guerrilla Movement in Northwest China: The Origins of the Shensi-Kansu-Ninghsia Border Region," *China Quarterly,* Nos. 28 and 29 (October–December, 1966 and January–March 1967), 63–81, 61–81.

Tsou, Tang. "The American Political Tradition and the American Image of Chinese Communism," *Political Science Quarterly,* LXXVII (December 1962), 570–600.

Unpublished Study

Iriye, Akira. "The Twenties (1922–1931)." Unpub. Paper, American-East Asian Relations Research Conference, Cuernavaca, Mexico, January 2–4, 1970.

Index

*Americans and
Chinese Communists, 1927–1945*

Designed by R. E. Rosenbaum.
Composed by Vail-Ballou Press, Inc.,
in 11 point linofilm Baskerville, 2 points leaded,
with display lines in Weiss Roman.
Printed offset by Vail-Ballou Press
on Warren's 1854 text, 60 pound basis,
with the Cornell University Press watermark.
Bound by Vail-Ballou Press
in Interlaken AVA book cloth
and stamped in All Purpose foil.